A PORTRAIT OF MARGINALITY

☆☆☆

A PORTRAIT OF

EDITED BY
MARIANNE GITHENS
Goucher College

David McKay Company, Inc.
NEW YORK

The Political Behavior of the American Woman

MARGINALITY

AND

JEWEL L. PRESTAGE
Southern University

A Portrait of Marginality:
The Political Behavior of the American Woman

Copyright © 1977 by David McKay Company, Inc.

MANUFACTURED IN THE UNITED STATES OF AMERICA

DEVELOPMENTAL EDITOR: Edward Artinian
EDITORIAL AND DESIGN SUPERVISOR: Nicole Benevento
INTERIOR DESIGN: Bob Antler
COVER DESIGN: Bob Antler
PRODUCTION AND MANUFACTURING SUPERVISOR: Donald W. Strauss
COMPOSITION: Typographic Services, Inc.
PRINTING AND BINDING: Colonial Press

Library of Congress Cataloging in Publication Data

Main entry under title:

A Portrait of marginality.

Includes bibliographical references.
1. Women in politics—United States—Addresses,
essays, lectures. 2. Marginality, Social—United States
—Addresses, essays, lectures. I. Githens, Marianne.
II. Prestage, Jewel Limar, 1931–
HQ1391.U5P67   301.5'92   76–58484
ISBN 0-679-30333-2 pbk.

To Stanley and Jim
and Jeffrey, Sharon, Julie,
Jonathan, Terri, Grady, Eric,
Kay, and Jay.

Acknowledgments

Anthony Orum, Roberta Cohen, Sherri Grasmuck and Amy W. Orum, "Sex, Socialization and Politics," *American Sociological Review* 39 (April, 1974): 197–209, is reprinted by permission of the authors and the publishers of the *American Sociological Review*.

Barry Bozeman, Sandra Thornton and Michael McKinney, "Continuity and Change in Opinions About Sex Roles," is reprinted by permission of the authors. Originally presented at the 1975 Annual Meeting of the Southwestern Political Science Association.

Reprinted from "Sex Differences in Black Political Beliefs and Behavior," *American Journal of Political Science* 17, No. 2 (May, 1973), by John Pierce, William P. Avery and Addison Carey, Jr. by permission of the Wayne State University Press.

Cornelia Flora, "Working Class Women's Political Participation: Its Potential in Developed Countries," is reprinted by permission of the author and the American Political Science Association. Originally presented at the 1974 Annual Meeting of the American Political Science Association.

"A Case Study in Patriarchial Politics: Women on Welfare," by Lynne B. Iglitzin, is reprinted from *American Behavioral Scientist* Vol. 17, No. 4 (March/April, 1974) pp. 487–506 by permission of the Publisher, Sage Publications, Inc.

Marcia Lee, "Toward Understanding Why Few Women Hold Public Office: Factors Affecting the Participation of Women in Local Politics," is reprinted by permission of the author and the American Political Science Association. Originally presented at the 1974 Annual Meeting of the American Political Science Association.

Naomi Lynn and Cornelia Flora, "Societal Punishment and Aspects of Female Political Participation: 1972 National Convention Delegates," is reprinted by permission of the authors. Originally presented at the 1975 Annual Meeting of the Southwestern Political Science Association.

Virginia Currey, "Campaign Theory and Practice—The Gender Variable," is reprinted by permission of the author. Original version presented at the 1975 Annual Meeting of the Southwestern Political Science Association.

John Soule and Wilma McGrath, "A Comparative Study of Male-Female Political Attitudes at Citizen and Elite Levels," is reprinted by permission of the authors and the American Political Science Association. Originally presented at the 1974 Annual Meeting of the American Political Science Association.

Marianne Githens, "Spectators, Agitators, or Lawmakers: Women in State Legislatures," was originally prepared for delivery at the 1974 Annual Meeting of the Southern Political Science Association, New Orleans, Louisiana, November 7, 1974.

Charles S. Bullock III and Patricia Findley Heys, "Recruitment of Women for Congress: A Research Note," *Western Political Quarterly* 25 (September, 1972): 416–23, is reprinted with the permission of the author and the University of Utah, Copyright Holder.

Edmond Costantini and Kenneth H. Craik, "Women As Politicians: The Social Background, Personality and Political Careers of Female Party Leaders," *Journal of Social Issues* 28 (1972): 217–36, is reprinted by permission of the *Journal of Social Issues.*

Barbara C. Burrell, "A New Dimension in Political Participation: The Women's Political Caucus," is reprinted by permission of the author. Originally presented at the 1975 Southwestern Political Science Association.

John Stucker, "Women As Voters: Their Maturation As Political Persons in American Society," is reprinted by permission of the publisher, from *Women in the Professions* edited by Laurily K. Epstein (Lexington, Mass.: Lexington Books, D. C. Heath and Company, 1975).

Elizabeth King, "Women in Iowa Legislative Politics," is reprinted by permission of the author and the American Political Science Association. Originally presented at the 1973 Annual Meeting of the American Political Science Association.

Frieda L. Gehlen, "Women Members of Congress: A Distinctive Role?" is reprinted by permission of the author.

Emily Stoper, "Wife and Politician: Role Strain Among Women in Public Office," is reprinted by permission of the author.

Mae C. King, "The Politics of Sexual Stereotypes," *The Black Scholar* (March–April, 1973): 12–23, is reprinted by permission of *The Black Scholar.*

Inez Smith Reid, "Traditional Political Animals? A Loud No," from *Together Black Women* by Inez Reid is reprinted with permission of the author and the publisher, Joseph Okpaku Publishing Company, Inc.

Marjorie Lansing, "The Voting Patterns of American Black Women," is reprinted by the permission of the author and of the American Political Science Association. Originally presented at the 1973 Annual Meeting of the American Political Science Association.

Herrington Bryce and Alan E. Warrick, "Black Women in Electoral Politics," *Focus* 1 (August 1973), is reprinted with the permission of the authors.

Jewel L. Prestage, "Black Women State Legislators: A Profile," was originally presented at the 1974 meeting of the Southern Political Science Association.

Contributors

William P. Avery is Assistant Professor of Political Science at the University of Nebraska at Lincoln. He holds the Ph.D. from Tulane University. His current research interests are global arms transfers, political development and modernization and international relations generally.

Barry Bozeman received the Ph.D. from Ohio State University and is now Associate Professor of Political Science at the University of Missouri at Columbia. He is now involved in research on science policy.

Herrington Bryce holds the Ph.D. in Economics from the Maxwell School of Public Affairs, Syracuse University and serves as research director for the Joint Center for Political Studies in Washington, D. C. He is now conducting research on planning problems in small cities.

Charles S. Bullock III is Professor of Political Science at the University of Houston. His Ph.D. was granted by Washington University in 1968. He is author of several books, including *Black Political Attitudes* (with Harrell Rodgers III) and *Law and Social Change*, as well as numerous articles in political science journals.

Barbara C. Burrell, currently pursuing the Ph.D. in Political Science at the University of Michigan, completed the article included in this volume as a part of her Masters thesis at Iowa State University at Ames.

Addison Carey, Jr., who is Professor of Political Science at Southern University—New Orleans, holds the Ph.D. in Political Science from Tulane University. His research and teaching interests include American politics, minority politics and urban politics. A former Ford Foundation Fellow, he is a past President of the Louisiana Political Science Association.

Roberta S. Cohen, Assistant Professor of Sociology at Princeton University, holds a Ph.D. from the University of Illinois at Champaign-Urbana. Her research interests are currently political socialization and quantitative methods.

Edmond Costantini is Associate Professor of Political Science and Department Chairperson at the University of California at Davis. His Ph.D. is from the University of California at Berkeley. His publications include *California Politics and Parties* (co-author), *The Democratic Leadership Corps in California,* and numerous articles in social science journals and periodicals. In addition he has been active in party politics in California.

Kenneth H. Craik is Associate Professor of Psychology at the University of California at Berkeley where he received his Ph.D. His current research interests include styles of humorous behavior and some aspects of environmental psychology.

Virginia Currey, Associate Professor of Political Science, Southern Methodist University, Dallas, Texas, received her Ph.D. in Political Science from the University of Iowa. A former Fulbright Fellow, she has long been active in Texas and national politics and teaches a course on Women in Politics.

Cornelia Butler Flora serves as Assistant Professor of Sociology at Kansas State University at Manhattan. Her Ph.D. was awarded by Cornell University and her research interests are sociology of women and sociology of religion.

Frieda L. Gehlen, an Assistant Professor of Sociology at the University of New Mexico, received her Ph.D. from Michigan State University. She is now doing further research on women in Congress and public opinion about strikes by police.

Sherri Grasmuck is a graduate student in Sociology at the University of Texas at Austin.

Patricia Lee Findley Heys was an undergraduate student at the University of Georgia where she worked as an assistant to Professor Charles S. Bullock III.

Lynne B. Iglitzin is Assistant Director of Undergraduate Studies and Lecturer in the Department of Political Science at the University of Washington in Seattle. She holds the Ph.D. in Political Science from Bryn Mawr and serves as Vice President of the American Civil Liberties Union of the state of Washington. Her publications include *Women in the World* (co-author), *Violence in American Society,* and numerous articles on feminist related issues.

Elizabeth G. King teaches Political Science at St. Norbert College in West De Pere, Wisconsin. A prior faculty appointment was at Drake University in Des Moines, Iowa. Her training in Political Science includes the B.A. from Emory University and the M.A. from the University of Missouri.

Mae C. King received the B.A. from Bishop College and the Ph.D. at the University of Idaho. She is presently Visiting Professor of Political Science at the University of Benin in Nigeria. From 1968–1975 she served as Staff Associate of the American Political Science Association in Washington, D.C. Dr. King, who taught at Texas Southern University, Virginia State College at Norfolk and Howard University, has published articles in the *Black Scholar,* the *Black Politician* and the *Social Science Quarterly.*

Marjorie Lansing is currently Associate Professor in Political Science at

Eastern Michigan University. Her Ph.D. is from the University of Michigan and she has written widely in the area of elections and voting behavior.

Marcia M. Lee is Assistant Professor at Rutgers University in Newark, New Jersey. Her Ph.D. is from Tufts University and her current research is on public policy and women in local politics.

Naomi B. Lynn is Associate Professor of Political Science at Kansas State University at Manhattan. Her Ph.D. was awarded by the University of Kansas in 1972. She was former President of the Women's Caucus for Political Science of the American Political Science Association. Her articles have been published in the *Journal of Military Sociology* and other periodicals.

Wilma E. McGrath is a doctoral candidate in Political Science at the University of California at Irvine.

Michael McKinney holds the rank of Associate Professor of Political Science at North Carolina Central University. His Ph.D. is from the University of Maryland. He is currently doing research on southern politics, voting studies and urban politics.

Amy W. Orum, Administrative Assistant to the City Manager, Community Services Administration, City of Austin, Texas, has done extensive graduate work in history and sociology. She holds the M.A. in Sociology from the University of Chicago where she completed all Ph.D. requirements except the dissertation. At Emory University all requirements for the Ph.D. in history were completed except the dissertation. Her current research is in the area of urban politics.

Anthony M. Orum is Associate Professor of Sociology at the University of Texas at Austin. His doctorate in Sociology is from the University of Chicago. His articles are published in a number of journals. At present his research is on political socialization and social movements.

John C. Pierce, Associate Professor of Political Science at Washington State University, received the Ph.D. from the University of Minnesota. He has served as an APSA Congressional Fellow and taught at Tulane University. His articles have appeared in the *Midwest Journal of Political Science, Journal of Black Studies,* and the *Journal of Social Psychology.*

Inez Smith Reid holds the Ph.D. from Columbia University and a law degree from Yale. She is Associate Professor of Political Science at Barnard College. Her research interests include African politics, women in politics, minority politics and public law. In addition she has served as Executive Director of the Black Women's Community Development Foundation.

John W. Soule, Assistant Professor of Political Science at San Diego State University, holds the Ph.D. from the University of Kentucky. His current research interest is congressional attitudes toward the future.

Emily Stoper serves as Associate Professor of Political Science at California State University–Hayward. In 1968 she was awarded the Ph.D. by Harvard University. Her research and teaching areas are American political institutions, urban politics and ethnic politics.

John J. Stucker, a recent recipient of the Ph.D. in Political Science from the University of Michigan, is Assistant Professor of Political Science at the

University of South Carolina. Research and teaching in American politics, political socialization, elections and voting behavior are his primary interests.

Sandra Thornton holds the position of Associate Professor of Political Science at Georgia Institute of Technology. Her Ph.D. is from Georgetown University and she is now engaged in research on Soviet affairs and women's studies.

Alan E. Warrick was a student assistant at the Joint Center for Political Studies while studying Political Science at Howard University.

Contents

PART

I Marginality: Women in Politics

MARIANNE GITHENS and
JEWEL L. PRESTAGE

1

☆☆☆☆☆☆☆☆☆☆☆☆☆☆☆☆☆☆☆☆☆☆☆☆☆☆☆

Introduction

Until about a decade ago, the political behavior
of women was largely an unexplored area
in the literature of political science. Maurice Duverger's *The Political
Role of Women* had examined the nature and extent of women's political participation, the unabridged version of *The American Voter* had
devoted one section to women as voters, and James David Barber had
discussed the contribution of women sitting in the Connecticut legislature in *The Law Makers: Recruitment and Adaptation to Legislative Life;*
but little systematic research had been done on women's role in politics.[1] Indeed, most studies either ignored women's political participation or mentioned it only in passing.

Given women's representation in public office, this omission
might seem reasonable. Despite the long and bitter suffrage struggle
and the subsequent adoption of the Nineteenth Amendment, women
voters did not materialize in anywhere near the numbers anticipated.
Gradually more women did go to the polls; but their voting did not
result in more female officeholders. There have never been more
than nineteen female members in the U.S. House of Representatives
at one time, and no more than two women simultaneously in the Senate. State legislatures today include only slightly more than 600
women out of a total of 7,700, or 7.98 percent; and this represents a
substantial increase from a decade ago when only 3 percent of the
state legislators were female.

Women account for only a handful of federal judges. In fact, a single woman sits at the federal appellate court level, and only 3 of 333 federal district court judges are women.[2] At the higher levels of the federal bureaucracy women are grossly underrepresented; only 2 percent of these positions are filled by females. In political party organizations, women are rarely found in decision-making positions. For all intents and purposes, female political participation might be considered too negligible to be worthy of study.

The resurgence of the women's movement in the 1960s brought into prominence the sexual, social, economic, and political inequality in which the American woman found herself and stimulated research on women within a variety of settings. An obvious area for investigation was politics. The ballot box has always been a key to political change. If women could be mobilized politically and elected to public office where they could press for equality, the status of women might be improved. For such a strategy to be viable, however, an accurate assessment of women's role in politics was needed. It was necessary to determine women's location in American political structures and their behavior within them. As the shocking underrepresentation of women in politics became more widely known, researchers sought specific reasons for the phenomenon. Each study raised more questions than it answered and encouraged further research.

The initial phase of the current work on women in politics was basically descriptive and centered around the distinctive characteristics of women who were participating in politics. What kind of women were they? How did they function? Such research provoked interest in three related questions. How did women who became involved in politics differ from women in general? Why did some women deviate from the established pattern of female noninvolvement? What were the constraints on political involvement? The second phase of research sought to answer these questions and provide a theoretical framework in which women's political behavior could be viewed.

To date, explanations of women's political behavior have emphasized the impact of socialization, which transmits to women and men clearly defined roles. The fundamental problem revolves around the fact that female political activists, by virtue of their sex, have an ascribed status, and their childhood and young-adult socialization prepares them to fulfill those functions that are compatible with this status. Political women seek achieved status as well, but their anticipatory socialization does not provide the necessary values and skills. In fact, research on achievement and educational opportunity suggests that women are often discouraged from acquiring the experience, knowledge, and techniques required to realize their ambitions in nontraditional roles.[3]

At best, women are taught that involvement in politics means participation at the citizen level only. Women grow up believing that they ought to vote; be informed on public issues, particularly as they pertain to the social well-being of the community; and be active in civic matters that affect home and family life. These orientations, consistent in many respects with female-ascribed status, prompt women who opt for a more active involvement either to move into nonpartisan and volunteer organizations specifically concerned with public-service issues or to pursue a supportive, service-directed position in male-dominated political organizations and institutions.

Of course, not all women accept the roles that their ascribed status assigns them. Motivated to achieve, they compete for positions of power and influence in politics. Their lack of training for such roles, however, as well as the societal norms that do not envision women in decision-making positions, impose restraints on female recruitment, participation, and performance. Consequently, women tend to remain in peripheral roles even when they have managed to enter the political elite.

The problems confronting women in politics have been attributed chiefly to the tensions between ascribed and achieved status created by female socialization. This explanation often tends to be diffuse and vague. It describes the peculiar tensions arising from the contradictory roles of woman and politician, but is static and limited in dealing with the problems of interaction that political women encounter in their relationships with nonpolitical women and political men. Yet women in politics continually articulate these concerns. An obsession with being well prepared, doing her homework, and being known for speaking only when she has something to say is stressed by most women politicians, and connotes anxiety about interaction with male politicians. Moreover, a higher degree of liberalism, unconventionality, and sense of adventure in political women over nonpolitical women implies the possibility of problems in interaction with other females. Nevertheless, the general methodological framework of socialization does not permit detailed, specific treatment of these themes.

To be sure, some clues about the dynamic of interaction emerge. Bardwick and Douvan's essay on "Ambivalence: The Socialization of

Women," which appears in *Women in Sexist Society,* suggests that, unlike boys, girls do not develop independent sources of esteem. Instead, girls rely on others' perceptions for their esteem. Consequently, girls' identity is derived from interpersonal success; and this is what conveys self-esteem.[4] Even here, though, the emphasis is on the transmission of particular values and norms to women, and on their reinforcement. Little consideration is paid to the tensions stemming from socialization beyond an identification of them. In short, the dynamic occasioned by interaction with other women and with men is basically ignored.

Marxist analyses of the condition of women, although seeing the root causes of female oppression as a product of capitalism, have also stressed socialization. Rowbotham, for example, sees the condition of women changing only in a socialist society; even then, she envisions this only when women conscious of their own needs work to resocialize their sisters and brothers.[5] Once again, the dynamic of interaction, aside from the question of resocialization, is barely touched. As a result, the problems involved in transforming socialist societies into ones of equality for women are not fully explained.

The leitmotif of research on women in politics is the contradictory values that the ascribed role of woman and the achieved role of politician create. One theory related to socialization seems to go a long way in explaining specifically the political behavior of the American woman. Ironically enough, it is the theory known as the Marginal Man.

The concept of marginality was first introduced by Robert E. Park and subsequently expanded by Everett Stonequist. This notion was initially developed to explain the difficulties confronting the ghetto Jew who sought to become assimilated in the Gentile world. Rejecting the values of his coreligionists and rebuffed by the group he wished to affiliate with, the Jew, a prototype of the marginal man, existed on the borders of two groups that placed contradictory demands on him. As Turner described him in *The Social Context of Ambition,*

> ... the marginal man is a person who seeks to change his identification from one stratum to another, but who is unable to resolve the related choices between value systems and between organized group ties. The choices are necessary because the strata have incompatible value systems, and because it is difficult to maintain ties across stratum boundaries.[6]

The condition of marginality manifests itself objectively by the position one holds—experientially by feelings of conflicting demands, and symptomatically by certain personality traits. Although marginality encourages some measure of unconventionality in thinking and a novel perspective, characteristics associated with creative thinkers and innovators, another set of traits is also related to marginality. These reflect anomie: rootlessness, isolation, and the absence of clear standards to guide conduct. These traits manifest themselves in problems with making decisions, hypersensitivity, irritability, lack of ease in interpersonal relationships, and inconsistent behavior.

Like the marginal man, the woman in politics is intensively involved with two groups, women and politicians. Each group represents a way of life; at the same time, each provides an identity and strong social ties. Women who seek to enter the male-dominated political elite reject, whether they want to or not, at least some of the values and norms of most women. Like the Jew, the political woman no longer feels comfortable with nonpolitical women; she has problems engaging in informal conversation and in acknowledging other women's evaluations as criteria for her own self-esteem. On the other hand, the politician group, where she wishes to establish contact, displays reticence in accepting her. The woman in politics thus finds herself isolated from both groups.

Crucial to marginality is the inability to choose between two groups. Internal pressures derived from socialization to the role of woman and aspirations to achieve in politics leave the woman in politics in a dilemma. To select one fully and reject the other is difficult, for self-esteem is threatened whichever choice is made. Moreover, choosing is not solely her prerogative, for the politician group does not fully accept her.

If Bardwick and Douvan are correct in asserting that female socialization creates special identity problems for women and makes interpersonal success the measure of female self-esteem, marginality must create an acute anxiety for women in politics. The socialization to dependence and the other-directed thrust that it implies means that women caught between two conflicting groups are very vulnerable and that their experiential marginality is intensified.

The literature dealing with upward mobility attaches great importance to learning values appropriate to one's ambitions. Ideally, anticipatory socialization allows upwardly mobile people to become familiar with the values and norms of the group to which they aspire. Characteristic of the upwardly mobile marginal person is the separation of ambition from such learning. This intensifies marginality because the perspective for consolidating the social position that an occupation conveys and the values that will enhance personal acceptance at the higher level is absent.

Although not upwardly mobile in the classic sense of movement from one social class to the next, women seeking achieved status confront the same problems, probably because their ascribed role has traditionally had a low status. As a result of their anticipatory socialization, women do not have the opportunity to develop talents, values, and skills necessary to higher-status aspirations.[7] This is often true for women in politics, who have no occasion to learn values or engage in activities that permit the required perspective to be internalized or personal acceptance to be facilitated. Their preparation for the role of political activist comes from their involvement in women's political activities: public-service groups or "women's work" in political party organizations. Neither can be thought to provide meaningful credentials for entrance into the political elite; in fact, they provide no qualifications that could lessen marginality.

Problems are compounded for the political woman when she encounters prestige isolation in her interaction with her original group. Her intimacy with women declines even as she is viewed as a role model for women. This prestige identification, in many respects, exacerbates the problem for the political woman, for it creates a situation in which she finds her loyalties divided.

Evidence of this condition of marginality pervades the research in this book. Women who have moved into the political elite feel intensely the pressures of the two conflicting groups. Much time, effort, and energy goes into seeking some reconciliation of the roles of woman and politician. Political women want to be respected by their male colleagues; yet they also feel the need to serve dinner on time, clean house, and so forth. Women on the fringes of politics, who participate actively on the citizen level but do not seek more visible political roles, may really be hoping to escape the anxiety of marginality that more competitive involvement entails. Explanations that concentrate on the incompatibility of the demands of wife and mother with politician may be only partially correct for this category of female political participant. Political women at the citizen level may be guided as much by self-interst in avoiding anxiety as by the service-to-others orientation which is almost invariably attributed to them.

The marginality that white women experience is more acute for the black woman in American politics. The black political woman finds herself in an even more value-conflicted situation. She is marginal because she is a woman wishing to achieve in a male sphere, and marginal because she is a black entering a traditionally all-white preserve. The marginality of blacks in American society has been noted by a host of social scientists and writers for some time. W. E. B. DuBois, Richard Wright, James Baldwin, and others have dealt with the tragedy of the American black operating in a white world that wants no part of him. As a consequence, he exists in both the black world and white world, but is a part of neither. The coupling of racism and sexism leaves the black woman in politics rejected by males and by whites. Her loyalties are badly divided. Moreover, the stereotypes applied to black women are fundamentally different from those attached to white women, which makes her situation genuinely unique. The special setting in which the black woman in politics finds herself necessitates specific research on her as a minority within a minority, and warrants a separate section on her in this volume.

This book is divided into seven parts, of which this Introduction is part 1. Part 2 deals with female socialization and the particular problems that it creates for women in their quest for achieved status in politics. Part 3 focuses on a variety of barriers to female recruitment to politics at both the citizen and elite levels. Part 4 explores the area of female political participation and the impact of socialization and recruitment on political activity. Part 5 discusses female performance in the political domain and some issues involved in evaluating women's role in politics. Part 6 considers the special condition of the black woman in politics, the consequences of sexist and racial stereotypes, the special patterns of recruitment for black women, and participation and performance at the elite level. Part 7, the conclusion, examines the theme of marginality and its ramifications for women political activists.

NOTES
1. "A Symposium: Masculine Blindness in the Social Sciences," *Social Science Quarterly* 55 (December 1974): 563–656.
2. Doris Sassower, "Women in the Law: The Second Hundred Years," *American Bar Association Journal* 57 (April 1971): 309.
3. Pamela Roby, "Institutional Barriers to Women Students in Higher Education," in *Academic Women on the Move,* ed. Alice S. Rossi and Ann Calderwood (New York: Russell Sage Foundation, 1973), pp. 37–56.

4. Judith M. Bardwick and Elizabeth Douvan, "Ambivalence: The Socialization of Women," in *Woman in Sexist Society,* ed. Vivian Gornick and Barbara Moran (New York: Basic, 1971), pp. 151–52.

5. Sheila Rowbotham, *Women, Resistance and Revolution: A History of Women and Revolution in the Modern World* (New York: Pantheon, 1972), pp. 170–99.

6. Ralph H. Turner, *The Social Context of Ambition—A Study of High School Seniors in Los Angeles* (San Francisco: Chandler, 1964), p. 109.

7. Ralph H. Turner, "Some Aspects of Women's Ambitions," *American Journal of Sociology* 70 (November 1964): 271–85.

II The Problem of Being a Minority: Sex, Socialization, and Politics

Perhaps the most widely utilized explanation of sex differences in political participation lies in political socialization theory. Essentially this explanation seeks to attribute sex differences in adult political behavior to sex-related differences in childhood socialization. Among adults, women participate less than men at almost all levels of political involvement.

Early studies on the development of political attitudes in children document the existence of similar differences.[1] Herbert Hyman in 1959 offered data supporting greater interest in politics on the part of boys. Among differences reported by Hess and Torney were the tendency of girls to be more attached to personal figures in the political system, a greater trust in and reliance on the inherent goodness of the system by girls, and an inclination on the part of boys to be more task-oriented and more willing to accept and see benefit in conflict and disagreement. No differences were detected in levels of basic attachment and loyalty to the country. Work by Fred Greenstein found boys to be invariably more political than girls. Boys scored higher on

11

political information, were more likely to favor political change in the world, were more able to name news stories and more interested in national news. In addition, boys were more likely than girls to select public figures as the person they most admired. Both boys and girls tended to prefer the father as a source of political advice. Other studies on more generalized socialization practices tend to support the existence of different processes and different behavior norms for growing youngsters depending on their sex.[2] The net result seems to be a situation in which females find themselves socialized to a concept of femininity that excludes those qualities that make for success in the political arena. What is the current status of political socialization research findings relative to sex differences in childhood? Are there changes taking place in the larger society that might impact upon the socialization of women? To what extent do conditions faced by women after they reach adulthood influence their political orientations? Are there significant deviations from the prevailing pattern among selected racial or economic groups? In what ways do public policy priorities and sanctions affect the adult socialization of women?

In "Sex, Socialization, and Politics," the authors examine the political socialization explanation of sex differences in political involvement by American adults. Essentially, this explanation holds that political habits are formed before individuals reach adulthood and that adult participation-pattern differentials result from the same dynamics of childhood learning as other sexual differences. Boys become boys by modeling men and being reinforced for acting like men while girls model women and are reinforced for behaving like women. Because women are largely excluded from meaningful political involvement, at an early age girls, taking cues from the adult world, become less interested in politics; boys, for the same reason, are led toward interest and involvement.

Testing this explanation, the authors sample over 2,000 students, cutting across sex and race lines, and probe their views on a number of political dimensions. Results do not offer confirmation of the political socialization assumption. Political differences between boys and girls uncovered in the study were, in general, minor. This pattern is at odds with previous findings and raises serious questions regarding the reliability and validity of these earlier findings. Speculations offered as to the possible sources of these divergencies range from reservations about aspects of previous studies to closer examination of components of the present study to the citing of more recent studies in which findings are closer to those of the present study. Concluding with an affirmation of faith in the validity of their current findings, the authors suggest that the socialization explanation may need further critical assessment, modification, or revision.

Bozeman, Thornton, and McKinney provide an interesting overview of the evolution of opinions about sex roles in America. Major data for the study are taken from a 1972 study by the Survey Research Center and focus on five issues: role of women, abortion, layoffs of women in the labor force, women in politics, and women's liberation. Utilizing eight variables, the 1972 findings are analyzed and compared with relevant data from earlier studies. The variables were: age, education, income, sex, race, marital status, and geographic region. On the role of women, a most startling finding was that sex is of little importance in accounting for differences in attitude; more education and more urban origins are associated with more egalitarian views. On abortion, more favorable attitudes occur among those of higher education, younger age groups, higher income groups, and whites from regions outside the South and in more urbanized sectors. The question of layoffs of women in the labor force generated a pattern in which equal treatment of women was more highly associated with younger age groups, those with more education, nonwhites, men, urban residents, and those of nonsouthern origins. Strongest support for involvement of women in politics was associated with education and marital status. Married persons are more inclined to favor such involvement. On the liberation question, only race was an especially useful variable in accounting for differences in attitudes.

While attitudes on the questions posed have changed over time, cumulatively the authors view the status of the thrust toward equality for women at this juncture in history as one in which a majority of the population remain unconvinced of the desirability of such equality. They speculate that mass popular support is not likely to develop for some time to come. Nevertheless, the dominant role of upper-class men in decision making and their increased support of equality coupled with the low cost involved in changing opinions about sex roles may provide some basis for optimism. A significant mitigating element is the stake that women in traditional roles have in the continuation and reinforcement of sexist socialization.

"Sex Differences in Black Political Beliefs and Behavior" focuses on possible deviations from typical voter behavior on the part of black men and women using a sample of adults from a southern city. On the basis of the atypical behavior frequently attributed to blacks by social scientists studying other areas, the authors hypothesize that black men and women may exhibit patterns of political participation and beliefs different from those found in more general populations in America. This hypothesis is examined by directing attention to sex differences among blacks in three areas: levels of traditional and protest participation, beliefs about politics, and relationships between beliefs and participation.

Regarding traditional and protest political activity, the authors found no significant differences in participation levels of men and women. Women participated on a par with men in both traditional and protest activities; however, women exhibited greater propensity toward dual involvement. When results are controlled for income, lower-class women participate more than lower-class men; at the highest level, men predominate. Occupation control yields differences in contrast to those yielded from income control. Lower-class men dominate in participation only when education is utilized as the status indicator. Even here, as education increases the difference disappears. The net result of these findings is that sex differences found in the general population do not exist in the same proportions among black adults.

When political beliefs are examined, the findings are partially at odds with those of the larger population. For example, unlike white women, black women do not look more favorably on people in politics than do black men. But, like white women, they exhibit less efficacious feelings toward politics than do the males of their race. When a relationship between beliefs and participation is made, the authors conclude that personal perceptions of the political system are better predictors of the political behavior of black women than black men.

Collectively, the findings of the study would seem to cast doubt on the validity of the thesis of universal dominance of the male in participation in American politics and consequently on the universality of the apolitical socialization of females in America.

Cornelia Flora's "Working-Class Women's Political Participation: Its Potential in Developed Countries" is directed toward women who are disadvantaged in the political process both by sex and by economic position. In ferreting out possible factors that may lead to political mobilization among working-class women, she uses industrial sociology and three major models of political participation: political socialization, differential selection, and political mobilization. Political socialization research suggests that part of an individual's learned sex-role behavior includes attitudes about participation in politics and that socialization does not end with childhood but accommodates role transition during adulthood. Differential selection focuses on the structure of individual characteristics which predispose political activism. Such research points to the high degree of association between numerous high-status measures and high political participation and between central involvement in a variety of social networks and extensive political activity. The third model, political mobilization, focuses on mechanisms by which adults acquire attitudes and skills necessary for political participation. Under all three models working-class women are at a disadvantage because basic tenets of each model entail elements inconsistent with conditions associated with these women.

Turning to industrial sociology, Flora finds that it has a bias hindering development of a definitive model of female participation. Because it examines what actually transpires in the work situation, however, industrial sociology holds some potential for generation of hypotheses. Flora attempts to test out some suggested relationships between labor-force participation and political participation for working-class women employing data from the 1972 American National Election survey. Some 2,705 U.S. citizens, 18 years of age or older, are included. In particular, responses to a political efficacy item are examined by occupation and sex. Women are compared to men and to other women. Females are divided into four groups: homemaker, white-collar worker, industrial worker, and blue-collar worker. Deleting the homemaker category for men results in the use of three groups.

Flora found that by comparing political efficacy systematically by sex and occupation, there appears to be a strong interaction between certain aspects of political socialization, selective characteristics, and job-related structures that predispose persons toward political participation. Industrial employment has a great leveling effect in rates of political participation. For females, such employment seems to be much more important than the socialization and selective attributes characterized by education. Low education seems to lead to low degrees of political efficacy in freer work situations, but labor-force participation in either white-collar or industrial jobs appears to overcome this tendency somewhat. Nevertheless, differences among white-collar women and industrial-worker women are great at the higher education levels. Flora suggests that these two groups of women might have different class interests in the political process and that the higher participation of one might well be at the expense of the other. Finally, Flora feels that industrial workers, by their homogeneity in terms of sense of political efficacy, have the potential for developing a common identity. But the job situation, while it has this potential, has not mobilized this group of women in America.

Lynne Iglitzin, in her article "A Case Study in Patriarchal Politics," focuses on aspects of the Aid to Families with Dependent Children program as it affected women recipients in Seattle in 1972. She argues that public welfare reinforces the socialization of women into the feminine stereotype by encouraging a set of "feminine" personality traits—by supporting the traditional wife-mother role, by continuing to enforce an outdated standard of morality, by its "women's work" orientation, by pitting women against women, and by inculcation of feelings of apathy and powerlessness. Being on welfare appears to reinforce passivity, docility, dependence, and resignation in women. Especially devastating to women is the policy of creating "woman to woman" adversary situations in the administration of welfare programs. Men hold the top positions in the program, but the daily interaction is between women. Reforms suggested by Iglitzin include initiation of policies permitting change in the self-image of welfare recipients, elimination of the husband-protector disposition, bringing the welfare system in line with the needs of recipients, a cessation of moral judgment by the system, better education and employment opportunities for women, and waging war on patriarchalism.

The research in this section clearly suggests some differences in the political socialization of women and men, although not to the extent that some earlier studies indicated. The differences which do emerge, however, have significance for women's participation in and recruitment to politics, and contribute to the marginality of political women.

NOTES

1. Herbert Hyman, *Political Socialization* (Glencoe, Ill.: Free Press, 1959); Robert D. Hess and Judith V. Torney, *The Development of Political Attitudes in Children* (Chicago: Aldine, 1967); Fred Greenstein, *Children and Politics* (New Haven: Yale University Press, 1965), esp. chap. 6; David Easton and Jack Dennis, *Children in the Political System* (New York: McGraw-Hill, 1969).

2. See for example, Judith Bardwick and Elizabeth Dovvan, "Ambivalence: the Socialization of Women," in *Woman in Sexist Society*, ed. Vivian Gornick and Barbara Moran (New York: Basic, 1971).

ANTHONY M. ORUM, ROBERTA S.
COHEN, SHERRI GRASMUCK,
and AMY W. ORUM

2

☆☆☆☆☆☆☆☆☆☆☆☆☆☆☆☆☆☆☆☆☆☆☆☆☆☆

Sex, Socialization, and Politics*

Jack and Jill went up the hill,
To fetch a pail of water;
Jack fell down, and broke his crown,
And Jill came tumbling after.
(children's rhyme)

The rough-and-tumble world of politics, like
that of water-fetching, is one in which males
have long been dominant. In the United States in particular, men typ-

*These data were collected as part of a study of the political socialization
of black and white youth conducted under the auspices of the Survey Research Practicum, Department of Sociology, University of Illinois at Urbana,
Illinois, 1970–71. The study was funded by the University of Illinois. The
Practicum was directed by Anthony M. Orum assisted by Gregory Arling and
Gordon Lurie. Students who participated in the Practicum were: Roberta Cohen, Kay Darnell, McKinley Jones, Marilyn Klohr, Janice Perrier, Dennis
Roncek, and Leonard Thornton. The authors are quite grateful to each of
these persons for their aid and to Seymour Sudman and Matt Hauck of the
Survey Research Laboratory at the University of Illinois who provided the
Practicum with able guidance during the design of the study. Judith V. Torney also provided helpful advice in developing and constructing the questionnaire. Finally, we would like to thank Joan Huber and Adreain Ross for
their helpful and insightful comments on a previous draft of this paper.
Naturally the authors accept sole responsibility for interpretations reported
herein.

ically have shown up more often at the polls, have engaged more often in political organizations, and have manifested greater political awareness and concern [24, 26].** Male dominance has been notable as well in the legislative and executive branches of government, where men have clearly overshadowed women in power and numbers.

In recent years, women in America have begun to respond to such inequalities by organizing political groups of women as women, e.g. the well-known National Organization for Women. Targets for change vary from the kinds of legal and extralegal restrictions which prevent women from having an equal voice and stake in politics to attempts to elevate the social and political consciousness of women as a group. Coming under special fire are stereotypes of the ways men and women are supposed to act, including the anachronistic notion which asserts that women should be confined to *die Kinder, die Küche, und die Kirche.*

The purpose of this paper is to seek the origins of differences in political expression between men and women by looking at data on children. In so doing, we shall examine the validity of one explanatory model that has been used to account for the different political styles of the sexes.

Perspectives on the Origins of Sex Differences in Political Expression

There are two principal schools of thought concerning the sources of the divergent political styles of men and women. *Political socialization* assumes that the political habits of people are formed primarily before adulthood. The differences in the attention of men and women to politics, so this argument claims, result from the same dynamics of childhood learning as other sexual differences.[1] Generally speaking, boys become boys by modeling and being reinforced for behaving like men; whereas girls become girls by modeling and being reinforced for behaving like women. This process of sex differentiation is further accentuated by the dominant stereotypes present in the culture.

In the case of political learning in the United States, this process may be interpreted as follows: Throughout most American history,

---

**Numbers in brackets refer to numbered references at the end of the chapter.

women have been excluded from playing a full and equal part in the political arena. Even when women's suffrage came, it had little effect on equalizing the distribution of women in positions of political power. Furthermore, the vote did not measurably alter the sexual inequalities evident in other spheres of American life, particularly the economic and occupational. In addition, there have been certain prevalent cultural stereotypes regarding the proper role of men and women as, for example, that "a man must make the political decisions." Together both the realities and the symbols have produced a picture of the adult world that, at an early age, leads girls to become less interested and involved in politics than boys; or, conversely, leads boys to become more interested and involved in politics than girls.

Variations occur in these basic outcomes. Under some circumstances, boys will tend to be passive about politics, girls comparatively active. Such variations depend largely on the characteristics of men and women in a child's immediate family setting as well as the real and symbolic male and female role models associated with a child's subculture. For instance, in subcultural contexts in which women are more active or as active in politics as men, parallel differences can be anticipated among children. Finally, the political socialization viewpoint claims that the distinctive political attributes acquired by boys and girls may be irrelevant to their current situation as, for instance, particular forms of political partisanship or participation; but these and other types of political learning are assumed to prepare them for their expected political roles as adults.

While there are further variations on the above model and even differences in the school of political socialization itself, this general perspective has been advocated in recent years by a number of scholars. These include Hyman [21], who in 1959 presented data showing that males and females differed as early as elementary school in their semi- or quasi-political interests. His survey of the literature revealed that boys tended to be more interested than girls in news of politics or men of public affairs. Also supporting this viewpoint are the recent research of Greenstein [16], Hess and Torney [19], and, to a lesser degree, the work of Easton and Dennis [12].

The second major school of thought on male-female political differences emphasizes *situational* and/or *structural* factors. This school has at least two variants. We group them together here simply because each disregards the impact of early learning, and thus opposes the basic premise of the political socialization thesis.

Advocates of the situational viewpoint accept the idea that the sex roles and stereotypes of a culture help shape and perpetuate differences in political expression between men and women. They claim, however, that circumstances of adulthood as, for example, the nature of married life, are responsible for such differences. Lipset [26] remarks that

> the position of the married woman illustrates the problem of available time or dispensability as a determinant of political activity. The sheer demands on a housewife and mother mean that she has little opportunity or need to gain politically relevant experiences. Women might thus be expected to have less concern with politics, and in almost every country they do vote less than men. (p. 206)

The other side of this argument is that men, especially married men, are more involved in political life owing to their allegedly more frequent contact with a diversity of people and points of view as well as the obvious political concerns that spring from their work. (It follows, of course, that women probably would be as politically involved as men if they were freed from their chores as housewives and able to secure meaningful employment on a regular basis; and some results, like those which show a smaller difference in political activity among men and women from the middle classes as compared with those from the lower classes, can be construed as showing weak and partial support for such a conclusion.) Other scholars whose research and speculation support this kind of argument include Almond and Verba [1], Campbell et al. [5], and Lane [24].

The structural version of this thesis maintains that major societal forces lead to continuing conflict between men and women. According to this argument, sex-related differences and sex-role stereotypes are mainly reflections of and means for insuring the continuation of the power difference between men and women. Collins [6], for instance, has claimed that the political differences between men and women are a product of the fact that women are universally regarded as men's sexual property and compelled to remain so by men's monopoly over the means of physical violence. In contemporary industrialized societies, he argues, this situation diminishes somewhat as women have more time and opportunity to work and gain wealth on their own.

Another illustration of this structural argument has been put forth by Heiskanen [20]. Adopting a modified Marxian model, she maintains that the lesser political activity and participation of women derives, in part, from the nature of the modern capitalist economy, and, in particular, from its need for a large supply of cheap labor and spendthrift consumers. Traditional sex-role ideology, she goes on to argue,

> is not only a question of cultural lag, a leftover of traditional values, but also serves the prevailing economic interests. And, to the extent that issues concerning economic relationships ultimately concern that of political relationships, the content of traditional sex-role ideology is specially focused on discouraging women from participation in politics: (sic) from influencing the prevailing power structure. (p. 85)

Thus, the two main schools of thought, the political socialization and the situational/structural, establish different expectations about the origins of political differences between the sexes. Both agree that there are sex roles and dominant sex-role stereotypes in societies, but they disagree on the mechanisms whereby such sex roles and ancillary beliefs translate into political differences. Such differences among the explanations notwithstanding, a dynamic or processual interpretation of the origins of sex differences in politics is likely to involve different combinations of conditions working together. Thus, for example, inequities in opportunities identified by the situational argument may be both a starting point and a means of preserving patterns of sex differences established in childhood. On the one hand, the absence of equal occupational opportunities for men and women can produce political disparities between them which, in turn, are transmitted through political socialization practices to children; and, on the other hand, disparate expectations for political involvement established early in life for children may be fulfilled through a continuing system of unequal opportunities confronting adults.

In this paper we shall examine evidence which bears on the political socialization explanation. To the degree that parallel sex differences exist for children and adults, we may conclude that socialization mechanisms help account for sex differences among adults. The absence of consistent differences, however, frees us to adopt a variety of viewpoints, not the least of which would be that the situational or structural arguments are the only valid explanations of sex differences in political attitudes and behavior.

In this analysis we shall examine the political attitudes and behavior of boys and girls in the same school grades; such a control will act as a substitute for age variations. We also shall control for the effects of racial and socioeconomic background variations. Consistent with some evidence and arguments, we expect that political differences will be less pronounced between boys and girls from black families than between those from white families.[2]

Although it might appear useful to develop a similar kind of expectation for children from middle-class and lower-class homes, our sample, which was originally selected to represent large numbers of black children and white children, appears to underrepresent white middle-class children and, to a lesser extent, black middle-class children. Thus our data simply could not test such hypotheses as might describe differences between boys and girls from divergent socioeconomic backgrounds.

SAMPLE

The data for this study were assembled by means of self-administered questionnaires completed by 2,365 Illinois students in their classrooms in the spring and fall of 1971. The total sample consisted of approximately equal numbers of white students and black students as well as males and females. Children in the fourth through twelfth grades were sampled in four urban areas of the state; those in the fourth, fifth, and sixth grades completed a somewhat shorter version of the questionnaire given to older children. Each sample area was selected in order to acquire a particular combination of racial and socioeconomic characteristics, our ultimate expectation being that the sample would reasonably represent black schoolchildren and white schoolchildren of comparable socioeconomic backgrounds in Illinois. Fifty percent of the sample was drawn from an inner-city, lower-class predominantly black public school system. Ten percent of the sample was selected from an inner-city, middle- to upper-middle class integrated public school. Twenty percent of the sample consisted of a lower-middle to working-class public school system and 20 percent consisted of a middle-class public school system. The students in both systems were predominantly white.

FINDINGS ON THE NATURE OF POLITICAL ORIENTATIONS

Political Affect
Usually political affect among adults is examined in terms of the amount of interest men and women show in politics. Observers have

uncovered substantial differences, as noted above, with men expressing a greater degree of concern with politics, particularly of the ex-
tralocal form [2, 5, 10, 24, 25, 26, 29].

Research in the area of political socialization has generated a
broader conception of political affect as well as a multiplicity of indicators designed to tap it. Essentially political affect is represented by
the child's expressed feelings about different institutions and figures
in politics. Such sentiments are presumed to reflect the child's earliest
stance toward the political arena and to be least subject to modification later in life.

Most investigations of political socialization or related issues have
found that girls possess a more compliant and personalized attachment to social institutions. Ellis [13] for example, found that girls possess more favorable attitudes toward social groups and institutions
than boys; while Forbes and Dykstra [15] discovered that boys attribute more negative traits to public authorities like the policeman,
judge, or fireman. Along similar lines, Hess and Torney [19] report
that girls are the more likely to possess a personalized and idealized
conception of government, a difference that continues unabated
through elementary school. Such differences among boys and girls
parallel, in rough fashion, Almond and Verba's discovery [1] that
women are somewhat more likely than men to express a "subject"
orientation toward government and politics.

Our own examination of the differences between boys and girls
in political affect covers three specific measures: the child's feelings
about the protectiveness and helpfulness of the President; the child's
sentiments about the helpfulness of local, state, and national govern-
ments; and the child's impressions of the integrity and honesty of the
government in general. Assuming that the political socialization
model of sex differences in political expression is valid, we expect boys
and girls to be different. In line with such research as Hess and Torney's [19], we expect girls to have a more compliant attitude toward
and favorable image of government.

The results of our analysis with respect to the child's view of the
helpfulness of the President are displayed in table 2.1[3] They are presented in the form of mean scores, classified by the sex, race, and
grade of the child, as well as controlled for the socioeconomic status of
the child's family, the latter variable measured by the occupation of
the chief wage earner. Besides the mean scores, we computed partial
correlation coefficients that measure the degree of the sex difference
within each grade and for each racial group, separately, controlling

TABLE 2.1. Sex, Race, Grade in School, and Occupation of the Chief Wage Earner by Image of the President (mean scores on image of President)

		Race			
		Black		White	
Grade	Sex	CWE Occupation		CWE Occupation	
		White-Collar	Blue-Collar	White-Collar	Blue-Collar
4–6	Female	2.74 (39)	3.23 (49)	3.34 (128)	3.81 (40)
	Male	3.07 (24)	3.13 (46)	3.00 (101)	3.44 (32)
		Partial correlation: −.029		Partial correlation: +.166[a]	
7–8	Female	2.54 (42)	2.57 (74)	2.99 (69)	3.17 (17)
	Male	2.40 (33)	2.61 (93)	2.91 (65)	3.00 (17)
		Partial correlation: −.018		Partial correlation: +.063	
9–10	Female	2.45 (28)	2.41 (86)	2.48 (25)	2.91 (46)
	Male	2.43 (33)	2.63 (80)	2.74 (27)	2.99 (57)
		Partial correlation: −.124		Partial correlation: −.051	
11–12	Female	2.47 (25)	2.48 (100)	2.88 (55)	2.88 (70)
	Male	2.55 (27)	2.56 (107)	2.70 (39)	2.68 (65)
		Partial correlation: −.034		Partial correlation: +.110	

NOTE: The numbers of cases are in parentheses in each subcell of the table.

[a]$p \leq .05$. Tests of significance will be reported here and elsewhere in this paper for interested readers. Although we have no reason to believe that the schools included in our sample were any different from other schools attended by black children and white children, save for the fact that middle-class youngsters are underrepresented, the principle of probability sampling underlying the application of significance tests is not met by our sampling procedures and, therefore, the meaning of such tests must be interpreted with caution.

for the effect of socioeconomic status. We calculated these partials by transforming the sex and the chief wage earner's occupation into dummy variables, assigning females a score of "1" on sex and males a score of "0," and assigning white-collar workers a score of "1" on chief wage earner's occupation and blue-collar workers a score of "0" [33]. We transformed the variable of occupation to conserve the number of cases in each subcell of the table. Note that the magnitude of the partial correlations in this format did not vary appreciably from that obtained with the full range of major occupational categories derived from the U.S. census classification.

Like previous research [see 19], we find that older children and children from white-collar backgrounds hold less favorable views of the protectiveness and helpfulness of the President. But unlike the findings of previous research, few differences of any magnitude are noted between boys and girls. The only statistically significant difference is found among the youngest white children, where girls hold the more positive images of the President; that difference is hardly substantial in view of the subcell sample sizes and the range of scores for the scale. Among white-collar black children of the same age, we find a sex difference of almost the same magnitude but in the opposite direction—boys hold the more positive image; beyond the sixth-grade level we are hard pressed to find a sex difference of even a fifth of one standard deviation for the black youngsters. Among older white children, we may observe a consistent pattern of small differences: with the exception of the ninth- and tenth-grade whites, girls are slightly more apt to rate the President as helpful and protective. The deviation of the ninth- and tenth-grade children from this pattern for white youngsters helps confirm the conclusion that the differences between boys and girls are negligible.

Similar analyses were undertaken on two related indices of political affect, our government benevolence scale, and our political cynicism scale.[4] These analyses yielded virtually identical results to that of the image of the President scale.[5] On each, a statistically significant but minor difference was found among the youngest white youth, girls expressing more positive sentiments than boys. On the benevolence scale, the white girls retained more positive feelings through the eighth grade, then the differences between the sexes dropped to virtually zero; while on the cynicism scale the white girls remained the less cynical—through not statistically so—through the eighth grade, but only among white-collar youth. Among black youngsters, no differences between boys and girls were observed.

In sum, we find only the slightest evidence of sex differences with respect to political affect, and then only among the youngest children. Among young whites, girls are the more apt to express positive and favorable sentiments, a finding noted in earlier investigations. But, in contrast to previous investigations, e.g., Hess and Torney, these sex differences cease to exist among older children, or take on highly random qualities. We also note some slight support for the hypothesis that the sex differences will be less pronounced among black youngsters. However, such a conclusion can only be tentative in view of the fact that very few differences were uncovered in these data.

Political Knowledge and Participation
Although the affective dimension of political orientations is believed to be the first to develop among children [16, 19], the dimen-

sions of cognition and behavior doubtlessly are the most often studied. The reason for this is self-evident; the cognitive and particularly the behavioral facets of political orientations represent the ways in which the public influences the political process. Among children, too, the same or somewhat similar dimensions have been examined quite carefully, the assumption being that the cognitive and behavioral expressions evident at this stage of growth provide the groundwork for patterns manifested in early adulthood.

To assess the possible sex differences in the cognitive dimension of political orientations, we developed a scale of political knowledge that consisted of six items extracted from a standard civics test.[6] Illustrative of these items was the following query: "Who is the present governor of Illinois?" Answers to each of these questions were scored as right or wrong, assigned scores, respectively, of "1" and "0," and then summed to create a cumulative index with total scores ranging from "0" through "6." Table 2.2 presents the results of this analysis.

Inspection of the mean scores in this table reveals some relation-

TABLE 2.2. Sex, Race, Grade in School, and Occupation of the Chief Wage Earner by Political Knowledge (mean scores on knowledge)

		Race			
		Black		White	
Grade	Sex	CWE Occupation		CWE Occupation	
		White-Collar	Blue-Collar	White-Collar	Blue-Collar
4–6	Female	1.07 (43)	.75 (52)	.66 (125)	.45 (40)
	Male	1.25 (24)	1.06 (49)	1.07 (101)	.77 (34)
		Partial correlation: −.098		Partial correlation: −.212[a]	
7–8	Female	1.88 (42)	1.23 (62)	1.46 (74)	1.11 (18)
	Male	2.10 (30)	1.43 (74)	2.27 (63)	1.20 (15)
		Partial correlation: −.053		Partial correlation: −.267[a]	
9–10	Female	2.48 (25)	2.29 (80)	2.39 (26)	1.62 (45)
	Male	2.66 (29)	2.53 (58)	3.00 (27)	2.59 (56)
		Partial correlation: −.095		Partial correlation: −.267[a]	
11–12	Female	2.44 (23)	2.54 (93)	2.48 (52)	2.37 (68)
	Male	3.36 (22)	2.56 (88)	3.49 (39)	2.77 (62)
		Partial correlation: −.081		Partial correlation: −.229[a]	

NOTE: The numbers of cases are in parentheses in each subcell of the table.
[a]$p \leq .05$.

ships comparable to those uncovered in previous research: for instance, older children and those from white-collar families are more apt to have higher scores on the knowledge index. Sex differences, we observe, are reasonably pronounced among white children, with boys consistently scoring higher than girls. Among black youths, the same pattern holds; however, the differences between the sexes are not statistically significant. There also seems to be no tendency for the magnitude of the sex differences to diminish with increasing age among black or white children. These general patterns among white children, we should mention, confirm virtually all previous political socialization research which had dealt with white youngsters, including that cited in Hyman [21] as well as the original research of Dowse and Hughes [9] in Great Britain, Heiskanen [20] in Finland, and Greenstein [16] and Merelman [28] in the United States.

The possibility of sex differences in the behavioral facets of political orientations was investigated with two different scales, one of reported types of actual participation, the other of forms of political discussion.[7] Anyone familiar with studies of political behavior among adults is aware of the consistency of those findings concerning the differences between men and women: in particular, men are observed to be more likely than women to vote, and also more apt to belong to and participate in social and political organizations [5, 24, 25, 26, 29, 32, 35]. (But cf. Booth [4] for some differences.) Thus, to the degree that a political socialization model accurately explains the differences in political behavior between men and women, we would expect to find parallel kinds of differences between the boys and girls in our sample.

Among the children in this study, we find a much less consistent pattern of differences in actual participation and no differences at all in some subcells of our table. Table 2.3 presents these findings. An inspection of results shows boys as being the more likely to report some form of participation; however, the differences between the two sexes are extremely small and statistically significant only among the youngest whites and the oldest blacks. We observe some tendency for these small differences to diminish with increasing age through the tenth grade, and to increase in the eleventh and twelfth grades. Nevertheless, the possibility of simple random effects is sufficiently great that it would be a mistake to attach any meaning to this reversal in the highest grades. Finally, we may note that there is no difference between black youths and white youths in the magnitude of the sex differences.

TABLE 2.3. Sex, Race, Grade in School, and Occupation of the Chief Wage Earner by Political Participation (mean scores on participation)

		Race			
		Black		White	
		CWE Occupation		CWE Occupation	
Grade	Sex	White-Collar	Blue-Collar	White-Collar	Blue-Collar
4–6	Female	2.82 (38)	2.50 (48)	2.55 (118)	2.43 (35)
	Male	2.80 (22)	2.76 (51)	2.75 (94)	2.65 (35)
		Partial correlation: −.120		Partial correlation: −.144[a]	
7–8	Female	2.67 (39)	2.73 (59)	2.80 (71)	2.57 (18)
	Male	2.81 (30)	2.89 (68)	2.94 (60)	2.61 (14)
		Partial correlation: −.097		Partial correlation: −.101	
9–10	Female	2.84 (27)	2.64 (79)	2.79 (24)	2.63 (45)
	Male	2.66 (27)	2.75 (60)	3.06 (26)	2.58 (56)
		Partial correlation: −.031		Partial correlation: −.045	
11–12	Female	2.53 (25)	2.64 (82)	2.51 (53)	2.35 (68)
	Male	2.79 (24)	2.74 (92)	2.70 (38)	2.46 (62)
		Partial correlation: −.157		Partial correlation: −.122	

NOTE: The numbers of cases are in parentheses in each subcell of the table.
[a]$p \leq .05$.

An identical analysis was performed on the political discussion scale. On that scale, boys and girls did not differ significantly in any subcell comparison. Among the white children, girls were less apt to report taking part in political discussions; while among the black children the opposite was true, but again only slightly, with boys reporting the lesser tendency to participate. The differences were so small that we can reject any notion that boys and girls actually differ on political discussion in this sample.[8]

In short, then, the sex difference is evident in only one of the three indicators of the behavioral and cognitive dimensions of orientations, and then is significant only among white youngsters. In the case of political knowledge, as in the case of political participation to a markedly lower extent, boys are more apt to be "politicized." White children display greater differences by sex on the political knowledge index than do black youngsters; but there are no differences to speak of between the races with regard to sex differences on the measures of political behavior.

Political Partisanship

Political partisanship, the evaluative facet of political orientations, is regarded by scholars of the political socialization school to have its origins in late childhood or early adolescence. Its significance derives from the fact that it acts as both a screen and anchor for an individual's political perceptions and beliefs, guiding the thrust of one's activity in politics. We are interested in assessing whether boys and girls vary in their tendencies to become socialized to definite partisan preferences.

We examined the partisan preferences of boys and girls by asking children to indicate which political party they would vote for if they could vote. Children's responses were grouped into two separate clusters, the one representing a preference for a definite party, e.g., Republican, the other representing responses of no party preference, e.g., "independent," or "I'd vote for the man, not the party."[9] These data then were analyzed as the previous data and no sex differences were uncovered. Such a result conflicts with the observations of Merelman [28, p. 127] who found that boys in the sixth and ninth grades were somewhat more likely than girls to express definite partisan preferences.

Notes on the Reliability and Validity of the Findings

The political differences between boys and girls uncovered in this study are, in general, minor. They represent a departure from the results of previous investigations of sex differences in childhood and/or adolescent political orientations. In light of this, we must ask whether this study has characteristics that might artificially produce a general absence of political differences between boys and girls.

Let us consider our sample first. Originally selected to compare the patterns of political expression among black students and white students in Illinois, we concluded, after some preliminary analyses, that the sample underrepresented schoolchildren from middle socioeconomic groups, particularly white children. This affects the results of the study in the following respects only: among whites and, to a lesser degree, blacks, the possible variation explained in the dependent variables by our measure of socioeconomic status is reduced; and the pattern of differences between boys and girls classified as white-collar will not represent the patterns in the population. The most reliable observations of the sex differences, then, are to be made among children classified as blue-collar; yet, among them, we find no sharp or consistent pattern of sex-linked differences. This general absence of differences is all the more significant since most research suggests that the sex differences should be most pronounced among children in this socioeconomic group [1, 9, 20]. In other words, the lack of overall sex differences in this kind of sample is the strongest evidence that they may not exist in the larger population of children, lower or middle class. (It is possible, of course, that being confined to a single state, our sample is unrepresentative in some other way that might affect the pattern of boy-girl differences.)

Another source of error may be the kinds of questions and the indices used in this analysis. Again, we are inclined to dismiss these as suspect. Our questions, in fact, were adapted from the path-breaking analyses of Easton and Hess [12, 19], a study whose results greatly supported the idea that sex differences in political orientations emerge early in life. Our analysis of the results differs somewhat from the analyses of these other investigators, particularly Hess and Torney [19], inasmuch as we relied almost exclusively on factor analysis and the resulting factor scores to assess the sex differences; whereas their analyses relied partly on single items. On particular kinds of dimensions, however, like the affective one above, we would expect to find more pronounced differences between boys and girls than these researchers, assuming that such differences existed in the population. That is, factor scores represent a more complete and representative picture of a single attitude or belief dimension than single items. Thus if sex differences exist in the general population, then the scores resulting from the factor analysis should discriminate better between the sexes than those on single items. As above, the lack of pronounced and consistent differences between the boys and girls on our indices strongly confirms that there may be no such differences of any magnitude in the population.

The case for the reliability of our results is made even stronger when one notes parallel results from recent studies of political socialization. In particular, Merelman [28] in a study of white California schoolchildren in 1968 found few large or consistent differences between boys and girls. Many indices differed from those studied here, but some tapped the same general domain of content as, for example, indices of children's attitudes toward minority rights, freedom of speech, liberalism, or sense of civic obligations. Merelman also uncovered substantial differences only on the cognitive dimension. Note also that two recent studies of sex differences in political interest and information among children in Finland [20] and Great Britain [9] concur with our results.

CONCLUDING OBSERVATIONS

In the most recent textbook in political socialization, Jaros [22] has remarked:

> Are women socialized to . . . nonparticipatory orientations as children? If they are, girls ought to differ from boys on such dimensions at very early ages. On most measurements they do, with girls decidedly less political. Girls are less oriented to various kinds of political action and are decidedly less informed. Moreover, these sexual differences are evident as early as the fourth grade. Despite increased efforts to involve women in the political world, despite all the recent attention, there is a cultural tradition of feminine nonparticipation transmitted in childhood. (pp. 44–45)

Our findings indicate that such a statement—and this general perspective—may need revision, ranging from discarding the statement altogether, to modifying the underlying theory.

Since alternative interpretations flow from ours and Merelman's [28] comparable results, it is important to outline them carefully and cogently. The first assumes that there are virtually no differences between boys and girls in our sample; by this account, the difference on the cognitive dimension among the white children is either a deviant pattern, which calls for no explanation, or the last vestige of a sex difference in political orientations. Accordingly, then there are only two possibilities regarding the applicability of the political socialization thesis to sex-role differences in political expression. The first is simply that the political socialization model no longer applies to the explanation of sex differences in political expression. Sex differences may or may not come about as these children and others like them grow to adulthood and are affected by situational or structural circumstances; but clearly such differences *do not emerge* in childhood.

The second possibility involves one form of linking the political socialization explanation together with either the situational or structural explanation: in effect what we are observing now in the 1970s is the disappearance of the childhood basis for political differences. Presumably, then, certain changes are occurring in the real and symbolic sex-role models currently available to children, in particular, diminished differences in political expression between adult males and females. In support of this line of thinking is recent evidence of only minor and apparently diminishing differences in the rates of political participation and activity among men and women in the United States [see 34].

The two interpretations above operate on the assumption that no sex differences are to be observed in these results or, if so, they are so minor as to be discounted. The third interpretation, which also involves linking the political socialization explanation with the situational, is more speculative, and applies mainly, perhaps exclusively, to white children. Starting with the fact that white children in this and virtually every other study differ consistently and prominently on the dimension of political knowledge, this interpretation is that in childhood the sexes will only differ politically in information and interest. Boys and girls begin to differ early, so this interpretation goes, in their attention to the public spheres of social activity largely as a means of anticipatory socialization. That is, anticipating that, as men, they will enter the public world of work, boys become more interested in public affairs, generally, one manifestation of which is their interest in politics. Girls, in contrast, anticipate at an early age their more private existence as women, confined to the home and local community; thus, they typically devote less attention to the world of public affairs than boys. For girls this finds expression in their lesser knowledge of and interest in politics. For each sex, the experiential and symbolic world presented to them by adults offers different sex-linked pictures of appropriate interests and channels them into greater, or lesser, interest in the public spheres of social activity. In other words, socialization to politics does differ for boys and girls in childhood, but its effects are confined mainly to the cognitive realm.

The other differences between males and females, this argument continues, occur in adulthood. Boys and girls have prepared themselves for adult roles, boys by cushioning the otherwise difficult impact of occupations and the public life through their early attention to public affairs, girls through their attention to more private home-related affairs. Different levels of participation and discussion, so often observed among adults, are the result of events that occur contemporaneously in the lives of men and women. As the situational thesis puts it, women generally take a less active role in politics largely because they are confined to their homes; while men are more active because of the demands of their jobs and ancillary activities. Finally, this interpretation would claim that the development of the well-known differing levels of political efficacy among men and women [5, 29] occurs concomitantly with participation itself: in effect, males, as adults are thrust into the political arena and, hence, develop a greater sense of efficacy; while the reverse happens to females. Such an interpretation would help explain why Easton and Dennis uncovered no sex differences in political efficacy among their sample of children.

What this scheme does not and cannot easily account for is the relative absence of sex differences on the affective dimension of political orientations as compared with the presence of such differences in the Hess-Torney data assembled more than ten years ago. The most plausible option to follow is to dismiss the significance of those differences, much as Easton and Dennis [12, pp. 342–43] did in their interpretation of the same data.

To us the three schemes outlined above represent equally plausible ways of explaining the general patterns of our results. Unfortunately, we cannot embrace any of these arguments as the most correct since we, like other observers of similar dimensions among youngsters, have no crystal ball that would show us what, in fact, will happen to these children as they mature and enter the adult world. We hope more research will be forthcoming.

NOTES

1. Our discussion here relies mainly on a social-learning theory point of view; however, there are many overlaps between this interpretation and the cognitive-development interpretation of sex differences; and the reader is advised to compare the discussions of both Mischel [30] and Kohlberg [23] for such differences and similarities as exist.

2. A variety of suggestive bits and pieces of evidence support this expectation. In his definitive survey and profile of black Americans, Pettigrew [31], for instance, cites a number of empirical studies which suggest that black male children do act in ways less characteristically masculine than their white counterparts; while black female children act less feminine. The most important and relevant of these studies is one by Lott and Lott [27] which finds that the boy-girl differences among black children are much less sharply pronounced than among white ones over a wide range of beliefs and values. A most often cited reason for this sort of race-sex interaction is that a greater proportion of black than white families in America are headed by females; Farley and Hermalin [14], for instance, found that in 1969 almost 30 percent of the black families in America were headed by females as compared with almost 10 percent of white ones. As a result, it is believed that black males are less apt to be continuously exposed to the influence of a male role model during childhood and, in turn, are more likely to act in ways less

"masculine" than those of white males. Evidence on the effects of father absence suggest such an outcome, but is by no means incontrovertible on this point [3].

3. The questionnaires administered to our sample of children consisted, in part, of items adapted from scales used in previous investigations. To assess the internal consistency of these and other scales, and to discover whether there might be some unanticipated dimensions in these items, we subjected two thirty-six variable sets to principle components factor analysis. The resulting vectors were then rotated using Varimax rotation, producing the most clearly delineated set of factors. Seven factors were produced by this method; all seven represented dimensions we had expected to tap with our items, a circumstance of no little gratification. Next, the items which possessed the highest loading on each of these factors were incorporated into a scale representing that factor; for these purposes, we chose a loading of approximately .40 or better. As the reader will note below, only two items, in fact, possessed loadings of .39 with their respective scales, all others possessing higher loadings.

Three scales were used to analyze the political affect items. The first one, the image of the President scale, with a range of values from 1.53 to 5.63, consisted of the following items:

Would the President always want to help you if you needed help?
(Loading = .51)

Does the President protect you more than anyone else?
(Loading = .53)

When you write to the President do you think he cares about what you think?
(Loading = .49)

4. The government benevolence scale consisted of three items, each asking: "Does the ＿＿ government make things better for most people, make things sometimes better, sometimes worse for most people, make things worse for most people, or make no difference at all?" Of the three items, one referred to the U. S. government, one to state government, and one to local government. The range of scores for this scale was from 2.18 to 8.72.

The political cynicism scale for fourth through sixth graders, which has scores ranging from .64 to 2.56, consisted of the following items:

Does the government make a lot of mistakes?
(Loading = .71)

Can the government be trusted?
(Loading = .68)

Are there some big powerful men running the government who do not care about us ordinary people?
(Loading = .61)

The political cynicism scale for seventh to twelfth graders is made up of the same items as those for the younger children plus the following items:

Rich people are the ones who decide what goes on in government.
(Loading = .39)

The United States needs a complete change in its form of government.
(Loading = .51)

5. The results of these analyses are available on request from the authors.

6. Items included in the political knowledge scale are as follows:

How many years does a United States senator serve?
What country does Marshall Tito lead?
How many members are there on the United States Supreme Court?
To what political party did President Franklin Roosevelt belong?
Who is the present governor of Illinois?
Who is the mayor of your city?

The values on this scale ranged from 0 to 6.

7. The political participation items and loadings are as follows:

Have you ever worn a campaign button for a candidate?
(Loading = .66)

Have you helped a candidate by doing things for him such as handing out buttons or papers with his name on them?
(Loading = .79)

Have you, yourself, ever been involved in a political demonstration, like a march, a picket line, or a strike, other than a union strike?
(Loading = .54)

The scores on the political participation scale ranged from 1.99 to 3.98.

The political discussion items and loadings are as follows:

Have you talked a lot with your friends about a candidate?
(Loading = .67)

Has your teacher told you about the candidates?
(Loading = .56)

Have you talked with your parents about a candidate?
(Loading = .74)

The scores on the discussion scale ranged from 1.97 to 3.94.

8. These data are available on request from the authors.
9. These data are available on request from the authors.

REFERENCES

1. Gabriel Almond and Sidney Verba. *The Civic Culture.* Princeton, N.J.: Princeton University Press, 1963.

2. Bernard Berelson, Paul F. Lazarsfeld, and and William N. McPhee. *Voting.* Chicago: University of Chicago, 1954.

3. Henry B. Biller. "Father Absence and the Personality Development of the Male Child." *Developmental Psychology* 2 (March 1970): 181–201.

4. Alan Booth. "Sex and Social Participation." *American Sociological Review* 37 (April 1972): 183–92.

5. Angus Campbell, Phillip E. Converse, Warren E. Miller, and Donald E. Stokes. *The American Voter.* New York: Wiley, 1960.

6. Randall Collins. "A Conflict Theory of Sexual Stratification." *Social Problems* 19 (Summer 1971): 3–21.

7. Richard Dawson and Kenneth Prewitt. *Political Socialization.* Boston: Little, Brown, 1969.

8. Jack Dennis, ed. *Socialization to Politics: A Reader.* New York: Wiley, 1973.

9. Robert E. Dowse and John A. Hughes. "Girls, Boys and Politics." *British Journal of Sociology* 22 (March 1971): 53–67.

10. Maurice Duverger. *The Political Role of Women.* Paris: UNESCO, 1955.

11. David Easton and Jack Dennis. "The Child's Acquisition of Regime Norms: Political Efficacy." *American Political Science Review* 61 (March 1967): 25–38.

12. David Easton and Jack Dennis. *Children in the Political System.* New York: McGraw-Hill, 1969.

13. Joseph Ellis. "The Effects of Same-Sex Class Organization on Junior High School Students' Academic Achievement, Self-Discipline, Self-Concept, Sex-Role Identification and Attitude Toward Attitude." Educational Resources Information Center, U.S. Office of Education, Project Number 7-E 115, 1968.

14. Reynolds Farley and Albert I. Hermalin. "Family Stability: A Comparison of Trends Between Blacks and Whites." *American Sociological Review* 36 (February 1971): 1–17.

15. Joseph Forbes and Dale Dykstra. "Children's Attribution of Negative Traits to Authority Figures as a Function of Family Size and Sex." *Psychological Reports* 28 (April 1971): 363–66.

16. Fred I. Greenstein. "Sex-Related Political Difference in Childhood." *Journal of Politics* 23 (May 1961): 353–71.

17. Fred I. Greenstein. *Children and Politics.* New Haven, Conn.: Yale University Press, 1965.

18. Murray Hausknecht. *The Joiners.* New York: Bedminster, 1962.

19. Robert D. Hess and Judith V. Torney. *The Development of Political Attitudes in Children.* Chicago: Aldine, 1967.

20. Veronica Stolte Heiskanen. "Sex Roles, Social Class and Political Consciousness." *Acta Sociologica* 14 (1971): 83–95.

21. Herbert Hyman. *Political Socialization.* Glencoe, Ill.: Free Press, 1959.

22. Dean Jaros. *Socialization to Politics.* New York: Praeger, 1973.

23. Lawrence Kohlberg. "A Cognitive-Developmental Analysis of Children's Sex-Role Concepts and Attitudes." In *The Development of Sex Differences,* ed. Eleanor Maccoby. Stanford, Calif.: Stanford University Press, 1966. Pp. 82–173.

24. Robert E. Lane. *Political Life: Why People Get Involved in Politics.* Glencoe, Ill.: Free Press, 1959.

25. Paul F. Lazarsfeld, Bernard Berelson, and Hazel Gaudet. *The People's Choice.* New York: Columbia University Press, 1968.

26. Seymour Martin Lipset. *Political Man.* New York: Doubleday, 1960.

27. Albert J. Lott and Bernice E. Lott. *Negro and White Youth: A Psychological Study in a Border-State Community.* New York: Holt, Rinehart & Winston, 1963.

28. Richard M. Merelman. *Political Socialization and Educational Climates: A Study of Two School Districts.* New York: Holt, Rinehart & Winston, 1971.

29. Lester W. Milbrath. *Political Participation.* Chicago: Rand McNally, 1965.

30. Walter Mischel. "A Social-Learning View of Sex Differences in Behavior." In *The Development of Sex Differences.* Stanford, Calif.: Stanford University Press, 1966). Pp. 56–81.

31. Thomas F. Pettigrew. *A Profile of the Negro American.* Princeton, N.J.: Van Nostrand, 1964.

32. John C. Scott, Jr. "Membership and Participation in Voluntary Associations." *American Sociological Review* 22 (June 1957): 315–26.

33. Daniel B. Suits. "Use of Dummy Variables in Regression Equations." *Journal of the American Statistical Association* 52 (December 1957): 548–51.

34. Sidney Verba and Norman H. Nie. *Participation in America: Political Democracy and Social Equality.* New York: Harper & Row, 1972.)

35. Charles R. Wright and Herbert H. Hyman. "Voluntary Association Membership of American Adults: Evidence from National Sample Surveys." *American Sociological Review* 23 (June 1958): 284–94.

BARRY BOZEMAN, SANDRA THORNTON,
and MICHAEL McKINNEY

3

☆☆☆☆☆☆☆☆☆☆☆☆☆☆☆☆☆☆☆☆☆☆☆☆☆

Continuity and Change in Opinions About Sex Roles

Since Genesis, a subordinate social role has been assigned to women; it has been rationalized on religious, social, biological, economic, and/or psychological grounds. These attitudes pervade law, mores, and public opinion, yielding sharp gender-role stereotypes. In the United States feminism made significant inroads in entrenched discriminatory practices until stalled by the Great Depression and the post-World War II enthrallment with the ideal of domesticity.

Not until the 1960s did law and public policy affecting the status of women begin to change dramatically, concomitant with the development of a new and increasingly militant feminism.[1] This defiance of traditional beliefs about sex roles originated in intellectual and political elites[2] and has received a mixed reception by the general public. The purpose of this research is to analyze patterns of public opinion about sex roles, examining the relationship of certain demographic variables to these attitudes.

LITERATURE OVERVIEW[3]

Sexist beliefs are derived from, among others, Genesis, Aristotle, Saint Thomas Aquinas, and Freud. Sex roles are ubiquitously perceived, especially in Freudian theories, as biologically determined: anatomy is destiny. The woman is an incomplete, "castrated" (Freud), "misbegotten" (Aquinas) male; hence she is weak, intellectually inferior, passive, intuitive, masochistic, submissive, nonproductive, emotional, inconsistent, and of weak superego.[4] The male is the opposite of these traits (strong, superior, dominant, aggressive, rational, etc.); the adjectives "feminine" and "masculine" connote these respective groups of characteristics. The female is defined by the male, creating a conflict in the female between the conceptions of what she should be and what she is; hence she strives to conform to the feminine ideal or refuses to be reconciled to her "inferiority" and thus is unable to resolve her "penis envy." The male view is also ambivalent, especially because of the problem of reconciling the notion of inherent female inferiority with Eve, hoodwinker of Adam. The result is a severe ambiguity in the historical male views of women: evil and good, whore and virgin, sexually insatiable and frigid, "mothers and the others."[5] As a consequence, an enormous body of law and social policies has developed to assure that women do not rise above the station to which their natural inferiority assigns them.[6]

A fair amount of psychological and sociological research on sex roles has been done in the twentieth century. Most of it, not surprisingly, confirms the traditional religious view, which Freud "scientifically" validated.[7] One of the most ambitious empirical studies on the nature of masculinity and femininity was conducted by Terman and Miles in the early 1930s.[8] The pair created a 910-item questionnaire designed to determine a numerical masuclinity score for each person tested. The scale ranged from +1 to −1, most masculine to most feminine. Those scoring *highest* on the *masculinity* scale were female college athletes of high intelligence, female Ph.D.s and M.D.s, female college students of high intelligence, and homosexuals (active and passive). The most *feminine,* more so than all female groups, were male adults in their sixties, male Protestant theological students, male clergymen, male adults in their seventies and eighties, male artists, and male passive homosexual prostitutes.[9] Nonetheless, the index was considered to provide a reasonable bifurcation of sex-linked personality traits (although no claims were made as to whether the source of these traits was cultural). Thus empirical research confirmed cultural expectation by declaring the nonconformists to be deviant sex-traitors. Bright women are "masculine," artists are "effeminate."

Anthropologists and sociologists are more likely than psychologists to view gender roles as culturally determined. While the reproductive sex-role division cannot vary, attitudes toward child rearing, sex typing of occupations, and the characterization of a particular trait as "masculine" or "feminine" do. What *does* seem common to most cultures is the higher valuation placed on the male role, whatever that role may be.[10] The persistence of patriarchy has also inspired an androcentric ethology and anthroplogy, documenting the significance of aggression (and the greater male physical and hormonal capacities for it) as the basis for the superiority of male over female.[11] On the other hand, there is one rather journalistic anthropological study that could be called estrocentric.[12] Elaine Morgan's *The Descent of Woman* traces human development via female adaptations to the environment, in effect locating the "missing link" in the sea to which the ape was forced to flee for protection.

By and large, there is little disagreement in any kind of literature that male domination is the norm—economically, socially, politically. Differences occur over its origin and necessity. Marxism[13] provides the most developed, nonbiological, theoretical explanation of gender-role differentiation—as an aspect of the class struggle that will be resolved with the achievement of communism. Shulamith Firestone, a revisionist Marxist *and* Freudian, views the sex struggle as more significant than the class struggle but resolvable via a technology that permits women to control and even eliminate their role in the reproductive function.[14] Less teleological explanations of the influence of culture on gender role examine stratification, the socialization process, and stereotyping. Myrdal in 1944 described women as a caste akin to that of the Negro[15]; Hacker in 1951 elaborated this idea, describing how women are perceived as, and act the part of, a minority group.[16]

Well-developed empirical data exist to support this view, particularly in regard to the inferior position of women in the economy.[17] While women are increasingly represented in the labor force—43.3 percent of all women in 1970 worked, representing 38.1 percent of the total labor force—the occupational distribution places the majority of women in sex-stereotyped, lower-paid occupations (such as nursing and secretarial).[18] In 1970 income statistics indicate that as a percentage of white male income for full-time work, nonwhite males earned 70 percent, white females 58 percent, and nonwhite females 50 percent. Less than 5 percent of women had incomes over $10,000; less than 1 percent, over $15,000.[19] Women are almost invisible in top professional positions; indeed, the number of women Ph.D.s as a percentage of the whole is smaller now than in 1930.[20] The percentage of working married women and working mothers has increased sharply, with education the major correlate of women's longevity in the labor force.[21] Women are clearly a major factor in the operation of the economy, particularly certain sex-stereotyped sectors, but form subordinate strata to men at all occupation levels.

Women are repressed socially as well as economically. Because a woman's social status is that of her husband, this factor is more complicated to research although there have been initial efforts.[22]

Political and legal repression have been dealt with more extensively.[23] The common-law fiction that husband and wife are one effectively eliminated the legal identity of the majority of women. Although most of these legal disabilities are gone, women have not become the political force that the suffrage movement anticipated. Women vote less than men, and there is no apparent political-issue polarization along sex lines. There are indications, however, that the "women's vote" is more likely to support peace issues, gun control, conservation, consumerism, day-care centers, domestic spending over military spending, and is more likely to oppose capital punishment and criminal treatment of addicts. Nonetheless, the expected women's vote did not materialize for George McGovern in 1972—any more than did the men's—although he was the first presidential candidate to identify with "women's issues."[24]

The number of women in elected political office has increased in recent years, especially black women (probably because of different black/white socialization patterns, to be discussed later). Women elected officials tend to be Democratic and more liberal.[25]

One other sex differential that could have political salience now that women may no longer be excused from jury duty on the basis of sex alone is that there is some indication that the presence of women on juries tends to favor verdicts for lower-status litigants. All male juries, by contrast, generally favor the superior-status litigant.[26]

As with blacks, the achievement of equal legal status for women will no doubt be attained first, but achievement of equal political and economic status will be much slower. An equal role for women in politics appears more attainable than an equal role in the economy, perhaps because women have a minuscule presence in current American politics, and politics are held in bad enough odor that the addition of women may be at worst viewed as not harmful.

Sex stratification in American society is not an accident; it is the result of a socialization process that begins in the cradle. The male is socialized to assume the primary role, the female the secondary. Socialization appears to be particularly effective with women, to the extent that the intellectual parity of boys and girls (and the intellectual superiority of girls in certain areas) statistically disappears by the time of high school.[27] Girls who fail to yield to the pressure of family, school, and media to conform to the feminine stereotype are made to feel deviant.[28] As the Kenistons suggest, "The most effective forms of oppression are those with which the victim covertly cooperates."[29] This pressure creates a high level of ambivalence, however, particularly for the bright woman. She, Horner's research indicates, is motivated to avoid success in achievement situations outside the home and to adjust her ambitions to the culturally expected.[30] The toll this exacts is particularly illustrated by indications that the housewife (i.e., the woman who has fulfilled the stereotype) is more likely to be the victim of nervous disorders, neuroses, and psychoses. Bernard notes the double standard of mental health maintained by analysts: one for "healthy adults" and "healthy males," the other for "healthy women"—the latter passive, submissive, dependent, etc. Thus, a person who exhibits traits of assurance, dominance, independence, and the like will be classified as "healthy" if male and unhealthy or neurotic if female.[31] What appears to be happening is that women are severely cross-pressured by cultural demands and their own aspirations, with the result that they may express a greater identity with their assigned gender role than they in fact have.[32] The opposite would appear to be true of the educated male; research indicates that he verbalizes a greater degree of sex-role egalitarianism than he actually grants in the marital situation.[33]

The black woman does not appear to be socialized to the feminine stereotype; in contrast to the white woman, she is more likely to be encouraged by her family to excel and is unlikely to exhibit the success-avoidance syndrome.[34] The fact that black mothers are less likely to read Spock and other experts on child rearing[35] may help explain this, as will the higher proportion of black female heads of households.[36]

The socialization literature supports the view that both women and men accept their gender-role assignments, although there is greater ambivalence among better-educated whites and less effective socialization among blacks. The notion that "women are their own worst enemies" is given credence by the evident success of socialization as indicated both in academic research and in public opinion.[37]

Given that ideology places woman in the home while economic reality—and increasingly, counterideology—draws her out of it, it is not surprising that there should be stress and ambivalence. In particular, the rise of antinatalism sparked by environmentalists directly challenges the traditional ideology for woman's raison d'être. The conflict is highly visible on the abortion issue; legalization of elective abortion undercuts the legal and social status accorded the wife and mother. Recent research among whites indicated that the *only* group significantly favorable to elective abortion were upper-class males; that legislatures and courts overrepresent this group explains the change in public policy vis-à-vis abortion.[38] The possibility of controlling reproduction via simple and effective contraception and abortion, never before present in woman's history, offers both an opportunity for equality and a serious identity conflict to the traditionally socialized woman and, for that matter, man.

Although the literature of the Women's Liberation Movement has been discussed throughout, it is appropriate to isolate the movement here as a significant political and social event of the 1960s bearing on perception of sex roles.[39] The John the Baptist of the movement was Betty Friedan, whose 1963 book, *The Feminine Mystique,* was an instant best seller. In 1966 she organized NOW (National Organization for Women), currently viewed as the more conservative wing of the movement. The strength and visibility of the movement grew largely from younger women who had been radicalized by participation in varying aspects of the New Left—black civil rights, peace movement, counterculture, etc.—particularly as they discovered that their male "radical" counterparts were actually very traditional when it came to gender-role stereotyping. WLM achieved a separate identity—and is the main survivor of the late 1960s New Left. Nonetheless, WLM "consciousness raising" among males has been most effective in the younger age group, particularly those who had participated in New Left activities. This is quite noticeable among blacks: the Julian Bond who cosponsored the ERA in the Georgia Senate in 1975 is the same man who opposed elective abortion as "genocide."

It is clear that the women's movement of the late 1960s and 1970s has inspired a voluminous empirical and theoretical literature to challenge prevailing gender roles.[40] The purpose of the research reported here is to contribute new and more recent information about public attitudes concerning sex roles in society and politics and, where possible, to compare these findings to similar data from the past.

DESIGN

The scope of the research reported here is relatively modest. There is no broad-scale consideration of the meaning of sex roles in society; instead, the design focuses on the explanation of opinions about several issues related to sex roles. Each of the issues is currently highly visible and has far-reaching implications for the status of women in society.

The Data

While several supplemental data sources were employed, the heart of the study is the responses to five questions that were posed in late 1972 to a national sample of 2,708 respondents by the University of Michigan's Survey Research Center. The questions are given below along with the designations that have been given each for purposes of convenient discussion in this paper:

ROLE Recently there has been a lot of talk about women's rights. Some people feel that women should have an equal role with men in running business, industry, and government. Others feel that women's place is in the home. Where would you place yourself on this scale? [Seven-point scale, 1 = equal role, 7 = women's place is in the home.]

ABORT There has been some discussion about abortion during recent years. Which one of the opinions on this card best agrees with your view? [1 = abortion should never be permitted; 2 = abortion should be permitted only if the life and health of the woman is in danger; 3 = abortion should be permitted if, due to personal reasons, the woman would have difficulty in caring for the child; 4 = abortion should never be forbidden, since one should not require a woman to have a child she doesn't want.]

LAYOFF Sometimes a company has to lay off part of its labor force. Some people think that the first workers to be laid off should be women whose husbands have jobs. Others think that male and female employees should be treated the same. Which of the opinions do you agree with? [1 = lay off women first; 2 = treat male and female employees the same.]

POLITICS Do you agree or disagree with the statement, women should stay out of politics? [Five-point scale, 1 = agree, 5 = disagree.]

LIB (As a feeling thermometer item) Women's liberation [affect scale, 0–100.]

Independent variables were chosen that had been commonly considered in previous studies and that seem intuitively to be of interest in relation to sex roles and opinions. A list of the independent variables is given below:

x_1 Age
x_2 Education
x_3 Income
x_4 Sex (1 = male, 2 = female)
x_5 Race (1 = white, 2 = nonwhite)
x_6 Marital state (1 = married, 2 = single)
x_7 Raised (1 = country, 2 = town, 3 = city)
x_8 Region (1 = non-South, 2 = Border, 3 = South)

While there was no attempt at detailed hypothesizing, certain basic patterns were anticipated. It was expected that those most in favor of abortion would be better-educated, higher-income white males of all ages and young, better-educated white females; those most opposed would be Catholics, southerners, lower-income persons, less-educated persons, older white females, and blacks.[41] It was further expected that an expression of support for an equal role for men and women would be positively related to youth, better education, higher income, and, to a more moderate degree, being female and black.

Methods and Techniques of Analysis
The first and most important step in analysis involved the calculation of gamma for the relationship of each of the predictor variables to the five opinion items.[42] After analyzing the gammas, partials were calculated in cases that seemed appropriate.

Another important element of the analysis involved calculation of descriptive statistics for the original data. Finally, in order to lend some time perspectives and to assess change, results of relevant Gallup poll questions were examined.

FINDINGS

Each of the opinion items will be considered and explained separately. There is also an effort in this section to generalize and give accounts for the relationships that appear, with additional generalization and speculation provided in the Conclusions.

Role

This item is especially important because it is very general and perhaps the single true attitudinal item of the five.[43] A view on role could be considered an attitude, and the other four questions as expressions of opinion that are specific applications of that basic attitude. Table 3.1 gives the gammas for the relationships of the independent variables to Role.

In the case of correlation with Role, and all the correlations, the focus is on gammas in excess of ± .15. With such a large n (2,708), even relationships that are very small in magnitude are significant at the .01 level; thus a somewhat more conservative criterion is appropriate.[44]

Perhaps the most striking finding in connection with Role is that the independent variable sex is of little importance (gamma = .046) in accounting for differences in attitudes about the role of women in society. This is an expected result of the sexist socialization process described earlier: women are trained to be no more sexually egalitarian than men. Also, although the question measures the direction of affect and (roughly) intensity, it does not measure saliency. Another explanation that must be taken into consideration in the case of the relationship of sex to all the dependent variables is that some men may have been less honest in their responses to the sex-role question than women. As indicated, educated males are likely to be more egalitarian in theory than in practice. It would not be unreasonable to assume that male respondents, particularly the sociopolitically aware, might somewhat exaggerate support of sexual equality. On the other hand, women tend to exaggerate their support of *inequality;* however, the circumstances of the 1970s provide an atmosphere more conducive to female honesty, as least on the part of the younger woman.

TABLE 3.1. Gamma Correlations—Equal Role by Independent Variables

Age	Education	Income	Sex	Race	Raised	Region
−.098	.259	.132	−.046	−.032	.218	.120

Thus, it is possible that the data are somewhat distortive of reality, probably bringing the sexes closer together than in fact they are.

With these caveats, then, it should be noted that only 30 percent of all respondents (30 percent of men and 31 percent of women) took a position closer to the nonequal role than to the equal role end of the scale. There was, in fact, very little admitted variance by sex on any of the seven points of the scale.

Education, on the other hand, appears to be a much more significant variable (gamma = .26). Individuals with college degrees are considerably more likely to be supportive of an equal role for women, and moderate differences appear when education is looked at by sex. The less-educated men are somewhat more likely than less-educated women to be supportive of an equal role for women, while female respondents with some college are moderately more likely to be supportive of an equal role than their male counterparts. Of women under age thirty holding a college degree, 51 percent reported the top value on the scale of equality, and only 7 percent responded with scale values nearer to "women should stay at home." By contrast, only 28 percent of women who did not attend college reported the top value of equality, while 36 percent responded with scale values nearer the "women should stay at home" end of the scale.

No matter how the data were broken down, older respondents within every subgroup were less likely to support equal roles (gamma = −.16). Among all those fifty-five years or older, only 39 percent responded with values closer to equality. Among this group, men were considerably more likely to support equal roles; a majority of the men (53 percent) responded with one of the three values in the direction of equality. This is in marked contrast to responses to a 1938 Gallup poll: 82 percent of men and 75 percent of women in the sample answered "no" when asked if a married woman should work if she had a husband capable of supporting her.[45] In that question, young women were more likely to be supportive of working women than were young men, yet when that same generational cohort is questioned in 1972, the male attitude toward equal roles has shifted more dramatically than the female attitude. This may be because most women over fifty-five have never had careers, even though they may well have been anticipating careers early in life. For them, acceptance of "woman's place is in the home" may be a defense mechanism that has been invoked to rationalize a way of life. In addition, the 1930s depression, with public support, forced married women out of the job market. A less egalitarian attitude is to be expected in bad economic times, a phenomenon we are witnessing again.

A final variable that is important in understanding responses to Role concerns the demographic origins of the respondent—whether raised in a rural area, small town, suburb, or city. The .19 gamma indicates that more urban origins are associated with a view of women as equal.

In summation, the young well-educated female is, to no one's surprise, most likely to feel that women should play an equal role. But the next most likely supporter of equal roles is her male counterpart. The group that is most likely to feel that women should stay at home is the group that has most often done so—older, less-well-educated females.

Abort

The gammas for all but two of the independent variables and the abortion item were in excess of ± .15. As is indicated in table 3.2, the variable sex is of little use in explaining differences of opinion regarding abortion (gamma = −.07).

Support for abortion has increased dramatically in both sexes, with Gallup reporting somewhat more variation of opinion by sex in 1962 than in 1972. In response to a 1962 Gallup question concerning whether a woman who had taken the drug thalidomide (a drug discovered to be related to birth defects) had done the right or wrong thing in obtaining an abortion, 54 percent of the women and 50 percent of the men interviewed said that she had done the right thing, 30 percent of the women and 33 percent of the men said that she had done the wrong thing.[46] In the 1972 question, only 11 percent of the men and 12 percent of the women indicated that no consideration, including health, was sufficient to warrant an abortion. Our findings

TABLE 3.2.[a] Gamma Correlations—Abortion by Independent Variables

Age	Education	Income	Sex	Race	Raised	Region
−.256	.365	.234	−.069	−.168	.228	.224

[a]Coded so that more "liberal" answers are correlated positively with increasing age, education, income, being female, black, city raised, non-South.

are, however, somewhat contradictory of the Blake study, which found disproportionate support for abortion only among educated white males.

One of the best documented explanatory factors regarding abortion is religion. In the 1972 Gallup study, 49 percent of the Catholics interviewed said that the women who had taken thalidomide were wrong in obtaining an abortion, whereas, only 27 percent of the Protestants held that opinion.[47] While religion was not employed in the present study as an across-the-board predictor variable, it was employed in connection with abortion. The operationalization was simply Catholic/non-Catholic. The gamma was .227, suggesting a substantial but not overwhelming relationship between being Catholic and being less supportive of abortion. Perhaps more interesting than the positive relationship between Catholics and opposition to abortion is the fact that only 18 percent of all Catholic respondents were unalterably opposed to abortion. A majority favored abortion in cases where the mother's health seemed threatened and nearly 19 percent were in favor of abortion on demand—slightly more than were unqualifiedly opposed. Catholic males were more likely to be supportive than were Catholic females.

Younger people were substantially more likely to favor abortion than were older people (gamma = −.25). Among people over fifty-five years, 17 percent of both men and women were unqualifiedly against abortion, while 18 percent of the men and 15 percent of the women were in favor of abortion on demand. By contrast, 32 percent of those under age thirty were in favor of abortion on demand, and among women under thirty with college degrees, 42 percent were in favor. The data indicated that among younger people, women were moderately more likely than men to be in favor of abortion; among older people, men were slightly more likely than women to favor liberalized abortion.

These findings may be contrasted to a 1969 Gallup question concerning the legalization of abortion on demand.[48] At that time 46 percent of those under thirty and 38 percent of those over thirty were in favor of abortion on demand. This is in contrast to the SRC data in which 32 percent of those under thirty and 21 percent of those over thirty favored free abortion. This could mean that there has been a move toward conservatism in abortion in those three years, but more likely the differences are primarily attributable to the fact that the Gallup question was dichotomous (abortion on demand or not), whereas the SRC question gave three pro-abortion choices—abortion on demand, abortion due to inability to care for the children, and abortion due to health problems. This view is reinforced by the fact that only 11.2 percent of the SRC respondents were unqualifiedly against abortion.

Higher family income was associated with support for liberalized abortion (gamma = .23), and the finding appeared to have some theoretical importance rather than simply being an artifact of its association with education. A partial correlation was computed between income and abortion, controlling for education. The zero-order correlation (Pearson's r) was .11, significant at the .001 level, whereas the first-order partial between those two variables was .16. This finding indicates the explanatory effect of income is more substantial than is apparent in the findings in table 3.2.

The relationship between education and abortion is the strongest both in terms of the gammas and the Pearson coefficients. But an examination of the relationship of those variables with income held constant reveals that the simple correlation of .26 is reduced to a partial of .20 after income is introduced as a control. Thus, it appears that both education and income are useful as predictors of "unique" variance in regard to abortion.

The findings in regard to the relationship of race to support for liberalized abortion indicates that whites are generally more supportive than nonwhites. The relationship between race and support for abortion might be accounted for by a third variable known to be related to both race and support for abortion: income. That whites have a higher average income may account for their greater support for abortion. Such an argument, however, is not supported by the partial correlation. Controlling for income did not diminish the relationship between race and support for abortion. We may speculate that greater opposition to abortion among blacks may be explained by their traditional family and social patterns. For example, there is little stigma attached to illegitimacy among blacks, and the concept of the extended family retains strength. Another element may be the previously noted black opposition to abortion because it is viewed as genocide.

Both the type of area (i.e., city, town, country) in which one was raised (gamma = .22) and the region of the country in which one resides (gamma = .22) affect opinions about abortion. The more urbanized the area in which the respondent was raised, the more likely it is that the respondent will support liberalized abortion. This finding is not unexpected. It has been frequently observed that city dwellers are generally more likely to be both personally and politically liberal and that the cities are consistently the fountain of social change. Likewise, the finding in regard to region is consistent with broad interpretations of acceptance of change. The South has long been pointed to as the curator of traditional social values.

Layoff

Table 3.3, which gives the gammas of the independent variables in relation to Layoff, shows that the strongest "predictor" of opinion about whether women should lose their jobs before men is the variable age. As in all cases where age is associated with opinion about sex roles, younger people are more likely to be supportive of equal status for men and women. Among all respondents fifty-five years or older 58.1 percent said that women should lose their jobs before men. By contrast, in the most "liberal" category—females under thirty years with a college degree—only 28.8 percent said that women should lose their jobs before men.

A 1952 Gallup poll question that is somewhat comparable indicates that the relationship between age and views of working women has not changed dramatically in two decades. The Gallup sample was asked, "Do you think mothers who are working should or should not be allowed in figuring their federal income tax, to deduct from their taxes the amount they have to pay baby-sitters?"[49] While the majority of all respondents supported the deduction, among those over age fifty, 61 percent supported the deduction; among those under fifty, 75 percent supported this deduction.

In the case of Layoff, like in the cases of Role and Abort, the more-educated respondents are more likely to express opinions of equality (gamma = .21). One point of interest here is that the "cutting line" seems to lie between college-degree holders and those not hold-

TABLE 3.3.[a] Gamma Correlations—Layoff by Independent Variables

Age	Education	Income	Sex	Race	Raised	Region
−.377	.234	.041	−.161	.298	.125	−.098

[a]Coded so that more "liberal" answers are correlated positively with increasing age, education, income, being female, black, city raised, non-South.

ing a degree. There is no difference in opinion about Layoff between those who attended college (but did not graduate) and those who never attended college. This is in contrast to findings concerning the relation of education to the other dependent variables—in those cases there was a graduation of opinion with as much and usually more difference between those who attended college and those who did not versus those who attended and those who received a degree. A possible explanation is that the "attended college" respondents, while generally more likely to be supportive of equality than the "no college" respondents, feel as threatened by job insecurity as those who did not attend, and both groups feel much more threatened than holders of college degrees. Those not attending college often develop trades and industrial skills, whereas those attending but not graduating are likely to be employed in the more dispensable white-collar jobs; thus the two groups may feel equally vulnerable and their feelings of insecurity may cancel out the general tendency of those attending college to be somewhat more egalitarian than those who have not attended.

The fact that men are somewhat more likely to express the view that women should be treated equally in layoffs (gamma = −.16) might seem to contradict the argument just outlined since it is based on vulnerability of *male* workers. But women, even working women, are also greatly concerned about their husband's job security, and it is likely that in most cases married women would be more likely to respond on the basis of their concern for their husbands' vulnerability rather than in terms of a more abstract concern about equal opportunity. A reflection of this greater concern is the fact that 43.1 percent of married women and 56.6 percent of widowed women said that women should lose their jobs before men, whereas only 30.9 percent of women never married support this view. For male respondents, marital status is not an important explanatory factor in regard to opinions about Layoff.

The findings indicate that nonwhites are more likely to be supportive of equality in regard to Layoff than whites (gamma = .29). Among all whites, 48.1 percent said that women should lose their jobs before men; and among all nonwhites, 33.3 percent feel that women should be laid off first. The apparent explanation here is that while both white and nonwhite women are working in increasing numbers, nonwhite women are more often heads of households; and even in cases where both wife and husband are working, a higher proportion of nonwhite women than white women may be working to provide necessities.

Significant changes have occurred in attitudes toward layoffs since this question was posed by a Roper survey for *Fortune* magazine in 1946.[50] At that time, 72 percent of those polled would lay off an efficient married woman in preference to a less efficient family man; 57.9 percent would lay off an efficient single woman rather than a less efficient family man, while 68 percent would lay off an efficient single man rather than a less efficient family man. In other words, those polled were interested in distributing jobs on the basis of need rather than ability, a development that *Fortune* found troublesome.

In a related question, only 21.7 percent of males and 28.5 percent of females thought that women should have equal employment opportunity regardless of whether they were self-supporting or not. The responses to both these questions indicate the continuing strength of depression psychology in the postwar period.

Politics

The issue of women in politics is of special interest because it is the single issue concerning the status of women for which there is survey research data extending over a long period. One factor that has changed dramatically in the last forty or so years is the perception of men in regard to the participation of women in politics. Table 3.4 shows that the relationship between sex and opinions about women in politics is minimal (gamma = .066).

The SRC item (women should stay out of politics) has a low "difficulty" factor; that is, if one's opinion is not on the extreme lower end of a continuum of inequality to equality, one can be expected to respond "disagree." Thus, it is helpful to look at other questions from other polls that require a similar level of commitment to equality.

In 1937, this question was put to a Gallup sample: "Are you in favor of permitting women to serve as jurors in your state?"[51] The difficulty level here would not seem to be greatly in excess of that for the SRC question, yet 31 percent said that women should not be ac-

TABLE 3.4.[a] Gamma Correlations—Politics by Independent Variables

Age	Education	Income	Sex	Race	Raised	Region
−.225	.592	.390	−.066	−.064	.220	.129

[a]Coded so that more "liberal" answers are correlated positively with increasing age, education, income, being female, black, city raised, non-South.

corded the not very exalted right of jury duty, whereas only 21 percent of the SRC respondents said that women should stay out of politics. While the questions are not entirely comparable, there is still a suggestion of remarkable change in the opinions of men.

The change in opinions about women in politics can be traced through the years. In 1945, in response to a Gallup question asking whether more women should hold important jobs in government, 26 percent of the men and 38 percent of the women said yes.[52] In 1949 another Gallup question asked respondents whether or not they approved of President Truman's decision to appoint a woman as ambassador to Luxembourg; 48 percent of the men and 60 percent of the women approved.[53] In 1955, in response to a question concerning support of a "best qualified" woman for President, 52 percent of the women and 48 percent of the men indicated they would support the candidate.[54] In 1963 a similar woman President question was asked (with "qualified" replacing "best qualified"); 58 percent of the men and 51 percent of the women respondents reported that they would vote for the woman candidate.[55] A 1970 Gallup question asked whether respondents would vote for a qualified woman if she were nominated for Congress; 83 percent of the men and 84 percent of the women said yes.[56]

In summation, both sexes have become more supportive of political activity by women, but the most drastic change has been in men's opinions, which have gone from reticence on the least difficult questions to widespread support for questions with a high difficulty factor. In a 1971 Gallup question about voting for a woman nominated for President, 65 percent of the men (and 67 percent of the women) interviewed responded that they would vote for a woman President—14 percent more than would have supported women simply serving on juries in 1937. By way of further comparison, 27 percent of the men and 41 percent of the women in the 1937 sample indicated that they would vote for a qualified woman to be President.[57]

The strongest correlation between any single independent variable and any single dependent variable was that between education and Politics (gamma = .63). However, the correlation between income and Politics (.38) suggested that a degree of statistical confluence might be involved. The effect of computing a first order-partial, controlling for income, was to drive the Pearson's r down from .30 to .23. Employing the same procedure and reversing the control variable had the result of reducing the Pearson's r for income from .21 to .10. Moreover, despite some complications resulting from redundancy, both income and education have a degree of independent explanatory power in connection with politics although education appears to be more important. This is not unexpected, given that numerous studies of political participation have shown that women (and men) from higher socioeconomic backgrounds are much more likely to participate in politics at all levels—voting, electioneering, and running for office.[58]

The relationship between marital status and the respective dependent variables exceeds ± .15 only in the case of Politics (gamma = −.19). The findings indicate that married persons are somewhat more inclined than single persons to favor political participation by women. This should not be greatly surprising given the known tendency for married people to be more active in politics than those who are single.[59] Also, political participation, especially in the traditional, nonprotest mode, is a family affair. Further, it has been demonstrated that married individuals perceive that they have greater stakes in political outcomes.[60]

There is, however, an important footnote to the relationship between marital status and opinions about women in politics. A breakdown of the variables in terms of whether the single person was divorced, separated, widowed, or never married indicated that those never married were somewhat likely to agree that women should stay out of politics (17 percent "agree" among marrieds, 16 percent "agree" among never-marrieds); but those who are divorced, separated, or widowed are much more likely to agree that women should stay out of politics (23 percent, 22 percent, and 34 percent respectively). Thus, it appears that several explanations may be relevant here. First, married people do participate more and are therefore likely to support women's participation in politics; and, second, people who have never been married are not as likely to participate but are likely to support women's participation simply because the average age of all nonmarried persons is the lowest and age is associated negatively (gamma = −.25) with agreement that women should participate in politics. The disproportionate opposition of divorced and separated persons to women in politics may be related to a perception that the marital failure was in part attributable to a breakdown of traditional male/female roles.

Lib

The independent variables had much less explanatory power in connection with the Woman's Liberation feeling thermometer question than with any of the other dependent variables. Table 3.5 shows that only race was especially useful in accounting for differences in perception of Lib (gamma = .36).

This single important relationship is even more pronounced when nonwhites are viewed by sex. Whereas white men and white women as a group have similar perceptions of women's liberation, nonwhite women are much more likely than nonwhite men to be supportive (62.1 percent to 37.9 percent).

While the direction of the correlation between age and supportiveness of women's rights remains the same, the magnitude is much smaller (gamma = −.12). Given the across-the-board relationship of age and the other dependent variables it is curious that the correlation is no higher for the controversial issue of Women's Liberation.

Further, the variables income and education, which are related to every other sex-equality item, show very low correlation with Women's Liberation. It is highly unlikely that perceptions of Women's Liberation are as near random as it would seem by the account rendered here (multiple R^2 = .011); certainly other explanatory variables must be explored.

CONCLUSIONS

The study provides evidence for both continuity and change in regard to acceptance of equality of the sexes. It is significant that, despite the steady trend toward the acceptance of sex equality, the United States is entering the last quarter of the twentieth century with the majority of the population unconvinced. Only the most "militant" of the strata analyzed here—young women with college degrees—was more likely than not to favor full equality for women (in terms of

TABLE 3.5.[a] Gamma Correlations—Women's Liberation by Independent Variables

Age	Education	Income	Sex	Race	Raised	Region
−.121	.022	.048	−.004	.355	.095	−.042

[a]Coded so that more "liberal" answers are correlated positively with increasing age, education, income, being female, black, city raised, non-South.

Role). Even among this most supportive subgroup, only 51 percent believed that women should be fully equal.

While comparatively little support exists for full equality of woman's role in society, there is considerably more support for complete parity in the political sphere. In all likelihood "conservers" are less likely to feel directly threatened by the appearance of women in politics. Furthermore, there are very few women in politics (probably about 1 percent of all elected officials; 7 percent in 1974 of state legislators) and virtually none in high positions (1 governor, 1 lieutenant governor, 1 cabinet officer, no senators, 18 House members, 1 House committee chairmanship). The threat, if any, is potential.[61]

Full equality in regard to political participation is perhaps also made more palatable by the fact that political activism by "some other woman" is less likely to be viewed as personally disruptive, socially or economically. Another factor that may be of secondary importance in explaining the increasing acceptance of "political woman" is that the traditional "women's issues"—peace, conservation, civil rights—have been more salient in the past few years than before. Additionally, political participation by women is made more "respectable" by the fact that even traditional, family-oriented, antiliberation woman are active in elective politics.

Issues that involve social change and potential legal change evoke much less enthusiasm. While it is significant, for instance, that only 11.2 percent of the SRC respondents were against abortion under any circumstances, it is equally significant that only 24 percent were in favor of abortion on demand. Nonetheless, legislatures and courts have made elective abortion a matter of public policy.

In regard to layoffs, there have been important changes in the attitudes toward equal treatment of women in the labor market since World War II. It is interesting, however, that as many as 38 percent of those who have attended college, 50 percent of females, and 44 percent of people with incomes over $12,000 oppose equal layoffs for men and women. Public policy to prohibit sex discrimination in employment is not as much in advance of public opinion as it is in the case of abortion. Nonetheless, it would appear that federal requirements for affirmative action to achieve equal employment standards may be a threat to a significant proportion of the population. Moreover, we may expect that such opposition may increase if affirmative action, under court pressure, becomes more effective than it has been thus far.

Probably the most important finding in this study is the dramatic change in men's opinions that has come about in the past decade or so. Men are generally no less likely (or only a little less likely) to be supportive of equality of the sexes than women. The critical variable now appears to be age: younger people are consistently more likely to be supportive of equality. Better-educated, higher-income urban residents tend to have more egalitarian attitudes toward sex roles, but the age variable is by far the most significant.

It appears from this study that a critical mass of popular support has not developed in connection with full equality of the sexes and possibly will not develop for some time to come. Nonetheless, law and public policy are changing, despite the lack of public support. Such changes apparently occur because belief systems are articulated by elites and internalized by masses, with a time lag between the origination of an idea or belief set in the upper classes and its trickling down to the lower classes. In the process of transmission, a conviction is likely to be simplified or vulgarized, and the consequent belief system is apt to exhibit few constraints.[62] Mass convictions are based more on faith, authority, and tradition than on reason. Consequently, changes in prevailing belief systems are slow to be accepted by the general public, particularly if the challenged beliefs are well entrenched and there is no severe social crisis that shakes the roots of conviction.

The traditional belief system concerning sex roles has been thoroughly articulated, as the literature overview indicated, by elite authority: God, the founding fathers,[63] and Freud. Small wonder that there is common conviction that women are inherently inferior and that there is great reticence to accept a contradictory policy. Nonetheless, changes in belief systems happen, almost always originating in the elite—frequently at the behest of rebellious youth—and slowly permeate the rest of society, however unevenly. Our study indicates that the process of change in the traditional belief set about sex roles has started, but it has not diffused very far beyond its origins in the elite (and young), and indeed, egalitarianism has not become a uniform conviction of even the elite. The fact that resistance to change is weakest in the well educated and the young, and strongest among older people, rural residents and the less educated, helps explain why legal and social forces for change have had a strength beyond their numerical popular support: public policy as well as belief systems originate in the elite.

This factor, plus the dramatic upsurge of male support for women's rights, explain changes in law favorable to equality between the sexes: upper-class men virtually monopolize political decision making. Moreover, this large-scale change in men's opinions about sex roles augurs well for those who favor the further use of legislative avenues to equality of status. Though it appears that the time for "mass movement" politics in women's rights is still not completely ripe, it is likely that selective lobbying of officials should continue to be more and more successful if the trend for supportiveness among young educated men continues. It is also likely that the state legislatures, with lower median ages of legislators than is the case in Congress, will prove an important source for new women's rights legislation. The exception here is likely to be state legislatures dominated by rural interests.

While there are several policy implications of the findings, particularly for political coalition building, some basic cues about socialization are also implicit in the findings reported here. In the first place, it appears that higher education mitigates sexism. Among both men and women, higher education is continually associated with increased support for equal status. In this respect it appears that sex discrimination is not unlike race discrimination. Further, women are clearly no less likely and perhaps more likely than men to have instilled in them fundamental beliefs about the subordinance of women in society. The feminine counterpart of the Uncle Tom is not only very much in evidence but is much more common than adamant egalitarians. Moreover, the socialization process is far more pernicious for women than men. There is typically less cost involved in a man's changing his opinion about sex roles. Women, however, often have a stake in reinforcing sexist socialization if they are engaged in a traditional role, the rationale for which is contingent on the values of subordinate status. A woman in such a position has, in a sense, a psychological stake in inferiority—a great deal of time and effort and sometimes a lifetime have been devoted to a traditional secondary role. The psychological costs are enormous in confronting the logic or desirability of not only one's own role but also the framework of sex stratification in society. Indeed, the great psychological costs to many women may help explain why the increase in support for equal status among women in recent years has been modest, while the increase among men has been much greater.

NOTES
   1. For example, The Equal Pay Act of 1963; the Civil Rights Act of 1964 (Title VII); Executive Order 11246 of 1965 as amended in 1967 by Executive Order 11375

(requiring nondiscrimination by federal contractors); *Griswold* v. *Connecticut* in 1965 (declaring contraception a protected right to privacy); abortion-law reform (beginning in 1967 in California); the Equal Employment Opportunity Act of 1972; the Higher Education Amendments of 1972; *Roe* v. *Wade* and *Doe* v. *Bolton* (abortion as a constitutional right); *Frontiero* v. *Richardson* (a Supreme Court plurality holding that sex is a suspect classification under the Fourteenth Amendment); the proposed Equal Rights Amendment.

2. In contrast to issues involving black civil rights, the Supreme Court has followed rather than led Congress and state legislatures; and at a respectful distance at that.

3. Extended bibliographies and bibliographic essays include Wilma Rule Krauss, "Political Implications of Gender Roles: A Review of the Literature," *American Political Science Review* 68 (December 1974): 1706–23; Vern L. Bullough, *The Subordinate Sex* (Urbana: University of Illinois Press, 1973), pp. 355–56; Committee on the Status of Women of the Midwest Political Science Association, "Women and Politics: Selected Course Syllabi and Bibliography," (1974); William H. Chafe, *The American Woman* (New York: Oxford University Press, 1972), pp. 321–41; Arlie Russell Hochschild, "A Review of Sex Role Research," in *Changing Women in a Changing Society*, ed. Joan Huber (Chicago: University of Chicago Press, 1973), pp. 249–67; Annotated Bibliography compiled by Robert M. Oetzel in *The Development of Sex Differences*, ed. Eleanor E. Maccoby (Stanford: Stanford University Press, 1966), pp. 223–321; "Classified Summary of Research in Sex Differences," in ibid., pp. 323–49; Jeanne Spiegel, ed., *Sex Role Concepts* (Washington, D.C.: Business and Professional Women's Foundation, 1969).

4. See Sigmund Freud, "Psychological Consequences of Anatomical Distinctions Between the Sexes," "Three Contributions to the Theory of Sex," "Female Sexuality," "Civilization and Its Discontents," in *Complete Psychological Works* (London: Hogarth Press, 1953); Naomi Weisstein, " 'Kinder, Küche, Kirche' as Scientific Law: Psychology Constructs the Female," in *Sisterhood Is Powerful*, ed. Robin Morgan (New York: Random House, 1970), pp. 205–20; Natalie Shainess, "A Psychiatrist's View: Images of Women—Past and Present, Overt and Obscured," in ibid., pp. 230–45. Freud is the particular bête noire of the Women's Liberation Movement, because Freudianism has so permeated popular culture in attitudes toward female sexuality, child rearing, and gender role. See also Susan Lydon, "The Politics of Orgasm," in ibid., pp. 197–205; Ann Koedt, "The Myth of Vaginal Orgasm," in *Notes from the Second Year: Women's Liberation*, ed. Shulamith Firestone and Ann Koedt (New York, 1970); Alix Shulman, "Organs and Orgasms," in *Woman in Sexist Society*, ed. Vivian Gornick and Barbara Moran (New York: Basic, 1971), pp. 292–303; Betty Friedan, *The Feminine Mystique* (New York: Norton, 1963); Jessie Bernard, *Women and the Public Interest* (Chicago: Aldine-Atherton, 1971), esp. chap. 12 on the WLM view of sexism; Phyllis Chesler, "Patient and Patriarch: Women in the Psychotherapeutic Relationship," in Gornick and Moran, *Women in Sexist Society*, pp. 362–92; Phyllis Chesler, *Women and Madness* (Garden City, N.Y.: Doubleday, 1972).

5. Eva Figes, *Patriarchal Attitudes* (New York: Stein & Day, 1970). This ambivalence toward women is particularly evident in religion and literature. Simone de Beauvoir, *The Second Sex* (New York: Knopf, 1952), is a classic treatise on woman as the "other" as defined by men.

6. This point is made in John Stuart Mill's "On the Subjection of Women" (1869). Some particularly good works on the legal disabilities of women are Leo Kanowitz, *Women and the Law: The Unfinished Revolution* (Albuquerque: University of New Mexico Press, 1969); Kenneth Davidson, Ruth Ginsburg, and Herma Kay, *Sex Based Discrimination: Text, Cases, and Materials* (St. Paul: West Publishing, 1974); Susan Ross, *The Rights of Women* (New York: Avon, 1973); "Sex Discrimination: Supreme Court Cases," Annotation 27 L. Ed. 2d935, pp. 935–49. Pauli Murray and Mary Eastwood,

"Jane Crow and the Law: Sex Discrimination and Title VII," *George Washington University Law Review* 34 (1965): 232; Robert Allen Sedler, "The Legal Dimensions of Women's Liberation: An Overview," *Indiana Law Journal* 47 (Spring 1972): 419–56; Faith A. Seidenburg, "The Submissive Majority: Modern Trends in the Law Concerning Women's Rights," *Cornell Law Review* 55 (1970): 262–272; John D. Johnston, Jr., and Charles L. Knapp, "Sex Discrimination by Law: A Study in Judicial Perspective," *New York University Law Review* 46 (October 1971): 675–747. Entire issues: *Harvard Civil Rights Law Review,* March 1971; *Yale Law Journal,* April 1971; *New York University Law Review,* October 1971; *Valparaiso University Law Review,* Fall 1970; *University of Chicago Law Review,* February 1972.

7. Freudian and variations on Freudian theories of women include Helene Deutsch, *The Psychology of Women* (New York: Grune & Stratton, 1944–45); Karen Horney, *New Ways in Psychoanalysis* (New York: Norton, 1939); Erik Erikson, *Childhood and Society* (New York: Norton, 1950); F. Lundberg and M. F. Farnham, *Modern Woman: The Lost Sex* (New York: Harper & Bros., 1947); Karl Stein, *The Flight from Woman* (New York: Farrar, Strauss & Giroux, 1965). See also Nancy Reeves, *Womankind: Beyond the Stereotypes* (Chicago: Atherton-Aldine, 1971).

8. Lewis M. Terman and Catherine Cox Miles, *Sex and Personality* New York: Russell & Russell, 1936.

9. Ibid., pp. 580–87.

10. Margaret Mead, *Male and Female* (New York: Morrow, 1947); Mead, *Sex and Temperament in Three Societies* (New York: Morrow, 1935).

11. Lionel Tiger, *Men in Groups* (New York: Random House, 1970); Konrad Lorenz, *On Aggression,* trans. M. Wilson (New York: Harcourt, Brace & World, 1966); Desmond Morris, *The Naked Ape* (New York: Dell, 1967); Robert Ardrey, *The Territorial Imperative* (New York: Dell, 1966); Steven Goldberg, *The Inevitability of Patriarchy* (New York: Quadrangle, 1974); A. Storr, *Human Aggression* (New York: Bantam, 1970). Goldberg suggests that intelligence may be hormonal, thus providing a noncultural explanation for boys testing lower than girls on essentially all measures of intelligence until after puberty. See Maccoby, *Development of Sex Differences.*

12. Elaine Morgan, *The Descent of Woman* (New York: Bantam, 1972). See also Ashley Montague, *The Natural Superiority of Women* (rev. ed.; New York: Collier, 1974).

13. F. Engels, *The Origin of Family, Private Property and the State* (New York: International Publishers, 1970); V. I. Lenin, *The Emancipation of Woman* (New York: International Publishers, 1934); August Bebel, *Women Under Socialism,* trans. Daniel de Leon (New York: Source Book, 1970); Leon Trotsky, *Women and the Family* (New York: Pathfinder, 1970); Juliet Mitchell, *Woman's Estate* (New York: Random House, 1975); Shulamith Firestone, *The Dialectic of Sex* (New York: Bantam, 1970); Herbert Marcuse, *Counterrevolution and Revolt* (Boston: Beacon, 1972); Marlene Dixon, "Why Women's Liberation?," in *Female Liberation,* ed. Roberta Salper (New York: Knopf, 1972).

14. Firestone interprets Freud metaphorically rather than literally, with masculinity standing for power. Penis envy is a metonym for the woman's desire to be a man because of her entirely accurate perceptions that males yield power in society. Cf. Firestone's view of the social impact of technological society with Karl Bednarik, *The Male in Crisis,* trans. Helen Sebba (New York: Knopf, 1970).

15. Gunnar Myrdal, "A Parallel to the Negro Problem," *An American Dilemma* (New York: Harper & Row, 1944), 2:1073–78.

16. Helen Hacker, "Women as a Minority Group," *Social Forces* 30 (October 1951): 60–69.

17. See, for example, Kirsten Amundsen, *The Silenced Majority* (Englewood Cliffs, N.J.: Prentice-Hall, 1971), chaps. 2–3; Bernard, *Women and the Public Interest,* Pt. 3;

Caroline Bird, *Born Female: The High Cost of Keeping Women Down* (New York: McKay, 1968), Chafe, *American Woman,* chaps. 9–10; Janet Saltzman Chafetz, *Masculine, Feminine, or Human* (Itasca, Ill.: Peacock, 1974); Davidson, Ginsburg, and Kay, *Sex Based Discrimination,* pp. 419–61; Clarice Stasz Stoll, *Female and Male: Socialization, Social Roles and Social Structure* (Dubuque: Wm. C. Brown, 1974), chap. 3; Shirley Bernard, "Women's Economic Status: Some Clichés and Some Facts," in *Women: A Feminist Perspective,* ed. Jo Freeman (Palo Alto, Calif.: Mayfield, 1975), pp. 238–41; Francine Blau, "Women in the Labor Force: An Overview," in ibid., pp. 211–26; Valerie K. Oppenheimer, "Demographic Influence on Female Employment: The Status of Women," in Huber, *Changing Women,* pp. 184–99; Larry E. Sater and Herman P. Miller, "Income Differences between Men and Career Women," in ibid., pp. 200–212.

18. Blau, "Women in the Labor Force," pp. 216–22.

19. Bernard, "Women's Economic Status," pp. 234–40.

20. Bernard, *Women and the Public Interest,* p. 122.

21. Davidson, Ginsburg, and Kay, *Sex Based Discrimination,* pp. 419–61. This is a particularly useful study of female employment patterns. On women in academia, see Jessie Bernard, *Academic Women* (University Park: Penn State University Press, 1964); Alice Rossi, ed., *Academic Women on the Move* (New York: Russell Sage Foundation, 1974); Marianne Ferber and June W. Loeb, "Performance, Rewards, and Perceptions of Discrimination among Male and Female Faculty," in Huber, *Changing Women,* pp. 233–48; Patricia Graham, "Women in Academe," *Science,* 25 September 1970, pp. 1284–98; Ann S. Harris, "The Second Sex in Academe," *AAUP Bulletin* (Fall, 1970): 283–96; Modern Language Association Commission on the Status of Women, *Academic Women, Sex Discrimination and the Law* (rev. ed.; 1975); Pamela Ruby, "Structural and Internalized Barriers to Women in Higher Education," in Freeman, *Women,* pp. 171–93; Bernice Sandler, "Sex Discrimination, Educational Institutions, and the Law: A New Issue on Campus," *Journal of Law and Education* 2 (October 1973): 613–35. The most recent statistics on salary by sex are contained in "Two Steps Backward: Report on the Economic Status of the Profession," *AAUP Bulletin,* Summer 1975.

22. See Joan Acker, "Women and Social Stratification: A Case of Intellectual Sexism," in Huber, *Changing Women,* pp. 174–83. See also Naomi Weisstein, "Woman as Nigger," *Psychology Today* 3 (October 1969): 20.

23. See note 6.

24. Carolyn Setlow and Gloria Steinem, "Why Women Voted for Richard Nixon," *Ms.* 1 (March 1973): 66–67; 109–10. Their answer is that women lost confidence in McGovern's ability to end the war. See also *Ms.* (July 1972) on women's voting patterns, and Naomi Lynn, "Women in American Politics: An Overview," in Freeman, *Women,* pp. 364–85; Roper Organization, Inc., *The Virginia Slims American Women's Poll,* vol. 2 (1972).

25. See Lynn, "Women in American Politics"; Susan Dworkin, "Running for Office: Victory with Honor," *Ms.* (April 1974): 61–63; "Women Who Win," *Ms.* (March 1973): 68.

26. Eloise C. Snyder, "Sex Role Differential and Juror Decision," *Sociology and Social Research* 55 (1971): 442–48.

27. See esp. Maccoby, *Development of Sex Differences;* Weisstein, in Morgan, *Sisterhood Is Powerful.*

28. Lenore J. Weitzman, "Sex Role Socialization," in Freeman, *Women,* pp. 105–44. On socialization, see also Dair L. Gillespie, "Who Has the Power: The Marital Struggle," in ibid., pp. 64–87; Judith Bardwick and Elizabeth Douvan, "Ambivalence: The Socialization of Women," in Gornick and Moran, *Women in Sexist Society,* pp. 225–41; Sandra and Daryl Bem, "We're All Unconscious Sexists," *Psychology Today* 4

(November 1970): 22; Nancy Chodorow, "Being and Doing: A Cross Cultural Examination of the Socialization of Males and Females," in Gornick and Moran, *Women in Sexist Society*, pp. 259–91; M. Kent Jennings and Kenneth Langton, "Mothers versus Fathers: The Formation of Political Orientations Among Young Americans," *Journal of Politics* 31 (May 1969): 329–58; Jean Lippman-Blumen, "How Ideology Shapes Women's Lives," *Scientific American* 226 (January 1972): 34–42; William H. Sewell and Vimal P. Shah, "Social Class, Parental Encouragement and Educational Aspirations," *American Journal of Sociology* 73 (March 1968): 559–72; Marjorie U'ren, "The Image of Women in Textbooks," in Gornick and Moran, *Woman in Sexist Society*, pp. 318–28; Fred I. Greenstein, "Sex Related Political Differences in Childhood," *Journal of Politics* 23 (May 1961): 353–71; Alice Rossi, "Equality Between the Sexes: An Immodest Proposal," *Daedalus* (Spring 1964): 607–52; Chafetz, *Masculine, Feminine, Human*, chap. 3; Stoll, *Female and Male*, chaps. 5 and 6; Fred I. Greenstein, *Children and Politics* (New Haven: Yale University Press, 1965) pp. 107–27; Barbara Harrison, *Unlearning the Lie: Sexism in School* (New York: Liveright, 1973); National Education Association, *Sex Role Stereotyping in the Schools* (Washington, D.C., 1973); Lynn White, Jr., *Educating Our Daughters* (New York: Harper & Bros., 1950).

The socialization process is reinforced by peripheral sources such as literature, language, and music. The Women's Liberation Movement has drawn attention to these more subtle manifestations. See, for example, Alma Graham, "How to Make Trouble: The Making of a Non-Sexist Dictionary," *Ms.* 2 (December 1973): 12–16; Wendy Martin, "Seduced and Abandoned in the New World: The Image of Woman in American Fiction," in Gornick and Moran, *Woman in Sexist Society*, pp. 329–46; Kay F. Reinartz, "The Paper Doll: Images of American Woman in Popular Songs," in Freeman, *Women*, pp. 293–308; Kimberly Snow, "Women in the American Novel," in ibid., pp. 279–92; Diana Trilling, "The Image of Women in Contemporary Literature," in *The Woman in America*, ed. R. J. Lifton (Boston: Beacon, 1965); Kate Millet, *Sexual Politics* (New York: Doubleday, 1970); Diana Scally and Pauline Bart, "A Funny Thing Happened on the Way to the Orifice: Woman in Gynecology Textbooks," in Huber, *Changing Wmoen*, pp. 283–88; Lucy Komisar, "The Image of Women in Advertising," in Gornick and Moran, *Women in Sexist Society*, pp. 304–17; Lyvia M. Brown, "Sexism in Western Art," in Freeman, *Women*, pp. 309–22.

29. Ellen Keniston and Kenneth Keniston, "An American Anachronism: The Image of Women and Work," *American Scholar* 33 (Summer 1964): 355.

30. Matina S. Horner, "Toward an Understanding of Achievement Related Conflicts in Women," *Journal of Social Issues* 28 (1972): 157–75; idem, "Fail: Bright Women," *Psychology Today* 3 (1969): 36. See also Saul Felman, "Impediment or Stimulant? Marital Status and Graduate Education," in Huber, *Changing Women*, pp. 220–32.

31. Chesler, "Patient and Patriarch"; Jessie Bernard, "The Paradox of the Happy Marriage," in Gornick and Moran, *Woman in Sexist Society*, pp. 145–62; Gillespie, "Who Has the Power"; Walter Cove and Jeannette F. Tudor, "Adult Sex Roles and Mental Illness," in Huber, *Changing Women*, pp. 50–72; Keniston and Keniston, "American Anachronism," pp. 355–75; Bernard, *Women and the Public Interest*, chap. 8.

32. See "The Great God Security," *Fortune* (August 1946): 4–6, 8, 10, 14; George Gallup and Evan Hill, "The American Woman," *Saturday Evening Post*, 22 December 1962, pp. 19–32.

33. Gillespie, "Who Has the Power"; Robert O. Blood and Donald M. Wolfe, *Husbands and Wives: The Dynamics of Married Living* (Glencoe, Ill.: Free Press, 1960); Mirra Komarovsky, "Cultural Contradictions and Sex Roles: The Masculine Case," in Huber, *Changing Women*, pp. 111–22; William Goode, *World Revolution and Family Patterns* (Glencoe, Ill.: Free Press, 1963).

34. Weitzman, "Sex Role Socialization"; Cynthia Fuchs Epstein, "Positive Effects

of the Double Negative: Examining the Success of Black Professional Women," in Huber, *Changing Women,* pp. 150–73; Denis B. Kandel, "Race, Maternal Authority, and Adolescent Aspirations," *American Journal of Sociology* 76 (May 1971): 999–1018.

35. Zena Smith Blau, "Exposure to Child Rearing Experts: A Structural Interpretation of Class-Color Differences," *American Journal of Sociology* 69 (May 1964): 596–608.

36. See Weitzman, "Sex Role Socialization." See also Mae C. King, "Oppression and Power: The Unique Status of the Black Woman in the American Political System," *Social Science Quarterly* 56 (June 1975): 116–28; and Elizabeth Almquist, "Untangling the Effects of Race and Sex: The Disadvantaged Status of Black Women," ibid., pp. 129–42.

37. The *Fortune* (1946) and *Saturday Evening Post* (1962) surveys about women's role indicated that male/female agreement was remarkably high. Gallup concluded his survey as follows: "The American Woman reflects what she helps to create—a wholesome, God-fearing, stable society. And she likes not only the Society she is molding but her role in it. As one woman told us, 'Being a woman is wonderful.' " An interesting experiment conducted by Philip Goldberg indicated the willingness of women to denigrate writings attributed to women, while praising the identical writings when they were attributed to men. "Are Women Prejudiced Against Women?" *Trans-action* (April 1968): 28–30.

38. Judith Blake, "Abortion and Public Opinion: The 1960–1970 Decade," *Science* 171 (12 February 1971): 540–49. Interestingly, although the South was a bastion of antiabortion sentiment, Georgia was one of the first states to pass a liberalized abortion statute. The availability of abortion has drastically reduced the illegitimacy rate, regardless of antiabortion attitudes. See June Sklar and Beth Berkov, "Abortion, Illegitimacy, and the American Birth Rate," *Science* 185 (13 September 1974): 909–15.

39. For accounts of the development of the WLM, see Jo Freeman, *The Politics of Women's Liberation* (New York: McKay, 1975); Firestone, *Dialectic of Sex,* pp. 15–40; Mitchell, *Women's Estate,* pp. 19–98; Roberta Salper, "The Development of the American Women's Liberation Movement," in Salper, *Female Liberation,* pp. 69–83; Chafe, *American Woman,* pp. 226–44; Jo Freeman, "The Women's Liberation Movement, Its Origins, Structures, Impacts, and Ideas," in Freeman, *Politics of Women's Liberation,* pp. 448–60.

40. In addition, to the works on WLM previously cited, see Edith·Altbach, ed., *From Feminism to Liberation* (Cambridge, Mass.: Schenkman, 1971); Mary Daly, *The Church and the Second Sex* (New York: Harper & Row, 1968); Karen De Crow, *Sexist Justice* (New York: Random House, 1974); Germaine Greer, *The Female Eunuch* (New York: Bantam, 1972); June Sochen, *Movers and Shakers* (New York: Quadrangle, 1973); Cynthia Fuchs Epstein, *Woman's Place* (Berkeley: University of California Press, 1970); Elizabeth Janeway, *Man's World, Woman's Place* (New York: Morrow, 1971), and *Between Myth and Morning* (New York: Morrow, 1974); Edwin Lewis, *Developing Women's Potential* (Ames: Iowa State University Press, 1968); Jacquelyn Mattfeld and Carol Van Allen, *Women and the Scientific Professions* (Cambridge, Mass.: MIT Press, 1965); Juliet Mitchell, *Psychoanalysis and Feminism* (New York: Pantheon, 1974); Sheila Rowbotham, *Women, Resistance, and Revolution* (New York: Random House, 1969); Miriam Schneir, ed., *Feminism: The Essential Historical Writings* (New York: Random House, 1972). For comparative reviews, see Carol Ehrlich, "The Woman Book Industry," in Huber, *Changing Women,* pp. 268–82; and Sheila Tobias, "In the Balance: The Study of Women," *Choice* (December 1971): 1295–1304.

41. See Blake, "Abortion and Public Opinion."

42. Gammas were computed because most of the data were not interval level. While they were not the chief focus of the study, Pearson *r*s were also computed so that when partials were computed, the degree to which the original correlation was changed

could be noted. In such cases assumptions of interval level were violated, but there seemed to be no greatly damaging effects.

43. We were not greatly concerned with distinguishing precisely between opinion and attitude, but the distinction noted seems to follow that given in Robert Lane and David O. Sears, *Public Opinion* (Englewood Cliffs, N.J.: Prentice-Hall, 1964).

44. It should be noted, however, that gamma is not conservative in the strength of relationship required for a perfect correlation. A given magnitude of gamma is "equivalent" to a lower magnitude for Pearson r.

45. American Opinion Institute (George Gallup poll), Survey #13-B, 25 December 1938.

46. Gallup poll, Survey #662-K, 19 September 1962.

47. Ibid.

48. Gallup poll, Survey #793, 30 November 1969.

49. Gallup poll, Survey #4910TPS, 2 May 1952.

50. "The Great God Security," pp. 4–8, 10.

51. Gallup poll, Survey #67, 21 February 1937.

52. Gallup poll, Survey #360-K, 15 December 1945.

53. Gallup poll, Survey #444-K, 30 July 1949.

54. Gallup poll, Survey #543-K, 15 February 1955.

55. Gallup poll, Survey #678-K, 15 November 1963.

56. Gallup poll, Survey #810-K, 26 August 1970.

57. Gallup poll, Survey #67, 21 February 1937.

58. See, for example, V. O. Key, *Politics, Parties and Pressure Groups,* (New York: Crowell, 1942); Angus Campbell, Phillip Converse, Warren Miller, and Donald Stokes, *The American Voter* (New York: Wiley, 1960); Gerald Pomper, *Elections in America* (New York: Dodd, Mead, 1970).

59. See, for example, Angus Campbell, Gerald Gurin, and Warren E. Miller, *The Voter Decides* (Evanston, Ill.: Row, Peterson, 1954).

60. Campbell et al., *American Voter.*

61. See *Congressional Quarterly* (1974), pp. 941, 3104. Including the 6 women elected to Congress in 1974, a total of 92 women have served in Congress since Jeanette Rankin was elected in 1917. Of these, 10 were in the Senate and only 1, Margaret Chase Smith of Maine, served in both houses. The largest number of women in the Senate at one time was 3, in the 83rd Congress; prior to the 94th Congress, the largest number of women in the House was 17, in the 87th. See *Congressional Quarterly Almanac* 28 (1972): 1035. See also Patricia Barstein and Marlene Cimons, "Women Who Won," *Ms.* (March 1973): 68–71; 84–88.

62. See Philip E. Converse, "The Nature of Belief Systems in Mass Publics," in *Ideology and Discontent,* ed. David E. Apter (New York: Free Press, 1964).

63. See L. H. Butterfield, ed., *The Adams Papers,* series 2, *Adams Family Correspondence* (Cambridge, Mass.: Harvard University Press, 1963) pp. 76–402.

JOHN C. PIERCE, WILLIAM P. AVERY,
and ADDISON CAREY, JR.

☆☆☆☆☆☆☆☆☆☆☆☆☆☆☆☆☆☆☆☆☆☆☆☆☆

4 Sex Differences in Black Political Beliefs and Behavior

Whether through choice, systematic exclusion, or norms of role allocation, women generally exhibit lower rates of political participation than men.[1] Yet, the unanimity with which this conclusion has been reached is weakened by the scant attention directed to subcultural variations, particularly in those subcultures thought to have unique patterns of expected behavior for men and women. In the United States, many scholars consider the black subculture (and the black lower-class community in particular) to possess such atypical expected behaviors for men and women.[2] Higher rates of male absence from the family, with an increase in demands on the female, and the historical subjugation of the black male are alleged to have led to *matrifocality* among lower-class blacks.[3] Matrifocality is that collection of norms and actions through which women are expected to take many of the roles, responsibilities, and duties assigned to men. As Helen I. Safa notes,

> These forces . . . have curtailed (the male's) role as economic provider, as leader in his community, and as spokesman for his family in dealing with the outside world. As a result, the woman has been forced to take over many traditional male roles.[4]

66

Politics is part of that "outside world" with which black men and women must deal. Consequently, we are drawn to the hypothesis that black men and women may exhibit patterns of participation and beliefs different than those found in more general populations. In this note we examine that hypothesis by focusing on sex differences among blacks in (1) levels of traditional and protest participation, (2) beliefs about politics, and (3) the relationships between beliefs and participation.

The attitudinal and behavioral differences between black men and women are evaluated through an analysis of a survey of a three-stage random cluster sample of 300 black residents of New Orleans conducted in late 1969 and early 1970. Appropriate pretesting preceded extensive personal interviews, all of which were taken by black interviewers.

PARTICIPATION

While many studies have looked at black political behavior,[5] few have examined sex differences. Among those few, however, Matthews and Prothro concluded that "the old sex differences still show up among Southern Negroes at all (status) levels."[6] Also, Seasholes decided that sex related differences in political participation do not result from "matriarchal" family structures in the two black communities he studied.[7] Yet, neither study examined both traditional and protest participation, the relationship between the two forms of participation, and the influence of several indicators of class or status. The findings in this section are directed toward filling those gaps.

In order to measure traditional participation levels, the respondents were asked if they had tried to register to vote, voted, discussed politics, attended political meetings, helped in political campaigns, or contacted public officials. A ten-point index subsequently was collapsed into three levels: low, medium, and high. The same process created a protest participation index from respondents' reports of talking protest, boycotting, marching, picketing, and sitting-in.[8]

Table 4.1 shows that in our sample no significant differences obtain in the participation levels of men and women. For both types of participation, the small differences are short of those which would indicate that they occurred by anything other than chance. In both areas, then, we find black women participating on a par with black

TABLE 4.1. Levels of Protest and Traditional Participation
Among Black Men and Women in New Orleans
(in percentages)

Participation Level	Participation					
	Protest			Traditional		
	Men	Women	Difference[a]	Men	Women	Difference[a]
High	16	13	+3	20	16	+4
Medium	38	43	−5	56	56	0
Low	46	44	+2	24	28	−4
Total	100	100		100	100	
Number of cases	130	170		130	170	

[a] A positive difference means a higher percentage of men at that level of participation.

men. Another question is the degree to which men and women exhibit dual or isolated channels of participation. Is there a higher association between degrees of behavioral involvement in the two types of political activity among either the women or the men? In answer, we obtained a gamma of .64 for the women and .48 for the men. Consequently, in addition to the equality in participation levels for black men and women, women have the greater propensity to participate in both types of behavior, given an initial involvement in politics.

In their study, Matthews and Prothro took "education as an index of social status."[9] There is reason to believe that education may not be the most valid indicator of class status, both generally and in the black community.[10] Thus, in table 4.2 the participation levels of the men and women are compared, controlling for income, occupation, and education. Employing income levels as a measure of status supports the hypothesis that among lower-class blacks the women participate more while at the highest level the men predominate. Moreover, these differences are greater on the protest measure than on the traditional measure. The occupation control produces differences in contrast to those achieved with income, and occupation's influence depends on the type of participation. Only with education as the status measure do the "lower-class" men participate more in both types of politics than the "lower-class" women, and as education increases even this difference disappears. These New Orleans results, then, run counter to both the general proposition that men participate more than women, as well as the more narrow contention that sex differences in the political participation of blacks are unrelated to class or status.

TABLE 4.2. The Proportion of Black Men and Women with High or Medium Levels of Participation, Controlling for Income, Education, and Occupation[a]

| Status Measures | Participation | | | | | |
| | Protest | | | Traditional | | |
	Men	Women	Difference[b]	Men	Women	Difference[b]
Income						
$0–3,999	.42	.51	−.09	.62	.67	−.05
4–7,999	.50	.67	−.17	.82	.88	−.06
8,000+	.84	.64	+.20	.90	.73	+.17
Occupation						
Other	.57	.52	+.05	.64	.67	−.03
Service/Labor	.45	.53	−.08	.69	.76	−.07
Sales	.59	.67	−.08	.69	.76	−.07
Professional	.67	.86	−.19	1.00	.93	+.07
Education						
0–8 years	.52	.42	+.10	.74	.56	+.18
8–12	.46	.59	−.13	.74	.79	−.05
12+ years	.70	.73	−.03	.83	.88	−.05

[a]The entry in each cell is the proportion of those respondents of that sex and that category on the status variable with high or medium levels of participation on that type of political behavior. No cell contains less than eleven cases.

[b]A positive difference indicates a higher proportion of men; a negative difference indicates a higher proportion of women.

BELIEFS

Women are thought to be more likely than men to personalize politics and to look to individuals rather than institutions for protection and as objects of political attention and trust.[11] Therefore, one might expect black women to have more confidence than men in those who hold public office or who have been candidates for political office. The counter hypothesis would suggest that greater female responsibility in the black community would nullify the more general patterns. Our findings show that the black women in New Orleans do not look any more favorably on the people in politics than do the black men (table 4.3: questions 4–6). If the demands and the norms of the black community on its female members involve relatively greater interaction with public officials, this personal experience with individuals may contribute to the lack of any significant differences in the orientations of the men and women in our sample.

Previous research also has shown women to be less efficacious

TABLE 4.3. Beliefs About Politics and Participation
(in percentages)

Item	Men	Women	Difference[a]
People like me don't have any say about government.	32	43	−11
Politics and government seem so complicated to me.	40	55	−15
Nothing or little can be gained through traditional political methods.	19	25	−6
Public officials don't care what people like me think.	73	79	−6
Black candidates never keep promises to Negroes.	17	20	−3
White candidates never keep promises to Negroes.	55	58	−3

[a] A positive difference indicates that more men than women agreed; a negative difference indicates that more women than men agreed.

than men.[12] Women are less likely to feel that their participation has an impact on government and politics. Unlike the findings directly above, we obtain a pattern consistent with those other studies (table 4.3: questions 1–3). In each case the women have less confidence in their ability to understand or influence politics. The overall equal participation manifested by the women is not mirrored in equal feelings as to its effectiveness. One might hypothesize that white women feel less efficacious than white men at least in part due to the norms which are contrary to very active involvement, while black women feel less efficacious than black men because the norms support their involvement, but that involvement results in a feeling that their impact is weak. Thus, similar beliefs may stem from dissimilar sources.

To this point, we have a picture of the black female equal to the black male in participation, but less likely to view that participation as having an impact on political outcomes. The following section examines the relationship between levels of participation and those political beliefs.

BELIEFS AND PARTICIPATION

Positive feelings about the impact of political behavior are related to active involvement in political affairs, both for whites and blacks.[13]

Yet, with the above findings we might expect that association to be lower for the women than for the men, for with greater cynicism toward the system and relatively equal levels of participation, one would expect a number of women to be participating out of obligation— rather than a feeling of accomplishment. The relationship between beliefs and behavior found in the New Orleans sample is presented in table 4.4. In all cases, higher associations (gamma) are present for the women. The differences are both larger and more uniform in the area of traditional participation. At the same time, among both the men and the women the associations are consistently lower in the area of protest behavior. Overall, then, the personal perceptions of the political system are more important in predicting and, presumably, causing the behavior of black women than the political behavior of black men.

Several possible reasons may be proffered for the higher associations among the women. If one accepts the matrifocal thesis, we may surmise that the patterns reflect a greater relative role of the black

TABLE 4.4. Correlation of Beliefs About Politics with Two Types of Participation[a]

| | Participation | | | | | |
| | Protest | | | Traditional | | Differ- |
Belief	Men	Women	Difference[b]	Men	Women	ence[b]
Public officials don't care what people like me think.	.00	−.04	−.04	.12	.32	−.20
People like me don't have any say about government.	.02	.08	−.06	.24	.39	−.15
Politics and government seem so complicated to me.	.01	.21	−.20	.13	.27	−.14
Nothing or little can be gained through traditional political methods.	.32	.43	−.11	.37	.53	−.16

[a]The gamma measure of ordinal association is employed here. A positive correlation indicates a negative answer to the above statements is associated with higher levels of participation.

[b]A positive difference indicates a higher correlation among the men; a negative difference indicates a higher correlation among the women.

woman in dealing with the agents of the system as representative of the household. Those who had discouraging experiences in such a role and also feel a low sense of efficacy would have confirmation of their feelings of powerlessness, and thus would refrain from extended participation in attempting to influence the system. On the other hand, those with successful experiences may feel efficacious, perceive confirmation of those feelings, and be moved to further attempts to influence the system. The woman's greater interaction with the system in the "subject" role (receiving services) would bring her participation as a "citizen" into greater congruity with her actual orientations to that system. At the same time, apart from actual experiences with government, the greater responsibility attributed to women within nonpolitical areas of the black community may contribute to a general feeling of independence. This general independence may result in a greater freedom to act in accord with one's motivational level in the political world, independent of the expectations of others.

In this paper we examined some aspects of the political beliefs and behavior of black men and women in a major southern city: New Orleans. This interest stemmed from two previous patterns of research conclusions. First, women generally manifest lower levels of participation in politics. Second, black women are held to take many of the roles taken by men in other American subcultures: the notion of matrifocality. As a result of our inquiry we found: (1) only minimal overall differences in the amount of protest and traditional participation of black men and women; (2) a higher association between the two forms of participation among the women; (3) that in both types of political behavior, lower-class women participate more than lower-class men when income is used as the measure of class, but educational and occupational controls for status result in mixed findings; (4) that black women have less positive feelings about the political system than black men; and (5) that beliefs about the political system are more important predictors (higher correlates) of levels of participation for the women than for the men.

While these findings are confined to a single city, they cast doubt on the universality of male dominance in participation in American politics. These patterns are not only inconsistent with studies of the general population, but they also run counter to the few studies of sex differences among blacks. We suggest, then, that conclusions about the relative roles of men and women in politics must be sensitive to potential subcultural variations which may be based on different perceptions as to the relative roles men and women ought to take. Moreover, within those subcultures separate communities may differ in the degree to which men and women share political activism. Thus, further research is needed which will clarify the social, political, and economic dimensions contributing to cultural, subcultural, and community level variations in sex differences in political behavior.

NOTES

1. Gabriel A. Almond and Sydney Verba, *The Civic Culture* (Boston: Little, Brown, 1965), pp. 324–35; Angus Campbell, Philip E. Converse, Warren E. Miller, and Donald E. Stokes, *The American Voter* (New York: Wiley, 1960), pp. 483–93; Maurice Duverger, *The Political Role of Women* (Paris: UNESCO, 1955); Robert E. Lane, *Political Life* (New York: Free Press, 1959), pp. 209–16; Seymour M. Lipset, *Political Man* (Garden City, N.Y.: Doubleday, 1960), pp. 187–89, 193–94, 206–7, 210, 216–17; and Lester W. Milbrath, *Political Participation* (Chicago: Rand McNally, 1965), pp. 135–36.

2. See, for example, Lee Rainwater, "Chronicle of Identity: The Negro Lower-Class Family," *Daedalus* 95 (Winter 1966); St. Clair Drake, "The Social and Economic Status of the Negro in the United States", *Daedalus* 94 (Fall 1965); Daniel P. Moynihan, *The Negro Family: The Case for National Action* (Washington, D.C.: U.S. Department of Labor, 1965); and John Aldous, "Wives Employment Status and Lower-Class Men as Husband-Fathers' Support for the Moynihan Thesis," *Journal of Marriage and the Family* 31 (August 1969).

3. Helen I. Safa, "The Matrifocal Family in the Black Ghetto: Sign of Pathology or Pattern of Survival," in *Health and the Family*, ed. Charles O. Crawford (New York: Macmillan, 1971), pp. 35–59.

4. Ibid., pp. 38–39.

5. Among studies of "traditional" black participation are: Anthony M. Orum, "A Reappraisal of Social and Political Participation of Negroes," *American Journal of Sociology* 72 (July 1966); William Brink and Louis Harris, *Black and White* (New York: Simon & Schuster, 1966); Oscar Glantz, "The Negro Voter in Northern Industrial Cities," *Western Political Quarterly* 13 (December 1960); Donald R. Matthews and James W. Prothro, "Social and Economic Factors and Negro Voter Registration in the South," *American Political Science Review* 67 (March 1963); and James Q. Wilson, *Negro Politics* (Glencoe, Ill.: Free Press, 1960). Among studies of black protest activity are: James W. Vander Zanden, "The Non-Violent Resistance Movement Against Segregation," *American Journal of Sociology* 68 (March 1963); Ruth Searles and J. A. Williams, "Negro College Students' Participation in Sit-Ins," *Social Forces* (March 1962); John M. Orbell, "Protest Participation Among Southern Negro College Students," *American Political Science Review* 61 (June 1967); Allan P. Sindler, "Protest Against the Political Status of Negroes," *Annals of the American Academy of Political and Social Science* 344 (January 1965); James Q. Wilson, "The Strategy of Protest: Problems of Negro Civic Action," *Journal of Conflict Resolution* 5 (September 1961): 291–303; David O. Sears and John McConahay, "Participation in the Los Angeles Riot," *Social Problems* (Summer 1969); and David O. Sears and T. M. Tomlinson, "Riot Ideology in Los Angeles: A Study of Negro Political Attitudes," *Social Science Quarterly* 49 (December 1968).

6. Donald R. Matthews and James W. Prothro, *Negroes and the New Southern Politics* (New York: Harcourt, Brace & World, 1966), p. 68.

7. Bradbury Seasholes, "Negro Participation in Two North Carolina Cities" (Ph.D. dissertation, University of North Carolina, Chapel Hill, 1969), pp. 128–49.

8. Some activities are given more weight than others, depending on the number engaging in the particular activity. The fewer the number engaging in the activity, the greater the weight it was given, and the weights ranged from one to three. The cutting points for the three levels of participation differ slightly between the two measures because the protest uncollapsed distribution was centered to the left (below) that of the traditional. Therefore, the lines dividing low, medium, and high levels are lower for the protest measures. Consequently, comparisons between the measures are in relative and not absolute terms of the index scores. Using the same cutting point for protest as for traditional does not change the conclusions about the relative participation rates of men and women within each area. It would, of course, alter the percentages at each level of protest, but the purpose here is to compare men and women within types of behavior and not to contrast either across types of behavior.

Also relating to the construction of the indices, it is apparent that "talking politics" and "talking protest" involve the same activity: talking. However, the substance of the talking differs. That they may overlap to some degree is only to say that at some point the two types of behavior may approach convergence. It is to be expected, then, that this point of convergence would be the activity of talking, for it is the behavior most engaged in by the members of our sample in both areas of participation.

The respondents also were asked if they had participated in violent protest. Less than 1 percent admitted to it. This may result from either the general absence of violent political activity in New Orleans up to the time of the interviews, or from a general reluctance to give out such information. In either case, the inclusion of the violence item in the index would have added nothing to our ability to discriminate among respondents according to their levels of protest participation.

9. Matthews and Prothro, *Negroes and the New Southern Politics,* p. 68.

10. Marie R. Haug and Marvin B. Sussman, "The Indiscriminate State of Social Class Measurement," *Social Forces* (June 1971): 563–67. The reservations expressed in the Haug and Sussman article are the basis for not constructing a more elaborate index of class by combining several indicators.

11. Robert Hess and Judith Torney, *The Development of Political Attitudes in Children* (Chicago: Aldine, 1967), pp. 167–78; Angus Campbell, Gerald Gurin, and Warren E. Miller, *The Voter Decides* (Evanston: Row, Peterson, 1954), p. 155; and Duverger, *The Political Role of Women,* pp. 70–73.

12. Campbell et al., *American Voter,* p. 490; Lane, *Political Life,* p. 213; and Almond and Verba, *Civic Culture,* p. 331.

13. In particular, see Campbell et al., *American Voter,* p. 105; Robert A. Dahl, *Who Governs: Democracy and Power in an American City* (New Haven: Yale University Press, 1961), p. 286; and John C. Pierce and Addison Carey, Jr., "Efficacy and Participation: A Study of Black Political Behavior," *Journal of Black Studies* (December 1971): 201–23.

CORNELIA BUTLER FLORA

☆☆☆☆☆☆☆☆☆☆☆☆☆☆☆☆☆☆☆☆☆☆☆☆☆☆

5 Working-Class Women's Political Participation: Its Potential in Developed Countries

Participation in politics implies collective action aimed at the polity to reinforce or to change existing policy or personnel. It implies an awareness of a collective identity and an ability to carry out actions which serve to further the interests of that collective. Ideally, perhaps, each citizen acts in light of the collective interests of the nation-state of which he or she is a part. In practice, the social and economic situation of that individual creates subgroups whose betterment is presumed to lead to improvement of the general welfare. "What is good for General Motors is good for the country" can be generalized as the slogan of any member of any pressure group. When the different interest groups in a society are equally mobilized, with equal access to the seats of political and economic power, the general welfare can be furthered without too much damage to any one sector. (This model presumes that different groups within a nation state do have diverse interests and that furthering the interests of one group can definitely harm the interests of another group.) But when a group is not mobilized, other groups can direct "general welfare" policies at the expense of the unmobilized segments. Altruism cannot be counted on to assure that exploitation of unmobilized groups will not take place, even when such groups make up a substantial portion of the total society.

Thus it is crucial, when considering political participation, to set down the dimensions which (1) allow a group to develop a sense of common identity (and to deal with the question of false consciousness, or identification with the very group which is oppressing you); and (2) facilitate the mobilization of members of that group to act in a political fashion toward their collective interest. Thus political participation in this paper refers to more than simply voting, which can be thought of more as civic than political activity, and will focus on conditions which optimize the political participation of groups within a society. Particular attention will be focused on working-class women, a group which, in many developed countries, is doubly disadvantaged in the political process, due to both sex and economic position. Female industrial workers will receive the most detailed analysis.

The title of our panel, and the intellectual tradition from which it has sprung, can serve to disguise, rather than clarify, the position of women in society (a point made by many others, including our panel organizer, Elsa Chaney [11]).* The analogy of minority group is much less useful in terms of political participation than is the concept of class. "Minority group" is really a false term, resulting from historical accident and reflecting a basic belief in the democratic nature of society, including politics, namely, if we just get enough on our side, we will win. Blacks, the most studied and discussed "minority," were and are under 50 percent of the population of the United States. In the South, where blacks were probably most exploited, they were the majority: a necessary yet powerless majority whose labor was utilized to support the minority group which dominated them.

Often exploited groups have been majorities, as Indians are in many Latin American countries, as Africans are in South Africa, and as the women are in developed countries. Medical technology has assured women a greater life span through decreasing risks in child bearing, thus giving them a biological-numerical advantage. Women have not gained concomitant economic or political advantage. Such exploited *majority* groups are marginal to the distribution of power

*Numbers in brackets refer to numbered references at the end of the chapter.

and wealth in a society, but *absolutely necessary* for its functioning. It is the availability of the labor of the dominated group at the right price (free, in many cases, for women) that keeps the powerful in their positions of power. Dominated groups, as Memmi [35] points out and as Hacker [24] shows, do internalize the myths of their own inferiority, myths perpetuated by the dominant groups to rationalize their own privilege. It is not a question of numbers that causes this inferiority to be felt most keenly, but a question of power, power which stems in large measure from a group's relation to the control of the means of production.

These groups, which are so successfully dominated (uniquely so in the case of women, who are allowed to assume the social status of their sexually superior male owner and thus truly assume the characteristics of marginals [53]) have great potential power because they perform the essential services of the society. Dominated groups, and women in particular, have been a long time in realizing their potential power, identifying as a group with common interests, and mobilizing to defend these interests. Furthermore, the unique relationship that women have to the dominant group (men) allows many women, even if they first identify with women, to put their class position in the forefront of their political struggles.

The cross-currents of class and sex is a problem with which certain segments of the women's movement in the United States are currently struggling (see especially the "Ain't I a Woman" collective in Iowa City and the paper "Triple Jeopardy" out of New York City). It is clear to some that even though we as women share many mutual problems, there is a large gap caused by social class which allows middle- and upper-class women to gain power in the women's movement— and then in the established system. Having gained power, these women continue the domination of their working-class sisters, who they resent paying decently for child care and housework, and whose problems they like to think will simply be solved by electing more women to office. These women presumably will be more altruistic than their husbands who previously occupied these offices. It is at least arguable that the best group to defend a group's interests is the membership of that group itself, and that altruism or charity has never resulted in real redistribution of wealth or power in any situation.

Many middle-class women have acquired a sense of common female identity, through deliberate and effective measures of consciousness raising. In the United States, where the myth of a classless society is still entertained, it is assumed that feminine consciousness raising is enough. The absence of U.S. working-class women in the movement is a much-lamented fact. In European countries, where social class has long been a factor in the political calculus and is much more salient in an individual's self-evaluation, working-class women have been more active in organizing for their own behalf [50]. Aware of their double exploitation both as women and as workers and as wives of workers, the predisposition to collective political activity exists, but the mechanisms to facilitate mobilization of working-class women are still lacking to a large extent.

Research that has been done on the question of political participation has sprung from the survey research tradition of North American social science and has focused on the individual as the unit of analysis (Verba and Nie [52] is just one of the many examples of such work). Thus, instead of examining the context of collective identity and political behavior, these studies have assumed that it is individual characteristics which lead to political activity, which is measured in individual actions. Analysis of this data very much suggests the need for a new methodology which takes context into account in studying the mobilization of interest groups. The following discussion deals with the findings of the studies of political participation, which generally do not look at women, especially working-class women, as a separate group, as well as the studies from industrial sociology, which were originally carried out not to find out how workers best mobilize to protect their own interests but to discover the way to get the greatest productivity for the lowest cost. These studies do give us important clues about the mobilization of working-class women, however, because of their emphasis on the context of the working situation.

MODELS OF POLITICAL PARTICIPATION

Three major models of political participation are of use in ferreting out the factors which may lead to the potentials of political mobilization among working-class women: (1) political socialization, (2) differential selection, and (3) political mobilization. Theorizing and research using each of these models can be combined to determine the possibilities and the obstacles to organizing working-class women.

Political Socialization

Political socialization research has long examined differences in political participation by sex (Dawson and Prewitt [16] have a good review of this research). It suggests that part of the learned sex-role behavior of an individual includes that of whether or not it is proper to participate in politics [41, 23]. In addition, an individual's sex determines whether or not one acquires the skills necessary to become a viable political actor. This research has focused on childhood socialization, and, interestingly enough, shows that change in the dominant ideology regarding sex roles does result in a decline in the differences between political behavior among primary and secondary students [41, 2].

Socialization does not end with childhood. The learning of sex-appropriate behavior continues into adulthood, being particularly strong at points of role transition [20]. This leads one to focus on the changing situational circumstances surrounding an individual, whether or not that system rewards or punishes behavior, especially whether it views such behavior as political participation as sexually deviant or appropriate (see Levy [28] for discussion of systemic punishment leading to an individual choosing behavior in line with role expectations).

Among middle- and upper-class women who enter the political sphere, there is an attempt to justify such sex-inappropriate behavior as politics in terms of traditionally feminine roles. Lynn and Flora [33] have demonstrated how this occurred among 1972 national convention delegates, Chaney [12] has shown how the "supermadre" image is presented externally and internalized by women in politics in Peru, while Flora and Harkess [19] have demonstrated the use of sex-appropriate imagery to justify their political participation in newspaper coverage of female politicians in Colombia.

Working-class women, however, are less skilled in the manipulation of symbols and in an environment where sex roles are more intensely stressed [31, 42]. They are less likely, in a system which generally disapproves of female political activity, to enter politics. Pressures at home are more intense, with more division of labor by sex. Their husbands are likely to be jealous of their association with other men that politics so often requires (because few females participate). They are also unsocialized in the tools of political activism, which include meeting new people, actively expressing a point of view, and taking leadership roles among people who are not neighbors or kin [45, 34].

Political socialization also differs by class, and working-class individuals in general are less likely to acquire either the sense of political efficacy or the interpersonal skills to become viable political actors. However, when one realizes that political socialization is an ongoing process, being put in situations which require a high degree of interaction and legitimize the taking of leadership can overcome some of the barriers sex and class place on an individual's political activism.

Differential Selection

Research based on the model of differential selection does not deny the political socialization model of political participation. Instead, it focuses on the structure of individual characteristics which predispose political activism, rather than the process by which these characteristics cause a particular level of political activity. This research points to the high degree of association between a variety of measures of high status—including both class and sex—and high political participation [44, 52, 18]. This has been generalized by Milbraith [36] into a center-periphery argument, whereby those who are central to a system because of their position in a variety of social networks are more likely to be politically active. This empirical regularity is explained in terms of the intermediate variable of positive political attitudes occasioned by a high-status individual's higher stake in the ongoing system and their general belief in the efficacy of groups, due to a greater feeling of group awareness and more positive feedback from previous group activity. Higher-status persons also have a greater sense of personal efficacy, which is related to political activity [27, 52].

Working-class women, then, are low status by at least two important dimensions: sex and class. This should lead to a low degree of personal efficacy and a low level of belief in groups as an effective mechanism for social change. These attitudes tend to be reinforced because of the objective difficulty of bringing about change in a system already rigged against working-class women. While middle- and upper-class individuals are mobilized to defend their vested interests, which are already being served to one degree or another, low-status individuals must muster whole new mechanisms of political input if their interests are to be included in the political calculus.

Thus this body of research, which best utilizes a one-point-in-time survey technique, stresses qualities of an individual, presumably stemming from social positions, which influence political activity directly.

Political Mobilization

A third school of research on political activity has focused on mechanisms by which adults acquire the attitudes and skills necessary for political participation. Again, this research and theory does not directly challenge either of the two schools of thought presented above, but focuses on a different aspect of political participation. In this framework, involvement in voluntary organizations is seen to encourage individuals to become politically active [40]. This can be seen as an extension of the political socialization thesis, in that the voluntary organization provides the training ground and the supportive atmosphere in which political attitudes and skills may be learned [32]. The research behind this thesis has not focused on the individuals and the processes themselves, but merely on the number and types of memberships in voluntary organizations that an individual possesses [40, 1, 52].

High-status individuals are more likely than low-status individuals to join voluntary organizations [9, 25]. This finding suggests that there may be an overlap or tautology between this theory and that of differential selection: high-status individuals join more organizations, including political ones. Researchers aware of this potential dilemma have controlled for measures of socioeconomic status and found that organizational involvement exerts an independent effect on political participation [45, 40]. This model, according to Rogers, Bultena, and Barb [45], assumes that (1) group involvement makes political issues more salient; (2) the new relationships from voluntary associations draw individuals into public affairs; (3) involvement in organizations increases members' information, trains them in social interaction and leadership skills, and provides other personal resources essential for effective political activity [40]; and (4) encourages a sense of satisfaction with democratic processes and with participation in political activity. Few studies have actually examined these assumptions, which rest on the processes involved, and have chosen instead, through dependence on survey research methodology, to concentrate on the static structure of an individual's voluntary association memberships.

Again, even by this theory, working-class women are at a real disadvantage. Several studies suggest that the function of voluntary organizations—and thus their potential for political mobilization—varies according to the class of the women participating. Both Domhoff [17] and Moore [38] suggest the importance of voluntary associations of upper-class women in performing a vital function for the class to which a woman belongs and reinforcing her membership in this class. For middle-class women, Moore [38] found most voluntary activities to be gratifying and noncompetitive with domestic functions. The role of wife is highly compatible with group membership. Among working-class women, the wife role instead conflicts with that of member of a voluntary association [48, 34]. There are few alternative self-definitions favoring membership [49], thus making such participation much more negative for working-class women. As Smith points out: membership in voluntary associations reinforces "class boundaries among women, as reflected by the self-righteousness of middle- and upper-class women who have the time, money, educational resources, and eligibility" [49].

Because of their sex and their class, working-class women are not as likely as men to belong to voluntary associations [3]. Correlates of social class also keep them from membership. Lopata [30] has found that formal education, highly related to social class, is a major requirement for the social engagement of women. When working-class women do belong to groups, they are not likely to belong to organizations which are likely to further political attitudes or skills. Women are more likely to join church and recreational groups, while men join governing boards, job-related, and fraternal service groups, which directly involve an individual in the public sphere [8, 4].

CONTRIBUTIONS OF INDUSTRIAL SOCIOLOGY

It has been argued that participation in the labor force decreases the differences in sexual privilege, including political participation, between men and women [5, 14, 41]. These arguments are based on women acquiring more economic power, resulting in more power within the home, equalizing division of household tasks, and thus freeing them for political activity. Often participation in the labor force simply adds to the total work requirement of a working-class woman, doubling the demands on her time. Any skills a woman might learn at the workplace cannot be utilized because she is too busy in her dual role to think of political behavioral options. Labor-force participation, besides providing the economic means for women's liberation at home, can simply add an alienating office or factory job to the already pressing labors required in the nuclear family.

The Marxian view of how workers are organized suggests another aspect of labor-force participation which could result in an increase in female political participation. Women in group work conditions, particularly when cooperation is required to complete a task, are removed from the isolation of the home and placed in situations where political attitudes can be fostered and supported and where interpersonal skills necessary for successful political mobilization can be learned. Participation in decisions affecting day-to-day job conditions, through cooperative self-management or union participation, can build a sense of personal efficacy which leads to greater political participation. Perhaps more important, the work group itself becomes a viable group for collective political activity. It is here that industrial sociology can aid us, as it introduces a methodology based on observing process, rather than simply focusing on individual characteristics.

Industrial sociology, too, has a bias which hinders developing a definitive model of female political participation. Most studies in industrial sociology of the plant situation are aimed at increasing production. If anything in these studies relates to worker organization and mobilization in their own defense, it is gauged to cut off such activity as quickly as possible (see, for example, in the famous Hawthorne studies. When the "girls" in the relay assembly test room began to get together to complain about their conditions, the instigators were fired and operators with a more cooperative attitude were brought in [10]). Because of its history of examining what actually transpires in the work situation of blue-collar workers, industrial sociology is invaluable as a source of hypotheses concerning the potential political participation of working-class women who enter the industrial labor force. Only a few studies have actually explicitly examined female industrial workers [13, 43]. However, we can generalize at least partially here from the male experience as well as the uniquely female aspects of entry into the industrial labor force.

One hypothesis that is at least partially borne out in empirical studies is that participation on the job in both formal and informal groups leads to a higher degree of off-the-job political participation. French has defined participation as "a process in which two or more parties influence each other in making certain plans, policies, and decisions. It is restricted to decisions that have further effects on those making the decision and by those represented by them" [21, p. 3].

Studies which have documented participation among industrial workers can show the mechanisms by which women, especially working-class women, leave the isolated home environment and become integrated into new social networks. As homemakers, they are cut off from direct socialized production, isolated in the home, and denied possibilities of social life outside the neighborhood and kin.

This in turn deprives them of social knowledge and social education, confirming to society and themselves the myth of female ineptitude [15, p. 76]. A number of interesting studies demonstrate under which conditions workers gain in participation [54, 29, 6].

The "social climate" of the job has been minutely examined in terms of its effect on worker productivity and satisfaction. While such studies have been accused, probably correctly, of being aimed at worker manipulation (Gomberg [22] and Carey [10] present convincing evidence that this is their primary motivation. and use), they do overwhelmingly demonstrate that workers in democratic situations are more likely than workers in authoritarian settings to be socialized into the skills and attitudes necessary for participation [54]. The degree of participation of workers in determining the work conditions is related to their degree of informal interaction—and their potential for further mobilization [6].

Other aspects of work structure and organization affect the interaction of workers and their possibilities of gaining a political-group consciousness and the ability to act to further group ends. Lipset, Trow and Colemen [29] found that a large-size unit increases the politicalness of the atmosphere, heightening political awareness and presumably political mobilization. Persons in larger shops are much more active in unions than are those in smaller shops [29].

Union membership itself is important in furthering political participation among women [43]. The typical union member is higher in pay, skill, seniority, and general job status than the inactive or nonunion worker. The union worker has a greater number of friends within the plant and is more likely to belong to other formal organizations. The union worker is also much more likely to be male [51, pp. 746–47]. Participation in unions may be a key to women's on-the-job socialization and mobilization to political action, yet it is a participation than has been systematically denied them. Not only does this have direct financial implications for women, since the impact of union membership is greatest for social groups that experience wage discrimination [46], but it denies women entry into a climate where her overt political behavior is positively sanctioned. It must be noted in this context that unions in the United States are much more conservative politically than are European unions, and are more pragmatic than ideological, thus not providing the range of political skills and attitudes they potentially could [7].

Even despite the fact that U.S. unions are not utilizing their full conscienticizing potential, they still offer important avenues for women to increase their political participation. Why are women such a small minority of the organized workers in the United States? Miner and Miner [37] state several reasons why so few women are unionized:

> In the past, the majority of women viewed their work as a short-term matter; they were not career-oriented and thus expected little benefit from the dues they had to pay a union. Furthermore, they viewed unions as essentially male organizations. This conception was often fostered by the unions themselves; little was done to recruit female members except in industries with predominantly women workers. (p. 462)

As women think in terms of lifetime careers, evident to an increasing extent in the 1960s and 1970s, a higher proportion of female union members might be hypothesized. However, "while the number of female union members increased during the 1960s, the ratio of women union members to the total number of women in the labor force actually declined" [37, p. 462].

Other reasons for low female union membership and low participation of female union members have been posited. Unions, like politics, are unfeminine, and severe societal punishment accrues to the woman who breaks convention by becoming active. It is difficult for women to attend the meetings, which often are at night, when women are afraid to travel alone, and where no child care is provided. Unions have ignored the "women's issues" in the past, and have discouraged special-interest collective bargaining for women. Furthermore, working-class women themselves lack confidence in themselves and feel organization would be fruitless [47]. In an intensive study by the New York School of Industrial and Labor Relations of Cornell University of the barriers that keep working women who are union members from participating more fully in their trade-union organizations, it was found that female participation "at every level of union activity is jeopardized by lack of information, training, and experience on the part of most women, not by lack of desire" [47, p. 2]. The need for fewer home responsibilities and the need to feel more competent were also important barriers to union participation by women already in unions.

INDUSTRIAL LABOR FORCE PARTICIPATION AND POLITICAL PARTICIPATION: A NATIONAL SAMPLE

In order to test out some suggested relationships between the labor-force participation of working-class women and their political participation, an analysis of data from the 1972 American National Election survey was undertaken. The study includes 2,705 respondents who were U.S. citizens and eighteen years of age or older any time on or before election day, November 7, 1972. The sample is designed to be representative of the adult population of the United States. These data have a number of weaknesses in being used for this purpose, in that they were not gathered to look explicitly at labor-force participation. Further, they cannot show many of the crucial processual and context variables that the examination of past research and theory deems essential. However, they are a readily available sample that allows for analysis.

The measure used for political participation was an attitudinal one, used in past analyses to demonstrate predisposition toward political participation and to be highly predictive of a variety of political behavior [33]. This variable, which can be referred to as a sense of political efficacy, can be viewed as a kind of threshold item showing the potential of an individual mobilizing to attempt to influence policy. It does not show collective identity, but is presumably necessary for collective action to occur. The respondents were asked, "Would you say that voting is the only way people like you can have any say about the way government runs things, or that there are lots of ways that you can have a say?" Those who replied that voting was the only way were determined to have low political efficacy; those that said there were more ways than voting to influence the government had high political efficacy.

In the following analysis, differences in political efficacy are examined by occupation and by sex, comparing women to men and women to other women. Female occupations were divided into four groups, using the three-digit census classification: (1) homemaker; (2) white collar, which included all occupations from professional technical to clerical and sales which are usually included in this category; (3) industrial workers, which included all occupations of a production nature which involved group activity (foremen and craftsmen were included in this category); and (4) other blue collar, which were mainly service workers in the case of females. Three types of male occupations were analyzed, leaving out the homemaker category, since the total number of males in this category was exceedingly small. Controls for education and marital status are introduced in order to examine the interaction between industrial labor-force participation and the major mechanism for political socialization discussed in the past, formal education, and to see the impact of the hypotheses of alternative time demands and role pressures present among women with heavy home responsibilities. Other control variables were introduced, and will be discussed briefly.

Political Participation by Sex and Occupation

As expected, men had a significantly higher level of political efficacy, with 40.5 percent of the total sample classified as high political efficacy compared to 34.7 percent of the women (see table 5.1). This difference held for each occupational group except industrial workers. This group of males had the lowest political efficacy rate (27.6 percent) which was not significantly different from that of the women in the same occupational position. For women, however, the occupational group representing other blue-collar occupations— those women working in isolated blue-collar jobs—had a lower rate of political efficacy, with only 20 percent of these women having high political efficacy. (The males in this group had a high degree of political efficacy, perhaps due to the differential nature of their jobs compared to women in this category. They were likely to be in all male occupations, work outside, and had considerable autonomy in their work.)

While women did achieve equality in political efficacy with males in the industrial workers category, they are still significantly below the housewife in political efficacy. The literature on political participation

TABLE 5.1. Percent with High Political Efficacy by Sex and
          Occupation

	Male	*Female*
Homemakers	—	31.7 (717)
White-collar workers	51.9 (518)	47.0 (460)
Industrial workers	27.6 (519)	25.5 (137)
Other blue-collar workers	42.5 (80)	20.0 (175)
Total	40.5 (1,168)	34.7 (1,537)

suggests that an increase in political efficacy should be expected to take place with labor-force participation, with the factory being a more political source of mobilization than the home or neighborhood [26]. The difference between housewives and female industrial workers could simply be a function of social-class variables implying differential socialization or selection: housewives tend to be of all social classes, and thus have an initial level of political participation far above that of their working-class sisters.

Education, Occupation, and Sex

When the two female occupational groups are compared by education, it becomes clear that the differences between them found in table 5.2 are due to differences in educational level and the social-class background characteristics implied by it. The only comparisons of housewives and industrial workers where the differences are statistically significant are among the women with at least some college (chi-square probability less than .05). There are very few female industrial workers in the sample with any college education, and they have less than half the participation rate of college-educated homemakers. They also have a participation rate well below that of high school graduates who are industrial workers, but this difference is not statistically significant.

When male and female industrial workers are compared within educational groups, the differences still are not significant, although

TABLE 5.2. Percent with High Political Efficacy by Occupation and Education

| | Grade School Only | | Grades 9–11 | | High School | | At Least Some College | |
	Male	Female	Male	Female	Male	Female	Male	Female
Homemakers	—	16.2 (179)	—	21.4 (154)	—	36.1 (263)	—	59.9 (147)
White-collar workers	30.9 (55)	25.0 (20)	36.4 (44)	34.0 (53)	42.2 (128)	41.6 (185)	63.4 (287)	58.3 (199)
Industrial workers	16.6 (157)	23.5 (34)	28.6 (112)	19.1 (47)	31.3 (166)	35.6 (45)	42.9 (77)	25.0 (8)
Other blue-collar workers	10.5 (19)	18.4 (49)	30.0 (10)	14.3 (49)	56.3 (32)	24.6 (57)	64.7 (17)	29.4 (17)
Total	19.5 (231)	18.1 (282)	30.7 (166)	22.1 (303)	38.0 (326)	36.7 (550)	59.3 (381)	59.1 (357)

the men show a systematically increasing pattern of political participation by education and the women do not. One could conclude that in an industrial setting education aids men in gaining a sense of political efficacy, but does not give women the same advantage. Further, education is a good predictor of female political efficacy in all the other occupational groups. In all the educational categories except that of women with at least some college, white-collar women have the highest degree of political efficacy. For those women with a college education, white-collar workers and homemakers have similar high degree of political efficacy. Education makes more of a difference in political efficacy among white-collar workers than any other group except males in other blue-collar jobs and homemakers. Here are two groups of people that have more freedom to control their own environment, either positively or negatively, and where prior political socialization and selective factors have the greatest impact. Among industrial workers, on the other hand, situational factors seem very important. Participation is much less dependent on prior political socialization or personal characteristics.

Marital Status, Occupation, and Sex

A major situational factor, ignored by industrial sociologists who take a systems approach to their research, are the off-the-job demands and obligations of an individual. In the case of middle-class women, being a mother—assuming that role and the various responsibilities and statuses that went with it—served to reduce political efficacy. The total demand on women's time (total number of children) did not make a difference on their political efficacy. Instead, it was an internalized set of norms which altered their fundamental self-conception and resocialized them politically [20]. Motherhood did not make a comparable impact on working-class women, whose political participation was already considerably lower than that of the middle-class group.

Another indicator of the alternative demands on an individual's time is marital status. Never-married individuals presumably have less time demands off the job than their divorced or separated coworkers. Among women, those who are divorced, widowed, or separated have the job of running a total household alone (often with children present) and have a higher level of time demands than do even married women. For divorced or separated women, however, the situation parallels that of the single male. His ex-mate is the one who almost automatically takes over the children and other household responsibilities, while he gains a great deal of free time.

For the sample as a whole, this was the pattern followed (see table 5.3). Never-married men and women had the highest level of political efficacy (45.5 percent and 46.7 percent, respectively), and no differences by sex were present. Married individuals of both sexes had the next highest level of political efficacy, significantly lower than that of never-married individuals. Here, however, men had a small but statistically significant advantage over married women: 39.6 percent were politically efficacious compared to 36.2 percent of the women. Divorced men had the same degree of political efficacy as married men, but divorced, separated, or widowed women had a rate of political efficacy well below that of married women, being the lowest of all the categories (27.7 percent).

In comparing women by marital status among the different occupational groups, the pattern of higher efficacy for never-marrieds, followed by marrieds, holds. Divorced, widowed, and separated women have the lowest level of political efficacy. Among white-collar women workers the difference between married and divorced women is not significant. This group of women probably has the skills and capital necessary to hire husband-substitutes to fulfill their family obligations. For female industrial workers, the spread is greater, but also not significant. The differences among married and divorced women is greatest among homemakers· and other blue-collar workers, who

TABLE 5.3. Percent with High Political Efficacy by Occupation and Marital Status

	Married Male	Married Female	Never Married Male	Never Married Female	Divorced Male	Divorced Female
Homemakers	—	34.8 (543)	—	44.2 (43)	—	22.3 (157)
White-collar workers	51.8 (389)	46.4 (237)	54.5 (66)	53.4 (89)	50.0 (62)	44.6 (130)
Industrial workers	25.8 (403)	26.0 (73)	35.3 (51)	37.5 (16)	35.7 (56)	21.3 (47)
Other blue-collar workers	55.3 (47)	24.6 (77)	41.2 (17)	29.4 (17)	7.1 (14)	14.3 (77)
Total	39.6 (839)	36.2 (930)	45.5 (134)	46.7 (165)	39.4 (132)	27.7 (411)

probably have less resources to mobilize for family tasks as well as for political activity.

When marital status is controlled, difference in political efficacy by sex among industrial workers is significant only for divorced, widowed, or separated persons. Divorced male industrial workers have the same high rate of political efficacy as do never-married male industrial workers, while female industrial workers who are divorced, widowed, or separated have a rate that is lower than all the other marital-status groups.

Among white-collar workers, differences by marital status between the sexes occurs only when the women incur differential home responsibilities: never-married men and women have the same high level of political efficacy, while the differences between married white-collar men and women and divorced white-collar men and women is about five percentage points. For other blue-collar workers, where the difference between men and women is greatest anyway, large differences occur at each marital status *except* for divorced individuals. Here the male rate is lower than the female rate, but the difference is not significant, except that the status of being divorced appears to be much more alienating for men in blue-collar jobs than in other occupational categories.

Differences among women by occupation when marital status is controlled appear much as before. White-collar women in all marital-status categories have the highest rate of political efficacy, followed by homemakers, female industrial workers, and finally female workers in other blue-collar jobs. The differences between homemakers and female industrial workers are greatest among the never-married, although the sample size here is so small that the results are not statistically significant. Being married seems to make about the same amount of difference for both groups—a reduction of about ten percentage points in rate of political efficacy. However, among divorced women, the rate of political efficacy is almost identical for homemakers and industrial workers. This group was by far the most disadvantaged among the housewives, but rather similar to married women among industrial workers.

These results suggest that there is something about being married that decreases political efficacy among women—but it also decreases political efficacy among men. If one subscribes to the alternative use of time theory, then one would conclude that male industrial workers are very egalitarian in the division of labor at home, and the lack of differences in political efficacy by sex among married industrial workers is due to equal time demands at home for men and women. However, a political socialization theory might explain this difference in terms of the differential sex roles required of married vs. unmarried males. Married males have fulfilled their societal obligations by having a family, which may then create explicit but sexually differentiated demands on their time. Unmarried males must find other justifications of their manly responsibility. Clearly this requires further research.

CONCLUSIONS

This analysis of the structure of sociodemographic characteristics and political efficacy in light of a variety of theories of political participation and job-related characteristics which influence political participation raises more questions than it answers. By comparing political efficacy systematically by sex and occupation, there appears to be a strong interaction between certain aspects of political socialization, selective characteristics, and job-related structures that lead to persons being predisposed to being a political participant. Such static research needs to be augmented by studies of the processes involved, especially the processes that occur at the interfaces of the job, the home, and political participation. Industrial employment shows a great leveling effect by sex in rates of political participation. For women, such employment seems to be much more important than the socialization and selective attributes characterized by education. In freer work situations, low education seems to lead to a low degree of political efficacy and a kind of anomie, which labor-force participation in either white-collar or industrial jobs overcomes to some extent. (However, the differences among white-collar women and female industrial workers are particularly great at the higher education levels, requiring a greater understanding of the relation between job structure and political socialization. These women clearly have a greater stake in the political process than do the female industrial workers, and their political activities, while they may be feminist, may also be more inclined to support their own class interests rather than furthering the welfare of all women. Indeed, the white-collar women's political participation may be at the expense of the political participation of the other female blue-collar workers.) Industrial workers, by their homogeneity in terms of sense of political efficacy, seem to have the potential for developing a common identity. However, the job situation, despite its potential, does not seem to facilitate the mobilization of this group in the United States.

REFERENCES

1. Robert T. Alford and Harry M. Scoble. "Sources of Local Political Involvement," *American Political Science Review* 62 (December 1968): 1192–1206.

2. Jo Ann Aviel. "Changing the Political Role of Women: A Costa Rican Case Study." In *Women in Politics,* ed. Jane S. Jacquette. New York: Wiley, 1974.

3. Nicholas Babchuk and Alan Booth. "Voluntary Association Membership: A Longitudinal Analysis." *American Sociological Review* 34 (February 1969): 31–45.

4. Nicholas Babchuk, R. Marsey, and C. W. Gordan. "Men and Women in Community Agencies: A Note on Power and Prestige." *American Sociological Review* 25 (1960): 399–403.

5. Margaret Benston. "The Political Economy of Women's Liberation." *Monthly Review* 21 (September 1969): 13–27.

6. Paul Blumberg. *Industrial Democracy: The Sociology of Participation.* New York: Schocken, 1968.

7. Derek C. Bok and John T. Dunlop. *Labor and the American Community.* New York: Simon & Schuster, 1970.

8. Alan Booth. "Sex and Social Participation." *American Sociological Review* 37 (April 1972): 183–92.

9. Alan Booth, Nicholas Babchuk, and Alan B. Knox. "Social Stratification and Membership in Instrumental-Expressive Voluntary Associations." *Sociological Quarterly* 9 (Autumn 1968): 427–39.

10. Alex Carey. "The Hawthorne Studies: A Radical Criticism." *American Sociological Review* 32 (June 1967): 403–16.

11. Elsa M. Chaney. "The Mobilization of Women in Allende's Chile." In *Women in Politics,* ed. Jane S. Jacquette. New York: Wiley, 1974.

12. Elsa M. Chaney. "Women in Latin American Politics: The Case of Peru and Chile." In *Female and Male in Latin America: Essays,* ed. Ann Pescatetto. Pittsburgh: University of Pittsburgh Press, 1973.

13. Frank Clemente and G. F. Summers. "Rapid Industrial Development and Relative Status of the Sexes." Working Paper RID 72.15, December 1972, University of Wisconsin–Madison.

14. Randall Collins. "A Conflict Theory of Sexual Stratification." *Social Problems* 19 (Summer 1971): 3–21.

15. Mariarosa Dalla Costa. "Women and the Subversion of the Community." *Radical America* 6 (January–February, 1972): 67–102.

16. Richard Dawson and Kenneth Prewitt. *Political Socialization.* Boston: Little, Brown, 1969.

17. William C. Domhoff, *Who Rules America?* Englewood Cliffs, N.J.: Prentice-Hall, 1967.

18. William Erbe. "Social Involvement and Political Activity: A Replication and Elaboration." *American Sociological Review* 24 (April 1964): 198–215.

19. Cornelia Flora and Shirley J. Harkess. "Women in the News: An Analysis of Media Images in Colombia." *Revista-Review Interamericana* 4 (Summer 1974).

20. Cornelia Flora and Naomi B. Lynn. "Women and Political Socialization: Considerations of the Impact of Motherhood." In *Women in Politics*, ed. Jane S. Jacquette. New York: Wiley, 1974.

21. J. R. French, Jr., Joachin Israel, and Dagfinn As. "An Experiment in Participation in a Norwegian Factory." *Human Relations* 13 (February 1960): 1–17.

22. William Gomberg. "The Trouble with Democratic Management." *Transaction* 3 (July–August 1966).

23. Fred J. Greenstein. *Children and Politics.* New Haven, Conn.: Yale University Press, 1965.

24. Helen Hacker. "Women as a Minority Group." *Social Forces* 30 (October 1951): 60–69.

25. Herbert H. Hyman and Charles R. Wright. "Trends in Voluntary Association Membership of American Adults." *American Sociological Review* 36 (April 1971): 191–206.

26. Christian Lalive D'Epinay. "Sociedad Dependiente, 'Clases Populares' y Milenarismo." *Cuadernos ed la Realidad Nacional* 14 (October 1970): 96–112.

27. Robert E. Lane. *Political Life: Why People Get Involved in Politics.* Glencoe, Ill.: Free Press, 1959.

28. Sheldon G. Levy. "The Psychology of Political Activity." *The Annals of the American Academy of Political Science* 391 (Summer 1970): 83–96.

29. Seymour Martin Lipset, Martin Trow, and James Coleman. *Union Democracy.* Garden City, N.Y.: Doubleday, 1956.

30. Helen Lopata. "The Effect of Schooling on Social Contacts of Urban Women." *American Journal of Sociology* 79 (November 1973): 604–19.

31. Helen Lopata. *Occupation: Housewife.* New York: Oxford University Press, 1971.

32. Naomi B. Lynn and Cornelia B. Flora. "Societal Punishment, Amateurism, and Female Political Participation." Ms., Kansas State University, 1974.

33. Naomi B. Lynn and Cornelia B. Flora. "Motherhood and Political Participation: The Changing Sense of Self." *Journal of Political and Military Sociology* 1 (Spring 1973): 91–103.

34. Kathleen McCourt. "Politics and the Working Class Woman: The Case on Chicago's Southwest Side." Preliminary Report, Center for the Study of American Pluralism, National Opinion Research Center, University of Chicago, 1972.

35. Albert Memmi. *Dominated Man: Notes Toward a Portrait.* Boston: Beacon, 1968.

36. Lester W. Milbrath. *Political Participation.* Chicago: Rand McNally, 1965.

37. John B. Miner and Mary Green Miner. *Personnel and Industrial Relations: A Managerial Approach.* New York: Macmillan, 1973.

38. Jo Ann W. Moore. "Patterns of Women's Participation in Voluntary Associations." *American Journal of Sociology* 66 (May 1961): 592–98.

39. New York School of Industrial and Labor Relations, Cornell University. "Trade Union Women's Studies." New York City, 1973. Mimeographed.

40. Marvin E. Olsen. "Social Participation and Voting Turnout: A Multivariate Analysis." *American Sociological Review* 37 (June 1972): 317–33.

41. Anthony M. Orum, Roberta S. Cohen, Sherri Grasmuck, and Amy Orum. "Sex, Socialization, and Politics." *American Sociological Review* 39 (April 1974): 197–209.

42. Lee Rainwater, Richard P. Coleman, and Gerald Handel. *Workingman's Wife: Her Personality, World, and Life Style.* New York: Oceana, 1959.

43. Edna E. Raphael. "From Sewing Machines to Politics: The Woman Union Member in the Community." Paper presented at the Annual Meeting for the Study of Social Problems, 1973.

44. David L. Rogers and Ken Barb. "Impact of Social Positions on Political Perceptions and Behavior." Paper presented at the Annual Meeting of the Rural Sociological Society, 1973.

45. David Rogers, Gordon L. Bultena, and Ken H. Barb. "Voluntary Association Membership and Political Participation: An Exploration of the Mobilization Hypotheses." Paper presented at the Annual Meeting of the Midwest Sociological Society, 1974.

46. Paul T. Schollaert. "The Wage Impact of Blue Collar Union Membership." Ph.D. dissertation, University of Wisconsin at Madison, 1973.

47. Nancy Seiler. *Absent from the Majority: Working Class Women in America.* New York: American Jewish Committee, 1973.

48. Carol Slater. "Class Differences in Definition of Role Membership in Voluntary Associations Among Urban Married Woman." *American Journal of Sociology* (May 1960): 616–19.

49. Leticia M. Smith. "Women and the Double Standard: A Feminist Reevaluation of Volunteerism." Paper presented at the Annual Meeting of the Midwest Sociological Society, 1974.

50. Evelyne Sullerot. *Women, Society, and Change.* New York: McGraw-Hill, 1971.

51. Arnold S. Tannenbaum. "Unions." In *Handbook of Organizations,* ed. James G. March. Chicago: Rand McNally, 1965. Pp. 710–63.

52. Sydney Verba and Norman H. Nie. *Participation in America: Political Democracy and Social Equality.* New York: Harper & Row, 1972.

53. Joyce Jennings Walstedt. "Women as Marginals." *Psychological Reports* 34 (April 1974): 639–46.

54. R. K. White and Ronald Lippitt. *Autocracy and Democracy.* New York: Harper & Row, 1960.

LYNNE B. IGLITZIN

6

☆☆☆☆☆☆☆☆☆☆☆☆☆☆☆☆☆☆☆☆☆☆☆☆☆☆☆☆

A Case Study in Patriarchal Politics: Women on Welfare

Patriarchal thinking, which instills the idea of male superiority, is still widespread throughout the major institutions of our society, despite efforts of feminists and others to dispel it. Policies which reflect what has variously been referred to as patriarchal, paternalistic, and sexist attitudes and beliefs are daily being made and implemented in our schools, churches, and governmental and business bureaucracies.

As contemporary women's liberation writings have been pointing out, the result of the institutionalization of patriarchal politics is that the vast majority of women of all social classes are socialized into "femininity," that is, into being subordinate, dependent, docile persons who meet the sex-role stereotypes for women. In this article the focus is on a particular group of women who are caught in an institution, public welfare, which reinforces and encourages "feminine" (dependent, passive) behavior. While all women are oppressed by sex-role socialization, welfare women, poor and often nonwhite, are additionally burdened by pressures integral to the institution of welfare.

This presentation will deal both with the policies of a major federal institution, the Aid to Families with Dependent Children (AFDC) program of the Department of Health, Education, and Welfare, and the application and implementation of these policies at the state and local level. As a case study, aspects of the AFDC program, as it affected women recipients in the city of Seattle during spring 1972, receive major emphasis. A participant-observer project under the direction of the author provided data on attitudes, feelings, and behavior of welfare women. Participants in the research (referred to hereinafter as the Seattle Project) befriended women recipients and talked with them about their lives, their grievances, and their complaints. Others in the project joined the local welfare rights organization and assisted in ongoing organizational efforts of women recipients. All participants in the project kept daily journals, from which many of the following observations and reflections are drawn.

Statistics on poverty and governmental assistance justify focusing on public welfare's special impact upon women. Families headed by women are disproportionately represented among the aged, rural, and urban poor. Among whites, 36 percent of households headed by women with dependent children were poor in 1968. Almost two-thirds (62 percent) of all nonwhite families headed by women were poor. The largest category of public assistance, approximately 85 percent, goes to dependent children who live in families headed by women. Statistics from the U.S. Department of Health, Education, and Welfare Social Rehabilitation Service [17, p. 1]* cite 2.7 million families receiving AFDC support in 1971.

The central focus of this essay is on the ways in which the institution of public welfare reflects society's image of the proper role of women, and the specific double bind this creates for AFDC women. It is argued here that public welfare reinforces the socialization of women into the feminine stereotype by encouraging a set of "feminine" personality traits—by supporting the traditional wife-mother role, by continuing to enforce an outdated standard of morality, by its "women's work" orientation, by its pitting of women against women, and by its inculcation of feelings of apathy and powerlessness. Some policy recommendations which might begin to counter the pressures of patriarchal politics upon welfare women conclude this essay.

WELFARE AND THE FEMININE STEREOTYPE

The "Feminine" Personality
Even a cursory reading of the existing literature and research on

*Numbers in brackets refer to numbered references at the end of the chapter.

AFDC mothers makes apparent the degree to which personality traits and attitudes associated with femininity come to characterize welfare recipients. Being on welfare appears to reinforce those traits into which women, qua women, have already previously been socialized: passivity, docility, dependence, and resignation.

Dependency is the most prominent of these traits since the social worker exercises discretion over the distribution of benefits and has control over social services the client badly needs. It is in this context that social workers in one study [9, p. 129] reported "an ingratiating, embarrassing type of dependency" among their clients. Similarly, another study of welfare recipients' views about themselves and the welfare institution [2] elicited submissive attitudes toward authority as well as a strong sense of obligation and gratitude to the agency. In the Seattle Project, interviewers reported recipients unwilling to make a fuss or to challenge the system in any way. Both recipients and the employees with whom they dealt felt that to receive public assistance branded one as a failure. The recipients were ashamed, and often delayed making their initial application as long as possible. When they did come in, they expected and accepted the patronizing and demeaning manner in which, often unconsciously, the welfare employees treated them. As humiliating as it is to receive public assistance, the fear of getting no subsistence at all is worse, and in order to avoid that, recipients were willing to put up with the loss of dignity which goes along with the bestowal of aid. One observer in the project described this attitude in a woman she was helping:

> Another old woman was in to get her check. She had the sweetest smile-wrinkled face, and walked with a cane because she had broken her hip. I helped her with the forms and she kept thanking me. When her check finally came down, she thanked me profusely for being so nice and had a tear in the corner of her eye.

People in need are made to feel that they are guilty of something, that they are asking for something they do not deserve, and thus they come to feel that the welfare system has the right to regulate their lives.

Feminine stereotypical traits such as dependency and submissiveness are also reinforced by the recipients' view that decision making in welfare agencies is a highly complex, mysterious process. Respondents in the Briar study [2] felt that it was all right for the agency to ask so many questions, to make searches, and to check on how funds are being spent, since the agency was supporting them. A lack of understanding of the rules and regulations, and an even more basic lack of certainty as to exactly what the department could and would do for them at some future date, combine to create a feeling of awe and mystery in regard to the whole operation. There are so many un-certainties to be encountered—people checking one's house, regula-tions changing all the time, no assurance that the same financial or case worker will continue to handle your case. Seattle Project partici-pants found that in some offices a deliberate policy of daily rotation on all cases exists which involves constant repetition by the recipient of all the facts at each interview, so that it is almost impossible for anyone to know what to expect, let alone demand. Recipients will live with doubts and suspicions, reluctant even to ask questions, afraid to call attention to themselves.

In our society, women particularly are socialized into traits, such as resignation and satisfaction with one's lot, which also happen to make them most cooperative as welfare recipients. One student in the Seattle Project became personally involved as she made a welfare ap-plication of her own, and consciously attempted to analyze her own prior socialization as a woman:

> Some of the qualities I noticed in myself were extreme patience, gratitude (we are very used to receiving financial support) and an unwillingness to take action on my own behalf (I have always been quick to champion someone else's cause before my own). Women are also taught to be more intimidated by authority than are men, and I felt this strongly in myself when confronted by the forms and its many directions.

After several months of interaction with a group of AFDC mothers in one office, one interviewer commented that

> the women were reluctant to talk about the Stoneway office and the treatment they were getting there. Those who spoke most freely smoothed over any complaints that they had, with apologies for the system. An example of this was one woman who failed to receive a check for two months and almost didn't survive. Even if she had received the check each month, she commented, the money scarcely covered essentials. She followed this statement by excusing the frantic workers and explaining that now she was getting her checks on time.

Most of the women the students encountered had been on welfare before and expressed little hope of ever becoming self-supporting. Their overwhelming attitude appeared to be one of resignation. In contrast, men recipients were more extreme in their feelings of shame and humiliation and often expressed more bitter feelings against the welfare system. The longer one is on welfare, the more the system encourages feelings of resignation and acceptance. Women recipients who reported they were "satisfied" or "expressed some complaints timidly" were common. The longer period seems to teach recipients how to work with the system with the least hassle to both the department and the client. Seattle Project interviewers found a correlation between the more children a woman had (more financial assistance) and her greater expressions of satisfaction with the system.

Although payments are low and services generally inadequate to meet the needs of their families, many of these women have no viable alternative to remaining on AFDC, and are thus realistic in resigning themselves to it. In the Handler and Hollingsworth study [9, p. 179], 25 percent of the AFDC mothers interviewed said they could not foresee any time in the future when they would no longer require AFDC assistance or some kind of welfare aid. For women with large families and few job skills, the prospect of being able to support themselves is dim, and the options to remaining on welfare are severely restricted.

Still another trait traditionally associated with the feminine stereotype, which is reinforced and perpetuated by the welfare institution, is a sense of powerlessness. The powerlessness of women may extend to a lack of economic independence, a lack of decision-making power over their own bodies, or a lack of physical power to defend themselves against assault.

Women on welfare, who share all of these conditions because they are women, are subject to even more profound pressures. They often feel futile and apathetic regarding their ability to bring change in their own lives. Because they sense their total economic dependence upon the largesse of the state, and because they have been socialized into thinking they ought to be grateful for its beneficence, most welfare women have little incentive to try to change their situation, or even to protest inequities and injustices.

The "Caretaker Relative": Wife and Mother

A central aspect of the "ideal" woman has been her identity as wife and mother. Society has bequeathed to women the role of upholders of the institution of the family. This feminine stereotype of woman's role as housewife/mother is one of the core concepts of the AFDC program. Public welfare institutions reinforce and perpetuate the "mother-in-the-home" image for their women recipients.

Regulations issued by the Department of Health, Education, and Welfare make continual reference to the goal of maintaining and strengthening family life. Policies designed to implement this goal range from programs to prevent or reduce out-of-wedlock births, to family-planning services to help individuals limit family size, to programs for establishing paternity and securing financial support for children born out of wedlock. Such policies have been in effect since before the Mother's Pension Laws were federalized in 1935. "Home life is the highest, finest product of civilization. Children . . . of reasonably efficient and deserving mothers who are without the support of the normal breadwinner should as a rule be kept with their parents," according to a 1909 White House Conference on Children [3, p. 91]. According to the 1935 Report of the Committee on Economic Security, which submitted the initial draft of the Social Security Act, "the purpose of ADC has been to prevent the disruption of families on the ground of poverty alone and to enable the mother to stay at home and devote herself to housekeeping and the care of her children" [7].

Over the years the AFDC philosophy for parental roles has not changed: mothers stay at home and care for children: fathers work and are the breadwinners for the family. When the latter are absent, public welfare is called for.

Such a division of labor is still part of the AFDC program, even though many federal regulations have substituted the nonsexist phrase, "individual caretaker relative" for "mother" when referring to child care. Assistance codes of many states continue to reflect the old assumptions that it is, of course, mother who cares for the children. For example, recent regulations of the Washington Administrative Code have two different bases for terminating eligibility for assistance: when the mother resumes care of the children; or when a father or stepfather receives his first pay for full-time employment. Thus, even in 1973, welfare policies reflected the widespread view that men work at jobs while women care for children.

Pressures to be mother and homemaker are combined with an even more subtle message which continually tells the woman that her troubles will cease, or at least diminish, if she can reconcile with her husband (or the father of her children) and lead a "proper" family life. One way of doing this is to insist on the mother's cooperation with law-enforcement agencies in forcing the absent father to meet his obligation to care for and support his children. This enforced cooperation, which has been agency policy since the NOLEO Amendment of 1960, has a double purpose. It puts pressure on a man and woman to fortify traditional marital and familial institutions and it also serves to perpetuate the idea of the male as breadwinner.

Public welfare subtly focuses the efforts of its women recipients on "getting a man." Getting married, reconciling with one's husband, or being lucky enough to find another man who will marry a woman with a ready-made family, is seen by many as the ideal solution. One respondent in the Seattle Project told the interviewer that finding a husband would be the solution to all her troubles. In their study of AFDC mothers who left the program, Handler and Hollingsworth [9, p. 181] found that for about one-fifth, marriage was the principal reason for leaving. Others planned to get married, while still others had husbands who returned or recovered from illness or came back from prison. In sum, according to the authors, "combining all groups, over 40 percent of the women leaving AFDC returned to or created families headed by males. Clearly, the availability of men plays an important role in welfare exits."

Johnnie Tillmon [16], past president of the Welfare Rights Organization, argues that the institution of welfare is designed to punish women for failing to live up to the feminine stereotype of wife and mother. A husbandless woman is a deviant, and welfare regulations are constructed so that women pay the price of their nonconformity to the marriage institution. According to Tillmon:

> Society needs women on welfare as "examples" to let every woman, factory workers and housewife workers alike, know what will happen if she lets up, if she's laid off, if she tries to go it along without a man. (p. 112)

Guarding Feminine Virtue

Even within the supposedly sexually liberated climate of the 1970s, many people continue to view the welfare woman as immoral, involved in illicit sex not legitimized by marriage, and continuing to have children simply in order to get bigger subsidies from the government. Ironically, although the welfare institution exerts pressure, as we have seen, to have a man in the house, he is permitted to be there in only one carefully circumscribed role, that is, husband/

breadwinner. A relationship not legitimized by a marriage contract is frowned upon.

At first glance, welfare appears to be an egalitarian system, giving aid to those in need regardless of sex. But a careful scrutiny of the philosophy and practices which determine eligibility reveals that a double standard does exist. To be eligible for public assistance, a man must merely prove that he is destitute and that he is willing to accept work if it turns up. On the other hand, a mother who wishes to be eligible for AFDC benefits for her children must meet a whole set of noneconomic conditions. Not only must she adhere to a preestablished set of moral standards, but she must be willing to trade in a significant portion of her privacy and personal liberty. As Steiner [15, p. 119] puts it, "in accepting AFDC, the client has made Public Welfare the guardian of her morals and has contracted away any right to live in sin."

The assumptions and philosophy underlying these practices of the welfare system are rooted in mid-Victorian ethical standards still operative, at least for poor women. Moral behavior (living only with a man to whom one is married) has been an unstated condition of receiving benefits. In the original 1935 House and Senate Committee Reports setting up the Social Security Act, the states were left free to impose eligibility requirements relating to the "moral character" of the applicants. Many families were declared ineligible because children were not living in "suitable homes" due to the alleged immoral behavior of their mothers.

In the 1940s the "suitable home" provisions came under increasing attack as punishing needy children for the misdeeds of their mothers. Finally, in 1961, Secretary of Health, Education, and Welfare Flemming ruled that states could not deny assistance to needy children, no matter what the home conditions. Since that time federal public welfare policy has become more sophisticated and enlightened than it was in the past (it does not punish children by denying them aid) but its moralism is still in evidence, albeit more subtle. What federal regulations have done (*King* v. *Smith*, 1968) is to determine that immorality and illegitimacy should be dealt with through rehabilitation measures (children can be removed from unsuitable homes and placed in foster homes or institutions; states must provide programs to improve and correct unsuitable homes; agencies must provide voluntary family planning services to reduce illegitimate births) rather than measures that punish dependent children. Yet coerciveness has not been removed from AFDC regulations, since current regulations approve the withholding of aid from uncooperative mothers who fail to assist the agency in establishing the child's paternity and seeking support from the father.

Women Against Women

Still another aspect of feminine socialization noted by contemporary feminists, is the subtle way women are taught to be competitive with one another. Women learn from the time they are little girls to vie with each other for the attention of men, and it becomes difficult for them to form friendships and long-lasting relationships with other women. The welfare system contributes to this socialization by pitting women against women on an everyday basis. Nearly all the receptionists, secretaries, caseworkers, and financial workers that welfare recipients encounter, are women. Welfare workers, by the nature of their jobs, appear to wield huge discretionary power over the lives and pocketbooks of recipients (although the real power and decision making lies elsewhere).

Spending the day dealing with the problems of people who are angry, hungry, and depressed is a difficult and dehumanizing experience for many of the women workers within the system. Men dominate the top of the welfare bureaucracy (in one office 209 out of 247 employees were female; in another 11 out of 13 administrative positions were held by men), but the daily interaction is between women and women. One receptionist told an interviewer in the Seattle Project that she was quitting soon because it was too much of a strain, serving as a buffer between the miseries of the recipients and the relative unavailability of the caseworker.

Things are not much better when one finally gets past the mass of paperwork, the buzzers, and the receptionists, to the caseworker. Institutional operations have grown so enormously around the country that welfare workers are in bureaucratic routines that frustrate initiative for change. The case load of most workers is so high that the level of service is necessarily scanty. Previous research reports [10, p. 47] that the recipient-caseworker relationship is unstable because of the high percentage of caseworker resignations and frequent reassignments.

Although the majority of social workers are women, they view their clients less as sisters sharing problems due to their sex, than as lower-class people distant from their own middle-class values and morals. According to one source, Freudian training of most schools of social work tends to emphasize "individual readjustment" rather than reform of societal institutions, and the caseworkers in turn see poverty as an individual problem, apart from factors of socioeconomic or sex and race discrimination [10, p. 95].

The Narrow World of Woman's Work

Most people feel that anyone who is willing to work hard can find a job; thus, by implication, people on the relief rolls are simply malingerers who could support themselves if they really tried. The myth of the lazy welfare worker is a pervasive one. Yet, as everyone knows, myths often contradict one another, and this is particularly true in the case of women. On the one hand, they are subject to the woman-as-mother-in-the-house myth, and expected to stay at home caring for their children. On the other, they are included in the people-on-welfare-are-lazy myth, with its strong implications that anyone who really wants to can find a job. Yet widespread discrimination exists against women in hiring and salary policies: most women are channeled into low-paying "temporary" jobs such as typist or sales clerk, or into traditionally low-paying, female professions. Most communities lack the facilities that would enable mothers to work anyhow—that is, day-care centers and adequate public transportation.

A very limited number of vocational programs, all within the traditional female occupations such as secretarial and clerical work, constitute the full range of the welfare woman's job possibilities. Public welfare will not pay child care benefits for a woman who wishes to broaden her horizons vocationally and desires to go to college to do so. In spite of these restrictive provisions on single mothers, Wickendon [21] argues that many AFDC mothers have made heroic efforts to upgrade their employment qualifications by completing their higher education. Several respondents in the Seattle Project told interviewers of women cajoled and coerced into taking dead-end jobs because public assistance was not forthcoming while they attended school to try to better their employment prospects.

Cloward and Piven [4, p. 129] argue that a mother's fears of being dropped from public assistance if she refuses to work, put great pressure on her to remain in the marginal labor market, if she has been lucky enough to find a job at all. A number of respondents in the Seattle Project expressed such fears and an attitude of resentment. Mary Thomas's case was typical. She would like to quit her job as a saleswoman in a clothing store, in order to return to school and become a medical technician. Unfortunately, though welfare will subsidize the day care of her five children while she works at the store, it will not do so while she returns to school for four years. Nor will welfare pay for her tuition. It is thus difficult, if not impossible, for her to work in anything except a low-paying, dead-end job. Mary Thomas expresses her hopes this way: "I want to better myself; I'm tired of going down, I want to go up for once. . . . I don't want to be at Lerners the rest of my life."

Many of the women the students interviewed echoed Mary Thomas's hope for a good job where they could have independence and dignity. Yet the federal minimum wage of $1.60 an hour means that for all her hard labor, a woman who has several children will still be stuck in poverty. In fact, public officials such as Senator Russell Long and Elliot Richardson have argued that welfare recipients ought to work for less than the minimum wage ($1.20 an hour) if private industry jobs are unavailable.

Women in the Seattle Project say that they would like to work if proper care could be given to their children. Other research on AFDC recipients corroborates this. In one survey of AFDC mothers in New York City [14, p. 17], in response to a question, "Would you prefer to work for pay or stay at home?"—70 percent said they would prefer to work. In another national study of women who received or had applied for AFDC [13, p. 16] over 80 percent said they would like to work if they could find a steady job. Yet in the Seattle Project, the long-term recipient women lacked confidence in their own abilities, and were insecure about their chances of job success. In Goodwin's study [6, p. 51], mothers who were poor, heads of households, and marginal to the work force gave similar responses.

As a partial result of the enormous increase in the number of public assistance recipients during the 1960s, federal policies which encouraged the institution of programs of job counseling and retraining in order to assist AFDC mothers to work were developed. In 1967, Congress set up a new work incentive program (WIN) with local welfare departments required to provide day-care centers for children of mothers training or working.

Encouraging women to leave the role of full-time housewife/mother in favor of a job outside the home might at least seem to help destroy the traditional feminine stereotype. This however, was not the case. The unstated premise of WIN throughout its short history has been that welfare mothers must work at any job the Department of

Public Welfare regards as suitable, or risk losing eligibility. "Suitable" work seems to be mostly waitresses, scrubwomen, and maids: age-old, low-paying "women's work." Only 8 percent of AFDC mothers are employed in jobs that are skilled, clerical, or white collar, according to one recent study [4, p. 137]. Of these, a vast majority are white. Unskilled labor and service jobs occupy the remainder of the women. A triple type of discrimination is in evidence against sex, race, and class. Society treats low-income women differently than other women. As Bernard [1, p. 179] puts it: "For those in the lowest levels—on assistance rolls, policy has been designed to encourage—coerce would not be too strong a term—a two-role pattern of mother-breadwinner."

Although the commonly stated goal of the WIN program is to rehabilitate its clients and transform them into self-supporting persons, the actual functioning of the program, particularly for women, falls far short of this goal. Little financial incentive exists for a poorly educated AFDC mother to accept training for herself which would fit her only for some menial job when at the same time she can expect day care of at best uncertain quality. The inequities of the WIN program in the past have been clearly apparent. The work training program was mandatory for men and optional for women, and the federal regulations set up a referral system which puts mothers with preschoolers at the bottom of the list. In effect, the program discouraged women with small children from job training altogether, and gave top priority to men and young people over the age of sixteen. These priorities have come under increasing attack as possible violations of Title VII of the Civil Rights Act. Thus, we can expect to see more women admitted to job training programs. Nonetheless, the narrow selection of jobs available still limits most of them to low-paying maintenance work.

Furthermore, the job placement record for those graduating from the WIN program has not been good. According to statistics of the U.S. Department of Labor Manpower Administration [19, p. 22], of those terminated from WIN by 1970, only about 20 percent had jobs. Only about 10 percent of the 1.6 million public assistance recipients eligible for WIN in the first place (of whom 95 percent were AFDC mothers) were admitted into the program. Thus it becomes apparent that the program provided jobs for only about 2 percent of the total eligible welfare population. In his study of work orientations of black welfare women, Goodwin [6, p. 101] found that success or failure in obtaining a job after going through WIN affected one's orientation: "The 92 trainees who failed to obtain jobs after WIN not unreasonably felt greater dependence on welfare and even less confidence in themselves than they did at the start of their training." Thus failure in the work world makes women even more dependent upon public assistance.

The total work picture for welfare women is a bleak one: a low percentage of jobs are open after completion of work training; jobs that are available are largely in the low-paying, menial, and unskilled levels; a heavy concentration of jobs is in the traditional female occupations; high costs exist for child care; and, there is low motivation and expectation of advancement as well as little dignity in one's work. It is no wonder that existing research finds many welfare women longing for the traditional breadwinner/husband to support them.

BREAKING OUT OF THE MOLD:
SOME SUGGESTIONS FOR REFORM

In order to begin to change their patriarchal attitudes and practices, public welfare agencies need to stop reinforcing attitudes of submissiveness, suppliance, dependence, and passiveness among their clients. Recipients should be able to view themselves as responsible citizens, with rights and responsibilities, who simply, at this point in time, need to turn to the public realm for assistance. It is possible to provide aid without making clients feel the sense of awe, powerlessness, self-degradation and submissiveness to agency regulations that is presently the case. Specific policy suggestions, at the very least, might follow along the lines suggested by Briar [2, p. 60]:

—radical simplification of the eligibility and budgeting processes
—high visibility of agency decision-making in individual cases
—high visibility and accessibility of appeal procedures
—redefinition of social worker's role to that of advocate for the client

Welfare clients need to develop a sense that they have the means and power to criticize and challenge actions of officials. Moreover, the welfare system needs to end its paternalistic attitude toward recipients. This attitude is particularly harmful for women, socialized always to be dependent upon others. Clients need not be treated like children who lack the ability to control their expenditures and whose every action must be supervised. In addition to this paternalism, the welfare system's attitude toward AFDC mothers is that of husband-protector, equally damaging to the self-esteem and independence of women. Glassman [5, p. 102] describes welfare as a supersexist marriage, where women are still in their ancient role of economic dependence, with the welfare board simply taking place of the husband. One of the ways of putting an end to such a relationship, as Handler and Hollingsworth [9, p. 207] suggest, might be to refrain from using coercive rules which carry with them less-than-adequate protective standards. As these authors point out, rules which require the unwed mother to supply the name of the putative father or which make public aid contingent upon employment, are inherently coercive, no matter what protective standards are included. The vast majority of recipients, who must maintain a continuing relationship with the agency, are subject to the huge discretionary authority of the field worker. In such a context, protective standards do not ever fully protect welfare recipients.

Practices which reflect society's old view that recipients need to be punished because they are morally unworthy, ought to be changed. Public assistance is a right and eligibility should be based on need, not on how much sacrifice someone is willing to make. If this attitude were to change it would reduce the many delays and unnecessary verifications, as well as the violations of dignity, self-respect, and privacy, to which AFDC mothers are particularly vulnerable. The welfare system should get out of the business of making moral judgments about the sexual behavior and life style of those to whom it provides assistance. All too often judgments result in supporting only the traditional nuclear family structure and rejecting, by implication, other alternatives.

With respect to employment, public welfare should cease contributing to the channeling of women into low-paying, menial "women's work" jobs. Employment for AFDC mothers should not be simply a way of reducing the public assistance rolls but a method of providing a more satisfying and independent existence for women whose previous work experiences have been degrading and demoralizing. Some specific national policy changes which might begin to accomplish this end would include:

—permitting the mother to work without being penalized by an equal reduction in her assistance allotment
—ending wage differentials for males and females (which should

be easier as the Equal Rights Amendment gets passed in one state after another)
—providing adequate day-care centers and extensive preschool educational programs for children of working mothers
—expanding job training options for women within the WIN program to include a far greater range of possibilities than presently exist
—expanding financial aid to cover educational programs for women, from high school through higher education, payable as part of the usual assistance grant

These suggestions (influenced by Kriesberg [11, pp. 321–23]) might encourage women to view employment as a major portion of their lives, and not as a temporary stopgap until some man can be found to support them. They are small enough compensatory efforts to make up for the second-rate education which most welfare women have received simply because they are poor, female, and oftentimes non-white.

Few of the foregoing recommendations and policy changes will have much effect in helping reduce the feeling of powerlessness which public welfare reinforces in its women clients unless they themselves are made part of the process of change. Women must learn to develop political and organizational strengths so that they can influence the direction of these programs. No only will their input be valuable in shaping institutional policies, but the effort itself will contribute to the development of the political skills so many women—and poor women in particular—presently lack. The factor that might contribute the most to this goal is the growth of welfare rights organizations (WRO) around the country.

Where effective welfare rights organizations exist, significant changes in the feelings of powerlessness and dependency among recipients seem to occur. Participant-observers in the Seattle Project who worked with the local welfare rights organization noted the self-conscious feeling of power among the activists, who often had novel and innovative ways of exercising power. Such women, whose activities brand them as trouble makers, develop an inner strength to combat the resultant pressure on them. Major WRO efforts center on developing local community social service and day-care centers run by the women themselves.

Beyond these concrete issues, however, welfare rights organizations will prove their strength and effectiveness by the degree to which they are able to instill feelings of self-worth and dignity in women who are presently on welfare. Such feelings will emerge as the women come to recognize that part of the blame for their dependency is with the system. As one woman suggested while talking with a student: "many women begin to think they are going crazy because of the paranoia caused by the 'put offs' of the department, and often have themselves committed." As with the larger women's movement, women on welfare are coming to reject this personalized view of their own problems, and to look at broader social and political factors. Once they learn to look at the issues this way (and it is still only a small minority who do) the next step to organizing, demonstrating, protesting, and pressuring for change, is not far behind. The increased consciousness of women—of women who are poor, angry, and hungry—has been seen in many local welfare offices, as nervous and harried employees can testify.

As yet, only a small minority of all those on welfare are aware of the services of the welfare rights organizations and call upon them in need. An even smaller number are activists within the organizations, but their number is growing. Every student involved in the Seattle Project was struck by the contrasts between the sense of power, strength, humor, and wisdom displayed by the activist women they met, and the feelings of apathy, uncertainty, and resignation displayed oy so many of the other recipients.

In conclusion, the lot of the welfare women is intimately related to the lot of all women in our society. Only when we begin to educate women equally with men, when we offer them equal job and career opportunities and quality child-care facilities, when we cease socializing and channeling them into dependent, submissive, "femininity," will the conditions of women on public assistance really improve. The policy recommendations made in this paper will perhaps alleviate some of the most blatant sexist practices in the welfare institution, but similar efforts must be made to eradicate sexist and racist practices in every institution simultaneously if any meaningful social change is to be accomplished.

In the larger society patriarchal institutions function to isolate women, to keep them dependent and blaming themselves for problems they encounter in life. Public welfare operates in the same way. And the solution, as women are beginning to learn, is to oppose patriarchalism wherever it occurs in whatever form, by joining with one another in strength of purpose and solidarity.

112 ☆ LYNNE B. IGLITZIN

REFERENCES

1. Jessie Bernard. *Women and the Public Interest.* Chicago: Aldine-Atherton, 1971.

2. S. Briar. "Welfare From Below: Recipients' Views of the Public Welfare System." In *The Law of the Poor,* ed. J. TenBroek. San Francisco: Chandler, 1966. Pp. 46–61.

3. M. Calcott. *Principles of Social Legislation.* New York: Macmillan, 1932.

4. Richard Cloward and Frances Fox Piven. *Regulating the Poor: The Function of Public Welfare.* New York: Pantheon, 1971.

5. Carol Glassman. "Women and the Welfare System." In *Sisterhood Is Powerful,* ed. Robin Morgan. New York: Random House, 1970.

6. L. Goodwin. *Do the Poor Want to Work?* Washington, D.C.: Brookings, 1972.

7. L. Graham. "Public Assistance: Congress and the Employable Mother." *University of Richmond Law Review* 223 (1969).

8. J. Handler. "Justice for the Welfare Recipient: Fair Hearings in AFDC—The Wisconsin Experience." *Social Service Review* 42 (1969).

9. J. Handler and E. J. Hollingsworth. *The "Deserving Poor."* Chicago: Markham, 1971.

10. D. James. *Poverty, Politics and Change.* Englewood Cliffs, N.J.: Prentice-Hall, 1972.

11. L. Kreisberg. *Mothers in Poverty.* Chicago: Aldine, 1970.

12. J. Levin and P. Vergata. "Welfare Laws and Women: An Analysis of Federal Sexism." Rutgers Law School, ms.

13. P. Levinson. "How Employable are AFDC Women?" *Welfare in Review* 8 (July/August 1970).

14. L. Podell. "Families on Welfare in New York City." City University of New York, ms.

15. G. Steiner. *Social Insecurity.* New York: Rand McNally, 1966.

16. J. Tillmon. "Welfare Is a Woman's Issue." *Ms.* (Spring 1972).

17. U.S. Department of Health, Education, and Welfare, Social and Rehabilitation Service. *Public Assistance Statistics June 1971.*

18. U.S. Department of Health, Education, and Welfare, Social and Rehabilitation Service. "Service Programs for Families and Children" 34 *Federal Register* 18 (1969).

19. U.S. Department of Labor, *The Work Incentive Program* (Washington, D.C.: Government Printing Office, 1970).

20. U.S. House of Representatives, *Report of the Ways and Means Committee, 1972.*

21. E. Wickendon. "H.R.1: Welfare Policy As An Instrument of Control." New York: Center on Social Welfare Policy and Law, 1972.

PART

III Characteristics of Women in Politics: Problems in Recruitment

Socialization to female roles is the first hurdle confronting women in their efforts to achieve parity in politics. From childhood on, attitudes, values, and habits that are not consistent with adult roles of political involvement are transmitted to women. Consequently, many young women, particularly those who have effectively internalized societal norms, never aspire to active or effective participation in the political realm at either the citizen or elite level. The notion that politics is "too dirty," too demanding, or just too unfeminine is so ingrained that they shun active political involvement throughout their adult lives. In a small study of students at a prestigious women's college a few years ago, for example, the majority ranked politics as the most unfeminine of ten professions which included, among others, athletics. Although some women have been able to escape the limitations their training inculcates, the battle is by no means won. When women pursue more active political roles than those prescribed, they must still face the problems of entrance into politics. Indeed, recruitment poses a second and very serious barrier for women.

113

The problems of political recruitment cluster around a number of factors. There is, of course, the underlying issue of acceptance into those traditional organizations that facilitate access to politics. Part 5, dealing with performance, discusses the resistance of political parties to accept women on an equal basis, to incorporate them into decision-making roles, and to see them as either serious candidates for public office or sufficiently well qualified to stand for election. As pointed out there, women tend, as a result, to move into other kinds of organizations, especially nonpartisan and volunteer ones that address issues of unique concern to women but lack the clout to bring about political change, and refrain from running for elective office.

Then there are the characteristics considered necessary for a political career. Since socialization conveys different and antithetical values to women, a host of questions are raised. Must political women have special qualities that distinguish them from their less political or nonpolitical or apolitical sisters? If so, what are they? To what extent and in what areas are those traditional norms instilled in women absent in politically active women? Is there, in other words, a particular kind of woman who is more likely to be recruited into politics? If so, who is she? Can women manage to enter politics in significant numbers, or in isolated instances only?

Finally, there is the impact of women's responses to the contradictions of their dual role. Women must simultaneously avoid becoming separated from other women, be respected by their male political peers, and refrain from projecting a threatening nonfeminine image. This means that women must define a special place or function for themselves which allows them to reconcile notions of feminity with a nonfeminine enterprise such as politics. Is a reconciliation possible? How will it affect recruitment? What will be the impact on political style and effectiveness?

In a study of men and women participating in local politics in four municipalities, Lee examines some factors affecting women's recruitment at the elite level. Her findings indicate several interesting things. First, women devote more time to political activity than men. Second, social class as defined by income and education affects women's political participation more than men's. Thus, educated, affluent women spend more time in political activities. Nevertheless, despite the amount of time devoted and the educational and financial qualifications that characterize the women, they rarely hold leadership positions.

Several explanations for these findings are presented. Higher income levels free women from house-bound duties, and their education sensitizes them to the obligations of citizenship. The conclusion could be drawn that traditional female socialization does not preclude recruitment into lower-level elite participation. Baby sitters allow women to work in politics; however, the presence of children in the home acts as a restraint on seeking and holding public office. For the women in the study the roles of mother and professional politican were incompatible; when children were grown and the women felt free to take up a political career, they were not competitive with men who entered politics earlier and were therefore deemed more qualified. In addition, women themselves were ambivalent about a professional political role. Notions about what is proper for women coupled with perceptions of the sex discrimination they would encounter discouraged them from seeking more visible positions. Quite clearly, for the women in Lee's study the contradictions of women's dual role are a key issue in the inadequate recruitment of women into politics.

A similar theme runs through "Societal Punishment and Aspects of Female Political Participation: 1972 National Convention Delegates." In their views of a group of female delegates to the 1972 conventions, Lynn and Flora find both the same kind of concerns expressed by the women that Lee postulates as crucial and essentially the same sort of characteristics, at least insofar as party activity is concerned. Their analysis of the problem is somewhat different, however. They hypothesize that there exists a systematic punishment of women who deviate from traditional sex roles and that societal disapproval is perceived by women participating in politics. Attempting to avoid community disapproval the women cluster in James Wilson's category of "amateur." This political style, emphasizing self-sacrifice and dedication to others and eschewing personal political ambition, enables women to reconcile their contradictory roles of woman, wife, and mother on the one hand and political activist on the other. Although such a role orientation does not enhance chances for increasing power and influence, it nonetheless allows women an opportunity to be politically active. Furthermore, since women who can be described as professional tend to have belonged to groups that support such behavior, amateur status may well provide an important bridge between female citizen and professional, elite political participation.

Currey approaches the same questions, but from a different perspective. Drawing on her own experiences in running for elective office, she deals with a number of areas affecting political recruitment which she terms "gender variables." First, there is the relationship of primary-group urging and approval which she sees as significant in activating women to seek public office. Second, childhood socialization to politics, particularly to an activist orientation, modifies societal restraints internalized by young women. Third, in her case there were the backgrounds of professional political scientist familiar with research on political behavior, years of personal local political activity, and a number of general skills that must be seen as compensating for those resources available to candidates recruited through more traditional patterns.

Currey goes on to identify the problem of developing an image with broad-based appeal as one of the most significant gender variables. Appearance is fraught with difficulties for women. While the society prizes youth, good looks, and vitality in general, plus a Kennedy-style modification of these characteristics in male politicans, women who project them are viewed negatively. Political women are expected to be "serious, wise and gray," if they want community support; but this is not always easy to achieve or compatible with the female candidate's life style. Money and family are also seen as important gender variables. Indeed, differential access to financial resources may be most important. Though Currey sees limited finances as mitigated by women's experience in handling multiple demands more easily and efficiently, it nevertheless presents a constant worry and demands the channeling of creative and innovative energy into limited areas.

The inferences to be drawn from Currey's campaign are that women, or at least a particular kind of woman, can be effectively recruited into politics; and although they face serious liabilities because of their sex, certain female talents can offset them. Lee, Lynn and Flora, and Currey would all agree, however, that women enounter serious problems in their political recruitment, that only a certain type of woman is likely to be recruited into significant positions of leadership, and that women must exhibit more outstanding and creative qualities than males.

The findings presented in this section pinpoint important aspects of marginality. The tensions between ascribed status and aspirations and the problems in choosing between two conflicting value systems are clearly portrayed. The women in Lee and in Lynn and Flora's studies exhibit attitudes and behavioral responses reflecting experiential marginality. Currey, on the other hand, suggests the importance of creating new groups, the Texas Women's Political Caucus in this case, that can synthesize the values of the two conflicting groups—women and politicians—and thereby reduce anxiety.

MARCIA M. LEE

☆☆☆☆☆☆☆☆☆☆☆☆☆☆☆☆☆☆☆☆☆☆☆☆☆☆☆☆☆

7

Toward Understanding Why Few Women Hold Public Office: Factors Affecting the Participation of Women in Local Politics

Few women hold elite positions of power at any level of government in America today, despite their having been granted full citizenship over fifty years ago and their presently comprising a majority of the American population.[1] This phenomenon runs contrary to the theory of democracy, yet few studies have been conducted by political scientists to explain the scarcity of women compared to men in public office and party leadership positions.

In an effort to do so this paper presents the results of a survey conducted among men and women participating in local politics in four municipalities of Westchester County, New York. The results show that certain factors affect women's political participation in such a way that for all practical purposes they lack equality of opportunity to obtain elite positions of power in our governmental system.

These findings are important in two respects. First, they contribute new information to research being conducted by psychologists and sociologists on women's failure to achieve success and prominence in occupations outside the home.

Psychologist Matina Horner, for example, has found that college women are discouraged from excelling in competitive situations because they fear that success will lead to negative consequences such as social rejection or loss of feminity.[2] Sociologist Cynthia Fuchs Epstein maintains that a more discouraging factor to women is the "punishment" they receive for achieving success because of the male-oriented values of our society.[3]

This particular study has a more specific focus than Horner's and Epstein's studies. It identifies factors which are instrumental in preventing women from achieving positions of power in one specific aspect of American society—government and politics.[4] In a number of respects the factors identified in this study differ from the more broadly defined factors identified by Horner and Epstein.

Second, these findings supply information which should be important to democratic theorists, especially those interested in the feasibility of providing equality of opportunity for all American citizens.

The study shows that a number of factors prevent American women from enjoying an equal opportunity to hold public office and participate in elite positions of power in our governmental system. The nature of the factors responsible for these inequalities is not such that they can be easily overcome. Democratic political theorists must come to terms with this and recognize that the notion of equality of opportunity will remain an unobtainable goal for a majority of Americans unless substantial changes occur in cultural role assignments and role expectations.

METHODOLOGY

In conducting this study a number of research methods were used. The most important was an opinion poll sent to 496 women and men in the four municipalities.[5] The poll was designed to obtain a broad cross section of views from local "political participants," people who had shown enough interest in local political affairs to be involved in some form of political activity, partisan or not. To include such people in the survey, the following definition of "political participant" was constructed:

> A political participant is a person who (a) holds public office by election or appointment or (b) who is a member of an organized group whose primary objective is to elect people to office or to influence the policies of government in the manner it feels appropriate.

Using this definition, a list of both male and female political participants was compiled. The list, however, was too large to be practical. Consequently, an operational definition was constructed. Three qualifications were inserted in the original definition to limit the number of political participants who would receive questionnaires: (1) people involved in "issue" groups temporarily formed over a controversial issue were excluded—only members of "ongoing" groups which stayed in existence over a number of years and were concerned with more than one issue were included; (2) only the most active members of these groups, in most cases members of the executive boards, were included; and (3) only those groups primarily concerned with local community issues and local government, as opposed to national issues, were considered. The operational definition reads as follows:

> A political participant is a person who holds a public office by election or appointment or who is a *board member* of an *ongoing,* organized group whose primary objective is to elect people to office or to influence the politics of *local government* in the manner it feels appropriate.

The four municipalities in which the survey was conducted— Bronxville, Eastchester, Scarsdale, and Tuckahoe—are located immediately north of New York City, in Westchester County, New York. They were selected out of the 18 towns and 22 villages in the county for their variation in population size, economic characteristics, ethnic and racial composition, and median age of the citizenry. Two of the suburbs are relatively large, with populations over 20,000; and two are small, with populations around 6,000. Of the two large communities, one is upper middle class with a large percentage of the work force employed in highly paid professional occupations. The

other is a middle- to working-class community with a major portion of
the labor force employed in lower-level white-collar positions. The
same differentiation exists for the smaller communities, one being
upper middle class and one being working class.

The ethnic composition of the suburbs also varies. One has a
black population of approximately 20 percent, one a large Jewish
population of about 40 percent. Two have Italian populations comprising 15 percent of one suburb and 22 percent of another. One is
almost completely Anglo-Saxon. Moreover, the village in Westchester
having a population with the oldest median age is included, as well as
one having among the youngest. The annual per family income
ranges from $13,000 in Tuckahoe, the village with the lowest per fam-
ily income in Westchester, to $42,550 in Scarsdale, the village with the
highest per family income. Eastchester with $20,000 and Bronxville
with $27,000 fall in between.

The return on the mail survey was reassuringly high. Of 496
questionnaires sent, 301 were completed and returned, a return rate
of 60.7 percent. Furthermore, the demographic characteristics of the
participants included in the return mail sample were highly representative of and proportional to the original mailing list. With regard to
sex, the return was almost proportional to the number sent out to
each sex. Fifty-three percent of the questionnaires went to men and
47 percent to women. Of those returned, slightly more than half came
from men (50.2 percent) and slightly less than half from women (49.8
percent). There was also a good response from people in each of the
four suburbs. In each case the return was at least 50 percent.[6] A
somewhat higher percentage of returns came from the two upper-
middle-class suburbs, however, so a slight bias in this direction occurs.

Further analysis also shows that the party identification of the respondents is roughly proportional to the enrollment of the population in each of the communities. Also, the racial and ethnic backgrounds of the respondents closely reflects the racial and ethnic composition of each of the four communities, and the median family income of the respondents closely reflects the median family income of
their respective communities.

THE EXTENT OF WOMEN'S POLITICAL PARTICIPATION

One of the findings that immediately stands out in reviewing the
results of the survey is the great amount of time and activity women

devote to local government and politics. In fact, women "political participants" reported that they spent more time in local political activities than the men.[7] As shown in table 7.1, nearly one-sixth of the women (16.2 percent) reported devoting over forty hours per month to political activities, while less than a tenth (9.2 percent) of the men did the same. Moreover, over half the men (54.6 percent) said they devoted less than nine hours a month to political activities, compared to only 36.5 percent of the women. The stereotype image of women not as active as men in local government and politics, therefore, must be discarded, at least with respect to this study.

These findings need to be qualified in two important respects, however. First, in contrast to men, only a select group of women actively participate in local politics. Second, the form of their political participation is extremely limited and appears to be attributable to a number of specific factors.

A CERTAIN TYPE OF WOMAN

Although women were found to devote a great amount of time to local politics, further analysis shows that they come from a very select group. The most active women in local politics are primarily from upper-middle-class families or better, and have college degrees. These findings are particularly noteworthy because the same is not true for men.

TABLE 7.1. Hours per Month Devoted to Political Activities by Sex

Response (in hours)	Women	Men
	(in percent)	
Over 40 hours	16.2	9.2
30 to 40 hours	12.2	5.9
20 to 30 hours	10.8	11.8
10 to 19 hours	24.3	18.4
9 or less hours	36.5	54.6
	100.0	100.0
	(N=148)	(N=152)

Cramer's $V = .207$

Income

Table 7.2 shows, for example, that a direct relationship between family income and the time devoted to political activities exists for women. Only 8.7 percent of the women with family incomes under $15,000 devoted more than twenty hours a month to political activities while one-fourth (25.9 percent) of those women with family incomes of $15,000–$24,000, and one-half (49.5 percent) of those with family incomes of $25,000 or more, devoted as much time.

TABLE 7.2. Time Devoted by Women to Political Activities by Family Income

Response	Income		
	Under $15,000	$15,000 to $24,999	$25,000 and over
20 hours or more	8.7%	25.9%	49.5%
19 hours or less	91.3%	74.1%	50.5%
	100% (N = 23)	100% (N = 27)	100% (N = 97)

Cramer's V = .323

In contrast, the relationship between income and time devoted to political activities for men is very little. Table 7.3 shows that almost the same percentage of men with incomes under $15,000 served twenty hours or more as those with incomes over $25,000.

TABLE 7.3. Time Devoted by Men to Political Activities by Family Income

Response	Income		
	Under $15,000	$15,000 to $24,999	$25,000 and over
20 hours or more	25.0%	21.1%	27.6%
19 hours or less	75.0%	78.9%	72.4%
	100% (N = 24)	100% (N = 38)	100% (N = 87)

Cramer's V = .063

The fact that differences in the degree of political participation exist among women of different incomes, and yet not among men, strongly suggests that for women family income plays a special role in their ability to participate in local politics. Its importance probably lies in the fact that money enables women to hire baby sitters and other people to do the chores around the house that they would otherwise have to do. Money, however, does not serve the same function for men. Most are at work during the day and cannot dismiss themselves anyway.

In the evenings either sex, of course, can take care of the children, but more than likely both partners consider the responsibility to be primarily hers. For her to engage in such activity on a large scale, therefore, probably will necessitate the hiring of a baby sitter, unless the husband is unusually cooperative.[8]

Education

The survey also shows that a direct relationship between education and time devoted to political activities exists for women. Only 15.0 percent of the women who had not gone beyond high school devoted more than twenty hours a month to political activities, while over one-third of those with some college experience (37.1 percent) and nearly one-half of those with college degrees (45.2 percent) devoted over twenty hours per month, as shown in table 7.4.

For the men, however, the level of education made little difference. Almost the same percentage of men with college degrees as without them spent twenty hours or more a month in political activities, as shown in table 7.5.

TABLE 7.4. Hours per Month Women Devote to Political Activities by Level of Education

Response	Level of Education		
	College Degree	Some College	High School or Less
20 hours or more	45.2%	37.1%	15.0%
Less than 20 hours	54.8%	62.9%	85.0%
	100%	100%	100%
	(N = 93)	(N = 35)	(N = 20)

Cramer's V = .257

TABLE 7.5. Hours per Month Men Devote to Political Activities by Level of Education

Response	Level of Education		
	College Degree	Some College	High School or Less
20 hours or more	28.4%	20.0%	26.1%
Less than 20 hours	71.6%	80.0%	73.9%
	100%	100%	100%
	(N = 109)	(N = 20)	(N = 23)

Cramer's V = .064.

There are a number of possible explanations for the greater amount of time devoted to politics by women with higher education than those without. One is that women who have college experience, in contrast to those who do not, have in the process of their education acquired a greater sense of citizen duty or have increased their level of interest in government and politics.[9] One would expect higher education to have a similar effect on men's participation, however. If it does, the results of the survey do not show it. Men with and without higher education devoted about the same number of hours to local politics per month. An additional factor probably accounts for the failure of college-educated men to devote more time to local politics. Very likely they are employed in professional and management occupations which require working late hours, especially when they are young. Consequently, they simply do not have the time.

Many women with college educations, however, are at home caring for children just as women without college experience. If they can afford a house cleaner and baby sitter to get away from the house, they can pursue other interests.

Another probable explanation has to do with the nature of an important organization through which women engage in political activities—the League of Women Voters. This nationwide organization, with over 150,000 members and 1,275 local chapters in all fifty states and territories, is one of the main ways women pursue their interest in government and politics. The organization, however, is not an ordinary social group. A considerable amount of its activity is conducted in small study sessions where members undertake extensive research, discuss problems of government at a fairly high intellectual level, and compose well-documented reports on their findings. A number of Leagues have even published books.

Interviews with various women lacking college experience indicate that they are intimidated by the intellectual bent of the organization and feel that they might lack the skills to participate. If this is the case, it helps to explain why education may be an important factor for women interested in participating in political activities.

Income and Education Compared

Since income and education are closely related variables in that people with high income usually have more years of schooling and vice versa, a multivariant analysis was undertaken to determine if a stronger relationship existed between one variable and the time devoted to political activities than the other.

Two things became apparent from the analysis. First, the level of education had little bearing on women whose annual family incomes fell below $15,000. Women in this lower-income bracket devoted considerably fewer hours to politics than men, no matter how many years of schooling they had received.

Second, above the level of $15,000 education had a considerable bearing on the amount of time women devoted to politics. In fact, women with college degrees in the income brackets above $15,000 devoted more hours to political activities than men with equal education in the same income brackets.

Both income and education, therefore, are important. Money, it appears, gives a woman the financial wherewithal to replace herself at home. Extensive formal education appears to influence the type of activity in which she will engage once she is outside the home.

In addition to these two factors, a number of others were considered to see if they also had a bearing on the time women and men devoted to political activities. They included age, number of children at home, regional origin of birth, marital status, ethnic background, religion, and racial background. None of them proved to be important.[10]

When it comes to participating in local politics, therefore, it appears that two factors in particular influence the amount of time women devote to political activities: income and education. The result is that, unlike male political participants who are drawn from a fairly broad socioeconomic cross section of the community, only an elite group of women, for the most part, are active in local politics. They are the wealthy and well educated.

THE LIMITED NATURE OF WOMEN'S PARTICIPATION

Given a wealthy and well-educated group of women willing to devote a considerable amount of time to local politics, one might think that many would be involved in decision making and leadership positions. This is not the case, however. In contrast to men, women's political participation is confined primarily to women's organizations or to party work at the lowest level of the party hierarchy. Few hold elected or appointed public office, and very few hold leadership positions in the parties.

The extent to which this is so is remarkable. In the four suburbs under study, only 6.7 percent of the elected public offices were held by women. Moreover, women held less than a fifth (18.7 percent) of the appointed public offices and comprised less than a third of the school boards (30.7 percent).

The situation in these four communities is indicative of the 18 towns and 22 villages in Westchester County. Only 3.5 percent of the 341 elected public offices at the village, town, and county level were held by women.[11] Only about one-sixth of the members of the Westchester county boards and commissioners were women. Among the Republican town committees, only 1 woman in 18 is chairman; among the Democrats the number is slightly higher: 3 in 18.

Many factors, no doubt, account for the limited number of women holding public office in local government. The results of this study identify three, in particular, which seem to be important. All are related in that they concern role assignments and role perceptions held by men and women in our culture.

Children at Home
As might be expected, one of these factors is children. Someone, of course, has to take care of them, and present cultural norms assign this task primarily to the mother. Such responsibilities do not appear to limit the ability of women to engage in most political activities except one—holding public office.

When women with children at home were compared to women having none, no significant difference was found in the time they devoted to political activities in general or whether they had served as a party district leader. An important difference, however, was found between those who had and had not run for public office. Only a small percentage of women (5.3 percent) who had one or more children at

home had run for public office, while more than a fourth of the
women with no children at home (26.1 percent) had done so, as
shown in table 7.6.

TABLE 7.6. Women Who Have Run for Public Office by Children
at Home

Response	Number of Children	
	None	One or More
Have run	26.1%	5.3%
Have not run	73.9%	94.7%
	100%	100%
	(N = 46)	(N = 95)

Phi = .277

For men there was also a difference between the percentage having children at home who had run for office (21.5 percent) and those
having none (38.9 percent), as shown in table 7.7.

TABLE 7.7. Men Who Have Run for Public Office by
Children at Home

Response	Number of Children	
	None	One or More
Have run	38.9%	21.5%
Have not run	61.1%	78.5%
	100%	100%
	(N = 36)	(N = 106)

Phi = .154

It appears, therefore, that children might also have an influence
on the willingness of men to run for office. The influence, if it does
exist, however, is not as great. When men are compared to women, as
in table 7.8, it can be seen that a substantially higher percentage of
men who have run for office have children at home (21.5 percent)
than women (5.3 percent).

TABLE 7.8. Men and Women With One or More Children at Home Who Have Run for Office

Response	Women	Men
Have run	5.3%	21.5%
Have not run	94.7%	78.5%
	100%	100%
	(N = 95)	(N = 107)

Phi = .220

The importance of children as a factor restricting women from running for public office is further supported by the low percentage of women running for office at child-bearing and child-rearing ages. Table 7.9 shows that only 5.9 percent of the women under 40 had run for public office and only 6.8 percent of those between 41 and 50. Between the ages of 51 and 60, however, when most of the children have left home, a marked increase occurred in the percentage of women who had run (26.7 percent).[12]

TABLE 7.9. Women Who Have Run for Public Office by Age

Response	Age			
	Under 40	41–50	51–60	Over 60
Have run	5.9%	6.8%	26.7%	16.7%
Have not run	94.1%	93.2%	73.3%	83.3%

Cramer's V = .255

This was not the case for men. As shown in table 7.10, almost the same percentage of men under 40 (23.1 percent) had run for public office as those 51–60 (27.0 percent). There was, however, a substantial increase in the percentage of men over 60 who had run for public office. The probable reason for this is that many men, as they reach retirement age, find more time to devote to local civic activities.

If children, in fact, inhibit women from running for public office, it is important to consider why; especially in light of the fact that children were not found to limit the time women devoted to political activities in general or to restrict them from serving as a party district leader.

TABLE 7.10. Men Who Have Run for Public Office by Age

Response	Age			
	Under 40	41–50	51–60	Over 60
Have run	23.1%	20.4%	27.0%	38.5%
Have not run	76.9%	79.6%	73.0%	61.5%
	100%	100%	100%	100%
	(N = 26)	(N = 54)	(N = 37)	(N = 26)

Cramer's V = .148

Explanations offered by women who were surveyed indicate that the most likely reason lies in the particular nature of running for and holding public office. As one mother who was surveyed put it:

It is not so much the amount of time—I can always hire a baby sitter as long as I know some time in advance when I am needed. I can always plan my time around a League of Women Voters' meeting. But holding public office involves work at unpredictable hours, and I can't cope with this.

If this woman's feelings are indicative of others, and responses indicate they are, it appears that odd working hours and spur-of-the-moment activities are the aspects of public office which discourage women from pursuing such activities. For men this is apparently less the case. Since they are not the ones primarily held responsible for childcare, they feel more free to engage in such activities.

The discouraging effect of children on women's desire to seek public office also probably influences their ability to run for public office after the children have left home. Because of children, women may fail to gain the experience in their twenties, thirties, and early forties that their male counterparts are acquiring. When at last they are free, they may lack the political know-how and political connections to compete effectively against the more experienced men. In short, most men interested in politics get a head start on women and it is very difficult for women to catch up.

Children, however, do not alone explain the lack of women running for and holding public office. The survey strongly indicates that a factor of greater importance is the perceptions women have regarding the "proper" role of women in politics.

WOMEN'S ROLE PERCEPTIONS AND POLITICS

It is apparent from the survey that many women do not feel that running for public office is a "proper" thing for them to do—that is, they do not include such activity in their image of a woman's role. This feeling is expressed in a number of ways. A large percentage of women, for example, do not feel others would approve of such activity. Over three-fourths (78.8 percent) of the women felt that "most men would prefer women to contribute to politics in ways other than running for office."

Not only do many women believe that most men would prefer they not run for office, but a large percentage of women also feel that members of their own sex would disapprove of such activity. Almost half (47.9 percent), in fact, agreed that "most women would prefer other women to contribute to politics in ways other than running for office."

A survey conducted nationwide by Louis Harris and Associates shows similar results. Fifty percent of the women polled agreed with the statement that "women should take care of running their homes and leave running the country up to men."[13] Almost two-thirds (63 percent) agreed that "most men are better suited emotionally for politics than are most women."[14]

The effect of this type of thinking is evidenced by the large percentage of women unwilling to run for local public office. Almost three-fifths (59.7 percent) of the women political participants surveyed in the four municipalities said they would never run for public office, while 40.3 percent of the men took the same position.

There are several explanations for this attitude. Certainly one of them is the perpetuation of past cultural norms which excluded women from participating in public affairs. The fifty years that have elapsed since women became full citizens in America seem long in terms of a human life span but are short in terms of history. The effects of the past cultural norms which excluded women from politics are still too close at hand for our culture to be entirely free from them.

Another explanation is offered by Robert Lane. Drawing on literature from sociology and anthropology, he hypothesized that the lack of women in elected public office can be attributed to the fact that our culture types the two sexes on the basis of ascendant, power-possessing males, and submissive, dependent females.[15] "Since politics is an area concerned with power," says Lane, "the women who seem too active in these areas seem to some people to have moved from the properly dependent role of her sex and to seek the masterful and dominant role of men."[16]

Whatever the explanation, it appears that an important barrier to women seeking public office is their own perceptions about what they should and should not be doing in politics. At present many women consider it acceptable to show an interest in politics and to engage in behind-the-scenes activity. When it comes to holding public office, however, the same is not true. This form of political activity is still considered by women to be unfeminine. In a very real sense, therefore, women hold themselves back. Consequently, if there is ever to be a substantial increase in the number of women holding public office, there will have to be a considerable change in the concept women have of the things they should do in politics, that is, in the image of their female role.

FEAR OF SEX DISCRIMINATION

One other factor, in addition to children and women's role perception, was found to discourage women from running for office. As might be expected, many women indicated a hesitancy to seek public office because they fear sex discrimination.

Responses to the survey show that over half of the women (56.8 percent) felt that "a woman would have problems different from men if she were to seek public office." Of the women who felt there would be special problems, almost three-fourths of them (74.7 percent) selected "not being accepted by men" as the main problem over others, such as not being accepted by other women, not having approval from their spouses, or other factors which they were free to write in the blank space. A slightly smaller percentage of men (69.2 percent) agreed with them, as shown in table 7.11.

The 1972 Virginia Slims survey also shows that many women feel sex discrimination exists. Almost one-fourth (23 percent) of the women respondents volunteered the statement that "men hold women back in politics" when asked why so few women are in politics in the United States today.[17] Furthermore, one-half of the women agreed with the statement that "women are mostly given the detailed dirty work chores in politics, while men hold the real power."[18]

TABLE 7.11. Most Important Problem for Women Running for Office, by Sex

Response	Women	Men
Not accepted by men	74.7%	69.2%
Other problems	25.3%	30.8%
	100%	100%
	(N = 83)	(N = 65)

Phi = .045

It is difficult to determine to what degree women's fears are valid. There is good evidence, however, that a large percentage of the male political participants in the four suburbs would prefer not to see women running for public office. Two-thirds (69.2 percent) of them agreed that "most men would prefer women to participate in politics in ways other than running for office."

The important point is not whether discrimination exists, however, but whether women believe it does. The mere belief in its existence serves to discourage women from seeking public office. The results of the local survey and the Louis Harris survey indicate that women do believe it exists. This factor, therefore, also must be included among those inhibiting women from running for office.

FACTORS NOT LIMITING WOMEN'S PARTICIPATION

Interestingly enough, two factors which were found by some political scientists to limit women's political participation were not found to be important when it came specifically to running for and holding public office.

Sense of Political Efficacy

One of these factors is a sense of political efficacy. Angus Campbell and associates found in their voter study surveys that men tend to believe to a greater extent than women that their participation in politics carries more weight in the political process:

Men are more likely than women to feel that they can cope with the complexities of politics and to believe that their participation carries some weight in the political process . . . what has been less adequately transmitted to the women is a sense of some personal competence vis-à-vis the political world.[19]

The male and female political participants polled in the four municipalities did express a difference in their estimate of their political effectiveness.[20] When asked, "Do you feel your participation in politics accomplishes much?" a larger percentage of men (68.2 percent) than women (58.9 percent) answered with a positive response, as shown in table 7.12.[21] The difference between these two percentages, however, is not great enough to warrant a firm conclusion.

What is noteworthy about these results, however, is the large percentage of women, nearly three-fifths, who expressed a positive sense of political effectiveness. With such a large percent of women feeling this way, this factor does not appear to explain why so few women hold public office.

More research is needed to prove conclusively that a low sense of political competence is not a factor in women's failure to hold public office. Personal interviews with women, however, revealed that many of them feel they are more able than men to hold public office. Many felt they knew more about their local government, had more time to devote to local political activities, and were more capable of solving local problems facing the community.

Politics Is Too Dirty

A second factor which is thought by some to discourage women from participating directly in politics is a stronger belief among women than men that politics is "too dirty." Robert Lane suggests this hypothesis. He cites David Riesman's article "Orbits of Tolerance, Interviews, and Elites" to support his contention that women are more moralistic than men.[22] The moralistic orientation arises, Riesman states, from maternal responsibilities and greater participation in re-

TABLE 7.12. Sense of Political Efficacy, by Sex

Response	Women	Men
Positive	58.9%	68.2%
Negative	41.1%	31.8%
	100%	100%
	(N = 146)	(N = 151)

Phi = .090

ligious activities. This, Lane maintains, tends to focus female political attention upon persons and peripheral reform issues, and causes them to shun what they consider the less respectable aspects of politics. Lane states:

> The net effect of this moralistic orientation has not only been to provide an ineffective and relatively "ego-distant" tie with political matters, but also, as Riesman has remarked, to limit the attention to the superficial and irrelevant aspects of politics.[23]

No doubt, a number of women in the United States shun participating in politics because they feel it is "too dirty." Slightly over one-third (35 percent) of the women polled in a 1972 Louis Harris survey agreed with the statement that "politics is too dirty a business for women to become involved in."[24] "Dirty politics," however, is not a factor capable of explaining why so few women "political participants" in the four suburbs hold public office. Few women in the survey felt that local politics was "dirty." Moreover, no significant difference in opinion was found between men and women. Only a small percentage of both sexes (3.4 percent of the men and 6.8 percent of the women) agreed with the statement that in their community "politics is dirty." This, therefore, does not appear to be a factor which discourages women who are interested in politics from seeking public office.

CONCLUSIONS

The concept of equality of opportunity is one which is highly prized by most Americans. The paucity of women holding positions of power in government is a reminder to all of us of the chasm which exists between this ideal and reality.

Clearly such inequity is not caused by a lack of women interested in participating in government. This study has shown that women devote a great amount of time to local political and governmental activities, in fact, more time than the male political participants claimed to devote. But the form of their political activity is limited primarily to the nondecision-making aspects of politics and government. Most are involved in politics either through women's organizations or as party workers at the lowest level of the party hierarchy.

Three factors, in particular, are identified in this study to explain the limited nature of women's participation and their failure to achieve positions of power in government. One is the presence of children at home, a factor which has both short-range and long-range effects. Another is a fear of sex discrimination. A third is the perceptions held by women themselves about what is "proper" and "not proper" for them to do in politics.

Solutions to these problems will not come easily. Considerable changes in current role assignments and role expectations will have to take place. Child care, in particular, is a problem with no easy solution. Day-care centers cannot entirely solve the problem because many political activities occur in the evenings, long after the centers close. For the same reason, surrogate mothers are not the answer except for the very wealthy who can afford full time live-in help. A more realistic solution would be for women to limit or forgo having children—a trend which is already under way—and to insist that the fathers share greater responsibility in caring for their offspring.

Women's own perceptions about their "proper" place in politics also will not be changed easily. Such perceptions can not be legislated out of existence. Changing them involves, instead, the gradual process, starting from infancy, of conveying to girls that there is no "woman's place" in government and politics, and that public office is an appropriate responsibility for them to assume. The schools can provide assistance by selecting books which show women as well as men involved in public office and party leadership positions. The real difficulty, however, is reaching the mothers of preschool children and convincing them of the importance of women's political participation so that they will convey these feelings to their daughters.

Sex discrimination also will not be ended overnight. In the last decade a number of laws have been passed to prevent it, but the law and reality are very slow to catch up with each other. Acceptance of women really comes through the process of moving them into positions of power and letting them prove themselves.

In a certain respect the plight of this majority is unique, not because it exists but because, for the most part, democratic theorists have failed to come to grips with it—that is, to study seriously the reasons for its existence and to advocate changes to remedy the situation.

Other minorities in the American populace have long been the concern of democratic theorists. Considerable effort has been devoted to identifying factors contributing to their inequality, such as poverty, ignorance, poor health, low social status, religious preference, and racial background. Moreover, great stress has been placed on developing programs that would remove these disadvantages. Billions of dollars have been spent on developing good public school systems and improving the educational opportunities for all students. Efforts to equalize income and give citizens of all ages some form of economic security have been initiated, and programs to provide equality of employment, and housing, and health care also are being attempted.

These programs may help women to some degree, but they will not bring them into elite governmental positions of power. They will not bring them into such power positions because they are not designed to overcome the problems which specifically prevent women from holding public office. Such factors as child care, women's own role perceptions about themselves, and sex discrimination must first be dealt with. Until solutions are found, equality of opportunity will remain a myth for the majority of American citizens.

NOTES

1. Currently there are no women U.S. senators, only 15 representatives, no women governors, and only a handful of women state senators and representatives.

2. Matina Horner, "Toward an Understanding of Achievement-Related Conflicts in Women." *Journal of Social Issues* 28 (1972): 157–75.

3. Cynthia Fuchs Epstein, *Women's Place* (Berkeley: University of California Press, 1971).

4. Few studies have been concerned with women's failure to hold public office and party leadership positions. A number of political scientists, however, have analyzed the participation of women in terms of their voting patterns and attitudes toward politics. Among the most notable are, in chronological order: Harold F. Gosnell, *Democracy the Threshold of Freedom* (New York: Ronald, 1948), chap. 4; Paul F. Lazarsfeld et al., *The Peoples Choice* (2nd ed.; New York: Columbia University Press, 1948), chap. 3; Louise M. Young, "The Political Role of Women in the United States" (paper presented to the Hague Congress of the International Political Science Association, 8–12 September 1952); James G. March, "Husband-Wife Interaction over Political Issues," *Public Opinion Quarterly* 18 (1953–54): 461–70; Talcott Parsons and Robert Bales, *Family Socialization, and Interaction Process* (Glencoe, Ill.: Free Press, 1955), chaps. 2 and 5; Louis Harris, *Is There a Republican Majority?: Political Trends 1952–56* (New York: Harper, 1954), pp. 104–17; Maurice Duverger, *The Political Role of Women* (Paris: UNESCO, 1955); Robert E. Lane, *Political Life* (Glencoe, Ill.: Free Press, 1959), pp. 209–16; Herbert Hyman, *Political Socialization* (Glencoe, Ill.: Free Press, 1959), chaps. 2, 3, and 4; Fred Greenstein, "Sex Related Political Differences in Childhood," *Journal of Politics* 23 (May 1961): 353–71; Angus Campbell, Philip E. Converse, Warren E. Miller, and Donald E. Stokes, *The American Voter* (New York: Wiley, 1964), pp. 255–61; Martin Gruberg, *Women in American Politics* (Oshkosh, Wisc.: Academia, 1968).

5. In addition to the survey, the presidents of the "ongoing" organizations, the village and town mayors, and the chairmen of the local parties were interviewed, either in person or by telephone. A statistical analysis of male and female political participation in the 18 towns, 22 villages, and 5 cities of Westchester also was taken to determine

if the four municipalities selected for intensive study were typical. The village and town weekly newspapers were read on a consistent basis for eighteen months, and the writer also regularly attended the meetings of the most active women's groups concerned with local government.

6. The return rate for each suburb: Bronxville, 77.6%; Scarsdale, 67.5%; Tuckahoe, 52.6%; and Eastchester, 50%.

7. Because some women and men are active in local politics in name only, it was decided to use "time devoted to politics" as the criterion for involvement in political activities. The term "political activity" includes elected public office, appointed public office, local political parties, nonpartisan political organizations or local-issue groups, excluding those groups which operate on an ad hoc basis.

8. Nonworking women without families and women whose children are grown fall into a different category, of course. They are free to pursue political activities without the costs of replacing themselves at home.

9. For a discussion on the relationship between education and a sense of duty and interest in politics, see Campbell et al., *American Voter*, pp. 251–54.

10. At first glance an important difference was found to exist between black women and white women and the time they devoted to political activities. Controlling for income, however, the difference disappeared. Income, not race, appears to be the underlying factor explaining the lower level of participation among black women.

11. Specifically, in the 22 villages there is not one woman mayor. There are currently only 2 women serving on the village boards out of 97 trustees, and none of the 24 village judgeships are held by women. At the town level there is only 1 woman town supervisor out of 18, 5 women town council members out of 75, and no woman town judge out of 36.

12. The small number of women respondents under forty without children prevents the use of multivariant analysis to confirm the fact that the children, not age, is the underlying factor limiting women's ability to run for public office.

13. Louis Harris and Associates, 1972 Virginia Slims Opinion Poll, pp. 16–19.

14. Ibid., p. 15.

15. Lane cites Gordon W. Allport's article, "Test for Ascendance-Submission," *Journal of Abnormal and Social Psychology* 23 (1928–29): 118–36, to support his hypothesis.

16. Lane, *Political Life*, p. 213.

17. Harris, 1972 Virginia Slims Opinion Poll, p. 19.

18. Ibid., p. 16.

19. Campbell et al., *American Voter*, p. 261.

20. The Guttman Scale for measuring strength of political efficacy developed by the Michigan Survey Research Center was not used in this study.

21. Positive responses included "always" and "most of the time." Negative responses include "sometimes, but not usually," "rarely," and "never."

22. David Riesman, "Orbits of Tolerance, Interviews, and Elites," *Public Opinion Quarterly* 20 (1956): 49–73.

23. Lane, *Political Life*, p. 213.

24. Harris, 1972 Virginia Slims Opinion Poll, p. 16.

NAOMI LYNN and CORNELIA BUTLER
FLORA

8

☆☆☆☆☆☆☆☆☆☆☆☆☆☆☆☆☆☆☆☆☆☆☆☆☆☆

Societal Punishment and Aspects of Female Political Participation: 1972 National Convention Delegates

Female role expectations are not conducive to full participation in the political process. Indeed, the demands of female traditional roles conflict with the aggressive behavior associated with the successful politician. For men, dominance is a desirable characteristic and is a natural prerequisite for leadership; for women, dominance is viewed as unfeminine and therefore deviant behavior. Defining behavior as deviant is based on the normative situation in which an individual is located. One of the major determinants of this normative situation in American society is sex. Sheldon Levy[1] suggests that the systemic punishment that results from deviant behavior leads to a preference for circumstances more compatible with role expectations. Thus it should not be surprising that women have been relatively uninvolved in politics.

Women who do get involved in politics may find it necessary to justify their deviant role behavior and minimize its resultant societal punishment by legitimizing their deviance in terms of traditional roles. Thus justification is more compatible with a political orientation described by James Q. Wilson[2] as that of the "amateur," who sees the political world in terms of ideas and principles rather than emphasizing gaining power. The amateur insists that issues be settled on their own merit with as little compromising as possible. This identification with causes, rather than power, can be interpreted as compatible with the stereotyped female role—spiritual superiority and concomitant rejection of "dirty" political maneuvering which, if necessary, should be carried out by men, who, presumably, will not be defiled (see Stevens for a discussion of this phenomenon in Latin America).[3] Most studies of amateurism find that issues mobilize an individual to political participation. That index can have a more complex interpretation. It may be that for women issues are the most socially acceptable mobilizer for individuals whose characteristics may predispose them toward political participation.[4]

The amateur's motivation, which provides legitimation for initial political activity, should be seen as a transitional phase that may lead to a more professional view of the political process, especially if women are allowed to gain positions of power. Amateurism is thus by implication a short-term phenomenon. Women will either become disillusioned and drop out, or they will find different motivations for justifying their political existence.

In order to test this hypothesized process of female political involvement, we undertook a study of nominally politically active women. We traced the development and structure of their political participation, stressing systemic punishment and reaction to it.

THE SAMPLE

Political scientists have found delegates to national presidential conventions convenient sources for research on political leadership and information about the ideology and political preferences of American elites. Since degree of activity and types of participation were of special interest, it was important to get a sample that had achieved at least a threshold degree of political participation and activity.

The 1972 conventions attracted special attention because McGovern reforms opened the Democratic party to groups previously denied equitable admission. That, in turn, undoubtedly influenced delegate selection to the Republican convention. An area of most apparent change was the increase in women delegates (from 13 percent in 1968 to 40 percent for the Democrats and from 17 percent to 30 percent for the Republicans). The 1972 conventions, therefore, were a potentially fruitful source of data on women in politics and women in the party system.

Our sample was drawn from women delegates attending the 1972 Democratic and Republican conventions from Nebraska, Kansas, South Dakota, and North Dakota. Fifty-seven delegates were surveyed—almost the complete universe from those states. We stayed at the hotel with the Kansas delegations at both conventions, thus having opportunity for close observation and informal discussion. We conducted tape-recorded, in-depth interviews (in hotel rooms, during meals, or in hotel lobbies during convention breaks) with 50 of the 57 members of the sample. The interviews ranged from one to more than three hours. Follow-up mail questionnaires were used to obtain information from those whose schedules prematurely cut off interviews and from the seven additional delegates we were unable to interview during the convention. In general, interviews were conducted in relaxed and amiable atmospheres.

The questionnaire used life-history, open-ended techniques and forced-choice questions. Problems of coding open-ended questions were overcome by two teams categorizing responses independently and refining categories until agreement was reached, or eliminating the question in cases of disagreement. Coding disagreements were few; consultation was necessary on less than 10 percent of the cases. The interviewing technique, unlike self-administered questionnaires, permitted follow-up questions to gain accuracy and depth about various issues.

SYSTEMIC REWARDS AND PUNISHMENT

Behavior psychologists consider systematic reward to have taken place when the individual receives real or psychological benefits that are compatible with his desires within the society. When these benefits fall short of these wishes, systemic punishment is considered to have

occurred.[5] Thus, passivity may be the 'negative consequence that results when women attempt to participate in areas that deviate from
traditional feminine roles, especially when the women compete
against men. Women have been found to associate excellence with loss
of femininity and social rejection.[6] Men who succeed in politics generally receive positive reinforcement, while a woman may be "punished"
for leaving her home. In the present cultural climate, success in politics may mean exposure to criticism as a poor wife and a worse
mother, especially when a woman has young children. Even when a
woman has confidence in her ability to handle the dual functions of
politico and mother, she may hesitate to seek political office and
choose instead equally time-consuming voluntary associations that
society has defined as suitable for a young matron.

While any woman who participates in politics risks societal
punishment, the woman who is also a mother with children at home is
especially vulnerable. The role of mother has been identified by
sociologists as crucial for women.[7] In order to determine how systemic
punishment affects women's political behavior, we focused many of
our questions on the sensitive interface of motherhood and politics in
the women's lives. The unusually large percentage of the women—21
percent—who were childless and the 42 percent who either waited
until their children left home or reported that their children were a
negative influence on their political activity confirms the power of
such punishment. In addition, only half as many women with children
as without children aspire to elective office—even when urged to de-
clare their "ideal" political ambition. One extremely active woman
leader said that she had not been blessed with children, but if she had
had children she most *certainly* would not be involved in politics. Her
emphatic response conveyed a measure of criticism toward those who
attempted to combine the two roles.

Motherhood had the strongest impact on political participation
of women from rural areas (places of fewer than 10,000) ($p. > .02$).
More than half (13 out of 21) of them reported no children, implying
that the choice was *either* motherhood or political activity. Lack of
child-care facilities in rural areas, coupled with more traditional views
of maternal obligations, keep rural women out of politics. Interestingly, the one woman in our sample who reported that her children
had a positive influence on her political activity represented a rural
area. Her son was of draft age, and she was vitally concerned about his
participation in the Vietnam war. In explaining her recent political ac-

tivism, she exclaimed: "What's a mother to do?" This justification is in harmony with the traditional female motivation. In this case, political activity enhances the motherhood role.

That fear of criticism (or punishment, in Levy's terms) has a real basis is borne out by ten women we interviewed who mentioned being criticized for going to the convention and leaving their children at home. One woman delegate on an important committee of the Democratic party sat next to a man whose political views were quite different from hers. She reported that when he could not counter her arguments on a rational basis, he would begin a tirade against her for not being home with her husband and children. Another delegate who had run successfully for the state legislature mentioned that her opponent had said, "The only thing I have to say about running a woman against me is that she should be home taking care of her children." We had too limited a study to judge the effectiveness of such antifeminist appeal. However, half the mothers reported that they had misgivings about their political activity because of their children. Nevertheless, children had no statistical effect on the women's non-political organization activity. In our sample, women with children—even those with eight children—were as likely to participate in as many organizations as those with no children or very few children. As one respondent stated, "Women have time to play bridge and things—they've got time for politics."

The claim that conflicting time demands keep women politically passive offers only a partial explanation. A fuller explanation may be found in the punishment-avoidance theory, which focuses on the legitimate role opportunities open to women.

WOMEN'S PERSONAL POLITICAL ALTERNATIVES

Levy states that "one major distinction between the politically active and the politically passive is that the former have a wide range of response and cognitive alternatives." This was certainly true of the majority of female delegates in our study, who saw themselves with very limited political possibilities. Levy attributes this narrow range of available political responses to the amount of past systemic punishment an individual has experienced.[8]

Two of the questions we asked our respondents dealt with their future political ambitions, both realistic and ideal. The most striking result was the lack of personal political ambition or even consideration among these women. Their ambitions were for their party, their candidate, or their husbands. Only 5 of 57 women delegates aspired realistically to an appointed office and only 4 aspired realistically to an elective office, compared to 30 out of 63 male delegates from these states who had concrete political ambitions.[9] When urged to use creative imagination and visualize themselves in the political future, 66 percent were still unable to come up with a personal ambition, compared to 21 percent of the male delegates from these states who were not able to visualize themselves in public office and 18 percent who were not interested in a party office. Eight women envisioned an appointive office, while 11—mostly Democrats—fantasized themselves in an elective office.

This inability of many female delegates to see personal political alternatives can be traced to a variety of circumstances, including (1) lack of role models, (2) systemic punishment for deviation from traditional feminine roles, and (3) lifelong socialization patterns which emphasized the virtue of female lack of personal ambition.

AMATEURISM—PROFESSIONALISM

As mentioned, it was in terms of self-sacrifice and dedication to others that women tended to be mobilized for political participation. That motivation leads, according to Wilson, to an amateur orientation to politics for both men and women. Those with the amateur orientation believe that issues should be settled on their own merits, with as little compromising as possible. In contrast is the "professional," who emphasizes gaining power and, therefore, stresses concrete questions and specific persons who will help assure victory.[10] To determine the political orientation of our respondents, we used questions with modified Likert-scale responses developed by Soule and Clark to distinguish amateurs and professionals.[11] Thirty-one percent of the sample were amateurs, 40 percent were semiprofessionals and 29 percent were professionals. Republicans were more likely than Democrats to be professionals, while the Democrats tended to be amateurs.

We found that degree of amateurism was related to the organizational and political activities of the delegates—activities which influenced their role perceptions. Of greatest importance were participation in voluntary organizations, holding party offices, and years of party involvement. Personal characteristics such as age and rural-urban residence were not associated with degree of professionalism.

Voluntary Organizations

Women in our sample were extremely active in their communities, belonging to an average of seven organizations each. No woman interviewed belonged to fewer than two organizations and one woman listed thirteen. They currently held a mean of 2.7 organizational offices. Only 11 percent were not currently holding at least one organizational office, and the office most commonly cited was president.

Only 3 of the women had held public office—1 as a state representative, 2 on school boards. (Of the 47 husbands, 10 had held public office—3 state administrative posts, 2 each had been state senator and state representative, 1 had held a national office, 1 a state office, and 1 had been a city council member. As expected, the husband's political status was generally higher than that of the wife, suggesting that their selection may have been familial rather than on autonomous political merit.)

We found that the greater the number of voluntary organizations a woman delegate participated in, the more likely she was to be classified as a professional on the professional-amateurism scale (gamma = .22). This moderate relationship suggests that experience in an organization serves as a socializing agent toward professionalism.

However, all organizational participation did not contribute equally to the political socialization process. Certain specifically political organizations seemed to provide women delegates with political socialization that helped develop self-confidence in male-dominated areas. For the college-educated women, the League of Women Voters provided a socially accepted means of learning the ins and outs of the political process. While it is an issue-oriented organization, it nevertheless has provided an initial training ground for women who later enter partisan politics.

For women from small towns and with less educational background, women's organizations in political parties provided the same service. As one delegate said: "I know I wouldn't have been involved if it hadn't been for the women's organization [in the party]. It gave me the opportunity to learn without walking into a smoke-filled room with a bunch of men. It takes a gutsy woman to do this and there aren't that many gutsy women even with women's lib [laugh]—I should say there haven't been in the past. . . . I got a little carried away with that but it really is a thing with me because I remember how I felt when I first got involved and started going. I became aware that there were occasionally party meetings, regular party meetings. Then as I became more involved it finally dawned on me that those men aren't one damn bit smarter than the women are, but they had us fooled. They've got most of the women in ____ fooled still, y'know—ah—but they'll learn. They'll learn."

Party Offices

Nearly 80 percent of the women had held party offices: 12 as precinct committeewoman, 11 as county secretary or treasurer, 7 on the state central committee, 6 as national committeewoman, 5 as state secretary or treasurer, and 1 each in a national party office, state campaign director, district chairperson, and county chairperson. They had held a mean of 2.4 party positions previous to being chosen a convention delegate. Of those married, approximately 50 percent of their husbands had held party offices.

If we are correct in stating that amateurism is a temporary yet socially acceptable state for women in politics, we would expect those who have held party offices to have moved into the professional category. When we tested the relationship between professionalism and party office we found a high association between the two variables (gamma = .96). Thus it appears that when women actually gain some political power, they move away from idealistic amateurism. We should be cautious in assigning causality here, for women with a professional orientation are probably most likely to seek party office. Once in office, they receive benefits that offset the punishment for role deviation experienced in the larger society.

Years of Party Involvement

While mobilization to politics for women was hypothesized to be related to idealism (amateur status), we suggest that that is a transitional phase from political passivity to professional activity. Thus, the greater the length of party involvement, the greater the likelihood of being a party professional.

The mean number of years of party involvement was 10.8, mode 12, median 9, range from 1 or less to 26. For males from the same states, the mean was 18.2 years, the mode 12, the median 14. The range was from 1 year or less to 60 years of activity in politics. Republican women delegates' participation averaged longer than the Democrats', as expected because of Democratic efforts to bring in new groups and Republican hegemony in these states. Only 14 percent of the women had been a convention delegate previously, compared to 34 percent of the male delegates representing their states. Seven had attended two previous conventions and one had attended three.

As expected, those with less time in party work had less professional scores on the scale (gamma = .56). No one with less than five years' experience ranked as professional.

However, the association between years of party participation and degree of professionalism was not absolute. Apparently it is possible to work in the party, especially if one performs the powerless traditionally feminine tasks, and not broaden one's range of alternatives. Envelope stuffing, coffee making, and telephoning are not a dramatic break from traditional female passivity. Hence it will be necessary for women to gain power-holding experiences before they can be fully integrated into the political system. Participation in all-female groups with instrumental goals forces women to take leadership positions, giving them the necessary experiences which are not societally punished. That positively sanctioned activity enables them to perceive broader political alternatives. Women who remained amateurs for long periods of party involvement tended to have quite peripheral roles in the party organization.

SUMMARY

In examining a select group of politically active women—delegates to the 1972 Democratic and Republican national conventions—we tested Levy's theory of systemic punishment. It offers a partial explanation of both the quantity and quality of women's political participation. We found societal punishment for women in the political sphere was centered around their deviance from traditional female roles, particularly the role of mother. That source of punishment contributed to the tendency of even these women to be political amateurs and to justify their political behavior in terms of self-sacrifice for higher causes.

The shift from amateurism to professionalism and the ability to see a wide variety of alternative behavior seemed to stem from experiences of achieving power in a group which supports such behavior.

Thus, number of organizations joined, years of party activity, and party offices held were related to the degree of professionalism a woman attained. Type of organization and type of party involvement were also important and need to be investigated further. Those structures provided a new normative environment in which deviance from traditional female roles could be gradually undertaken, power achieved, and new role alternatives perceived. No claim is made that the conclusions derived from a regional study have universal application. Nevertheless, the findings suggest some of the specific mechanisms at work in the process of female political participation.

NOTES

1. Sheldon G. Levy, "The Psychology of Political Activity," *Annals of the American Academy of Political and Social Science* 391 (September 1970): 83–96.

2. James Q. Wilson, *The Amateur Democrat* (Chicago: University of Chicago Press, 1962).

3. Evelyn P. Stevens, "Marianismo: The Other Face of Machismo in Latin America," in *Female and Male in Latin America: Essays*, ed. A. Pescatello (Pittsburgh: University of Pittsburgh Press, 1973), pp. 89–102.

4. Lester W. Milbrath, *Political Participation* (Chicago: Rand McNally, 1965), pp. 110–13.

5. Levy, *Psychology of Political Activity*, p. 84.

6. Matina S. Horner, "Toward an Understanding of Achievement-Related Conflicts in Women," *Journal of Social Issues* 28 (1972): 157–74.

7. Helena Znaniecki Lopata, *Occupation: Housewife* (New York: Oxford University Press, 1971); Cornelia B. Flora and Naomi B. Lynn, "Women and Political Socialization: Considerations of the Impact of Motherhood," in *Women in Politics*, ed. Jane S. Jacquette (New York: Wiley, 1974), pp. 37–53.

8. Levy, *Psychology of Political Activity*, pp. 85–86.

9. The comparison group for males was provided by the Center for Political Studies, University of Michigan. Included were 36 male delegates from the Dakotas, Nebraska, and Kansas to the Democratic convention and 27 male delegates from these states to the Republican convention, a total of 63 male delegates.

10. Wilson, *Amateur Democrat*, p. 4.

11. John W. Soule and James W. Clark, "Amateurs and Professionals: A Study of Delegates to the 1968 Democratic National Convention," *American Political Science Review* 64 (September 1970): 888–98. The items developed by Soule and Clark which were used to measure amateurism and professionalism were: (1) My party leaders often make too many arbitrary decisions without consulting with sufficient numbers of party workers (intraparty democracy). (2) As a convention delegate basically my only job is to choose a candidate who will win in November (preoccupation with winning). (3) The principles of a candidate are just as important as winning or losing an election (willingness to compromise). (4) Party organization and unity is more important than permitting free and total discussion which may divide the party (intraparty democracy). (5) I would object to a presidential candidate who compromises on his basic values if that is necessary to win (willingness to compromise). (6) Controversial positions should be

avoided in a party platform in order to ensure party unity (programmatic parties). (7) A good party worker must support any candidate nominated by the convention even if he basically disagrees with him (willingness to compromise). (8) Party platforms should be deliberately vague in order to appeal to the broadest spectrum of voters (programmatic parties). (9) Part-time volunteers play a more important role in the party's campaign than any other segment of a party (citizen's role). (10) Would you characterize yourself as someone who: (a) works for the party year after year, win or lose and whether or not you like the candidate or issues; or (b) works for the party only when there is a particularly worthwhile candidate or issue (self-characterization). (This question was more heavily weighted than the others.)

9

VIRGINIA CURREY

☆☆☆☆☆☆☆☆☆☆☆☆☆☆☆☆☆☆☆☆☆☆☆☆☆

Campaign Theory
and Practice –
The Gender Variable

Political rule books for women have yet to be written. For the novice political woman the first problem is like that of a girl who has learned only the rules for boys' basketball and then is sent into a game in which the referee is calling girls' basketball rules. Women entering politics who try to play by men's rules may rapidly encounter penalties because the rules for women in politics are still uncodified, even though they are enforced, cruelly, arbitrarily, unexpectedly.

This paper is an attempt at ferreting out the rules for women politicos by autobiographically recapturing a hectic four-month experience in 1974, my campaign, how I felt, what I thought then, and later what I think I learned.

A recent study of Oregon state legislators divides candidates into "reluctants" and "enthusiasts." Regarding "reluctants," it said: "When a candidate was predisposed not to run and at the same time had few incentives, he anticipated high costs and low benefits. . . ." And of "enthusiasts": "A candidate strongly predisposed to run, and with rewarding incentives, expected high costs and high benefits.[1]

150

The Oregon study found significant the relation between the nature of the candidate, the type of candidate-instigation occurring, and the subsequent campaign theory to be applied. My candidacy was partly "reluctant," partly "enthusiast," and the campaign was related logically to the nature of my candidacy and its instigation.

On Saturday, January 26, 1974, I attended the policy council meeting of the Texas Women's Political Caucus where I learned of a recent court ruling that all the members of the Texas State Board of Education would be required to run again in 1974 because of redistricting. I took down the information with little self-interest, although as a feminist I had been writing on the needs to eliminate sexism in schools and to get women into positions of power. As the meeting broke up, informal discussion ensued, urging me to run for the 24th District spot. My long involvement in feminist groups qualifies this as *primary-group* urging. The next few days, while nursing a cold, I consulted friends, activists, and my children, other primary-group people in my life.

I had already been aware of the calculation of a liberal challenger, that the new demography of the 24th Congressional District could make possible a victory over the incumbent conservative Democrat in Congress.

I knew absolutely nothing about the 24th District incumbent on the State Board of Education until that Saturday when I also learned that he was bad news for feminists. Two women incumbents on the board told me that 24th District incumbent Cravens was a multimillionaire lawyer and banker, was sixty-eight years old, and had a poor attendance record for board meetings.

While I had known previously something about the powers and functions of the board, I first learned on that Saturday certain important items: (1) the post was not a full-time salaried job (my salaried teaching position and the necessary support duty to my children would remain unaffected, win or lose); and (2) the statutes provided a limit of $1,500 on campaign spending. Experience had clearly made me apprehensive about political fund raising, so the limit was appealing; too many candidates get "carried away" by excitement and end up deeply in debt. A third fact was that the statutes forbade any board member's being on a state salary, which meant that all public school teachers and state college professors were ineligible to run, thereby limiting the field. Since I was employed by a private university, I would be eligible and enjoy some advantage in supporters and in understanding educational issues. Moreover, I knew that a private university person had been elected to and seated on the board in 1972.

The 24th District covers parts of two countries, and by quirk of family fate, I had lived seventeen years in Tarrant County, worked in Tarrant County politics, and been elected precinct chairman there in 1970. At the same time, my late husband's family still lived and worked in Dallas County, and for ten years I had been teaching in Dallas County and taking an active interest in Dallas County political affairs. So my two-county existence and name identification was likely to be somewhat unusual.

Finally, the eleventh-hour opening meant that few political gladiators had taken it into their plans; only those who moved quickly would be likely to file. I could not learn of anyone other than the incumbent planning to file. I could hope for a two-person race, thereby avoiding the Texas liberals' usual run-off problem. I also passed the word to a liberal "kingmaker" that I was likely to file; a leading black activist encouraged me with the assurance that no Dallas black person would file. I began to hope for liberal, labor, black, and teacher votes—in spite of my general sense of hopelessness regarding the affluent suburb in Tarrant County where I reside and have long been outspoken and critical of establishment policies. I had taken public stands against John Birch activities in the school, the Vietnam war, on zoning matters, in liberal-conservative Democratic battles, and in local races. My well-known position on separation of church and state was little understood, and strong conservative and fundamentalist opposition to my candidacy would develop. The mayor in Arlington regularly delivers a solid majority to the mayor's taste, and we had frequently clashed. In the past my children had experienced some problems with peers, teachers, and crank callers as a result; now the children made clear that they could take flak. To my suggestion that Jim Don should get a haircut for the campaign, however, he replied, "No way!"

In short, I was mainly an enthusiastic candidate in an urban single-party situation, but not totally "unsponsored." In ways I felt like a reluctant. But I was getting the feeling that "*this one* has my name on it—I cannot pass the cup." I experienced hypocritical guilt feelings when I was tempted to pass the chance by. My self-talk: "Are you the timid coward most women are? How can you with integrity go on urging other women to stick their necks out if you won't do it yourself? Okay, Currey, practice what you've been preaching."

What was I reluctant about? Fear for the children. Fear of humiliating failure at vote getting. Fear of not being able to keep up with my obligations because of lack of energy. Fear of vicious attacks by people with money and power, attacks destroying my reputation and breadwinning. Fear of rallying enough volunteers. Fear I would be considered having flipped out, lost in delusions of grandeur. Unreasonable fears? For nearly twenty years I had been violating an incredible number of taboos in conservative, fundamentalist territory. Besides, I was a widow with three children in a coupled-off suburb; I gave big parties, so I was a merry widow at that. I was a feminist, a smoker, a drinker of Scotch, a tinted blond, a McGovern supporter, a Unitarian, a former CIA researcher; I had been to Bolshevik Russia and even spoke Russian. Finally, I was a scholar sensitive to political science colleagues' criticism of too much activism, and I was coming up for promotion review. Seligman's "minority martyr" was more apt? I was certain every newspaper in the area would oppose me, and most did.

The final plus that pushed me out of reluctance to enthusiasm was the contemplation of the learning experience a campaign could be to my students. I felt the challenge all watchers of politics must sometimes experience—to try out the textbook. And the intriguing challenge—could a woman win a race in a congressional-size district on a shoestring? The board race seemed to say, "Here is a lab—jump in and give it a try." I became certain I would be able to make a respectable showing and avoid disastrous embarrassment.

During that week, one additional consideration I had to deal with was that I had already filed for precinct chairman, so I had to time my withdrawal from the chairman's race to the last minute and get a friend to file, in this way not alerting precinct conservatives to file someone. This delay may have hurt; perhaps the Dallas liberal might not have filed had I made absolutely clear my intention by an earlier filing.

Tuesday morning, February 5, I first learned of two opponents besides the incumbent: Richard Johnston, the liberal white lawyer in Dallas who had the support of a liberal kingmaker analyst; and Senator Oscar Mauzy, a friend of labor and Education Committee chairman. My hopes for labor endorsement dimmed, despite my past sympathy walks in picket lines. Then my black friend called in astounded dismay, having just read (as I had) of my other new opponent, Clay Smothers. Smothers was the black Wallace delegate who nominated himself for vice-president in 1972; he was an outspoken reactionary and a regular columnist for the conservative *Oak Cliff Tribune*. My friend moaned, "I never dreamed of Smothers' filing." My black volunteer Sadie put the significance of this succinctly: "Most blacks won't vote for Clay unless they don't know any other alternative, but they will vote for any black—even Clay—over any unknown white."

That morning, my dream of winning a majority in a two-person May primary evaporated. I retreated to the hope of getting into the runoff, now strategizing with all the worries a runoff entailed.

STRATEGY

My attention first went to the new election code. A trusted friend in Austin checked the filing papers of my three opponents at the secretary of state's office and at the state Democratic chairman's office. She reported that two opponents, Johnston and Cravens, had not designated campaign managers before filing the fifty-dollar filing fee, a court-ruled "campaign expenditure"—at least according to the dates she read on the applications. Unfortunately, she did not Xerox what she saw that day. On her word, I filed two suits alleging campaign violations and simultaneously issued press releases deploring two lawyers' obvious disdain for laws aimed at campaign corruption. Johnston was soon to file a countersuit, charging that I was ineligible because of my educational activity. A lawyer friend came forth insisting that I would be clobbered without an attorney, and I assented gratefully. While I prepared most of the briefing and questions, my attorney handled the oral courtroom work and succeeded in winning my cases with Johnston; but my charge against Cravens was dismissed because, by the time of the court suit, the dates on the documents had become remarkably in compliance. Having not Xeroxed at the right time, we could not support a charge of tampering—but I am convinced of it.

Skeptics asked why I had filed suits; had I done it just for publicity? While a cynical affirmative would not be unexpected from a political scientist, the reason was not that simple. The main factor was a kind of gender variable I had hoped would favor my candidacy, i.e., the Sharpstown and Watergate corruption being associated with males and the voters' being encouraged to turn to women candidates as somehow cleaner, more ethical, and more punctilious in observing election laws. More specifically, in apprehension about possible dirty tricks, I had hoped that by blowing the whistle early in February, I would serve notice that I was watching every opposition move. I felt I could win if the rules were followed. With my personal campaigning and volunteers I could stretch $1,500 farther than could a multimillionaire used to spending that on lunch! Finally, early attempts taught me that getting free media coverage on issues was going to be difficult. That only "bad news" is "good news" to the media explains why candidates are tempted into kamikaze activities; perhaps I reacted to this truism. My action may have been fired by an old anger at arrogance of many in the legal profession. Despite second thoughts, I had risked a course; halting the flow of consequences would have been difficult.

The suits did get me publicity—weighed in the balance, favorable publicity. I carefully provided reporters handout statements but limited my spontaneous responses as I left the courtroom. Learning to talk and what *not* to say to reporters could be a book. To illustrate, before a scheduled interview, while being photographed at the *Star Telegram,* I made some casual comments about my hair (just like a woman) and the story the next day carried the lead "Candidate Decides to Let Her Hair Down."

How many votes were lost or gained from the court activity cannot be known; court time and energy might have been better directed. Because I began the suits before planning my overall strategy I was thrust into the image of a righteous fighter, foreclosing a strategy of presenting an image of wise and quiet dignity. But then, let's face it: Bella Abzug is my ideal, not Margaret Chase Smith. Perhaps this campaign-opening salvo into judicial politics served to confirm my earlier intention of having a moderate platform, to project myself sincerely, without pretenses, trusting to the voters' judgment. That, after all, would be the best test of my laboratory experiment designed to answer the question "Can a simple Iowa farm girl from Clay Township (now an urban feminist) find success and happiness running for the State Board of Education in Texas—using only her wits and a shoestring?"

A lifetime of political observation and study meant I had deeply internalized some general rules on campaigning, though putting footnotes on those rules would be difficult. Past election reflections led me to probe motivational and psychic conditions of women politicos and to explain my own; the following Kogan and Wallach rule hit home: "Perceived risks are more salient than benefits when decisions are made under conditions of uncertainty."[2] In my case, many conditions of uncertainty were present in my decision-to-run period, contributing to my anxieties regarding risks.

Seligman's study of Oregon legislators suggests that social structure and competitive pattern determine the incentives to run in each district.[3] As a political scientist, my perception of social structure and competitive pattern and my own place in the perception undoubtedly produced my conviction that "this one has my name on it." Seligman's analysis is useful in explaining my self-dialogue: "Anticipated gains and losses were shaped by the *interaction* between the candidates' desire to run and incentives."[4] Even more relevant is his conclusion:

> Each candidate's expectations of gains and losses depended on how strongly the candidate wanted to run (enthusiast or reluctant) and the particular incentives that were found to be attractive.[5]

I manifested characteristics of both the enthusiast and the reluctant. Seligman also found that what constituted an incentive for a particular candidate depended in part on "his [sic] motivation for politics and is rooted in his [sic] early socialization."[6] Some of my earliest childhood memories are of FDR rallies, running up and down the aisles of the state senate to my father's desk, even sitting on the governor's lap, so I suspect my motivations for politics are rooted in early socialization; those early exciting associations with politics must be credited for tipping me from the reluctant class to the enthusiastic class Seligman describes. Seligman further concludes:

> Motivation underlies various orientations to politics; a commitment to an issue or ideology, a deep sense of civic responsibility, or an instrumental orientation toward politics as an avenue to power or income.[7]

These three orientations are manifested in my career, and while tempted to emphasize these, I could entertain the argument that, probably before age six, my decision to run forty years later for the board of education might have been forecast!

Among the risks I calculated were the factors of prefiling planning, incumbent advantages, and irrational chance elements such as place on the ballot. Regarding planning, Seligman found that sponsors prepare for the campaign several months before the filing dead-line.[8] My sudden decision meant ignoring this factor. Regarding run-ning against an incumbent, Seligman found: "A challenger must wage an intensive campaign to catch the attention of enough voters to win."[9] Moreover, Seligman warns:

> When the field consisted of unknown candidates, the primary election was like a lottery. An unusual name, or a name identified with a familiar one, a catchy slogan in the Voters' Pamphlet or a chance factor such as position on the ballot often proved decisive.[10]

A long ballot and a lottery nature are true in Texas primaries. While *Currey* is not *Smith*, it is not an unfamiliar name. A district attorney, a college president, and a former sheriff in the area are named *Curry*. The name *Cravens* (the incumbent's) signaled an old pioneer family, wealth, and civic distinction. Cravens' style was that of a dignified business elite, his name identification gained over several decades by presence on countless boards of directors. In February he gave the city a thirty-acre park to be named for himself, a nicely timed, if ex-pensive, campaign gimmick that was not reported on his expense dec-laration!

Another opponent had the common name of Johnston; the third, Clay Smothers, was a well-known former radio announcer, an out-spoken black Wallace supporter. For what the gender variable was worth, mine was the only female first name of the four running for the board of education in District 24. For voters who associate women with "clean up" in the year of Watergate, this may have been useful.

Before filing, my general internalized views about campaigns probably mirrored the following remarks from William Flanigan:

> Campaigns . . . provide the electorate with political information. For most the information is insufficient to motivate them to vote. For many voters, campaigns inspire some partisan enthusiasm and reinforce usual political commitments, and for others the campaign provides information which disturbs their customary vote patterns. The candidates . . . concentrate on arousing sym-pathetic responses in the electorate, but they must attempt this with an electorate whose opinions and loyalties are fairly set by the start of a campaign. For the most part they must work with situations they cannot greatly change. Strategies aim at gaining

an advantage in turnout among one's voters and at publicizing
themes and symbols which arouse favorable sympathies. The
outcome of an election is mainly a result of the political
preferences and patterns in the electorate and only slightly a
result of strategy and maneuvering. . . . Both make substantial
efforts during campaigns . . . their efforts may cancel one
another . . . neither . . . can afford to reduce efforts . . . even a
relatively modest impact can change the outcome of close
elections. . . . [Our electorate is] hardly a classical model . . . with
rational, well informed voters making dispassionate decisions
. . . [The electorate is] capable upon occasion to respond to issue
appeals both positively and negatively . . . but does not appear
easily moved by most appeals . . . traditional loyalties dominate
electoral patterns.[11]

In addition, publicity to the name of the candidate was a priority. I
frequently reminded volunteers, when the publicity wasn't favorable,
of P.T. Barnum's rule that comment could be good or bad, so long as
his name was mentioned. My reassurance to volunteers was for their
morale (and my own); nonetheless, my past observations had tended
to confirm Barnum's aphorism, giving me strength in risk taking.

I acknowledged the general stability in voter (and nonvoter) behavior and thus the need of economizing my effort by activating the
already likely supporters and ignoring the likely supporters of other
candidates and the incumbent. I knew also that "three mechanisms
have replaced parties as the dominant instruments in election campaigns; the candidate's own campaign organization, the media, and
professional consulting firms."[12]

Having observed many Texas primaries, I knew how much campaign overkill crowded the media during the last two weeks before
voting, with most attention going to the heated, bigger, and more
glamorous offices; thus, if I wanted media coverage, I would have to
start earlier and "peak" before voters turned to concentrate on the big
offices. I had learned such basics as being positive, not engaging in
personality attacks, running my own race and not getting involved in
the races of friends running for other offices, sticking to carefully
selected theme issues, avoiding marginal and controversial stands unless directly asked. I knew the importance of a favorable consistent
image—remembering my conservative brother's advice years ago
when I went job-hunting, "Decide on a hair color and stick with it."

Despite general rules, I could appreciate Sorauf's comment:

"... optimum campaign strategy depends on a great number of variables and the only general rule is that there is no general rule."[13] In Sorauf's view, strategy will vary with candidate skills; nature and size of constituency; the office sought; the electoral system; party and other organized resources; availability of money and labor; and norms, perceptions, and loyalties of voters.[14] The chief early test of campaign strategists is the sober evaluation of these variables and the consequent demands and limits they present.[15]

In *assessing the setting*, the first element involved assessment of my own skills. Through twenty-five years of working and teaching, being active in church, PTA, Girl Scouts, Democratic party activities, and other groups, I had learned talking and debating skills, writing, organizing, friendly interaction, pleasantry skills. I had the skill of rapid reading and comprehension of the basic outlines of a new problem and a large vocabulary for articulating the issues. I had lived and traveled widely, worked in blue-collar and egghead jobs, and been at ease in cosmopolitan jet sets. I understood business from close working with my late husband's stint as a wild-catter entrepreneur; and as a mother of three, I could communicate with parents. I knew something of the educational bureaucrat's mind, having dealt with it so long. And I knew a good deal of the formal and informal political relationships among the different levels and areas of government, the crucial points of power and status. At some time or other in my life, I had played, at least metaphorically speaking, the three great roles of woman—Eve, (temptress), Mary Magdalen (fallen woman), and Mother Mary (saint and custodian of morals). I learn foreign languages easily and had developed that important survival skill of women and the oppressed of adapting language, dialect, dress, and manner to the people I am with, a skill of ingratiating oneself that I do not always engage in with self-approval and easy conscience (e.g., do you laugh at ethnic and sexist jokes in certain company?). I had the skill of being stoically tough and forthright in criticism in public meetings, a skill that could be both a liability and an asset in a campaign depending on how judiciously used. I did have a reputation of honesty and trustworthiness, and to many I am sure, of recklessly telling hard truths when most listeners would have preferred the rhetoric of white lies. In some areas, I could be said to be presenting an authoritative judgment.

But all these skills applied in politics carried a counter-liability with some voters, a head-on role stereotype problem of women in

160 ☆ VIRGINIA CURREY

politics. While I had the skill of being perfectly at ease "with the boys," playing the "fallen woman," hard drinking, hard smoking, swearing, witty and sarcastic, and in such a role knew how to pick up useful political intelligence, that image, "tough earthiness" if you prefer that to "fallen woman," while acceptable for a Churchill or an LBJ, is not acceptable for public women. The camaraderie such a role develops is not usually a cashable chit, except possibly for a woman lobbyist. Moreover, it presents blackmail problems greater for women than for men. While Wilbur Mills got his comeuppance, I find it hard to imagine political survival for a Bella Abzug, a Barbara Jordan, or a Sissy Farenthold had it been bandied about that they were dirty-old-lady boozers after hours.

The role of temptress has its liabilities and assets as well, and the ambiguities in the electorate on this point present especially great problems. Wearing a clinging, low-cut gown at a political affair may ensure opportunity to speak to and get photographed with notables, and given the rewards our culture gives to classy sex objects (full credibility goes to the brainy woman who is also a "looker"), the female politician endures constant torment regarding her dress, facial expressions, and hairstyle. Nearly every woman politico I have interviewed attests to this problem being far greater for women than for men. To men, the only comparable criticism would be for beard or length of hair. Few men are constantly admonished, "Smile, don't look sad," as women are. Many voters expect a woman to be fashionable and glamorous. But young voters may find the same appearance suspect. My daughter facilely categorizes traditional women as "bubbles" (referring to their hairstyle) and as "polyester pant-suiters." Acceptable to her values, however, "if you must be traditional," would be a dress that was flashy and "far out." My campaign hairstyle was a compromise—bubblelike on top, long in back. I always wore a dress, not pants, during the campaign and followed the advice of Johnnie Marie Grimes, a Dallas board member, who told me she wore the *same* dress throughout the campaign to establish a familiar identity image. For many evening affairs, I wore a simple princess-line long pink dress with or without a velvet blazer, though few other women were in long skirts at such affairs. A candidate at a rally needs to stand out and carry something of a glamour aura, especially when there are many candidates present and the need to establish identity in the voters' minds is great; that is, by appearance one helps facilitate the answer to the voter's question, "Which one is the candidate?" by being obviously the person advertising for attention.

For the candidate in young or middle years, the image problem is especially great, because the voter really wants her to be a bit of the charming temptress—serving to titillate male voter fantasizing and to maximize female voters' empathetic identification—after all, our culture has taught them well that they are or ought to be temptresses. If one rejects using the assets of the temptress image altogether, the youngish candidate may run the risk of being regarded as a "frigid bitch," or worse, a "lesbian man-hater." Should she be opt for the mature, grandmother image—Mother Mary model—this too has to be credible. For a candidate whose life style hasn't really been that of a dignified, graying Athena, slipups are a likely hazard. Since my life style has been outdoorsy, informal, and earthy—high dignity is my short suit—I rejected that image, although my observations and reflections since my campaign have led me to believe it has the greatest potential for women. Though America has been in a period when youthful looks and behavior are prized in male candidates, this may be an important gender variable. Whereas the public may prefer an aggressive youthful Kennedy-type in males, the public wants its women candidates to be serious, wise, and gray. Next year, if you see me silver-haired, in a lacy blouse, I'm running for something. Finally, in terms of assets, good health and energy are terribly important. In my campaign they were crucial because I would be continuing full-time university duties and moonlighting as a mother-household manager.

Campaigning became my substitute for recreation and companion to my usual duties. My car carried signs, and I carried a fund-raising bucket covered with a campaign label together with my hand-bag wherever it went—every woman knows how constant a companion is her handbag! At the bank for a night deposit, I left campaign cards beside the deposit slips. At Thirty-one Flavors for cones, we gave flyers to the customers. I shook hands and gave cards to the fans at Little League games. Commuting, I followed a hundred different routes, shopping and campaigning. Entering and leaving the turnpike I "carded" the turnstile keepers. My liability was that I could not foreswear my usual duties to campaign full time, so I turned the liability into an asset. My daily twenty-five-mile commuting became a daily campaign swing, as did my dutiful-mother occasions to baseball games and ice-cream shops. The only limitation in deference to good taste was that I didn't campaign at funerals and weddings! Undoubtedly this aggressive behavior turned off some voters, but Barnum's aphorism rationalized that!

This gender variable applies to women candidates with money and family problems. Men get money easier, can contract for activities and services that women must expend time on. Liz Carpenter once advised that time spent under the hair dryer should be used to write campaign cards. Men are customarily freed to give singleminded attention to a task; few male candidates sit on a platform musing about who will baby-sit tomorrow and making mental notes to pick up eggs and milk on the way home. Having to handle several matters simultaneously is a gender liability *and* an asset and may explain why women candidates appreciate women volunteers and managers for their similar skills and empathy. In my at-home headquarters, the skillful volunteer who could work while dealing with my children was usually the female volunteer, though some males also had this capacity.

Turning to Sorauf's second aspect of setting—the geographic and demographic nature of the district—the outstanding feature was the fragmented and heterogeneous nature of my district. It was about 50 miles wide and 50 miles long, and crescent in shape; it included 109 precincts, 74 in Dallas County, 35 in Tarrant County; and all or parts of 8 municipalities and school districts. The district encircled state senatorial District 23 of Democratic Senator Oscar Mauzy, chairman of the Senate Education Committee, and a part of senatorial District 12, of Republican Senator Betty Andujar. All or parts of six Dallas House of Representatives seats were in the district. The congressional seat of Dale Milford, conservative Democratic incumbent, was being contested by attorney Martin Frost, a moderate seeking liberal and labor votes.

In this setting, my office was obviously overshadowed by more visible contested offices, was obscure to most voters, but well known to professionally affected clientele. The office, membership on the 24-member board, is nonsalaried and entails monthly meetings in Austin. The board makes policy for Texas secondary education primarily, directs an annual $2 billion funding and investment program, is charged with channeling federal funds, and advises the legislature on needed new legislation. Statutory limitations include a ban on anyone running for the office who is salaried by public funds or engaged in public education; unique to an elective post in Texas, candidates for the board are forbidden to spend more than $1,500 to be elected. Characteristically, board posts are filled by businessmen, lawyers, physicians, and bankers. Only two women were on the board in the spring of 1974, and one was redistricted and chose not to run.

The electoral conditions of the setting was the necessity of running in the Democratic or Republican primaries Saturday, May 4, with the possibility of a Saturday, June 1, runoff. If successfully nominated by the party, one must run in the November general election. This could mean three election ordeals for which one could expend no more than $1,500 (for all three) in a district with a potential voter constituency of 500,000 people, though registered voters totaled around 300,000.

The office was listed over halfway down the ballot. With three opponents, I was fortunate to draw first place on the Dallas County ballot and last place on the Tarrant County ballot, which is considered second-best to drawing first place. Since Texas is essentially a one-party state, attention centers on the Democratic primary; even voters who consistently vote for Republican Presidents in November cheerfully come to participate in the Democratic primary and runoff. Liberal Democrats must do extraordinarly well even to capture their party's nomination; voters in November usually get the choice of conservative Democrat Tweedledum or conservative Republican Tweedledee. The major contribution of party stems from the practice of appointing as election officials in each precinct Democratic precinct chairmen, and in both Tarrant and Dallas counties most of these judges are conservative, carefully on guard against qualifying a new voter a liberal candidate might have motivated to vote. With this in mind, I made some effort wooing 109 precinct judges; if nothing else, this would apprise a hostile judge that the candidate and her workers were watching election-day activities. Having been a Democratic precinct chairman, I had already cultivated relations with Tarrant County people, so I concentrated on calling and writing Dallas County precinct judges.

The Democratic party organization at the county level does provide the candidate some time-saving materials: the names, addresses, and telephone numbers of precinct chairpersons; maps; filing and reporting forms; notices of official party functions and deadlines. One must look to less official party groups, such as a Democratic Women's Club of Dallas County, to detect significant party help on a campaign. The Women's Club gave a fund-raising reception for all Democratic candidates, a good area for recruiting volunteers. I learned to be aggressive and graciously polite at gatherings of Democrats, conservative or liberal.

Similarly, I attended every possible event of candidates for every race but my own, primarily to smile, shake hands, and establish identity with each candidate's followers, hoping that in the voting booth, as their eyes moved down the ballot to my less salient race, they would remember my name favorably and pull my lever. This parasitism is common, and results in the comical situation of more candidates than voters being present at some affairs.

AVAILABILITY OF POLITICAL RESOURCES

While at the outset of my campaign I had sugar-plum visions of enthusiastic feminist friends and students volunteering full responsibility for a precinct each to analyze, walk, telephone, poster, and then deliver—idealistic dreams that only a political scientist could manufacture in lurid detail—these dreams soon dimmed dramatically. Still, the ideal persisted, and I generally tried to follow my highly decentralized plan. I both overestimated and underestimated students. I remained sensitive to possible criticism for "using" students, so campaign work for me instead of another candidate was kept merely a class option. Students can be counted on to do limited, carefully directed work but are notoriously likely to overpromise; with the press of studies, they often exit with carefully marked and irreplaceable registration lists. The candidate can only smile weakly, "I understand." After all, one can't *fire* volunteers, especially if they are also voters.

At the late date I filed, experienced friends were already committed to work for earlier filers. Raiding the volunteers of other candidates hardly seemed in good taste, but I did get piggyback assistance—invitations to their affairs, introduction to guests, permission to leave my literature, exchange of yard-sign locations. Organizations of others are limited political resources because other candidates also know the cardinal rule—run your own race.

Many people with professional skills volunteered; a speech teacher sent his debate book on educational finance, which helped simplify the issues. An advertising instructor designed my campaign card. A camera artist followed me for days, providing photographs for my literature. An art student did the final layout and shopped printers until she found the best price, then monitored the work. Printers, a candidate learns, are difficult creatures with minds of their own and may easily ignore directions. When my first printer—the only one nearby with a labor shop authorized to apply the precious labor "bug" on materials, a stamp essential for labor endorsement—failed to crop a photo as directed and printed 10,000 cards for which I was expected to pay. I refused to accept them, got him to agree to do 10,000 more, correctly, and then negotiated to take the "ruined" ones off his hands at a reasonable price. Ironically, since I ended up using both batches, I found the "ruined" batch in which my kindergarten friend Jennifer had not been cropped out had more sales appeal than the one with my face alone!

By the time we were ready to print a newsprint flyer, labor had endorsed Johnston, so we decided to find the cheapest printer, labor bug or not!

I learned to utilize any skill to the fullest extent possible. A former black student spent her air force leave with me, covered the phone, addressed envelopes, and helped to develop my support in the black precincts of Dallas. Easter, her minister warmly presented us to the congregation of her church. Another former student, an experienced gubernatorial campaigner, took over press releases and general alter ego management. Third chief angel was precinct neighbor Linda-on-the-spot who, between her classes, did everything from running errands, riding herd on my children (and hers), answering the phone, cleaning the house, preparing coffee and punch, trouble shooting, and accompanying me to rallies, bolstering my morale and state of appearance and generally bragging to others at the rally how great Dr. Currey is. Her devotion was possible because her equally devoted husband never complained about solo fathering at his house and surrogate fathering at mine during the campaign. It may be a gender rule that active political women cannot have grumpy, unsupportive men in their lives. While a cooperative, enthusiastic spouse is an asset to a male candidate, it may well be a sine qua non for the female candidate to have supportive men (or none at all) in her life. A female candidate cannot survive a campaign if there's trouble at home; a male candidate can more easily leave an unhappy wife and children out of the campaign and still make it.

Every volunteer's skill was utilized, unfortunately not always at the desired level; for at the times when certain jobs *had* to be done, the persons available were over- or underqualified. One college instructor addressed cards in a tedious map-and-look-up task for which she was overqualified. Several friends brought me organizational mailing lists, one bought the registered voter lists of the 109 precincts for a dollar apiece, one gave a kickoff coffee. Two students went to the courthouse and marked the voter list of key precincts for the actual hard-core conscientious voters as measured by two recent lackluster elections. They called these hard-core voters, using standard survey techniques. The results suggest an inexpensive way of assessing one's strength and establishing name identification. In Precinct 426, of 257 voters reached out of 360 the students attempted to reach, 90 were definitely interested in Dr. Currey, 167 not interested. On May 4 I carried that precinct with 98 votes, and my three opponents divided the other 199 votes.

Several students pledged to stand outside the distance markers at precinct polling places all day May 4 and hand out cards saying "Please vote for my favorite teacher;" my three children did the same re "my mother." I won every precinct where this was done. Unfortunately, college exam week started May 3, and many "pledgees" backed out. Noteworthy regarding this technique, the only Chicano precinct I did well in was "womaned" by my Chicano student Flores who sang my praises in Spanish and English that day, especially my support of bilingual education. In regard to priorities, *hiring* young people for this all-day task at target precincts would have been wise. The long ballot meant many voters hadn't considered my race; they were willing to please the eager supplicant, being rewarded with a smile when the voter reported, "I voted for your teacher." For marginally known offices and long ballots, this technique may be first priority.

From the beginning, all volunteers were invited to the house for Sunday afternoon work sessions: dull work like addressing is more fun done in company and more likely to get done; no matter how small one's contribution, a student can learn something of the total atmosphere of a campaign in the presence of discussion and campaign tasks being performed, and such sessions helped morale and teamwork. One Sunday volunteers climaxed the afternoon of work by descending en masse on a labor-sponsored reception for a congressional candidate, who was happy to see our warm bodies at this sparsely attended affair despite the fact that my students reproached every labor person they buttonholed with "Why did your union endorse Dr. Currey's opponent?" That became known as our "blitz."

Another "blitz" was on the cars parked at churches on Sunday mornings. Using a carefully marked route on our maps that could be covered in two hours, we would swoop into a church parking lot and quickly put flyers on car door handles. Junior high boys consider this task rather high adventure, and pizza after, a sufficient reward.

A tedious job—going to the courthouse to mark the hard-core voters on our registration lists—was done by volunteers. Expecting a low turnout, we would economize by mailing only to "sure" voters, and a good share of our "target" precincts did get this attention. Another technique of economizing was to hand a bunch of stuffed, addressed envelopes without stamps to affluent friends to mail. A volunteer showing skill and devotion was put in total charge of a given town or batch of precincts with responsibility for getting material out. While such decentralization is risky, the fact that I carried the precincts in these decentralized areas vindicated my confidence in those area captains.

I interviewed each volunteer to find tasks appropriate to the person's skills and tolerable enough to keep the person involved, for giving volunteers distasteful jobs only drives them away. As a result, tasks of lower priority often get done before more important, but duller, jobs.

My artist volunteers silkscreened and made yard signs, and my 15-year-old daughter gave two speeches on my behalf when I was speaking elsewhere; on both occasions the feedback suggested she presented a delightful change of pace after the array of usual candidate blather which proceeded her. The cost was the blackmail of a new dress—"After all, Mama, I can't wear jeans and sit on the platform." Luckily, her speech at a park rally for Sissy came after the press had left; it was reported that she assured the young voters still present that Mama favored legalization of pot, a platform plank of her invention, not mine. So one does have to be on guard against the zealous projections of ardent supporters!

Sorauf's final resource, money, presented the most important gender variable. While the amount needed for my race was small, wanting to experience the problem of fund raising for women candidates, I felt determined that I would not pay for my own campaign.

Almost immediately, friends and relatives sent me checks and warm wishes; the largest check was $100. The omnipresent bucket yielded about $400 throughout the campaign and was used as a conversation piece to dramatize my commitment to small contributions from many voters rather than "being bought" by a pressure group. In the year of Watergate, it was effective in conveying that concept; with its bright label, it was a walking advertisement of my candidacy and name. Perhaps it was too gimmicky, not dignified enough for the office; supporters occasionally would try to dissuade me from carrying it. It was an innovation, certainly, although successful women candidates in recent years have urged women to be innovative. I sent out a fund-raising letter suggesting a $10 gift to about 200 people, eventually raising the spending limits of $1,500, but by the time I had to contract for printing, I had not yet raised enough, so I had continually nagging worries about money and its allocation. The joyful part of my fund raising was that I truly felt "unbought and unbossed." While $1,500 is clearly too small a limit for such a large district, I came to appreciate the limit because it encouraged me to economize and innovate, to weigh priorities carefully. For the law (or the candidate herself) to set a limit at the outset of the campaign makes sense. Money worries are too distracting when the candidate is concentrating on projecting a favorable image and discussing important issues. The gender variable in campaign money primarily involves time. A woman must start early and expect small contributions; but this can be an asset, building name identification and commitment from more people, who are likely to follow up on their investment by going to the polls.

Sorauf's seventh variable concerns the nature of the electorate—their norms, loyalties, and perceptions. The conservative incumbent congressman's analysis of the political complexion of the newly drawn district was that it was now 30 percent liberal, 38 percent conservative, and 32 percent moderate,[16] and a similar estimate by a liberal analyst was encouraging to my self-assessment as liberal-to-moderate. Of 109 precincts in the district, 28 were predominantly black, 15 precincts had gone for Wallace in 1968 by 24 percent. The 23rd District had given Ralph Yarborough 50.4 percent in the 1964 primary and 55 percent in November 1964. Redistricting made research difficult, but using the 1972 Sanders-Tower race for U.S. Senate and McGovern's vote in 1972 enabled us to target precincts as primary, secondary, and IGNORE. We ignored precincts lost by both McGovern and Sanders by over 3 to 1, and settled on 42 out of 74 Dallas County precincts and 18 out of 35 in Tarrant County as targets. This first stratagem parallels Sorauf's observation, "a good deal of American campaigning has the effect of stimulating, activating, and reinforcing 'given' political predispositions . . . and directed more to getting people out to vote than to altering or affecting the nature of the voting decision itself."[17]

How did the electorate of District 24 perceive the issues in education and the state board candidates? Few people know much about the functions and power of the state board of education because it has by tradition played a low-key role publicly. *Board of education* to most people means their local school board. State board candidate names appear halfway down a long ballot, where a large percentage of voters never extend their interest, and often simple name familiarity might be enough to get their attention and votes. Besides attention to the name *Currey*, I wanted to educate voters to understand the importance of the board, hoping they would be motivated to vote in that race as well as in the more well-known races that had actually brought them to the polls.

On Saturday, May 4, 26,983 votes were cast in the state board race in the 24th District. Of these I got 9,125, or 34 percent, leading the four-person race, including the incumbent Cravens who garnered 29 percent. In such a race, Michigan Research Center work predicts nearly the opposite should have happened.

Divided by county, the incumbent's vote and mine were

	Tarrant	*Dallas*
Currey	3591	5534
Cravens	4711	3266

The vote in our Dallas targeted precincts shows the vote for Rich Johnston as the factor that kept me from getting a majority in the May primary and avoiding a runoff. The Smothers vote, though mainly conservative, could have come in part to me had I been able to reach more black voters. I did far better in Tarrant County than I expected, since my campaign efforts had been deliberately concentrated on Dallas precincts. My excellent showing May 4 was unfortunate in that my exhausted volunteers turned back to school and personal affairs, or went on vacation, confident of my victory in June. The runoff contest brought forth the last-minute religious smear tactics I had dreaded.

The first beautiful Saturday of June, runoff day, found voters and workers largely unaware of the election, at the lake, anywhere but at the polls. In Tarrant, the voting dropped 75 percent; voter turnout dropped 80 percent in Dallas County where I needed to pick up an offsetting margin to Cravens' Tarrant strength. Runoff results: Cravens 4,520, Currey 3,388. The Dallas low turnout is explained by the absence of any exciting "big" races; Tarrant had four heated runoffs. The Arlington establishment machine (in Tarrant) did its usual turning out its faithful. Of the total vote, 32 percent came from Arlington precincts and 74 percent of Cravens' vote came from Arlington precincts.

My major lesson from this briefly sketched experience is the necessity of prefiling exploration with political groups and sponsors with coalition potential, perhaps with negotiations and tradeoffs that avoid driving compatible coalition partners into runoffs with conservatives. Of course, this lesson applies only to change-oriented women candidates similar to myself. Conservative women maintaining the Mother Mary image and status quo positions could do very well in a runoff situation. In this sense, the change-oriented woman candidate must deal with essentially the same problems that have long faced Texas liberals and minorities; the gender variable present in building prefiling coalitions with liberal and minority males is that chauvinism may well prevail in "tradeoff" negotiation. Is it entirely accidental that I was not opposed in the May primary by a *female* liberal or *female* minority member, but two such *males?* Races such as mine are not failures for women, however. My excellent showing in the May 4 primary and my respectable showing June 1 can be used by other women in negotiation with coalition-potential groups to prove that, with cooperation, women candidates can win.

Liberal and minority brothers, please take heed.

NOTE: On September 6, 1975, the incumbent Cravens died. Currey tried unsuccessfully for interim appointment. Thwarted, she chose to seek the office through open election. In June, 1976, Currey was elected to a position on the State Board of Education by a margin of 73 votes.

NOTES

1. Lester Seligman et al., *Patterns of Recruitment, A State Chooses Its Lawmakers* (Chicago: Rand McNally, 1974), pp. 82–83.

2. Nathan Kogan and Michael Wallach, "Risk-taking as a Function of the Situation, the Person and the Group," in *New Directions in Psychology* (New York: Holt, Rinehart & Winston, 1967), p. 143.

3. Seligman et al., *Patterns of Recruitment,* p. 79.

4. Ibid.

5. Ibid., pp. 79–81.

6. Ibid., p. 78.

7. Ibid.

8. Ibid., p. 77.

9. Ibid.

10. Ibid., pp. 77–78.

11. William H. Flanigan, *Political Behavior of the American Electorate* (Boston: Allyn & Bacon, 1973).

12. Ira Katznelson and Mark Kesselman, *The Politics of Power* (New York: Harcourt Brace Jovanovich, 1975), p. 274.

13. Seligman et al., *Patterns of Recruitment,* p. 239.

14. Ibid.

15. Frank Sorauf, *Party Politics in America* (Boston: Little, Brown, 1968), p. 249.

16. Ibid.

17. Ibid.

IV
Characteristics of Women in Politics: Patterns of Participation

Women recruited into politics at the elite level must avoid becoming isolated from other women; enjoy the respect of their male political peers; and refrain from projecting a threatening, nonfeminine image. If their attitudes, values, and behavior are too different from those held by the bulk of the female population, they risk negative evaluations and responses from that segment of the electorate which can provide meaningful support both in the polling booth and during campaign activities. At the same time, they need to be taken seriously by their male political peers who are in power positions in recruiting groups and political institutions. This means that political women must demonstrate expertise, political know-how, and the ability to function in the rough and tumble of politics. In other words, they must articulate interests that men can accept as pressing and important and in a language and style that men can relate to. They must also possess those skills that will allow effective aggregation. Manifestations of qualities associated with the role of politician, however, automatically constitute problems for they entail behavior that women have been socialized to view as deviant and that is regarded as unfeminine both by males and females.

The problems of recruitment are compounded in the areas of elite participation and performance. Research has indicated that institutions tend to shape the behavior of those operating within them through subtle and sometimes blatant reward systems. Respect of colleagues, formal and informal influence groups, appointments, recognition, and the like, affect individuals, modify their responses, and alter their perceptions. For women holding positions in male-dominated political structures, special difficulties arise. If the women reflect the attitudes and values of the institutions, they run the danger of being branded unfeminine. If they do not, they will be judged ineffective. How do these divergent pressures affect female political participation at the elite level? Can women be assimilated at all in these institutions? If so, to what extent? Do the political institutions modify or change the women within them? To what extent does resocialization take place for these women?

Soule and McGrath address themselves to the problem of attitudinal differences between men and women at the citizen and elite levels. Some interesting differences between males and females at both levels and between women in each of the categories emerge. Although at the citizen level men and women differed little with respect to conventional forms of political participation, the women exhibited a lower sense of political efficacy and were somewhat less liberal on public policy issues. Furthermore, although increased education correlated with an increase in participation, efficacy and liberalism, it did not seem to have the same impact on women that it had on men. Indeed, a college degree did not seem to increase female levels of participation or efficacy beyond that normally expected. On the elite level, however, women were much more liberal than men. Two factors appear to have affected elite women: awareness of sex discrimination and experience with the Women's Liberation Movement.

In discussing the findings the authors advance two explanations for the pattern of female participation. One is the particular socialization of women that emphasizes civic duty but discourages more activist political pursuits. The second centers around skill differential between males and females particularly in decision making which leaves women less prepared for politics at the elite level. Thus, for Soule and McGrath, women who move into the elite level of politics are resocialized; but as a consequence they are neither like women at the citizen level nor like their male peers in the political elite.

In "Spectators, Agitators, or Lawmakers: Women in State Legislatures," the theme of skill differential is explored in more detail. Githens argues that certain informal occupational prerequisites exist for selection to positions of influence and prominence, especially at the committee level. Those careers that are considered valuable are male dominated, while those in which females and other minorities cluster do not provide respected credential for the more important legislative appointments and offices.

There are several significant consequences for female legislators. In the first place, women see themselves as essentially less expert and seek to compensate for supposed inadequacies by creating a reputation for being very well prepared and by abstaining from participation unless their conceptions of "having done their homework" are fully met. The effect of this is often passivity. Second, the women are unable to move into the more respected role style of expert except in those areas where women have been traditionally regarded as having a special vested interest: e.g., social welfare, particularly as it affects children. Although these areas are acknowledged as women's special province, they are not assigned the same priority by legislators as other economic and political concerns that are considered male preserves. Third, women are encouraged by their peers in the legislature to take the initiative in those matters that are logical extensions of traditional female roles. Furthermore, women's expertise on issues considered peripheral does not contribute to positive judgments about effectiveness. In other words, women are assimilated into the political elite to a limited extent only, and even then sexual stereotyping and role assignment limit their power and influence.

In "Recruitment of Women for Congress: A Research Note" Bullock and Heys examine the impact of recruitment on the participation of women in Congress. Comparing women regularly elected with widows filling dead husbands' seats, they show that women recruited through the ordinary channels are similar to males in terms of education; are relatively alike in occupational backgrounds, although they are much less likely to be lawyers; but have had somewhat greater experience in holding office and party activity. Widows, on the other hand, tend to be primarily housewives and are less likely to see politics as an ongoing career or to seek reelection. Despite these differences, regularly elected women as well as widows exhibit substantially the same patterns of participation with respect to roll-call votes and party loyalty. Bullock and Heys' explanation for the lack of difference in the behavioral responses of both groups of women implies that resocialization occurs and that political institutions do, indeed, modify the actions of their members.

Costantini and Craik's study of male and female politicans suggests, however, that resocialization is less than complete. It is their contention that males and females in the political elite not only have somewhat different background characteristics, but also that they play rather different roles. Males, their data show, are more likely to be concerned with personal enhancement and career advancement; women are more often motivated by concepts of public service and policy issues. Thus women show greater interest in the party, its candidates and programs. These differences are seen as having their roots in sex-role assignments which place the male in exterior roles and females in primarily interior ones. As a consequence, men are involved in instrumental functions and women in those that are expressive. In other words, socialization to specific sex roles learned in early life pervades adult patterns of political participation at the elite level and lessens the effect of institutional resocialization on women.

Burrell approaches the question of female participation from a different perspective. Responding to the limited recruitment of women into the political elite, she explores the ramifications of the Women's Political Caucus for female participation in politics. Her study is concerned primarily with two basic questions. The first is whether or not new feminist organizations such as the Women's Political Caucus are attracting new members or rechanneling the efforts of women who are already politically active. This phase of her research concentrates on the characteristics of women joining the Women's Political Caucus and their previous political activity. The second question deals with the potential for increased female political participation. Burrell's findings confirm other studies, at least insofar as education and social class are concerned. The women attending the state convention of the Women's Political Caucus, like women recruited into politics elsewhere, represent a higher status category. Members tend to be fairly young, highly educated, and ideologically liberal. Of particular significance, however, is the fact that these women had been active in politics prior to the caucus's inception. Nevertheless, the activist orientation of the Women's Political Caucus has important implications for female representation in the political elite. Indeed, it is Burrell's contention that the Women's Political Caucus acting as a supportive, urging primary group might well be responsible for the recent increase in women elected to public office, and will have a lasting influence on women's political participation.

These selections seem to confirm the condition of marginality that women in politics experience. Indeed, they display many characteristics of the marginal man. Women who have moved into the political elite are objectively marginal by virtue of the positions they hold, but they share with women involved in politics at the citizen level experiential marginality as well. Actually, the value conflict confronting elite political women may be much more intense than that which women participating at the citizen level encounter. Hence, women political activists operating within the elite stratum may feel greater experiential marginality. This may well explain their more liberal attitudes.

Marginality is probably also intensified for political women at the elite level by the fact that their anticipatory socialization does not provide the skills and values that would allow them to consolidate their new position in the social order and enhance personal acceptance. Ambition and learning, in other words, are effectively divorced for them. Thus women in politics display the same pattern of marginality as the upwardly mobile person. In another respect, too, they reflect the characteristics of the upwardly mobile. Although the research does not specifically refer to prestige isolation and prestige identification, the data certainly imply their existence. On these bases, the female political participant's condition would seem to be particularly illuminated by the concept of the marginal man.

JOHN W. SOULE and WILMA E. McGRATH

☆☆☆☆☆☆☆☆☆☆☆☆☆☆☆☆☆☆☆☆☆☆☆☆☆☆☆☆

10 A Comparative Study of Male–Female Political Attitudes at Citizen and Elite Levels

The purpose of this study is to measure political attitudes of men and women in the United States and to compare and contrast these findings with similar attitudes among men and women at the 1972 Democratic National Convention. Two data bases are necessary to achieve this comparison: a nationwide sample of adult Americans from 1956 through 1972 (SRC surveys obtained through the University of Michigan, ICPR), and a sample survey of 1972 convention delegates. With these two sets of data we are able to (1) make male-female comparisons at the elite level, (2) make male-female comparisons between citizens and elites, and (3) chart the nature and direction of attitude changes among citizens over the sixteen-year period 1956–72.

In social science research we are confronted with a peculiar anomaly about the theoretical utility of sex differences in the United States. One of the most fundamental distinctions we make among people is whether they are male or female. Sociologists and psycholo-

178

gists have noted the importance of sex-role learning from early child-hood continuing throughout an individual's life. As a result, the context of sex roles is a persisting, ongoing process influenced by parents, siblings, peers, teachers, coworkers, and others. What consequences have social scientists noted that appear to follow sex-role distinctions? Maccoby,[1] Rosenberg,[2] and Holter[3] have compiled summaries of major findings on behavior areas which are attributed to sex-role learning in various cultures at different points in time.[4] These findings involve personality characteristics such as aggression, anxiety, and nurturance; they involve socialization factors such as cognitive styles, achievement, suggestibility, and creativity; they involve work patterns, economic disparities, and prescriptions for social interaction. Although they are far too extensive to list here, the resulting accumulations of data serve to underline the importance of sexual distinctions in practically every aspect of social life.

To complete the anomaly, we need to note the peculiar lack of utilization of sex distinctions in studying political behavior. Explanatory variables such as race, SES, education, personality, ideology, and others have been used extensively to explain differences between the way individuals approach or avoid political objects and symbols. What little use has been made of sexual differences by political scientists is essentially descriptive and atheoretical.[5] Our scant current understanding about sex differences and political behavior in the United States can be summarized as follows:

1. Women participate in voting and other civic activities only slightly less than men.
2. Women are drastically underrepresented with respect to men in political activities that involve large amounts of time, money, and commitment, such as campaigning for public office.
3. No significant patterns of ideological differences exist between men and women on public policy questions.

In short, while sex is a fundamental explanatory variable in most of the social sciences, it has not been so conceived in the study of politics. Against this backdrop we can note the recent resurgence of the feminist movement. New awareness has been generated about the status of women in this society, and this awareness has been fed and nurtured by liberal doses of publicity.[6] Attempts have been made to expose the nonconscious nature of belief systems about sex differences which are so pervasive in our society. These beliefs form the basis for sex-role typing and in turn render women less able than men to control their own lives.[7] As women become more aware of the process of sex-role stereotyping, can we expect changes in respect to manifest political attitudes and behaviors among women? If the answer to this question is affirmative, then such changes should be observable by analyzing national public opinion data from 1956 to 1972.

MALE-FEMALE DIFFERENCES IN POLITICAL PARTICIPATION, 1956–72

We have reanalyzed the data from national surveys conducted by the Survey Research Center at the University of Michigan and made available to participating universities through the ICPR. Prior to 1972, a general pattern of lower voting turnout and higher levels of apathy among women has been noted by researchers.[8] These findings are brought up to date in table 10.1., which we culled from the SRC national surveys conducted before and after the presidential elections in 1956, 1964, and 1972.

The data in table 10.1 indicate, first, a good deal of stability for both men and women with respect to the eight different types of political activity that are fairly conventional in this country. Slight differences can be observed between men and women with women generally less participatory than men, but these differences are not dramatic. If any trend can be interpreted over the sixteen years, it is one of a very slight overall convergence between the sexes.

In the 1950s the authors of *The American Voter* found that educational differences between men and women were largely responsible for differences in voter turnout. At that time the average education for women was lower than for men. They speculated that as women gradually reached parity with men in terms of education, sex differences in political partication would erode, since high levels of political participation were closely related to education.[9] The data in table 10.2. illustrate that large differences continue to exist between citizens with different levels of formal education. These differences far exceed the differences between males and females regardless of educational level. These data indicate that: (1) more educated citizens of both sexes were far more likely to engage in all of the political activities that were included in the national surveys; (2) in both 1964 and 1972 differences in participation between sexes tended to be larger

TABLE 10.1. Types and Rates of Political Participation for Men and Women in the U.S., 1956–72

Type of Participation		1956	1964	1972
% who always vote in	Males[a]	47	53	51
presidential elections	Females	38	49	48
% who are definitely	Males	81	83	80
registered to vote	Females	70	79	77
% who contribute	Males	11	11	12
money to campaigns	Females	9	12	9
% who attend political	Males	9	9	[b]
rallies or meetings	Females	6	7	[b]
% who have worked	Males	3	5	4
for a candidate	Females	3	5	6
% who wear political	Males	19	19	14
buttons or stickers	Females	13	18	14
% who write public	Males	[b]	17	29
officials	Females	[b]	14	25
% who try to influence	Males	36	31	35
others on political issues	Females	22	26	26

[a] In this and future tables in this chapter, the actual number of males and females is not reported. The large sample size, even when controls are introduced, allows for an adequate number of cases in each cell.

[b] These cells indicate that data were not available from SRC surveys for that particular year.

among citizens who did not finish high school; (3) education affects the level of political participation more among women than among men; (4) women in 1972 were relatively less likely to participate than in 1964. In short, no trend toward an increase in female participation can be discerned even among college graduates.

Let us turn to the partisan direction of political participation. From 1956 through 1972 the percentages of women identifying themselves as strong Democrats were 19, 23, 31, 23 and 14 percent; percentages of men during the same period who were strong Democrats were 22, 23, 31, 22 and 15 percent. No significant partisan differences existed between men and women. Both sexes have become less likely to identify strongly with either party, with men being slightly more likely to identify themselves as "independents" (not shown in tabular form).

Turning to how people actually have voted in presidential elections, the only meaningful differences in the vote between men and women occurred in 1972 when, according to the SRC data, 37 percent

TABLE 10.2. Sex Differences in Rates of Political Participation Controlling Education, 1964 and 1972

Political Participation		Less Than High School	1964 College Degree or More	Differ-ence[a]	Less Than High School	1972 College Degree or More	Differ-ence[a]
%who always vote	Male	41	70	+29	38	70	+32
in presidential	Female	31	80	+49	31	74	+45
elections	Diff.[b]	(+10)	(−10)		(+7)	(−4)	
% who always vote	Male	61	48	−13	47	50	−13
same party	Female	69	52	−17	52	49	−3
	Diff.	(−8)	(−4)		(−5)	(+1)	
% who contribute	Male				16	52	+36
money	Female				13	46	+33
	Diff.				(+3)	(+6)	
% who attend	Male	5	20	+15	6	19	+13
meetings	Female	1	27	+26	3	20	+17
	Diff.	(+4)	(−7)		(+3)	(−1)	
% who are	Male	78	89	+11	77	92	+15
registered to vote	Female	72	92	+20	64	90	+26
	Diff.	(+6)	(−3)		(+13)	(+2)	
% who work for	Male	3	16	+16	1	10	+9
candidate	Female	2	18	+16	1	10	+9
	Diff.	(+1)	(−2)		(+2)	(−1)	
% who wear	Male	17	25	+8	13	20	+7
campaign button	Female	14	29	+15	7	24	+17
or sticker	Diff.	(+3)	(−4)		(+6)	(−4)	
% who write	Male	10	45	+35	16	52	+36
officials	Female	6	46	+40	13	46	+33
	Diff.	(+4)	(+1)		(+3)	(+6)	
% who influence	Male	27	47	+20	26	56	+30
others	Female	19	52	+33	20	41	+21
	Diff.	(+8)	(−5)		(+6)	(+15)	

[a]A positive sign indicates the number of percentage points by which liberal responses among college educated exceed those with less than high school education.

[b]A positive sign indicates the number of percentage points by which males exceed females in the liberal direction.

of the women reported voting for McGovern, compared to 30 percent of the men. In the recent past, women were more likely than men to support Eisenhower, Nixon (in 1960), and Johnson, but the differences between the sexes were very small. 1972, then, marked the first time women distinguished themselves from men in respect to their presidential vote, probably since Prohibition was a national issue in 1928.

SEX DIFFERENCES IN POLITICAL EFFICACY

Political efficacy, the feeling that one's own participation in politics has some effect on the outcome of public policies, has been one of the most potent predictors of political participation. If one feels inefficacious, it is, of course, logical to expect him or her not to participate. Women have been shown to be less efficacious than men and this difference is magnified among the less educated.[10] The data in table 10.3 evaluate sexual differences with respect to four items commonly used to measure political efficacy. Females were on the whole less efficacious than males. Both sexes were frustrated in 1972, as feelings of inefficacy rose to unprecedented heights.

Again it seemed advisable to evaluate sex differences while controlling for education, since education has been found to be highly correlated with feelings of political efficacy. Four items on the SRC surveys are relevant to political efficacy. Two of them ("people like me" and "public officials don't care") refer generally to respondent's feelings of estrangement or alienation from the political system; the other two items ("voting is the only way" and "politics is so complicated") deal more directly with feelings of civic competency. Political efficacy increases with education (table 10.4) for members of both sexes on all items. On the competency items, however, increased education has a less salutary effect on females than males; on items reflecting political estrangement, education helps both sexes equally.

TABLE 10.3. Political Efficacy by Sex, 1956–72

% who agree that:		1956	1960	1964	1968	1972
People like me have	Males	24	29	28	—	37
no say in government.	Females	32	28	31	—	41
Voting is the only way	Males	70	71	74	53	58
to influence government.	Females	76	75	76	58	64
Public officials don't	Males	27	24	39	42	48
care what I think.	Females	26	25	39	36	50
Politics is so complicated	Males	—	51	61	38	66
I can't really understand it.	Females	—	63	72	48	78

TABLE 10.4. Political Efficacy by Sex Controlling for Education

% who agree that:		1964 Less Than High School	1964 College Degree or More	Differ- ence	1972 Less Than High School	1972 College Degree or More	Differ- ence
People like me	Male	38	17	−21	51	18	−33
have no say	Female	44	10	−34	56	19	−37
in government.	Diff.	(−6)	(+7)		(−5)	(−1)	
Voting is the only	Male	84	46	−38	74	28	−46
way to influence	Female	84	60	−24	79	39	−40
government.	Diff.	(0)	(−14)		(−5)	(−11)	
Public officials	Male	52	16	−36	61	30	−31
don't care what	Female	54	17	−37	67	30	−37
I think.	Diff.	(−2)	(−1)		(−6)	(0)	
Politics is so com-	Male	78	31	−47	82	41	−41
plicated, I can't	Female	83	41	−42	89	58	−31
understand it.	Diff.	(−5)	(−10)		(−7)	(−17)	

SEX DIFFERENCES ON PUBLIC POLICY ISSUES

Thus far we have looked at sex differences with respect to political participation and efficacy. We turn now to the direction or quality of attitudes men and women in the electorate have toward selected issues of public policy. Again we rely on data from the SRC over a period of years in order to evaluate sex differences in response to issues and to assess any trend over a period of time. Since the definition of issues changes over four year periods and the questions about issues are generally reworded from survey to survey, the data in table 10.5 should not be used to detect any absolute attitude change among the electorate. For example, the questions on foreign aid involve foreign aid to underdeveloped nations in one year and aid to all nations in another year. Attention is more safely confined to observing male-female differences for each particular year.

The data in table 10.5. show men and women to have responded similarly to most of these controversial public issues. Prior to and including 1972, we can observe that fewer women responded in the liberal direction although the differences were small. In 1972, even on questions relating specifically to women, male respondents were more

TABLE 10.5. Relationships Between Sex and Public Policy Issues

% who respond in a liberal direction[a]		1956	1960	1964	1968	1972
U.S. should give foreign aid.	Male	70	62	55	64	43
	Female	75	59	50	57	51
Government should push for integration of schools.	Male	38	42	58	50	10[b]
	Female	39	50	59	57	9[b]
Favorable attitudes to communist nations.	Male	13	12	72	84	n.a.
	Female	14	14	72	76	
Favors Vietnam withdrawal.	Male	n.a.	n.a.	n.a.	n.a.	15
	Female					22
Favors rights of accused.	Male	n.a.	n.a.	n.a.	n.a.	14
	Female					13
Favors civil disobedience.	Male	n.a.	n.a.	n.a.	n.a.	18
	Female					14
Favors abortion.	Male	n.a.	n.a.	n.a.	n.a.	25
	Female					23
Legalize marijuana.	Male	n.a.	n.a.	n.a.	n.a.	13
	Female					9
Favors government health insurance.	Male	n.a.	n.a.	n.a.	n.a.	n.a.
	Female					
Amnesty for draft evaders.	Male	n.a.	n.a.	n.a.	n.a.	20
	Female					29
Favors equal rights for women.	Male	n.a.	n.a.	n.a.	n.a.	33
	Female					32
Lay women off jobs same as men (not first).	Male	n.a.	n.a.	n.a.	n.a.	57
	Female					48

[a]Cell percentages reflect proportions of SRC respondents answering in the affirmative.

[b]The question in 1972 deals with busing, hence accounting for differences from previous years.

liberal. Only on the questions of amnesty and Vietnam withdrawal did greater proportions of women respond in the liberal direction.

Since levels of formal education have been correlated with the direction of opinion on public issues in a variety of past surveys,[11] and since women as a whole have slightly less formal education than males, the issues in table 10.6 are analyzed again statistically controlling for education.

In every case except one (responses among male college graduates toward the issue of a Vietnam withdrawal) education increased the percentage of liberal responses for both males and

TABLE 10.6. Sex Differences on Public Policy Issues Controlling for Education in 1972

% who respond in a liberal direction		Educational Level		
		Less Than High School Graduate	College Graduate or More	Difference[a]
Favors foreign aid.	Male	34	59	+25
	Female	33	51	+18
	Difference[b]	+1	+8	
Favors government health insurance.	Male	20	22	+2
	Female	19	26	+7
	Difference	+1	−4	
Favors busing for school integration.	Male	5	9	+4
	Female	5	7	+2
	Difference	0	+2	
Favors civil disobedience.	Male	13	30	+17
	Female	10	21	+11
	Difference	+3	+11	
Favors legalizaton of marijuana.	Male	6	22	+16
	Female	5	14	+9
	Difference	+1	+8	
Abortions should not be denied by law.	Male	16	40	+24
	Female	14	31	+17
	Difference	+2	+9	
Favors immediate withdrawal from Vietnam.	Male	18	15	−3
	Female	21	22	+1
	Difference	−3	−7	
Favors amnesty for draft evaders.	Male	17	25	+8
	Female	21	40	+19
	Difference	−4	−15	
Favors equal rights for women.	Male	33	38	+5
	Female	25	46	+21
	Difference	+8	−8	
Lay women off jobs same as men (not first).	Male	49	68	+19
	Female	42	62	+20
	Difference	+7	+6	

[a] A positive sign indicates the number of percentage points by which liberal responses among college educated exceed those with less than high school education.

[b] A positive sign indicates the number of percentage points by which males exceed females in the liberal direction.

females. Higher levels of education also provoked greater divergence between the sexes, although the pattern was somewhat mixed. In general, however, the greatest divergence found males more liberal. Exceptions in order of descending magnitude are attitudes favoring equality for women, amnesty for draft evaders, and Vietnam with-drawal.

FINDINGS FROM THE 1972 CONVENTION STUDY

Turning now from survey samples at the mass level to the elite level, a sample of 326 delegates was interviewed in Miami Beach, which represented 10 percent of the total number of Democratic delegates. This sample was a carefully drawn quota sample from each state delegation based upon sex, age and race. The study of male-female differences in political outlook was only a part of the convention study, as it was initially undertaken to analyze participation of political amateurs.[12]

Thanks largely to the reforms initiated by the McGovern-Fraser Commission, women showed up at the Democratic convention in un-precedented numbers. Forty percent of the delegates were women—not alternates who vote if the delegates are absent, but bona fide voting delegates. Women delegates constituted a visibly distinct group with identifiable interests and issues, caucus leaders, publicized meetings, press releases, and convention strategies. As an indication that women were more than a symbolic manifestation of the party re-forms, we need only examine the data in table 10.7. When men and women delegates were asked to respond to ten controversial public is-sues, women were more liberal on virtually every item than their male counterparts at the convention. The items appear in descending order on the basis of those which generate the greatest differences be-tween men and women delegates.

Perhaps, we theorized, these sexual differences would disappear if we controlled for socioeconomic factors, such as race, education, age, region, residence, and income, that have been found previously to be correlated with liberalism-conservatism attitudes in many previ-ous studies. Consequently, we formed all ten items found in table 10.7 into a general index of liberalism-conservatism, ran the index[13] against sex while imposing these background variables as controls. Examination of the data in table 10.8. put an end to this notion im-mediately. In almost every subcategory presented in table 10.8., women were more liberal than men, i.e., black women were more liberal than black men, southern women were more liberal than southern men, rural women more liberal than rural men, etc. The few exceptions can be observed by noting the direction of the gamma in table 10.8 for

188 ☆ SOULE AND McGRATH

TABLE 10.7. Issue Preferences of Men and Women Delegates to
the 1972 Democratic Convention

Liberalism-Convervatism Items	% who Answer in the "Liberal" Direction	
	Men Delegates (N = 181)	Women Delegates (N = 145)
1. Amnesty should be granted to Vietnam draft evaders.	59	81
2. Marijuana should be legalized for consenting adults.	52	71
3. Free, safe abortions should be available to any woman upon request.	63	80
4. Law-enforcement agencies should not be allowed limited eavesdropping by wiretapping and other devices.	70	86
5. Communism has changed greatly and we must recognize most wars and revolutions are not communist inspired.	63	76
6. School children should be bused to achieve racial balance in our public schools.	52	63
7. People who advocate radical changes to our way of life are not overprotected by our laws.	75	85
8. The U.S. should withdraw all military forces from Vietnam before POWs are released.	59	67
9. I am in favor of a federally guaranteed annual income for every American.	64	72
10. Government should finance free day-care centers for children of working mothers.[a]	83	90

[a]Save for item 10, chi-square tests indicate male-female differences to be statistically significant beyond the .05 level on each of the other nine items.

each subcategory which is always negative, except in cases where men appeared more liberal on the index than women. The greater the negative gamma (gamma runs from +1.0 to −1.0), the more liberal women were than men in any particular category.

Another alternative explanation of female liberalism is that McGovern recruited a disproportionate share of female delegates. Since his appeal was definitely greatest among those with liberal views, the reason women appeared more liberal than men might be due to his candidacy. This hypothesis can be assessed with the data in table 10.8. under "Candidate choice." Regardless of which candidate delegates supported, females were more liberal than males, i.e., Wallace women more liberal than Wallace men, McGovern women more liberal than McGovern men, etc.

TABLE 10.8. Relationships Between Sex and Ideology Controlling for Race, Education, Age, Region, Residence, Income, and Candidate Choice

		Males		Females	
		% Liberal Responses in Parenthesis			
	Gamma	N	%	N	%
Original Relationship Between Sex and Ideology[a]	−.28	180	(39)	145	(58)
Candidate choice					
McGovern	−.07	95	(52)	94	(55)
Humphrey	−.31	33	(0)	13	(8)
Chisholm	−.20[b]	5	(40)	8	(50)
Wallace	−.41[b]	13	(8)	10	(0)
Race					
white	−.31	139	(31)	111	(45)
nonwhite	−.14	40	(28)	30	(37)
Education					
high school or less	.09[c]	37	(14)	26	(4)
some college	−.29	47	(32)	44	(50)
college graduate	−.63	25	(28)	37	(60)
advanced degree	−.26	71	(38)	35	(46)
Age					
under 21	.38[c]	13	(46)	13	(31)
21–30	−.34	38	(50)	42	(67)
31–40	.13[c]	28	(43)	32	(34)
over 40	−.48	76	(13)	46	(30)
Region					
West	−.25	29	(48)	30	(60)
Midwest	−.25	53	(26)	48	(38)
East	−.23	48	(33)	40	(45)
Border and South	−.25	49	(18)	27	(30)
Residence					
city	−.30	78	(28)	71	(45)
suburb	−.07	42	(48)	31	(51)
small town, rural	−.28	61	(20)	37	(30)
Income					
under $10,000	−.14	51	(35)	34	(41)
$10,000–$15,000	−.27	34	(32)	37	(51)
$15,000–$20,000	−.18	22	(27)	31	(39)
$20,000 plus	−.51	59	(25)	34	(41)

[a] For an explanation of the ideology index, see note 8.

[b] Small cell sizes urge caution in interpreting these particular associations and percentages.

[c] These positive gammas indicate a *reversal* of the original relationship, i.e., in these three subgroups males are more liberal than female delegates.

We were left, then, with the inescapable conclusion that female delegates differed consistently from male delegates on a wide variety of public issues, and that this difference could not be nullified by imposing a number of third variables as statistical controls. Our examination also determined that female delegates reported that, generally speaking, they had been favorably impressed by the women's movement and that they had personally experienced discrimination as women active in politics. The exact wording of these questions and their correlation with the ideological positions of women delegates is reported in table 10.9. Women who had been affected by the movement and who reported discrimination were significantly farther left on the liberal-conservative continuum than women unimpressed by the movement or who reported no instances of sexual discrimination.

These data have been published and described elsewhere[13] at greater length, and we note the findings here because of the sharp contrast they provide with our earlier findings on sex differences at the citizen level. Female convention delegates, of course, exhibit a markedly greater desire to participate in the political process than most women in the electorate. In addition, however, these "elite" women were ideologically distinct from male delegates, a finding which was not paralleled in the electorate. In our final section, we will attempt to bring these apparent contradictions into some sort of theoretical order.

TABLE 10.9. The Women's Movement, Felt Discrimination, and Political Ideology (women only)

How much has the women's liberation movement affected you?	Liberal (N = 58)	Moderate (N = 63)	Conservative (N = 15)	Total
Much (N = 51)	61	39	0	100%
Some (N = 65)	37	52	11	100%
Not at all (N = 20)	30	30	40	100%
	gamma = .49 p < .01			
Have you personally experienced discrimination as a woman?	Liberal	Moderate	Conservative	Total
Yes (N = 83)	50	44	6	100%
No (N = 51)	33	48	19	100%
	gamma = .36 p < .01			

DISCUSSION AND ANALYSIS

Thus far we have tried to present the data on convention delegates and on general samples of the adult public in the United States from 1956 through 1972 in a simple descriptive manner. Our findings can be summarized as follows:

1. Men and women at the elite level differed sharply on ten controversial public issues with women appearing significantly more liberal.
2. Sex differences in ideology between male and female elites were not due to SES factors, but appeared rather to be associated (among women) with awareness of sex discrimination and experience with the women's movement.
3. Men and women in the population differed very little with respect to conventional forms of political participation throughout the sixteen-year period.
4. Women in the population generally felt less efficacious about politics than males throughout the sixteen-year period.
5. Women in the population were slightly less liberal than men on a variety of questions on public policy, although the pattern is a mixed one.
6. Higher levels of education were consistently correlated with increases in participation, efficacy, and liberalism.
7. Education appeared to have a different effect on women compared to men, only in respect to some public policy issues. Otherwise, gaining a college degree for women does not increase their levels of participation or efficacy beyond that expected for both sexes.

We are left with the conclusion that despite recent changes toward a more equal status for women, political participation at the mass level does not reflect these changes. Other than the isolated exception of the Democratic convention in 1972, where large numbers of women participated on an equal basis with men for the first time, equal participation by women as political elites has not occurred, and female officeholders tend to remain exceptions to the rule. At this point it is much more difficult to generalize about the future behavior of female political elites than about females in the electorate.

One question that seems worth asking, however, is why sex-role typing apparently plays so small a part in political participation at the mass level. It is difficult to argue that sex distinctions have disappeared. In fact, to assume they are not major determinants of social status is impossible. Why, then, do our measures of political participation essentially confirm an equivalent input into the political system by both males and females? And why are women so vastly underrepresented in political elite groups? One answer, of course, is that participation at the mass level has generally been conceptualized as the influence which citizens exert on the selection of elites. According to Schumpeter, democracy is a process, a set of institutional arrangements, rather than an end goal.[14] If males and females can be shown to participate in roughly equal fashion in this selection, the requirements for democratic government have been met. Inequality in social structures becomes an artifact not of the political process, but of some other less accessible (hence more acceptable) cause.[15]

By and large, the type of political participation dealt with by our data on the mass level is essentially ritualistic and serves to symbolize the fact that we have a representative democracy in operation. Participatory behavior, such as voting, wearing buttons, or writing to officials, is largely supportive and helps to bind the citizen to his government. Such behavior does not require much time, energy, commitment,[16] or skills, and it does not involve competition in any personal sense. It requires only a minor sense of civic duty, and there is no reason to expect sex-role learning to affect men and women differently in this respect.

Participation at elite levels like the Democratic convention, however, requires a substantially different type of commitment and one that is much more likely to be adversely influenced by sex-role learning. To become a delegate, even after reforms are initiated that give women the opportunity to participate, takes time, aggressive energy, skills, and involves a substantial amount of competition. These same qualities would seem to be necessary, if not sufficient, conditions for political participation at any elite level in this country. Women do not often appear among political elites, but when they do we must expect them to be highly motivated and to have undergone unusual socialization or resocialization experiences. This explanation appears to fit our data at both mass and elite (convention) levels. In short, women in the United States seem just as capable of performing the supportive functions of civic duties as men, but less likely to participate as political elites.

Two separate but parallel explanations can account for this

mass-elite difference. First, sex-role typing signifies rather clearly that girls should avoid conflict; not concern themselves with controversial public issues; devote their time to parochial or family concerns; be expressive and nurturant; appear shy, retiring, or "feminine"; and have a host of other characteristics that ill equip them for serious political commitment. Learning one's sexual identity starts early in life and is continually reinforced throughout life by familly, school, peers, coworkers, children, etc. Sex-role learning explicitly concerned with politics is no doubt further reinforced when girls perceive the stark absence of female role models at elite levels. None of this learning, though, prevents women from participating in the milder, more conventional forms of political activity expected of all "good" citizens.

A second parallel explanation for sexual equivalency in participation at mass levels, and nonequivalency at elite levels, incolves a theory of political participation put forward by Carole Pateman.[17] She argues that for people to participate in any meaningful way in democratic politics, they must first have experienced participation in other more real, immediate, and personally salient arenas. Democratic skills must be learned, and citizens whose personal experiences are limited to nonparticipatory authority structures will not be prepared to participate in any significant way in the larger political system. Pateman is particularly concerned with the extent to which participatory experiences are available at the workplace, but her argument may be even more significant in relation to women. Not only are women generally less able to participate in decisions at work, but they are also rendered less powerful than males in most other social institutions as well.[18]

Just as sex-role typing socializes women to be less motivated or prepared for political participation beyond civic duties, so too does the absence of opportunities to share equitable amounts of power and influence in other more immediate social units. Without that opportunity, we cannot expect most women (and many men) to benefit from the experiences of meaningful participation. The educational benefits, argues Pateman, consist of (1) learning skills and know-how in actual political situations; and (2) experiencing a widening of horizons of social awareness, a desire to cooperate with others, and a general sense of empathy about others' needs.[19] Such an argument may well underlie the lack of differences between men and women in the United States, it may serve to explain the generally more "liberal" positions of elites compared to the masses,[20] and it may account for the widely divergent views between women who participate in politics at the citizen level and those who participate at the elite level.

NOTES
1. Eleanor E. Maccoby, *The Development of Sex Differences* (Stanford, Calif.: Stanford University Press, 1966).

2. B. G. Rosenberg and Brian Sutton-Smith, *Sex and Identity* (New York: Holt, Rinehart & Winston, 1972).

3. Harriet Holter, *Sex Roles and Social Structure* (Oslo, Norway: Universitetsforlaget, 1970).

4. For a summary of sex differences regarding political behavior, see Martin Gruberg, *Women in American Politics* (Oshkosh, Wisc.: Academia, 1968).

5. As an excellent exception, see Kirsten Amundson, *The Silenced Majority: Women in American Democracy* (Englewood Cliffs, N.J.: Prentice-Hall, 1971).

6. Examples of this publicity can be found in all issues of *Ms.* magazine; Betty Friedan's best seller, *The Feminine Mystique* (New York: Dell, 1963); Kate Millett, *Sexual Politics* (New York: Doubleday, 1970).

7. Daryl Bem and Sandra Bem, *Beliefs, Attitudes and Human Affairs* (Belmont, Calif.: Brooks-Cole, 1970), p. 89.

8. Angus Campbell et al., *The American Voter* (New York: Wiley, 1964).

9. Sydney Verba and Norman Nie, *Participation in America: Political Democracy and Social Equality* (New York: Harper & Row, 1972); Campbell et al., *American Voter*, p. 259.

10. Campbell et al., *American Voter*, p. 225–59.

11. Ibid., p. 260; Also Seymour Martin Lipset, "Democracy and Working Class—Authoritarianism," *American Sociological Review* 24 (August 1959).

12. John W. Soule and Wilma E. McGrath, "A Comparative Study of Democratic Delegates, 1968 and 1972," *American Journal of Political Science* 19, no. 3 (August 1975).

13. All ten public policy items were grouped into a rough liberalism-conservatism index or scale. Each delegate was classified as a "conservative," "moderate," or "liberal" based upon their responses to all ten items. This index is used as our indicator of ideology in computing the correlations in table 10.8. Index, or scale positions were calculated by setting arbitrary cutting points after summating Likert responses to the ten items shown in table 10.7. Respondents who failed to answer a question were assigned a neutral score of 3 on a 1-to-5 scale for each item. Point scores ranging from 50 to 100 were divided in thirds, which represented "liberals" ($N = 123$), "moderates" ($N = 156$), "conservatives" ($N = 47$). The liberalism-conservatism scale should be considered a multidimensional scale reflecting a variety of beliefs about controversial public issues. When the items are subjected to Guttman scaling the coefficient of reproducibility is $>.90$, indicating the lack of unidimensionality. At best this scale denotes a loose configuration of attitudes toward the use of governmental power for certain policy objectives.

14. Joseph A. Schumpeter, *Capitalism, Socialism and Democracy* (New York: Harper & Brothers, 1942), p. 269.

15. Bem, *Beliefs, Attitudes and Human Affairs*, p. 89. According to Sandra and Darryl Bem, beliefs and attitudes toward women form a nonconscious ideology—one that is accepted because "alternate conceptions of the world remain unimagined."

16. Verba and Nie, *Participation in America*, p. 259, make a similar distinction between different types of political participation.

17. Carole Pateman, *Participation and Democratic Theory* (London: Cambridge University Press, 1970).

18. See Carol Andreas, *Sex and Caste in America* (Englewood Cliffs, N.J.: Prentice-Hall, 1971), chap. 5.

19. Pateman, *Participation and Democratic Theory,* derives her theory largely from J. S. Mill and Jean-Jacques Rousseau, pp. 27–33.

20. Samuel A. Stouffer, *Communism, Conformity, and Civil Liberties* (New York: Wiley, 1955).

11

MARIANNE GITHENS

☆☆☆☆☆☆☆☆☆☆☆☆☆☆☆☆☆☆☆☆☆☆☆☆☆☆☆☆☆

Spectators, Agitators, or Lawmakers: Women in State Legislatures

Much research on the personality traits of women active in politics at the elite level has appeared within the last several years.[1] These studies indicate that female politicians appear consistently to rank higher on the liberal-conservative scale, display a greater degree of unconventionality and a more pronounced sense of adventure. Such findings would seem to be further confirmed by a variety of case studies of individual women, especially at the congressional level.[2] Although such attitudes are important to an understanding of female political participation, other related problems faced by women in politics have been mentioned only in passing. The ability to function effectively, to exert some power and influence, and to adopt role styles that facilitate participation are all issues of fundamental importance in an examination and evaluation of the patterns of female political participation. It is these aspects which this study of female state legislators attempts.

The data in this paper have emerged out of a much broader projected study focused primarily on the significance of race as a variable in the behavior of female state legislators. Other factors have surfaced, however, at least in the case of Maryland's female legislators, which warrant exploration.

A few basic facts about the Maryland legislature should be pointed out before proceeding to a specific discussion of the women legislators' role. There are two chambers: a Senate with a total membership of 43, and a House of Delegates which has 142 members. The legislature meets annually in regular session for approximately three months—from mid-January to mid-April. Although compensation has been increased recently, it still falls below the amount adequate to sustain a life style expected of a state legislator. This means several things. First, some additional source of income is necessary for those legislators who are self-supporting. Second, another job must be fairly flexible in its hours and commitments if it is to be successfully combined with the occupation of legislator. Law and business meet these prerequisites relatively satisfactorily. Legal and business interests are affected by legislation, and sitting at one's desk in the office is not the only way to further such interests. Social work and teaching, on the other hand, tend to require regular physical presence to a much greater extent, and are therefore more difficult second jobs. Third, prohibitions on drawing two salaries from the state make it virtually a necessity for legislators to be drawn from the private sector. On the surface this might appear to give those members who are independently wealthy and do not need a second income and those who are supported by a spouse some advantages; but for reasons to be discussed here, this is not the case.

In addition to the rather standard organization of the legislature, each house has a number of standing committees. In the Senate there are six: Economic Affairs, Executive Nominations, Finances, Judicial Proceeding, Entertainment, and Ethics. The House of Delegates has nine such committees. There is also a Legislative Council which proposes changes in existing legislation, new legislation, and sets agenda for the legislation session. It meets about a month prior to the regular session and is empowered to hold hearings and subpoena witnesses and records. This committee has thirty members: fifteen from the Senate and fifteen from the House of Delegates.

Given the characteristics of state legislatures in general and the compensation issue just raised, the composition of the Senate and the occupations reflected there hold few surprises. There are four white women (9.3 percent) and four blacks (9.3 percent), one of whom is a woman. The remaining thirty-six members are white and male; 46.5 percent are lawyers, 32.6 percent are drawn from the business sector (the largest cluster of which is real estate and constitutes 9.3 percent of the entire membership), 7 percent are educators; and there is one farmer, one newspaper editor-owner, one professional musician, a steelworker (a job description which affirms more an origin and commitment than the position which he now holds) a nurse, and a rather professional volunteer.[3]

This occupational distribution is not, however, reflected among either the white women or the black members. One white woman is a teacher, another a lawyer, the third a nurse, and the fourth the volunteer. A similar pattern exists for the black members: one in real estate, two teachers (one being a woman), and one steelworker.

Although lawyers constitute a little less than half the total membership, their representation is much greater in the organizational structures of the Senate. Four of the six standing committee chairpersons (66.7 percent) are practicing attorneys, the fifth is a businessman who also holds a law degree, and the sixth is also a businessman. If the criteria used is law degree, the percentage increases to 83.8 percent. These data might be interesting, but dismissed as somewhat abstract, except that the only woman lawyer is a standing committee chairperson, and no other chair is held by a woman, even though two of the other women have more seniority than male chairpersons.

TABLE 11.1. Standing Committee Chairpersons

Occupation	Male	Female	% of Total
Law	3	1	66.7
Business	2	0	33.3
Total	5	1	100.0

TABLE 11.2. Legislative Council

Occupation	Male	Female	% of Total
Law	8	1	60.0
Business	2	0	13.3
Education	0	1	6.7
Agriculture	1	0	6.7
Music	1	0	6.7
Volunteer	0	1	6.7
Total	12	3	100.0

The same general pattern prevails in the Legislative Council. Lawyers again constitute the largest group (60 percent), followed by businessmen (13.3 percent). The remaining members are drawn from education, agriculture, music, etc.

The secondary occupational affiliation is perhaps critical from another perspective as well. Two of the three women who list a career are, in fact, not presently engaged in it. Rather, it represents an initial prelegislative professional orientation. This is not true for the male legislators, who, for financial reasons, continue to be fairly actively involved in a second job.

The same general patterns, with some notable exceptions, appear in the House of Delegates. Of the members, 134 are male (94.4 percent) and only 8 are female (5.6 percent). This means that the number of women in the lower chamber is almost 4 percent less than the Senate. There are 13 blacks, 2 of whom are women (9.2 percent). In other words, the House of Delegates is less female; but the numbers are so small in comparison to the general population that the minimal losses are quite irrelevant. The number of lawyers is smaller, only 33.8 percent, while the number of businessmen is greater (38.7 percent). There are 8.4 percent of the delegates in education, 5.6 percent are professional, 4.9 percent hold some kind of state employment,[4] 2.1 percent have had careers in law enforcement; another 2.1 percent come from blue-collar occupations. In addition, 2.1 percent are in agriculture, 1.5 percent define their occupation as housewife, and there is one labor official.

Again the general occupational pattern is not reflected among

TABLE 11.3. Composition of the Maryland House of Delegates

Occupation	Male	Female	% of Total Membership
Law	48	0	33.8
Business	54	1	38.7
Education	11	1	8.5
Professional	5	3	5.6
Government employment	6	1	4.9
Law enforcement	3	0	2.1
Blue-collar	3	0	2.1
Farmer	3	0	2.1
Housewife	0	2	1.4
Labor official	1	0	.7
Total	134	8	100.0

the women members. One owns a small retail business (a candy store), two describe themselves as housewives, three were trained as economists, one is in education, and one is a state employee on the Human Rights Commission.

Once again, although lawyers constitute just about a third of the total membership, 55.6 percent of the standing committee chairpersonships are held by them. The remaining committees are chaired by businessmen.

Delegates sitting on the Legislative Council represent law even more heavily, with 60 percent being drawn from that profession. Five of the remaining members are businessmen (33.3 percent), and one is a farmer (6.7 percent). The one black member of this all-male group, interestingly enough, is from one of the dominant occupational groupings—business.

TABLE 11.4. Standing Committee Chairpersons

Occupation	Male	Female	% of Total
Law	5	0	55.6
Business	4	0	44.4
Total	9	0	100.0

As is the case for the women senators, the indication of an occupation or profession does not mean that it is still being pursued. The women are simultaneously holding two careers outside the home in only two cases. The other six women are principally involved in legislative activities and tasks more closely associated with middle-class housewives, that is, household management and community affairs.

If standing committee chairpersonships and appointment to the Legislative Council are used as a measurement of power or influence, and if they are indicative of peers' appreciation of their colleagues

TABLE 11.5. Legislative Council

Occupation	Male	Female	% of Total
Law	9	0	60.0
Business	5	0	33.3
Agriculture	1	0	6.7
Total	15	0	100.0

abilities, then it is quite clear that the women in the House of Delegates are not highly regarded. There is, to be sure, slightly higher esteem shown for women in the Senate; but factors other than feminist sentiments appear to be operating here. The key appears to be occupation rather than length of service or median years of education. Indeed, the median number of years spent in school is slightly higher for women senators and delegates than for men. When occupation is taken as a variable, two patterns seem to emerge. First, a relatively high level of esteem seems to be accorded to both lawyers and businessmen. Second, women (and this would appear to be true for blacks as well) who are involved in these occupations are more likely to enjoy esteem than women who are not.

The numbers of women in the Maryland legislative are so small, of course, that there is great risk in concluding anything much at all. Interviews with the women legislators and a sample of the male legislators, however, would seem to bolster this shaky hypothesis, at least somewhat. When asked which members of the Senate and the House of Delegates were most competent and well qualified, the male legislators named lawyers (60 percent) and businessmen (30 percent) most frequently, and in proportions roughly approximate to the representation of these two occupations on the standing committees and Legislative Council. When a woman was cited, it was almost always the woman lawyer. This would seem to suggest that in the minds of male respondents, certain specific occupations were perceived as preparing one better and providing a level of expertise which fellow legislators viewed as valuable. The same pattern also appeared in the responses to the question, "In your opinion, who are the five most competent and well-qualified members of the House of Delegates?" In the House as well as in the Senate, law and business were the major job categories of those viewed as competent and well qualified.

The women legislators interviewed all discussed an issue closely related to this—the necessity for being extremely well prepared. As one member of the House of Delegates put it, "I have been in the legislature now for eight years and have a reputation for speaking only when I have something to say. That's why I have some influence as a legislator." Another spoke of the amount of time required to study matters coming before the legislature in order to be taken seriously. But perhaps the most telling remark was, "The key is to know what you are talking about before you talk. It's a man's world. You have got to get along with men. You have got to obtain their respect.

Women have to work very hard to be effective." This emphasis on superpreparedness, the consciousness of having to be a kind of superstar, may well represent not only the impact of the societal conditioning of women that implies the necessity of being better, but also an unconscious acknowledgment of skill differential and its significance for being effective.

In "Women and Soviet Politics" Barbara W. Jancar claimed that "the late entry of women into the educational world has handicapped their chances to compete with men for higher positions. Discriminatory educational politics have contributed to that handicap."[5] While the first part of this observation does not accurately reflect the educational background of the female legislators in Maryland, the educational channeling of women away from law and business may, in part, account for the problem that they confront once they are elected, and as will be discussed later in this chapter, may well be important for the roles they play both inside and outside the legislature.

Although within a different context, entry does pose a hurdle for Maryland female legislators. Most of the women have become active in seeking public office in middle life. Several of them moved from activities in the League of Women Voters into more specific partisan involvement, stood for election to Maryland's Constitutional Convention, and then ran for the legislature. Those who have taken this route all complained about the difficulties of entering politics "too late." As one of the women put it, "The prevailing age of women is higher than that of the men. Most women do not run for elective office until their children are older." Another was even more blunt about it. When asked about her feeling about the future of women in politics, she replied, "They should get in at a much earlier age."

Late entry and skill differential may very well be evidence of two important, interrelated aspects of female legislative behavior. The first has to do with roles played by women legislators, the other with judgments about their effectiveness.

In "Changing Patterns of Political Authority: Psychiatric Interpretation," Alexander Mitscherlich discusses in some detail the historical development of patterns of authority and indirectly roles associated with them. Borrowing rather extensively from Max Weber, he identifies them as charismatic and bureaucratic. The forms of charismatic leadership which Mitscherlich sees as persisting are those which emphasize the concept of political leader as "political priest" and is exemplified by Charles de Gaulle, and those rooted in "the stereotype of middle-class paternalism."[6] But the really modern form, he asserts, as others before him have claimed, rests not in these charismatic styles but in the bureaucratic role model. He goes on to say:

> The truly modern form of authority is that of the specialist. The explosive increase of our knowledge has made the specialist irreplaceable. It is fact that knowledge became one of the ideals of our civilization, which had the concomitant effect of intensifying the increase of knowledge. Here the interest of times is focused. Molecular chains have replaced the *summae theologiae* of Thomas Aquinas as proof of knowledge. . . .
>
> Above the *polit-specialist* of our times there are no father figures of the kind against whom the age of Enlightenment stood up. The functionary is, as his name implies, a function of an institution; the institutions themselves are made up by functionaries in action. There is no "meta"—no metapolitics of a kind one can believe in—outside. Historically seen this is perhaps the essential point in the change political authority has undergone.[7]

Literature dealing specifically with legislative role style reflects this same theme. In *The Legislative System: Explorations in Legislative Behavior,* Wahlke, Eulau, et al. develop a typology of representational-role orientations which Eulau designates as trustee, politico, and delegate.[8] The role orientation of trustee comes very close, in many respects, to that of specialist or expert. As Eulau describes it, "the trustee sees himself as a free agent in that, as a premise of his decision making behavior, he claims to follow what he considers right or just, his convictions and principles, the dictates of his conscience."[9] This is not predicated on the charismatic political priest role, however, for it is rooted in the notion of specialized knowledge. As Eulau says, "The trustee is not bound by a mandate because his decisions are his own considered judgment based on an assessment of the facts in each decision, his understanding of all the problems and angles involved, his thoughtful appraisal of all the sides of the issues."[10] He continues, "The trustee may follow his own judgment because he cannot afford to allow himself to be influenced by persons who are committed or ill informed."[11] Delegates, on the other hand, do not accept the notion of independent judgment or principle conviction.[12] In assessing this role orientation the comment is made, "It is a matter of speculation whether the role orientation of delegate is based on a conscious majoritarian bias which he could elaborate and defend, or whether *it simply reflects lack of political articulation and sophistication.*"[13] Politico in this typology represents an overlap of trustee and delegate orientations, where the two roles are taken on simultaneously.[14] In the concluding remarks to his chapter, he takes this position:

> Under modern conditions, the trustee orientation is probably more realistic. Given the complexity of governmental problems, on the one hand, and the finding out what clienteles may want, the delegate orientation is probably the least functional from the point of view of effective representation. In the four states, many more legislators take the role of trustee than the roles of politico or delegate.[15]

While the women legislators indicated in their interviews some preference for trustee and politico role orientations, and while they seem to perceive these roles as more effective, they are undoubtedly more difficult and conflicting ones for women to play. Occupations associated with the development of specialists or experts are simply not those from which the overwhelming majority of Maryland's female legislators are drawn. Instead, their immediate backgrounds cast them in feeling, responsive, reactive roles rather than the thoughtful, detached, rational ones associated with specialist. Since trustee and politico roles require a specialist's undergirding, however, in order to be carried off successfully, most women are unable to move into them with ease, and are forced into the delegate role which Eulau feels is more difficult and conflicted, or into other charismatic role styles.

The relatively late entry of women into elective office only compounds the problem. In the first place, their activities prior to their entry are not viewed by their colleagues as properly preparing the women for their legislative careers. As a consequence, a woman must demonstrate competency to be a legislator also. Since this prerequisite is considered to be met by those being drawn from "professional" occupations, and since women do not usually come from those professions, their legislative apprenticeship is more difficult and protracted. Given the age at which they enter, this is a serious liability. It means, among other things, that they cannot move quickly either as an influential legislator or even an effective legislator.

Closely related to the problem of protracted apprenticeship is the question of political career expectations. Late entry limits the kind of career elective politics which can be anticipated. Some women may reasonably hope to move from the lower chamber to the Senate; but the chances for running for higher office—governor, Congress, mayor, county executive—are very slight. By the time they have distinguished themselves in the legislature, particularly given the peculiar problem of developing prerequisite competency, the women are too old to be considered viable candidates for higher office. Thus, for all but two of the female Maryland legislators, their present office was the highest one they anticipated. While the men interviewed thought of their legislative career as a steppingstone, the women, by and large, did not. They were content to be where they were and had no further political ambitions.

James David Barber argues in *The Lawmakers:*

One does not necessarily move through an apprenticeship as a party worker to some minor office at the local level and on up the ladder to state and national office. A great many national officials have held no previous local or state office. A number of governors have had little or no experience in other offices.[16]

While this is obviously so in general, it is not true for most women. The reason why it is not is clearly related to the fact that the majority of women do not move, as Barber suggests politicians do, from "an occupational role one has held for many years" nor do they break off connections with a regular, recognized occupational role and status, at least in the same sense that a man does when he enters the legislature. She does not because she does not have those connections to start with. Hence, late entry poses an entirely different and much more serious problem for her than it does for a man, as Barber would, I am sure, readily agree.

One final point might be raised here: the level of motivation to obtain compensatory skills after election to the legislature. The women interviewed all exhibited some concern about being prepared, knowing fully the issues involved, and speaking intelligently on matters coming to the floor. This may well indicate a preoccupation with acquiring and demonstrating prerequisite skills. However, the motivation and/or desire to move beyond these does not emerge very strongly. One might speculate that the implications of late entry for running for higher office and considered essentially unprepared for a legislative career do not inspire these women, on the whole, to be effective in the ordinary sense of that term. It may well be that their perception of a reasonable payoff is simply accepted by their peers. In other words, they are, like the spectators Barber describes, basically other-directed in their patterns of behavior in the legislature, even if not for the same reasons or in the same context he suggests. At the same time, the women do not seek the same broad community support as their male colleagues do, because they do not need it. They are not concerned with building the reputation that will allow them to run for higher office because their chances for success are so slim.

If women in the Maryland legislature are, for the most part, not able to move into the bureaucratic role model, are they the spectators Barber indicates them to be? The answer to that seems to be both yes and no. The spectator portrayed by Barber is low in activity, high in willingness to return. General legislative style is characterized as watching, being entertained; and background and expectations depicted as typically a middle-aged lower-status housewife of modest achievements, limited skills, and restricted ambitions. Further traits include little sense of individuality and other directedness, enjoying the drama and color but especially sensitive to approval and disapproval.[17] Some of these descriptions apply to the women legislators discussed here. Moreover, they are more accurate for them than for the men interviewed. At the same time, this concept does not seem to take into account certain aspects of the women's behavior. The issues which the women cited as important to them—their concern with the passage of legislation in the general area of social welfare, their generally positive orientation to equal rights for women and to at least some aspects of women's liberation, their perceptions of sex discrimination, and their view of their role both within the legislature and in their own communities which they defined as serving as a role model and as sensitizing others to social concerns—do not seem to jibe with the passivity attributed to spectators. Indeed, such a category seems to distort as well as to fail to come to grips with underlying issues.

If spectator is not satisfactory as a category for Maryland's female legislators, and the bureaucratic role model is virtually foreclosed to them because of skill differential problems, what role orientations and styles are open to them? Eulau's delegate role is clearly available. It is certainly consistent with the feeling, responsive, reactive role with which the nonspecialist is so often associated, and is also closely linked with societal notions about the feminine nature.

Once again, however, the category does not fully or adequately convey the role perceptions of the women interviewed. There does not appear to be an overwhelming concern on the part of the women to consult with their constituents in order to take action on legislation, or any clearly and sharply focused commitment to mirror accurately the sentiments of the electors, or even to be bound by popular mandate. One of the responses quoted by Eulau, "What the district wants me to do is my most important job. I carry out their decisions," is simply not reflected in the Maryland interviews. Commitments to legislation for the aged, against child abuse, etc., are too strong to fit the delegate conception completely.

The role orientation and style of the women seems rather to be a somewhat charismatic one which fuses a transmutation of middle-class paternalism into a middle-class maternalism and political priest in the form of an inspired cry for justice for at least the aged, women, and children. Its operational style is agitational—very low profile, to be sure—but nonetheless agitational. All the women speak of talking to the other legislators, convincing them of the merits of particular issues, and going back to their own communities addressing groups to let them know what is going on, to educate them, to serve as a role model. These things seem to be extremely important to the women, are repeated again and again and elaborated even when the questions are not directly pertinent or call only for a short response. The male legislators interviewed, even in their negative assessments, seemed to confirm this role orientation of the women.

If the agitational style and charismatic role orientation correctly interpret the behavior of women legislators, or if aspects of the delegate and spectator roles characterize their legislative activities, or if, and this seems more accurate still, they overlap, the implications for assessing the effectiveness of female legislators are great indeed. First, it means that if traditional criteria are used to determine effectiveness—such as the number of bills passed—women will appear rather ineffectual. That in combination with their activities outside the legislature can be viewed only as an inefficient use of time and energy. In other words, they can be described only as "typically middle-aged, lower-status housewives of modest achievement."

Such an assessment, of course, fails to comprehend the different conception of role which these women see themselves as playing. Consequently, a more accurate evaluation of their performance is impossible. Needless to say, it neither takes into account other activities which may be important, nor deals with the reasons why minorities such as women may have to supplement the more traditional legislative activities.

Second, the skill differential precludes most women in the Maryland legislature from playing a bureaucratic or specialist role and therefore leaves them little alternative but to move into some charismatic role that is not only more old-fashioned, or less modern, but also not very highly regarded. Although the women did not discuss this issue, and no questions were asked about it, one may speculate that they are aware of the pitfalls of charismatic role styles and seek to play, albeit weakly, a more specialist role by carving out for themselves areas of self-proclaimed expertise—matters concerning women, the family, children, the aged, etc. But even here, the legal terms in which these concerns are couched in the legislature mean that their expertise is limited. Thus the women find themselves facing a serious dilemma. They understand, to some extent at least, that the bureaucratic role style carries with it more prestige and recognition, but the prerequisites for playing it force them into other, less effective role styles.

The net effect of this is that women desire to run for and get themselves elected to public office. They achieve this objective too late, however, and without the "specialist" training that permits them to entertain further political ambition. The low status they enjoy because of their prior occupations limits them in their activities in the legislature once they get there, and forces them into somewhat dysfunctional role orientations and styles. Their compensatory activity both in obtaining "expertise" in the legislature in order to accomplish their goals and objectives, and their work outside the legislature in the community at large, are taken as indicators of their ineffectiveness and inefficiency. This in turn traps them more and more into those styles and roles that further diminish their prestige. In other words, the women find themselves in a vicious circle from which there appears to be little escape.

As pointed out at the beginning of this paper, Maryland is in many ways not a typical state. Patterns of behavior, role styles, orientations, and the like, may, in fact, be peculiar to this state. They are, however, interesting enough to warrant further investigation in other states to see if similar patterns exist elsewhere.

Even if Maryland's women legislators are unique in their patterns of behavior, serious questions must be raised about present modes of analysis and research trends. More important is the development of alternatives that will allow at least Maryland women legislators to function more effectively or be evaluated differently. One alternative is, of course, to upgrade the training of the women entering the legislature. A more reasonable, realistic, and just alternative may be to move away from analyses that distort or are insensitive to the roles which minorities such as women find themselves in today. Perhaps this will happen naturally as more and more women enter legislatures, and as political scientists turn their attention to the behavior of groups such as women. It may well be, though, that we must turn our attention to the more fundamental issue of specialism and expertise. Quite frankly, the latter course seems more promising and more significant.

NOTES

1. Emmy E. Werner and Louise Bachtold, "Personality Characteristics of Women in American Politics," in *Women in Politics*, ed. Jane Jaquette (New York: Wiley, 1974); Emmy Werner, "Women in State Legislatures," *Western Political Quarterly* 21 (1968): 40–50.

2. Marie Rosenberg, "Political Efficacy and Sex Roles: Congresswomen Hansen and Green" (Paper presented to the 1972 Annual Meeting of the American Political Science Association, Washington, D.C., September 1972).

3. All data here and following are compiled from *Manual State of Maryland 1972–1973* (Baltimore: Twentieth Century Printing, 1973).

4. The attorney general of Maryland has ruled that state and local government employees are ineligible to draw two salaries from the state (hold two offices of public trust) and must, therefore, resign their second job if they wish to remain in the Legislature. This has been challenged as discriminatory. If the original ruling holds, however, these legislators will have to find other employment or resign their seats.

5. Barbara W. Jancar, "Women and Soviet Politics" (Paper presented at the Annual Meeting of the American Political Science Association, Washington, D.C., September 1972).

6. Alexander Mitscherlich, "Changing Patterns of Political Authority: A Psychiatric Interpretation," in *Political Leadership in Industrialized Societies: Studies in Comparative Analysis*, ed. Lewis J. Edinger (New York: Wiley, 1967), pp. 28–29.

7. Ibid., pp. 33–34.

8. John Wahlke, Heinz Eulau, William Buchanan, and Leroy C. Ferguson, *The Legislative System: Explorations in Legislative Behavior* (New York: Wiley, 1962), p. 267 ff.

9. Ibid., p. 272.

10. Ibid., p. 273.

11. Ibid., p. 274.

12. Ibid., p. 276.

13. Ibid., p. 277. Emphasis added.

14. Ibid., p. 278.

15. Ibid., p. 286.

16. James David Barber, *The Lawmakers: Recruitment and Adaptation to Legislative Life* (New Haven: Yale University Press, 1965), p. 223.

17. Ibid., p. 214.

CHARLES S. BULLOCK III and PATRICIA
LEE FINDLEY HEYS

12

☆☆☆☆☆☆☆☆☆☆☆☆☆☆☆☆☆☆☆☆☆☆☆☆☆☆☆,

Recruitment of Women for Congress: A Research Note

While the vast majority of congressmen arrive on Capitol Hill having survived a November general election, this path is followed by only a plurality (45 percent) of all congresswomen. Almost as many congresswomen (41 percent) come to fill vacancies created by the deaths of their husbands. The remaining congresswomen fill mid-term vacancies but are not widows of the previous incumbents.

The intensity, duration, and direction of the political ambitions of the widows and women chosen in November general elections (referred to hereafter as "regularly elected") seem to differ. While Joseph Schlesinger is no doubt correct in saying, "No man [or woman] is likely to obtain a major political office unless he wants it,"[1] the aspirations of widows have lain dormant until the demise of their husbands. The regularly elected, their opportunities not blocked by an officeholding spouse, can launch a campaign for Congress whenever they judge conditions to be favorable.[2] Widows, on the other hand, have assets not usually possessed by aspiring congresswomen, resulting in advantages typically accruing only to incumbents. They benefit from greater voter recognition of their names and from the goodwill nurtured by their husbands. Moreover, widows may get some sym-

210

pathy votes. Other congresswomen, lacking the above attributes, must rely more on their own appeal and initiative to win office.

Since the method by which a regularly elected woman achieves her seat seems more indicative of a professional, long-term commitment to politics, recruitment is expected to be associated with background variables and congressional career patterns. The regularly elected will, we suspect, have often followed careers similar to those pursued by many males in Congress. Thus the regularly elected should generally be well educated, have occupational experience outside the home, and frequently have been politically active prior to entering Congress. Widows, in contrast, are expected to have backgrounds in which factors indicative of political aspirations are less evident. It is suspected that they will have less formal education, more often have been housewives, and have had less political experience than regularly elected congresswomen. The third category, women chosen to fill interim vacancies but who were not widows, has too few cases (11) to permit analysis and is excluded after the discussion of recruitment.

If the backgrounds of the regularly elected include prelegislative experiences typical of congressmen, their subsequent behavior may also more closely approximate that of the latter than should the pattern followed by widows. Specifically, more of the regularly elected are expected to demonstrate interest in a congressional career. This assumption will be tested by comparing reelection rates and norm adherence for the regularly elected and widows.

RECRUITMENT

Between 1917 and 1970, sixty-seven women sat in the House and ten in the Senate. Six of the women were appointed to the Senate, while all the others arrived on Capitol Hill after being scrutinized by the electorate. Of the ten female senators, nine, including four widows, filled mid-term vacancies. The one regularly elected senator, Margaret Chase Smith (R.-Me.), had earlier completed the House term of her late husband and therefore will be treated as a widow in this paper. Of the female senators, only four were elected and two of these won their husbands' seats. In contrast, 52 percent of the women in the House were regularly elected.

The disproportionate number of women coming to the Senate in mid-term bespeaks the greater difficulty a woman faces in reaching the upper chamber. Further evidence is the showing that most women in the Senate were tapped for honorific reasons, their tenure being measured in months and in the case of the first female senator, Rebecca Felton (D.-Ga.), days.[3]

SOCIAL AND POLITICAL BACKGROUND

Congressmen typically are well educated and pursue high-status occupations.[4] Women, in general, are less educated and less likely than men to have careers outside the home. Hypothesizing that the regularly elected have backgrounds more similar to congressmen than do widows, we expect that the former are better educated and more often career women than the latter.

As shown in table 12.1, while congresswomen were typically well educated, the regularly elected had more schooling than widows, with more than 80 percent of the former, compared with 68 percent of the latter, being college graduates.[5] Moreover, while only one widow pursued her education beyond the baccalaureate degree, 34 percent of those regularly elected had advanced training: they divided evenly between those who went to law school and those who entered graduate programs.

The greater formal education of the regularly elected frequently prepared them for professional careers. Conversely, congresswomen who succeeded their husbands were more likely to list housewife as their vocation. Widows, being married to successful men, had little economic incentive to work; and their social status, at least until re-

TABLE 12.1. Level of Education for Congresswomen, 1917–70

	Regularly Elected	Widows
Did not attend college	14%	23%
Attended college	83	68
Unknown and other	3	10
	100%	101%[a]
Graduate study	17%	3%
Law school	17	0
	N = 35	N = 31

[a]Error due to rounding.

cently, militated against their taking jobs. The almost universal job-holding among the regularly elected may be indicative of ambitions and a willingness to deviate from conventional feminine roles, which culminated in a congressional seat.

Table 12.2 shows that the regularly elected came most often from education and law, while education was the only career frequently entered by widows. Public school teaching is often considered a feminine career, and it is not surprising that many congresswomen had experience in this field. Law, however, is overwhelmingly male-dominated and is the vocation of a majority of all congressmen.[6] That a fifth of the regularly elected had legal experience buttresses the assumption that these women more often entertained political ambitions.[7]

In addition to being more experienced educationally and professionally the regularly elected had also been more politically involved than widows. Aspirants for high public office may invest time in party activities or hold various elective positions during their apprenticeships. As anticipated, the regularly elected were more likely (57 percent) to have a history of party work (see table 12.3). Widows, while they probably participated in their husbands' campaigns, infrequently (14 percent) listed party activities in their biographies.

TABLE 12.2. Occupations of Congresswomen, 1917–70, and All Freshmen in the House of Representatives, 1947–67

	Regularly Elected	Widows	All Freshmen[a] 1947–1967
Education	37%	21%	8%
Law	20	0	53
Journalism	11	11	5
Business	11	7	31
Agriculture	14	4	9
Other	11	14	11
Housewife	11	50	—
	115%[b]	107%[b]	117%[b]
	N = 35	N = 28[c]	N = 854

[a]Source: Charles S. Bullock III, "The Committee Assignments of Freshmen in the House of Representatives, 1947–1967" (Ph.D. Dissertation, Washington University, St. Louis).

[b]Totals equal more than 100 percent because some members listed more than one occupation.

[c]Data unavailable for three widows.

TABLE 12.3. Political Party Activity for Congresswomen,
1917–70

Level of Activity	Regularly Elected	Widows
Local	3%	0%
State	3	7
National	20	7
More than one level	31	0
Active in party	57%	14%
No party activities cited	43%	86%
	100%	100%
	N = 35	N = 28[a]

[a] Data unavailable for three widows.

Not only were more of the regularly elected active in their party, their participation seems often to have been fairly visible. Approximately a third of this group had worked at more than one political level and another 20 percent had been national committee women and/or delegates to national party conventions. Experience in these capacities intimates their political interest and capabilities. Moreover, through their party work they undoubtedly made contacts and alliances which facilitated their election.

Another type of political apprenticeship for Congress is holding state or local public office.[8] As with party activity, the regularly elected were more likely to have experience in this realm. Data in table 12.4 show that 69 percent of the regularly elected but only a tenth of the widows held public office before entering Congress. Those winning regular elections had most frequently used local office as a steppingstone, although some had served in a state legislature and/or held a variety of other state offices. Regularly elected women had had more experience in elective positions generally, with 57 percent having won some office prior to their congressional victories, in contrast to a mere 3 percent of the widows. Past electoral campaigns were probably particularly useful in developing voter identification and in learning campaign techniques.

Comparing the extent of precongressional political activity of the regularly elected with that of all freshmen in the House during the 80th through 90th Congresses provides a perspective on the more exacting prerequisites confronting women. Sixty-nine percent of the regularly elected, contrasted with 59 percent of all freshmen, had

TABLE 12.4. Public Officeholding Experience for Congress-women, 1917–70

Office Held	Regularly Elected	Widows
State legislature	26%	3%
Local office	34	0
State office other than legislature	20	3
Federal office	9	3
Officeholding experience	69%[a]	10%[b]
No previous officeholding	31	90
	100%	100%
Held elective office	57%	3%
	N = 35	N = 28[c]

[a]Some women had held offices in two or more categories.
[b]Rounding error.
[c]Data unavailable for three widows.

held public office before going to Congress. Also, 57 percent of the regularly elected women, but only 21 percent of all freshmen, listed party activities.[9] These data suggest that political experience is more crucial for women than men who wish to be elected to Congress. Men seem more often able to move laterally to a congressional seat after achieving success in nonpolitical careers.

CONGRESSIONAL ACTIVITIES

Having shown several differences in the backgrounds of widows and the regularly elected, we will briefly discuss whether the latter more frequently give evidence of an intention to make a career of congressional service than do widows. The two sets of women are compared on how frequently they offered for reelection and the length of their tenures.

The regularly elected were, as expected, far more likely to offer for reelection. Ninety-seven percent of these women displayed static ambitions, seeking second terms. In contrast, discrete ambitions were predominant among widows, 55 percent of whom retired upon completing their husbands' terms.[10] So limited have been the aspirations of some widows that they have announced their intentions not to seek reelection even before being selected to fill the vacancy. Recently, for example, Irene Baker (R.-Tenn.) was induced by local Republican leaders to seek her husband's seat as an interim replacement to prevent factional warfare.[11] Widows who often lack extensive political experience may find the work of Congress confusing and tedious, prompting them to retire. For the regularly elected, congressional service may be the culmination of long held ambitions and may prove quite rewarding.

Age does not seem to be the crucial factor in explaining differences in the frequency with which the two sets of women sought reelection. While widows were, on the average, somewhat older upon coming to Congress—a difference of 5.2 years exists between the sets—they were not too old (mean age of 52) to seek second terms if they desired to do so.[12]

The frequency with which women seek sophomore terms is a snapshot of ambition at a single point in time. Length of tenure provides an elongated view of both ambition and political skill. Table 12.5 shows that, contrary to expectations, the mean tenure of widows and regularly elected is approximately the same. The mean tenure for widows is skewed by the extended careers of Frances Bolton (R.-Ohio) and Edith Rogers (R.-Mass.) who served 15 and 17 terms respectively in the House, and Margaret Chase Smith who has been in Congress since 1940. As other data in table 12.5 show, these women are atypical of widows, for whom the median tenure is one term. Also of interest are figures showing that while a fourth of the regularly elected were one-term congresswomen, 61 percent of the widows served that briefly. Differences in reelection rates seem to be primarily a product of ambition. When only women who offered for reelection are compared, the regularly elected are only slightly more successful than

TABLE 12.5. Length of Congressional Tenure for Congresswomen, Measured in Terms,[a] 1917–70

	Regularly Elected	Widows
Mean	3.3	3.4
Range	1–13	1–17
Median	3	1
One term	25.7%	61.3%
	N = 35	N = 31

[a]A term is any part of a two-year Congress, with the exception of women who were simultaneously elected to the remainder of a vacant term and a full two-year or six-year term. To make House and Senate service comparable, six-year Senate incumbencies are treated as three two-year-terms.

widows: 77 percent of the former and 71 percent of the latter who sought second terms won.

The rate of reelection victories for congresswomen is, however, below that for all House members. During the 1950s and 1960s more than 90 percent of the incumbents seeking reelection were returned.[13] Among freshmen, 81 percent of those first elected between 1946 and 1966 triumphed in general election bids for sophomore terms.[14] The slightly lower success rate for first-term women may be further evidence of prejudices against women entering politics.

Since static ambitions were much more prevalent among regularly elected than widows, it was hypothesized that the former would be more receptive to learning congressional norms. One norm, which Matthews refers to as "work horse versus show horse," is that legislators should work diligently at their jobs, attending chamber and committee hearings in order to learn through observation and to share the less glamorous chores.[15] Acquiring the esteem of fellow members which is accorded those who faithfully attend to the routine tasks of Congress would seem more likely to be a goal of the regularly elected than of widows who so often spend less than a term in Congress. Adherence to this norm may be evidenced by frequency of participation on recorded votes.[16]

A second norm is that one should be a loyal party member.[17] The woman who has long aspired to serve in Congress and who intends to remain there might be more responsive to the requests of party leaders in hopes of winning their support, confidence, and the rewards they dispense. This consideration was popularized by the late Speaker Sam Rayburn who advised freshmen, "You have to go along to get along." Therefore it is postulated that the regularly elected more often vote with the majority of their party than do widows.

Data on first-term women since 1947 reveal only slight differences between regularly elected and widows in either roll-call participation or party-unity scores (see table 12.6). The absence of striking differences cannot be readily explained. There is research which shows that freshmen tend to be more loyal to their party than do more senior members. Davidson found that 70 percent of the freshmen he interviewed were loyalists or superloyalists, compared with 64 percent of those having two to five terms in the House and 48 percent of those with at least six terms' seniority. At the other end of the scale a third of the most senior, a sixth of the intermediate group, but none of the freshmen were party mavericks.[18] First termers, regardless of other factors, may be drawn to vote with the party leadership either in re-

218 ☆ BULLOCK AND HEYS

TABLE 12.6. Mean First-Term Scores on Two Voting Indices for Congresswomen, 1947–70

	Regularly Elected	Widows
Voting Participation		
Answered roll call	84.3%	80.1%
Party Unity		
Party support	79.3%	80.1%
	N = 21	N = 14

Source: Congressional Quarterly.

turn for the assistance provided by the leadership in finding staff, getting assignments, and otherwise adjusting to the life of a congresswoman, or because no other cue-giver has greater credibility.[19] This could explain why the groups display similar levels of party loyalty.

A second consideration with possible relevance for findings on both norms can be deduced from Ralph Huitt's analysis of Senator William Proxmire. From this case study, Huitt suggests that a legislator may purposefully opt for the role of an outsider. If this is so, it may be that those who choose to ignore the norms do so, like Proxmire, after having served a year or more in the chamber. If, as Huitt suggests, new members typically adhere to the norms, it is not surprising that no differences are observed between the sets of women during their first term.[20]

SUMMARY

As anticipated, congresswomen who win regular elections had background characteristics different from those of widows. The former were more similar to males in Congress than were the latter in terms of education, occupation, and political activities. Indeed, women winning regular elections more frequently had officeholding and party work experience than did first-term congressmen. While, unlike congressmen, the law was not the most frequent occupation among regularly elected congresswomen, 20 percent of the regularly elected but none of the widows were attorneys. Unlike the widows, regularly elected congresswomen tended not to be housewives and were somewhat better educated. Thus, on the criteria considered, the regularly elected more often had backgrounds similar to congressmen than did widows. The expectation that the regularly elected were more likely than widows to see Congress as a career was substantiated by the greater frequency with which the former sought reelection. Although three widows have served a composite of 94 years in Congress, widows generally were less likely to remain in Congress more than a single term. Differences in the two groups did not, however, extend to norm observance. Widows, even though less interested in remaining in Congress, participated almost as frequently on roll calls as did regularly elected women. The two groups were almost identical in their party loyalty.

NOTES

1. Joseph A. Schlesinger, *Ambition and Politics* (Chicago: Rand McNally, 1966), p. 4.

2. Husbands may be a limiting factor on the careers of the regularly elected. For example, Cora Knutson (D.-Minn.) lost a bid for a third term after her husband publicly appealed for her defeat so that she could return home.

3. Seven of the women senators served less than a year; five served less than half a year. Only Hattie Caraway (D.-Ark., 1931–46), Maureen Neuberger (D.-Ore., 1960–67), and Margaret Chase Smith (R.-Me., 1949–present) served full terms.

4. For a treatment of background characteristics of congresswomen, see Emmy E. Werner, "Women in Congress: 1917–1964," *Western Political Quarterly* 19 (March 1966): 16–30. Other sources of background are: Donald R. Matthews, *U.S. Senators and Their World* (New York: Vantage, 1960), pp. 11–67; Donald R. Matthews, *The Social Background of Political Decision-Makers* (Garden City, N.Y.: Doubleday, 1954); Roger H. Davidson, *The Role of the Congressman* (New York: Pegasus, 1969), pp. 34–59.

5. Biographical material was collected from various volumes of *Congressional Directory* (Washington, D.C., Government Printing Office), issues of *Congressional Quarterly Weekly Reports*, and the *Biographical Directory of the American Congress, 1776–1961* (Washington, D.C.: Government Printing Office, 1961).

6. In the 91st Congress, for example, 58 percent of the members were lawyers. *Congressional Quarterly Weekly Report,* 3 January 1969, p. 46.

7. The relationship between the legal profession and politics is dealt with in Heinz Eulau and John Sprague, *Lawyers in Politics* (Indianapolis: Bobbs-Merrill, 1964), and Joseph A. Schlesinger, "Lawyers and American Politics: A Clarified View," *Midwest Journal of Political Science* 1 (May 1957): 26–39, to cite two of the better works.

8. For a precise presentation of the officeholding career patterns of senators, see Schlesinger, *Ambition and Politics,* pp. 89–118. See also Matthews, *U.S. Senators,* pp. 50–58; and Davidson, *Role of the Congressman,* pp. 48–54.

9. Data on freshmen taken from Charles S. Bullock III, "The Committee Assignments of Freshmen in the House of Representatives, 1947–1967" (Ph.D. dissertation, Washington University, St. Louis, 1968). Bullock relied on publicly available sources for his data, as does this research note.

10. For a discussion of types of ambition, see Schlesinger, *Ambition and Politics,* p. 10.

11. *Congressional Quarterly Weekly Report,* 13 March 1962, p. 501.

12. By comparison, the mean age of the freshmen of the 91st Congress in the House was 47.6 and in the Senate 46.6. *Congressional Quarterly Weekly Report,* 3 January 1969, p. 44.

13. Charles O. Jones, *Every Second Year* (Washington, D.C.: Brookings, 1967), p. 68; Charles O. Jones, "The Role of the Campaign in Congressional Politics," in *The Electoral Process,* ed. M. Kent Jennings and L. Harman Zeigler (Englewood Cliffs, N.J.: Prentice-Hall, 1966), p. 24; Barbara Hinckley, "Seniority in the Committee Leadership of Congress," *Midwest Journal of Political Science* 13 (November 1969): 620.

14. Figures computed from Charles S. Bullock III, "Freshmen Committee Assignments and Re-election in the United States House of Representatives," *American Political Science Review* (September 1972).

15. Donald R. Matthews, *U.S. Senators,* pp. 94–95; Malcom E. Jewell and Samuel C. Patterson, *The Legislative Process in the United States* (New York: Random House, 1966), pp. 368–69.

16. Roll-call data were taken from the appropriate volumes of the *Congressional Quarterly Almanac.*

17. Charles L. Clapp, *The Congressman: His Work As He Sees It* (Garden City, N.Y.: Anchor Doubleday, 1964), pp. 354–56.

18. Davidson, *Role of the Congressman,* p. 152.

19. See ibid., pp. 152–53, and the sources he cites.

20. Ralph K. Huitt, "The Outsider in the Senate: An Alternative Role," *American Political Science Review* 55 (September 1961): 566–75, reprinted in *Congress: Two Decades on Analysis,* ed. Ralph Huitt and Robert L. Peabody (New York: Harper & Row, 1969), pp. 165–75.

EDMOND COSTANTINI and KENNETH H.
CRAIK

13

☆☆☆☆☆☆☆☆☆☆☆☆☆☆☆☆☆☆☆☆☆☆☆☆☆☆☆☆

Women as Politicians: The Social Background, Personality, and Political Careers of Female Party Leaders*

Women attaining high levels of political party leadership in California are the focus of this interdisciplinary study of personality and politics. The energies of female politicians tend to be directed toward a career within the political party. Compared to male leaders, they less often fashion a political career around the goal of public office and a political career serves less frequently as an integral part of a broad social career. Female leaders tend to express the forceful, effective, and socially ascendant style in an earnest, sobersided, and ambivalent manner; male leaders express the same personal style in a more easygoing, direct, and un-

*We would like to express our appreciation to the Institute of Governmental Studies and the Institute of Personality Assessment and Research, both of the University of California at Berkeley, for their generous support of this study and of the larger study of party leadership in California of which this is a part.

complicated way. The interplay among personality, sex-role typing, and political career is discussed.

In his work on the political role of women, Maurice Duverger [11]* commented that "women . . . have the mentality of minors in many fields, and, particularly in politics, they will accept paternalism on the part of men. The man—husband, fiance, lover, or myth—is the mediator between them and the political world" (p. 129). Stripped of its male chauvinism, Duverger's statement highlights what has become a virtual truism regarding women and politics. The political behavior literature is replete with evidence that at all levels of political action from discussing politics to voting, to political letter writing, to holding party or public office, women participate less than men. They appear to be less interested in politics, to belong to fewer organizations, to be less informed politically, and to display a lower sense of political involvement and political efficacy [7, 5, 11, 22, 1, 25, 6, 31, 4, 14, 33]. To one degree or another, women have tended to defer to the political judgment of men, in this country and elsewhere; sex roles have been so defined that politics is primarily the business of men.

There are other issues regarding women in politics besides their relatively low rates of political activity. When they do engage in politics, their pattern of political behavior is apparently not identical to that of male participants. Research suggests that women voters are more provincial (in the sense of focusing upon local issues), more conservative in their stance on policy issues, more responsive to issues with moral overtones, more likely to personalize politics and to be more sensitive to the personality of politicians, less sophisticated in level of concept formation, and less comfortable with political conflict and contention [1, 20, 7, 8, 27, 13, 29, 14, 22].

Moreover, despite aggregate sex differences in degrees of politicization and the pervasive social forces reflected in the relatively low level of participation of women, some women do enter the ranks of political leadership. The present study is concerned with women who have achieved leadership status within the political parties of a single (but highly significant) state. It seeks to advance understanding of "what it takes" in terms of background and personality for women to make their way in party politics, and to identify the distinctive roles, if any, female political leaders may play in present-day political life. More generally, the empirical study of female political leaders should

*Numbers in brackets refer to numbered references at the end of the chapter.

contribute to the increasing knowledge about outstandingly effective women engaged in diverse fields of endeavor. (Among studies of personality, Helson's [15–19] work on effective women is particularly notable.)

THE SAMPLE

The data on which the present study is based derive from questionnaires and other procedures designed for self-administration which were submitted to a wide range of party leaders in California. Over one thousand persons occupying the following positions within this major political system were invited to participate: legislators (congressmen and state legislators) holding office in 1965; members of the state's delegations (delegates and alternates) to the Republican and Democratic National Conventions of 1960 and 1964; members of the delegation slate (delegates and alternates) pledged to Nelson Rockefeller that narrowly lost to the Goldwater slate in California's 1964 presidential primary; and 1964 county committee chairmen of the two major parties. Transmission and receipt of research materials occurred by mail during the period between August 1964 and March 1965.

Over 50 percent of the political leaders meeting one or more of the criteria completed and returned the research instruments, including 264 (51 percent) of the Republicans and 282 (53 percent) of the Democrats. On four indices of representativeness for which information is available on both our sample and the research population—i.e., party affiliation, delegate versus alternate status on the delegations considered, geographic region (southern versus northern California), and sex—there is no evidence of significant sample bias. Ninety-seven respondents (18 percent) were women, including 46 Republicans (17 percent of the Republican sample) and 51 Democrats (18 percent of the Democratic sample).

SOCIAL BACKGROUND

Studies of political elites have regularly found an overrepresentation of persons of relatively high socioeconomic status. The present data are consistent with such findings: both male and female party leaders in California report large incomes and high educational attainments. These data also indicate significant class differences between the sexes at the leadership level.

It might well be expected that female leaders would be higher in social-class terms than male leaders. It is only at the higher socioeconomic levels that women achieve levles of political interest and involvement commensurate with those of men and where more traditional sex-role definitions have lost much of their significance; the greater personal resources afforded by higher income and educational attainment might be thought necessary if the woman is to overcome the barriers presumably created by sex-role typing in our society [7, 2, 31, 1]. However, such an expectation is not supported by the present data; indeed, the opposite relationship obtains. The male leaders are significantly better educated than the female leaders. For example, 72 percent of the males had completed college compared to 51 percent of the females, and 43 percent of the males had earned graduate or professional degrees compared to 12 percent of the females. Similarly, male leaders report significantly higher annual family incomes than their female counterparts: 19 percent of the men and 10 percent of the women had family incomes of over $50,000, while 37 percent of the men compared to 56 percent of the women had family incomes of under $20,000. The median family income of male respondents was $25,000, while the median family income of female respondents was $18,750. The direction of education and income differences between the sexes is the same for respondents from both parties.

Rather than reflecting compensatory factors, these findings may simply demonstrate that party elites are fairly representative of the differential socioeconomic opportunities and attainments of men and women in contemporary society. Additionally, an explanation of similar sex differences in class achievement among the Michigan delegates to the 1964 national party conventions offered by Jennings and Thomas [21] may be relevant: upper-class women who do participate in public affairs are more likely than men at the same socioeconomic level to prefer nonpartisan activities and organizations. In any event, the present data suggest that women party leaders—probably already handicapped by being engaged in an activity considered properly the domain of men—operate in politics with whatever disadvantages accompany relatively lower class achievement.

The question arises whether these women politicians differ from their male counterparts in ascribed social attributes—social background variables such as ethnicity, social origin, religion, and age, which the individual is virtually powerless to change—in the same way that they differ in the achieved social attributes of education and income.

The present data suggest that the relatively lower-class position of female political leaders may be somewhat balanced by ascribed social attributes which tend to be preferred according to societal standards. In both parties, women leaders are less likely than men to be affiliated with non-Protestant religious denominations: 8 percent of the female Republican respondents are either Catholic or Jewish, compared to 21 percent of the male Republicans: 29 percent of the female Democratic respondents are either Catholic or Jewish, compared to 43 percent of the male Democrats. Similarly, the women leaders are more likely than the male leaders to come from old-American stock: 49 percent of the Republican women are third generation or of even more distant foreign ancestry, compared to 44 percent of the Republican men; the comparable figures for Democratic women and men are 42 percent and 35 percent respectively. Such differences suggest the kinds of attributes which, in the absence of superior class status, may help some women overcome the handicaps of their sex in achieving party leadership. At the same time, these differences may be attributable to a greater persistence of traditional sex roles among Catholics, Jews, and those of more recent immigrant stock, with women from these groups being less likely than men to be interested in engaging in partisan political activity.

A similar conclusion may be reached from data on the social origins of our respondents. While the male political leader has apparently achieved a higher class status than the female leader, the reverse is true of his parents. In terms of class origins, in contrast to class achievement, it is the woman leader who is more likely to have come from those economic strata where traditional sex-role prescriptions are probably less operative. Thus, the educational attainment of the respondent's most educated parent is substantially higher in the sample of female leaders: 27 percent of the male respondents had a parent who completed college, compared to 43 percent of the female respondents; twice as many female (21 percent) as male (10 percent) respondents had at least one parent who had earned a graduate degree. Sex differences in parental education are significant for both parties' respondents. Similarly, the male leaders are more likely than the female leaders to have risen in class status during their lifetime; a significantly larger percentage of male leaders in both parties report that their present economic status is higher than was that of their parents when they were growing up.

That the female leaders' parents had significantly higher socioeconomic status than those of the male leaders, were of older-American stock, and presumably held less tradition-bound religious affiliations indicates the kind of family background which may have served to attenuate traditional sex-role typing among the female respondents. Since traditional political sex roles are most likely to be uprooted among the young [7], it would also be reasonable to expect the women leaders in our sample to be younger than the men. Again, this is not the case: Age differences by sex are inconsistent between the parties and are not significant for either [21]. It may well be that younger women, while relatively free of vestigial notions regarding the impropriety of members of their sex engaging in political activity, face special handicaps which make such activity difficult and which cancel out their comparatively greater psychological freedom to become involved. One such handicap would be the responsibility of childrearing and establishing a home, an explanation often offered for lower voting turnout among women. Another such handicap may be imposed by the men who dominate the political leadership stratum: For the woman to assume elite status in the parties she may be required to serve a longer period of apprenticeship than the similarly motivated male.

PERSONALITY CHARACTERISTICS

Systematic research into the personality attributes of political leaders has lagged well behind research into their social background. Standard procedures of contemporary personality assessment used by psychologists have rarely been employed in the empirical study of practicing politicians. The present research has employed one such procedure, the Gough-Heilbrun personality scales of the Adjective Check List (ACL). Each respondent was asked to describe himself by reading through a list of 300 adjectives commonly used in everyday life to describe persons and checking those terms which he considered self-descriptive. The ACL yields a rich fund of personological data and has already demonstrated its value in studies of highly effective persons in fields of endeavor other than politics [23, 3, 17]. Standard scores for each individual are computed on 24 established scales of the ACL, each composed of a cluster of adjectives having psychological significance when analyzed as a unit. A scale score indicates the individual's standing on that personality dimension, relative to general population norms. Thus, the use of this assessment instrument permits us to address the questions: what kinds of persons are female political leaders and what are their salient personality characteristics?

Table 13.1 presents the mean standard scores on the 24 ACL scales for the total samples of female and male leaders, as well as the mean scores for each party's respondents. To the extent that a scale score deviates from fifty, it deviates from general population norms for that scale among persons of the same sex.

Female Political Leaders

The female political leaders in both parties attain their highest mean scores on Self-Confidence, Dominance, Achievement, Number of Favorable Adjectives Checked, and Counseling Readiness. The titles of these scales, and the psychological dimensions underlying them, may suggest the broad personological implications of this pattern of scores. Its interpretation is further advanced by reference to the ACL Manual's concise sketches of the typical dispositions and personal styles characteristic of high (female) scorers on each scale. It is important to underline that fact that these sketches were formulated prior to this study, on the basis of previous empirical research findings, and are entirely independent of its data.

> SELF-CONFIDENCE: She is assertive, affiliative, outgoing, persistent, an actionist. She wants to get things done, and is impatient with people or things standing in her way. She is concerned about creating a good impression and is not above cutting a few corners to achieve this objective. She makes a distinct impression on others, who see her as forceful, self-confident, determined, ambitious, and opportunistic.

> DOMINANCE: She is a forceful, strong-willed and persevering individual. She is confident of her ability to do what she wishes and is direct and forthright in her behavior.

> ACHIEVEMENT: She is usually seen (by others) as intelligent and hard-working, and also *involved* in her intellectual and other endeavors. She is determined to do well and usually succeeds. Her motives are internal and goal-centered rather than competitive, and in her dealings with others she may actually be unduly trusting and optimistic.

TABLE 13.1. Adjective Check List Mean Scale Scores of Political Party Leaders

	Total Sample		Females		Males	
	Females $N = 93$	Males $N = 420$	Republicans $N = 44$	Democrats $N = 49$	Republicans $N = 208$	Democrats $N = 212$
Total number of adjectives checked	51.98	49.07	50.72	53.06	48.57	49.57
Defensiveness	54.32	56.92	55.86	53.00[a]	57.51	56.34
Number of favorable adjectives checked	59.28	53.29	59.86	58.94	53.88	52.70
Number of unfavorable adjectives checked	45.11	47.21	44.63	45.52	46.15	48.26[b]
Self-Confidence	61.65	57.39	62.53	60.88	56.60	58.17
Self-Control	53.27	50.77	53.79	52.82	52.40	49.18[b]
Lability	49.16	49.83	47.47	50.62	47.70	51.93[b]
Personal adjustment	55.53	51.72	57.07	54.30	53.43	50.04[b]
Achievement	60.70	60.15	61.79	59.76	60.54	59.77
Dominance	61.23	59.94	62.09	60.48	60.04	59.84
Endurance	56.41	57.39	57.65	55.34	58.67	56.13[b]
Order	55.33	55.79	57.00	53.90[a]	57.36	54.25[b]
Intraception	55.65	56.21	55.84	55.48	56.33	56.09
Nurturance	51.53	53.43	51.93	51.18	54.58	52.29[a]
Affiliation	50.30	52.52	50.00	50.56	53.23	51.82
Heterosexuality	49.41	50.08	49.49	49.34	50.45	49.72
Exhibition	53.06	51.90	52.81	53.28	50.45	53.33[b]
Autonomy	52.30	51.00	51.79	52.74	49.72	52.27[b]
Aggression	53.13	51.14	53.56	52.76	50.03	52.23[a]
Change	49.87	48.64	48.51	51.04	46.75	50.50[b]
Succorance	42.30	43.32	41.81	42.72	42.49	44.13[a]
Abasement	41.39	43.39	40.44	42.20	43.28	43.50
Deference	43.72	46.07	43.95	43.52	47.46	44.71[b]
Counseling readiness	58.10	45.24	59.37	57.00	45.03	45.45

[a]$p < .05$.
[b]$p < .01$.

228

NUMBER OF FAVORABLE ADJECTIVES CHECKED (a scale consisting of the 75 adjectives considered "most favorable" by panels of independent judges): She appears to be motivated by virtue of hard work and conventional behavior. The reactions of others is to see her as dependable, steady, conscientious, mannerly, and serious; there is also a suspicion that she may be too concerned about others, and lacking in verve and quickness of mind. Egotism and self-centeredness, which might be suggested by the way in which the variable was derived, is seldom salient in high-scoring subjects. The social desirability component, in other words, is not ordinarily a facade or an artifact but sincere concern with behaving appropriately and with doing one's duty.

COUNSELING READINESS (a scale designed to identify counseling clients who are ready for help and who seem likely to profit from it): She is predominantly worried about herself and ambivalent about her status. She feels left out of things, unable to enjoy life to the full, and unduly anxious. She tends to be preoccupied with her problems and pessimistic about her ability to resolve them constructively. In contrast, the low scoring person on this scale is more or less free of these concerns: she is self-confident, poised, sure of herself and outgoing; she seeks the company of others, likes activity, and enjoys life in an uncomplicated wav [12].

Clearly, compared to most other women, female political party leaders are forceful, effective, ambitious, and socially ascendant individuals. The low mean scores on Abasement, Succorance, and Deference achieved by both parties' female leaders reinforce this finding. However, their dominant and self-confident approach to life and their strong, purposeful style appear to be complicated by doubt and concern about their place in society and their push toward achievement seems constrained by a sense of caution and propriety.

COMPARISONS BY SEX AND POLITICAL PARTY

Female and male standard scores for the ACL scales have been established separately. Thus, direct statistical comparisons are not appropriate. However, examination of table 13.1 reveals that the ways in which female party leaders differ from most other women is remarkably similar to the ways in which male party leaders differ from most other men. In both cases, the highest mean standard scores are obtained on Self-Confidence, Dominance, and Achievement. Indeed, omitting Counseling Readiness, the correlation between the rank order of the remaining 23 ACL mean scale scores for the female and male political leaders is +.88.

The mean scores for Counseling Readiness offer the most dramatic contrast between the two profiles, ranking 5th in magnitude on the female leaders' profile and 22nd in magnitude on the male leaders' profile. Combined with the greater salience of Number of Favorable Adjectives Checked for female leaders, it suggests that while both sets of leaders are unusually capable, outgoing, socially skilled, and persistent persons, the female party leaders try harder and worry more. In addition, the relatively higher scores of the female leaders on Self-Control and lower scores on Nurturance and Affiliation provide further support for the notion that they tend to express their predominantly forceful, effective, socially ascendant style in a relatively earnest, sobersided, and ambivalent manner, while the male leaders express the same predominant style in a more easygoing, direct, and uncomplicated way.

The general similarity between the personality characteristics of Republican and Democratic female party leaders is noteworthy. Among male political leaders, in contrast, a pervasive pattern of personality differences is found: Republican male leaders attain higher scores on Endurance, Order, Nurturance, Personal Adjustment and Self-Control; Democratic leaders show higher scores on Exhibition, Lability, Autonomy, and Aggression. This relationship of personality to political orientation among male political leaders has been reported and analyzed extensively elsewhere [10].

In short, the present findings indicate that female political leaders differ from most other women in their tendency toward a serious and dutiful manner and in a fretful uncertainty about themselves and their situation, which is accompanied by a greater degree of anxiety and readiness for psychological change. These factors, which do not characterize male political leaders, may represent accommodations and consequences of dominant dispositions in women, or they may have unrelated antecedents. The issue warrants further research. Indeed, the study of female political leaders clearly offers an excellent opportunity to investigate in finer detail the social skills and psychosocial hazards encountered by effectively dominant women. The interaction of the dominant dispositions of female leaders with contemporary sex-role prescriptions would be a useful focus for further study of its expression and of the style of political leadership it engenders.

POLITICAL CAREERS

There are major sex differences among the leaders in two aspects of their political careers: position in the political arena and motives underlying participation in that arena. Regarding position in politics, the participants reported on the extent of their public officeholding and on their involvement in political party activities. Additionally, those who had served on delegations to the 1960 and/or 1964 national conventions appraised factors they saw as contributing to their selection. The findings can be presented within the framework of two nonexclusive styles of political careers, one which is public office oriented and one which is intraparty oriented. The former career style is more characteristic of the male politicians among our respondents. A substantially greater proportion of male (48 percent) than of female leaders (29 percent) had ever held elective public office. And at the time of the study, over 17 percent of the male respondents were holding elective state or national office, while only one of the female leaders was holding such office. Not surprisingly, female leaders also attributed significantly less importance to the status of public officeholder as a factor in their being selected to a national convention delegation; female party leaders must depend upon other avenues to that position of party recognition and responsibility (see table 13.2). Additionally, running for office was granted significantly less importance by the women respondents as a reason for their entry into political life (see table 13.3).

Accessibility
The severely limited access of women to elective public office is a nationwide phenomenon, well documented, for example, in two recent reports by Werner on congresswomen and female state legislators [32, 33]. Werner found that between 1917 and 1964 only seventy women had served in the United States Congress. Of these, about one half had had relatives in Congress and over half were either appointed or elected to fill a vacancy, often one caused by the death of a husband. The situation in state legislatures cannot be much more encouraging to the aspiring female political leader. In 1963–64, for example, only 4.5 percent of the state legislators in this country were

women, compared to 2.0 percent of the members of Congress. Moreover, the incidence of female legislators is particularly low in the most populous, urbanized, industrialized states. In California, the percentage of congressional or state legislative offices held by women has been below national figures in recent years, presenting what by any standard must be a discouraging prospect for politically ambitious women in the state, perhaps contributing to a tendency on the part of the female party leaders studied to discount public office as a career objective, and possibly leading career-minded women to channel their efforts into other, nonpolitical areas of endeavor.

It is notable that the most striking sex difference identified in the Jennings and Thomas [21] Michigan study was the female leaders' inaccessibility to public office. The authors suggest that the female political leaders' ambition for public office is constrained by the contemporary realities of their opportunities for attaining such office. Heeding the importance which Joseph Schlesinger [28] has attributed to office-seeking in his analysis of ambition and political careers, Jen-

TABLE 13.2. Importance of Factors Contributing to Selection as Convention Delegate (mean scores)

	Total Sample Female	Male	Republicans Female	Male	Democrats Female	Male
Public officeholder	1.3	1.9c	1.2	1.6a	1.2	2.2c
Party official	2.4	2.1b	2.4	2.0a	2.4	2.1
Supporter of current state party leadership	3.3	3.1	3.1	2.7	3.5	3.5
Financial contributor	1.7	2.2c	1.7	1.9	1.7	2.4c
Personal friend of someone important	2.6	2.4	2.8	2.4	2.4	2.5
Leader of the CDC or CRA	1.8	1.5a	1.1	1.4	2.2	1.6c
Leader of a politically significant nonparty group (e.g., labor union)	1.2	1.5a	1.2	1.4	1.3	1.6
Voluntary contributor of time and energy	3.8	3.0c	3.8	3.2c	3.8	2.8c

NOTE: Scoring was 1 = not at all contributing, 2 = very little, 3 = somewhat, 4 = very much.
a$p < .10$.
b$p < .05$.
c$p < .01$.

TABLE 13.3. Importance of Political Motives (mean scores)

Reasons for Initially Becoming Involved in Politics	Total Sample Female	Male	Republicans Female	Male	Democrats Female	Male
Concern for public issues	3.8	3.8	3.8	3.8	3.8	3.8
Strong party loyalty	3.3	2.8[c]	3.5	2.7[c]	3.2	2.9[a]
Sense of community obligation	3.6	3.5	3.7	3.5	3.5	3.5
Fun and excitement	2.1	2.1	2.1	1.9	2.1	2.3
Making social contacts and friends	1.6	1.8[a]	1.6	1.8	1.6	1.9[a]
An interest in running for public office	1.3	2.1[c]	1.2	2.1[c]	1.4	2.2[a]
Being close to influential people	1.5	1.9[c]	1.4	1.8[b]	1.5	2.0[c]
Making business contacts	1.2	1.6[c]	1.1	1.5[b]	1.2	1.6[c]
The appeal of a particular national leader	2.8	2.5[b]	2.6	2.2[a]	3.0	2.7
A search for power and influence	1.3	1.9[c]	1.2	1.6[c]	1.3	2.1[c]
The influence of a friend or friends	2.0	2.0	2.0	2.0	2.0	2.0
Reasons for Wanting to Attend Party's Presidential Conventions						
To help select the party's national candidates	3.8	3.5[b]	3.8	3.7	3.7	3.4[b]
To meet new friends, renew new old acquaintances, and generally enjoy a great American social occasion	2.2	2.3	2.0	2.1	2.4	2.6
To exchange views on the issues of the day and to help define the program of the party	3.6	3.3[c]	3.7	3.3[b]	3.6	3.2[b]
To demonstrate my loyalty to state party leadership	2.7	2.4[b]	2.8	2.2[c]	2.6	·2.5
To enhance my prestige in my locality and among my political friends and enemies	1.9	2.2[b]	1.6	2.0[b]	2.1	2.4

NOTE: Scoring was 1 = not at all contributing, 2 = very little, 3 = somewhat, 4 = very much.
[a]$p < .10.$
[b]$p < .05.$
[c]$p < .01.$

nings and Thomas [21] hypothesize that the differential availability of public office has a profound impact upon the entire pattern of the female political leader's political behavior; they conclude that "in the measure that [office-seeking] behaviors are the keys to power within the parties, women remain at a considerable disadvantage" (p. 483).

Interestingly, the striking sex difference in state or national officeholding among our respondents does not obtain at the level of local government: There is no significant difference between male and female leaders with respect to holding local elective office. Several factors may be operating to eliminate sex differences among our respondents in terms of holding such office. First, the functions of some local offices, particularly school board positions, may be considered to be in keeping with traditional sex roles and thus may be relatively acceptable both to potential female candidates and the electorate. Second, being nonpartisan and of relatively low visibility, campaigns for elective local office may be less contentious in nature than those for partisan office, and there is some evidence that females in general are more likely than men to find the contentious aspects of politics unappealing [13, 30]. Third, women political leaders may be more locally oriented in their political interests than male leaders. Such sex differences in area focus have been identified in several studies of political behavior [13, 24, 1]. The respondents in our own study were asked to rank local, state, national, and international politics in the order in which they were of interest. In each party, the female respondents were more likely than their male counterparts to rank local politics either first or second, a response pattern which may result, at least in part, from the relatively greater accessibility of local public office to the woman politicians. Fourth, an important consequence of the nonpartisan nature of local elective offices in California is that they are less likely than in other states to serve as stepping stones to higher partisan state or national office. Nor do they ordinarily provide the remuneration suitable for the political careerist. It is thus unlikely that these offices provide a major incentive or asset to the progressive office-seeking ambition that Schlesinger [28] considers the hallmark of professional political careers and that seems more characteristic of the male respondents in the present study. Women may be permitted to seek local office relatively unchallenged and, given their relatively limited career objectives, may be more willing to seek such office than to seek higher-level partisan office.

Career Style and Sex Differences

The inaccessibility of partisan elective office to women party leaders does not appear from the data to result from their lack of commitment to or involvement in the affairs of their party. As an institutional system in its own right, the political party offers an internal career pattern with a full array of positions, purposes, and satisfactions. The intraparty careerist operates predominantly within the institutional structure of the party to maintain its organizational viability and to facilitate the performance of its political functions. Sex differences in political party involvement suggest such a career style is more characteristic of female than male politicians.

In neither the Republican nor Democratic sample are women respondents more recent arrivals to the arena of party activity than the men. Indeed, the women are more likely to have been active in partisan affairs for ten or more years; 77 percent of the Republican women compared to 69 percent of the Republican men, and 89 percent of the Democratic women compared to 75 percent of Democratic men have achieved such longevity of service. A significantly larger percentage of female respondents were holding an official position within their party at the time of the study: 56 percent of Republican women and 77 percent of Democratic women compared to 50 percent of Republican men and 55 percent of Democratic men were party officers, although there was only one woman among the 52 country committee chairman respondents. Larger percentages of women (58 percent) than men (48 percent) attended a national party convention as a delegate or alternate prior to 1964. A significantly larger percentage of Democratic women than men were active members in the California Democratic Council, the organization which for a decade had been the volunteer grassroots arm of the party; there were no significant sex differences among the Republicans in terms of activity in the somewhat comparable California Republican Assembly. Only with reference to financial contributions to the party and its candidates do men respondents, especially among the Democrats, evince a greater partisan commitment of resources: 32 percent of the male respondents had contributed $1000 or more to their party or its candidates in 1962, compared to 18 percent of the female respondents. Even this difference is attenuated once sex differences in income are taken into account, i.e., when we consider contributions as a proportion of income.

The male-female pattern of party activity suggested by the above findings is underlined by responses to a question asking national convention delegation members in the sample to indicate the degree to which each of a series of factors contributed to their selection as delegates or alternates. Even more striking as a sex difference than the fact that male leaders attributed greater importance than female leaders to occupancy of the role of public officeholder is the relatively greater importance attributed by female leaders in both parties to taking on the role of voluntary contributor of time and energy. The role of party official is also considered to be somewhat more important as a factor for female than male leaders (see table 13.2.)

In terms of degree and longevity of party activity as well as perception of their own roles in the party then, it would seem that women leaders devote themselves as much if not more than their male counterparts to the workaday organizational burdens of their political party, through service in official and unofficial party organizations and through grassroots activity. Additionally, the data suggest that the political party is more likely to be the exclusive arena of social action for the female leader than the male leader, since the former belongs to and actively participates in significantly fewer community organizations in addition to her party than the latter. For example, the women respondents belong on an average to 5.13 nonparty organizations, compared to 7.88 for the men. This sex difference is similar in magnitude and is statistically significant for both parties.

Political Motivation

Yet despite her effort, the woman politician has not reaped the rewards and power potential which come with partisan public office or even with such notable party positions as county committee chairman. At least part of the explanation is suggested by turning to the question: Do women political leaders engage in political activities for different reasons than male leaders?

Participants in the present study were given two series of questions which bear on their political motivations. They were asked to record on a four-point scale the degree to which each of eleven reasons for initially becoming involved in politics was important in their own entry into political activity. And they were asked to record on an identical scale the degree of importance they attributed to each of five reasons for wanting to attend their party's national conventions in an official capacity. The responses to these questions are summarized in table 13.3.

The data display unmistakable sex differences in political motives among the political leaders surveyed. On the two most salient reasons for initial political involvement, "concern for public issues" and "a sense of community obligation," the two groups are alike in both parties; the great majority of respondents, male and female, agree that each of these reasons "very much" motivated their political entry. On twelve of the sixteen items, however, there are consistent (i.e., they appear among both parties' elites) male/female differences. In all but one of the twelve cases, these differences achieve significance at or beyond the .10 level for at least one party—and in half the cases, for both.

Seven of the items on which consistent sex differences appear involve motives which, in one way or another, are self-serving in nature: Some involve a desire for self-enhancement in power, influence, or material terms, namely the desire to run for public office, to be close to influential people, to achieve power and influence, to make business contacts, and to enhance one's prestige. Others include those motivations involving social or solidary factors (although even these are not necessarily without their influence payoffs), namely, the desire to make social contacts and friends, "to meet new friends, renew old acquaintances and generally enjoy a great American social occasion." On each and every one of these seven items, women in both parties achieve lower mean scores than men. The sex differences are particularly magnified on those items which most clearly tap a power orientation dimension, principally "an interest in running for public office" and "search for power and influence."

On each of the other five items on which consistent sex differences appear, the women achieve higher mean scores than the male leaders. These tend to tap the three dimensions of political motivation identified by students of voting behavior (e.g., Campbell et al. [8]) as critically involved in the average citizen's vote decision in that they relate to party loyalty, to an orientation toward the party's candidates or its leaders, and to the posture of the party on policy issues. Thus, the women leaders grant significantly greater importance than the male leaders to "strong party loyalty" as a reason for initially becoming involved in politics and, particularly among the Republicans, to indicate a stronger desire to attend national conventions in order "to demonstrate . . . loyalty to state party leadership." Thus, too, they are more likely to have become engaged in politics because of "the appeal of a particular national party leader" and to wish to be convention delegation members in order "to help select the party's national candidates."

Finally, although both men and women appear to have been more strongly motivated by a concern for public issues when they entered politics than by any other factor, and to equally high degrees, women leaders are significantly more interested in convention attendance in order "to exchange views on the issues of the day and to help define the program of the party."

Parenthetically we note the degree to which the women in the present study compare to the men on issues of public policy. Respondents were presented with a set of policy items designed to measure liberal-conservative attitudes. (The items and the way they successfully discriminate between parties and between factions within parties are reported in Costantini and Craik [9].) Within the Republican sample no significant sex differences appear. Among the Democrats, on the other hand, there is a discernible pattern, with the female leaders appearing significantly more liberal. Insofar as these attitudes are actually expressed within the political arena, female leaders in the Democratic party probably contribute to intraparty issue tensions and conflict and, more generally, widen interparty differences along the liberal-conservative dimension.

Politics for the male leader is evidently more likely to be a vehicle for personal enhancement and career advancement. But for the woman leader it is more likely to be a "labor of love," one where a concern for the party, its candidates, and its programs assumes relatively greater importance. If the male leader appears to be motivated by self-serving considerations, the female leader appears to be motivated by public-serving considerations.

The public office versus intraparty career styles and the self-serving versus public-serving motivational patterns reflected in the present data bear marked resemblance to often noted sex-role differences in the family. The male party leader, like the husband, is more likely to specialize in the instrumental functions of the system involved (whether party or family)—that is, in those functions related to the external world. The female party leader, like the wife, tends to specialize in expressive functions or those concerned with "the 'internal' affairs of the system, the maintenance of integrative relations between [its] members" [26, p. 47]. In general, she is relegated to, or relegates herself to, a supportive role of more or less selfless service to her family or party, while the male partner or copartyist pursues a career in the outside world.

The career styles and motivational differences between the men and women politicians studied are likely to contribute to male dominance of major public and party offices. Coupled with the sex differences in the personality characteristics of the respondents noted above, the motivational data lead to the conclusion that insofar as sex-role prescriptions affect the career patterns of female political leaders, they at least in part affect them through the traits and attitudes of the women themselves.

REFERENCES

1. Gabriel Almond and Sidney Verba. *The Civic Culture.* Boston: Little, Brown, 1965.

2. James D. Barber. *Citizen Politics.* Chicago: Markham, 1969.

3. F. Barron. *Creative Person and Creative Process.* New York: Holt, Rinehart & Winston, 1969.

4. W. Bell, R. Hill, and C. R. Wright. *Public Leadership.* San Francisco: Chandler, 1961.

5. Bernard Berelson, Paul Lazarsfeld, and William McPhee. *Voting.* Chicago: University of Chicago Press, 1954.

6. J. Blondel. *Voters, Parties and Leaders.* Baltimore: Penguin, 1963.

7. Angus Campbell, Phillip Converse, Warren Miller, and Donald Stokes. *The American Voter.* New York: Wiley, 1960.

8. Angus Campbell, G. Gwin, and Warren Miller. *The Voter Decides.* Evanston: Row, Peterson, 1954.

9. Edmond Costantini and Kenneth Craik. "Competing Elites Within a Political Party: A Study of Republican Leadership." *Western Political Quarterly* 22 (1969): 879–903.

10. Edmond Costantini and Kenneth Craik. "Personality, Party Leadership and Political Orientation: A Study of Democratic and Republican Elites." In *Personality, Belief and Participation,* ed. J. Citrin and P. Sinderman. Chicago: Aldine, 1972.

11. Maurice Duverger. *Political Role of Women.* Paris: UNESCO, 1955.

12. H. G. Gough and A. B. Heilbrun. *Manual for the Adjective Check List.* Palo Alto: Consulting Psychologists, 1965.

13. Fred I. Greenstein. *Children and Politics.* New Haven: Yale University Press, 1965.

14. Martin Gruberg. *Women in American Politics.* Oshkosh, Wisc.: Academia, 1968.

15. R. Helson. "Personality of Women With Imaginative and Artistic Interests: The Role of Masculinity, Originality and Other Characteristics in Their Creativity." *Journal of Personality* 34 (1966): 1–25.

16. R. Helson. "Personality Characteristics and Developmental History of Creative College Women." *Psychology Monographs* 76 (1967): 214–33.

17. R. Helson. "Sex Differences in Creative Style." *Journal of Personality* 35 (1967): 214–33.

18. R. Helson. "Generality of Sex Differences in Creative Style." *Journal of Personality* 36 (1968): 589–607.

19. R. Helson. "Women Mathematicians and the Creative Personality." *Journal of Consulting and Clinical Psychology* 36 (1971): 210–20.

20. Robert D. Hess and Judith V. Torney. *The Development of Political Attitudes in Children.* New York: Doubleday, 1967.

21. M. Kent Jennings and N. Thomas. "Men and Women in Party Elites: Social Roles and Political Resources." *Midwest Journal of Political Science* 12 (1968): 469–92.

22. Robert E. Lane. *Political Life.* Glencoe, Ill.: Free Press, 1959.

23. D. W. MacKinnon. "Creativity and Images of the Self." In *The Study of Lives,* ed. R. W. White. New York: Atherton, 1963.

24. James G. March. "Husband-Wife Interaction Over Political Issues." *Public Opinion Quarterly* 17 (1954): 461–70.

25. Lester W. Milbrath. *Political Participation.* Chicago: Rand McNally, 1965.

26. Talcott Parsons and R. Bales. *Family: Socialization and Interaction Process.* Glencoe, Ill.: Free Press, 1955.

27. P. G. Pulzer. *Political Representation and Elections.* New York: Praeger, 1967.

28. Joseph A. Schlesinger. *Ambition and Politics: Political Careers in the United States.* Chicago: Rand McNally, 1966.

29. S. Stouffer. *Communism, Conformity and Civil Liberties.* New York: Doubleday, 1955.

30. L. Terman and L. E. Tyler. "Psychological Sex Differences." In *Manual of Child Psychology,* ed. L. Carmichael. 2nd ed. New York: Wiley, 1954.

31. Herbert Tingsten. *Political Behavior: Studies in Election Statistics* London: King & Son, 1937.

32. Emmy E. Werner. "Women in Congress: 1917–64." *Western Political Quarterly* 19 (1966): 16–30.

33. Emmy E. Werner. "Women in the State Legislatures." *Western Political Quarterly* 21 (1968): 40–50.

BARBARA BURRELL

14

☆☆☆☆☆☆☆☆☆☆☆☆☆☆☆☆☆☆☆☆☆☆☆☆☆☆☆

A New Dimension in Political Participation: The Women's Political Caucus

The mass participation studies of the 1950s and early 1960s emphasized the lack of involvement in politics on the part of women. The results of empirical studies showed that "at all levels of political action from discussing politics to voting, to political letter writing, to holding party or public office, women participate less than men. They appear to be less interested in politics, to belong to fewer organizations, to be less informed politically, and to display a lower sense of political involvement and political efficacy" [2, p. 218].*

The decade of the 1960s saw the beginnings of a new feminist movement which has resulted in increased awareness of and participation in the political world on the part of women. Women have begun to demand equality in political affairs. They are no longer content to play only support roles. The changes that have taken place and

*Numbers in brackets refer to numbered references at the end of the chapter.

the potential that now exists for a greater say in power decisions have prompted Marjorie Lansing to call women "the new political class" [8].

Demands for equality and increased participation in politics by women are significant for the study of politics. If women as a group vote differently from men and if female political elites bring new experiences and attitudes to the decision-making levels of government, significant changes in public policy could occur. The questions of who participates, why, and how will all be affected. Among the many social movements of the past decade, the new feminist movement should influence the theories of elitism, pluralism, and participatory democracy.

The main organ of the movement promoting equality in and through the political sphere has been the National Women's Political Caucus. In their analysis of the Caucus, Judith and Jimmie Trent [12] suggest that it "is the instrument on which the entire feminist movement will depend for leadership" (p. 2). And in its account of the 1972 Democratic National Convention, *Newsweek* magazine [11] states, "By comparison [with the black movement] feminism proved an even more durable—and slightly more successful—force to be reckoned with. The backbone of the movement was the National Women's Political Caucus" (p. 32).

The National Women's Political Caucus was founded in July 1971 when approximately 324 women from 27 states gathered in Washington, D.C., "to awaken, organize, and assert the vast political power represented by women" (Statement of Purpose, 1971). Today, in addition to the national caucus there are local caucuses in all the states.

In their survey of American male and female attitudes toward women and politics, Louis Harris and Associates [3] concluded: "There is no doubt that greater involvement of women in the political processes of this country is desired by both sexes. In almost identical proportions, both men and women favor the formation, by leaders of the women's movement for equality, of 'new organizations' to strengthen women's participation in politics" (p. 19). But favoring an action and participating in such an activity are two different things. An in-depth study of the persons who seek or claim to represent over half the population in pressuring the government for change should provide greater insight into the expansion of political participation through one of today's numerous social movements.

Are the new feminist groups such as the Women's Political Caucus attracting new people into the political arena or are their members primarily those who are already involved and are merely rechanneling their efforts? Who are these participants, and how did they become interested in feminist activities?

The purpose of this study is to develop a profile of the women organizing to achieve political equality. The focus of this study is on the participants at the first state convention of the Iowa Women's Political Caucus.

The state convention of the Iowa Women's Political Caucus was chosen as the unit of study because of its geographical convenience to the author and its timeliness for research purposes. Having been involved in the formation of the caucus, the author had more access to the participants of this first state convention than might have been available to an outsider. The caucus's overall success, with relative ease, in attracting a large number of concerned women made it a significant choice for the study of women active in a movement generating social change through the advocation of political equality.

The 600 persons attending the state convention, nearly all of them women, make up the universe for this study. A questionnaire was prepared and distributed to all the participants during the convening session. A total of 405 questionnaires were completed, giving a 66 percent sample from which to make generalizations about the caucus population.

Regarding their relationship to the caucus, 64 percent of the respondents indicated they were members. This group presumably consists of persons who had paid the required membership dues. Another 8 percent considered themselves "members to be" who had not yet formally joined the organization, and 15 percent felt they were "supporters," although they apparently were not considering becoming members at that time. Ten percent, or 39 persons, classified themselves as "observers." A membership of approximately 300 for an organization only three months old is a significant indication of the growing latent and overt feeling on the part of many women that they were not receiving their fair share in the political arena.

For purposes of the following analysis, all "observers" have been excluded since any of their feelings of identification with or commitment to the movement were not expressed. Their reasons for attending the convention were not ascertained through this questionnaire. Thus the following analysis of the Iowa Women's Political Caucus is based on a sample of 366 members, members-to-be, and supporters who responded to questionnaires distributed at the 1973 convention.

THE PARTICIPANTS: DEMOGRAPHIC
CHARACTERISTICS

Demographic figures for caucus membership as a whole are not available so that the representativeness of this sample cannot be determined with great precision. However, it is possible to ascertain the representativeness of the convention participants geographically. The residence by county of the 1973–74 statewide membership and of the convention participants was determined. Both the convention participants and the statewide membership are overwhelmingly urban residents. The greatest number of members come from six of the seven most urbanized counties. The same is true of the convention participants. The percentage from each county for both groups is essentially the same.

The convention participants ranged in age from 16 to 73 years of age. The mean age was 32 years and the median 29, showing no major differences from the figures Carden [1] reported for members of women's rights groups nationally. Overall, the group consisted of relatively young women, although over one-fifth were over forty.

The participants were highly educated. Seventy percent had completed four or more years of college, and over 90 percent had had at least one year of college education. Of particular interest is the fact that over one-third of the respondents reported that they had continued their formal education beyond a bachelor's degree. In terms of education, they are a very elite group.

The largest number of participants listed occupations that would fall into the category of being professionally employed (36.8 percent). Of these professionals, a large plurality were educators, one of the few professional occupations traditionally employing large numbers of women. The second largest group of women classified themselves as homemakers (25.7 percent). Over one-fourth of the participants were not employed outside the home, an indication that women's rights organizations are beginning to expand beyond the world of the businesswoman. Nevertheless, as the education and income figures reveal, the movement still has a long way to go in successfully attracting significant numbers of women from lower socioeconomic status backgrounds.

The median family income of the participants was $14,560. The median income of the participants represents an above average income and is consistent with their high level of education. It differs considerably from the 1970 U.S. median family income of $10,999 [15, p. 328] and from the Iowa median family income of $9,018 for the same year [14, p. 217].

The presence of a fairly large number of students depressed the family income average as a number of these participants listed only their own earnings as opposed to their family income. Also, 20 percent of the respondents refused to answer the question on income which lowers the responses on that item to only about one-half of those present at the convention. Whether the family income of housewives is generally higher than the overall caucus average cannot be determined with any accuracy, but it does seem to point in that direction. Over one-fourth ($N = 29$) of the housewives listed their family income as over $25,000, while only one housewife listed her income as under $10,000. However, one-fourth of the housewives refused to respond to the question. Thus, only very tentative conclusions can be made about the income of the participants.

The participants were not directly asked what their marital status was, but the answers to the question "Has your spouse ever held party office or public office?" give some indication of their makeup in this regard as one response listed was "never married." Nearly one-fourth ($N = 74$, 20 percent) responded that they had never married. Sixty-four percent responded positively to this inquiry, and 16 percent did not answer at all. This is somewhat limited as it does not allow for any information on how many were divorced, but it does indicate that a majority of the participants were married women.

PARTISANSHIP

Nationally in 1973, 36 percent of American voters identified with the Democratic party, 41 percent considered themselves Independents, and 21 percent preferred the Republican party, while 2 percent were classified as apolitical [13]. In Iowa, traditionally considered a Republican state, a September 1973 poll showed the party preference breakdown for Iowa to be 38 percent Democratic, 30 percent Republican, 31 percent Independent, and 1 percent Other [6].

Did the participants in the first state convention of the Iowa Women's Political Caucus follow the national or the state pattern in terms of their partisanship? Or were they closer to the makeup of the national caucus and the women's movement in general in being over-whelmingly Democratic and Independent in party preference? If the Iowa Caucus has been more successful in attracting Republican women in larger numbers than the National Women's Political Caucus, then it would have come closer to being the multi-partisan organization it purports to be.

Nearly 60 percent of the Iowa Caucus respondents replied that they considered themselves to be affiliated with the Democratic party, while almost one-fourth felt they were political Independents. Republicans made up only 15 percent of the participants. Thus, in their political party preferences, the convention participants deviate rather strongly from the general Iowa and national electorate. Overall, they most closely follow the pattern of the women's movement nationally. Although a sizable minority of participants were affiliated with the Republican party, the caucus has not achieved a truly multipartisan representation considering the partisanship of the Iowa electorate.

Nearly one-half (47 percent) of the women who classified themselves as Independents stated that they had not participated in any of the traditional political activities listed in the questionnaire as opposed to 14 percent each of the Democrats and Republicans. This fact suggests that there is a fairly large segment of potentially active middle-class persons who have been propelled into the political arena as a result of appeals from feminist organizations to the importance of attaining women's political equality. Apparently, traditional political party activities did not appeal to them. What form their future political activity takes should provide further insights into participation in American politics.

Occupation and Partisanship

Were the partisanships of the participants significantly linked to their occupational backgrounds? Significant occupational differences were found among the respondents in relation to their party preferences. One-half of the Republicans were homemakers, while the largest percent of Democrats (35 percent) were professionals. Only about one-fourth of the Democrats were homemakers, with approximately one-fifth falling into each of the other categories. The Independents were made up mostly of professionals (46 percent) and students (29 percent).

The fact that so many of the Republicans were homemakers follows from traditional patterns of the occupational status of the two parties' adherents. Not only were the Republicans more likely to be homemakers, but 45 percent replied that they had a family income of over $25,000 as compared to 15 percent each for the Democrats and Independents. Thus, the high socioeconomic status usually ascribed to Republicans is reflected in the Republicans attending the convention. What is surprising is that these Republican homemakers came to the convention at all.

IDEOLOGY

According to the Iowa poll, 54 percent of Iowans consider themselves conservatives in politics, 34 percent regard themselves as liberals, and 12 percent are undecided [5].

The caucus respondents were asked to locate themselves on a liberal-conservative continuum. Feminist philosophy as part of the protest movements of the 1960s has been viewed as a liberal, if not radical, ideology. One would expect that, even though the caucus aims to work through the political system to achieve reform, its adherents would be almost exclusively "liberals" in their political outlook and thus would deviate substantially from the general populace in Iowa. The convention attenders in Iowa followed this pattern. Nearly 90 percent considered themselves to be either extremely liberal, liberal, or slightly liberal. Only 6 percent felt that they were conservatives.

Partisanship, Occupation, and Ideology
There was a significant difference among the respondents along political lines concerning ideology. Although a majority of all groups regarded themselves as liberals, Republicans were more apt to fall into the moderate to conservative categories compared with Democrats, and the Independents fell in the middle of these two groups. Thus the traditional political party patterns were reflected in the ideological orientations of convention participants.

No statistically significant differences existed among the respondents in occupational status on perceived ideology. However, a somewhat larger percentage of students called themselves extreme liberals than members of the other groups—29 percent as compared with 20 percent for professionals, 17 percent for the nonprofessionals, and 13 percent for homemakers.

POLITICAL INVOLVEMENT

Lester Milbrath [9] concludes from his extensive review of the research findings from a large number of studies of political involvement in the United States that "about one-third of the American adult population can be characterized as politically apathetic or passive; in most cases they are unaware, literally, of the political part of the world around them. Another 60 percent play largely spectator roles in the political process, they watch, they cheer, they vote, but they do not do battle . . . the percentage of gladiators . . . does not exceed 5 to 7 percent" (p. 21).

Iowans do not appear to differ significantly in their participation rates and interest from the national citizenry. An Iowa poll conducted in 1966 reported that few Iowans expressed an active interest in politics. Only 11 percent said that they had ever actively worked in a political campaign. Fifteen percent had a great deal of interest in politics, 52 percent felt they had some interest, and 33 percent had very little interest [4]. Only a minority of Iowans and the American voting-age population can clearly be classified as political activists. Where do the individuals who have come together to promote women's equality fall in this scheme of things?

One would assume that those persons attracted to a convention dealing with politics would at least fall into Milbrath's spectator category. Those who are politically apathetic or passive are not likely to possess the motivation to attend such a convention. But how active have these participants been in past political affairs? Were the convention participants already political activists, or has this segment of the women's liberation movement attracted new recruits to the political arena? (Of the delegates to the 1973 NWPC National Convention in Houston, 94 percent had had previous political experience. The national membership includes some of the most politically active women in the country) [10].

The respondents were asked how long they had been active in politics. Among those who indicated they had been active, the mean number of years of involvement was 6.0 years, with a median of 3.9 years. A total of 123, or 34 percent, of the respondents said they had not been active. Including the nonactives, the overall mean number of years the respondents had been active in politics was 4.63 years, and the median number of years was approximately a year.

The participants were also asked what kinds of public office, if any, they had held. A small number ($N = 23$, 7 percent) indicated that they had been elected or appointed to a public office. Thirty-five, or 11.4 percent, indicated that their spouse had held a public or party office.

While only a small minority of the participants had been elected or appointed to a public office, they had been extremely active in party politics prior to the convention. Seventy-eight percent of the respondents stated that they had engaged in at least one political party activity in the past. This is a significantly higher percentage than for the voting-age population as a whole although not as high as that of the participants at the national caucus level. Not only had over three-fourths of the respondents participated in previous political activities, but 65 percent had engaged in more than one activity and one-fourth had been involved in more than five different activities.

At the same time, the fact that nearly one-fourth of the participants reported no previous involvement in political party activities is an indication that the caucus is attracting new recruits into the political arena. (The discrepancy between the 22 percent figure used here and the 34 percent figure used when discussing the number of years the respondents had been active in politics is due to the fact that some of the respondents in terms of numbers said they had not been politically active but then checked that they had participated in one or more individual political activities.) Further research should include community activities other than partisan politics to more accurately gauge how active women's rightists have been.

Partisanship and Political Participation
There was little difference between the Democratic and Republican participants in the number of activities they had participated in. At all levels, no more than two percentage points separated the adherents of both parties. Individually, in only one activity was there a statistically significant difference between Republicans and Democrats. This main difference appeared in answer to the question concerning participation in their party's women's club. Forty-three percent of the Republicans indicated that they had a member of a women's club as opposed to only 13 percent of the Democrats. This finding most likely follows from the fact that the women's auxiliary of the Republican party has always been a more integral part of the party in Iowa than has been the case with the Democrats. The strong relationship between membership in the Republican party and being a homemaker also contributes to this difference.

Although not statistically significant, there were notable differences between Republicans and Democrats who have been delegates to a state convention and have given political speeches. The Republicans were more apt to have been delegates to a state convention. Forty-three percent had been delegates as opposed to 33 percent of the Democrats, which is interesting since the Democrats have been more vocal in recent years in advocating a greater role for women and minorities in the party decision-making process through quotas and affirmative action programs. While 25 percent of the Republicans had been speech givers, only 14 percent of the Democrats had performed this activity.

Occupation and Political Participation

Prior political participation of caucus participants appeared to be more closely linked to occupation than to partisanship. Women who were not employed outside the home appeared to have been much more involved in the traditional partisan activities than those employed outside the home or those attending school. For example, 34 percent of the homemakers had been precinct committeepersons as compared with 15, 16, and 13 percent, respectively, of the professionals, nonprofessionals, and students. They were also much more likely to have been delegates to state conventions, given speeches, conducted canvasses, contributed to a party's state sustaining fund, been members of a women's club, attended precinct caucuses, and participated in general campaign work.

The homemakers were not only the most active on several individual items but also appeared to have been the most active overall. Only 12 percent of the homemakers had not participated in any of the enumerated political activities as opposed to 29 percent of the professionals, 27 percent of the students, and 16 percent of the nonprofessionals. At the other end of the spectrum, over half (58 percent) of the homemakers had been involved in five or more activities. Only 17 percent of the professionals and 19 percent of the students had participated in this number of activities. The nonprofessionals fell in the middle, with 34 percent having engaged in five or more activities.

Their propensity for political involvement is probably a key variable in the attraction of the Women's Political Caucus for these homemakers and instrumental in overcoming any adverse feelings that they might have possessed toward the idea of women's liberation.

Political Career

In looking to the future, the participants were asked if they were interested in a political career for themselves. Over one-fourth expressed such an interest, one-fourth were not interested, and 42 percent were undecided.

The 25 percent who indicated a desire for a political career appears to be a significantly large number. Other studies of political elites (many of party functionaries) have not shown as high an incidence of public office aspirants [16, 2, 7]. One would expect that the interest in holding a public office would be higher for those who have already achieved success in seeking party office whereas there was no criteria such as election as a delegate for attendance at the Women's Political Caucus convention, although many of the participants had held party office. In regard to a political career, the Women's Political Caucus has attracted an outstanding number of aspirants, a very significant fact for the effect it could have on political participation at the elite level.

Partisanship, Occupation, and Political Career

There were no significant differences according to the party affiliations of Caucus participants and an interest in a political career. However, although the most active politically, the homemakers rejected the idea of a political career in a significantly higher proportion than members of the other groups. Forty-three percent of the homemakers were not interested in a political career, while 24 percent of the professionals, 23 percent of the nonprofessionals, and 21 percent of the students expressed no interest.

FEMINISTS, FEMALE POLITICIANS, AND WOMEN'S RIGHTS

Male-Female Differences

Politics has traditionally been a man's world. It took women over fifty years to gain the right to vote after they organized to achieve this goal. Since that time, few women have sought to achieve powerful decision-making positions in the political world. Women and men have been socialized into believing that women were not meant to participate in this aggressive power-seeking activity except to play the support roles of folder, envelope stuffer, and stamp licker in the back rooms. We have been led to believe that there are innate differences between males and females that make women unsuitable for leadership roles. As more women challenge the system and seek elective

office, whether they are successful depends on how they are perceived
by the electorate and whether these traditional attitudes toward them
as candidates are changing. Would they be more aggressive or idealistic than men? Would women who succeed in politics have to sacrifice
their "femininity?" Would they be more sensitive to problems of the
poor and underprivileged, or would the presence of women as government decision-makers not change things much?

After reporting on the feelings of his respondents on a series of
statements about "women who try to get ahead in politics" in the
Virginia Slims Poll, Harris [3] observes that

> while most women might prefer their responsibilities at home to
> those of public office, they are quick to recognize that some
> women are as capable—if not more capable—as men to fill
> positions of leadership in the public domain. . . . Women credit
> their own sex with idealism that could very well enhance the
> service of a public official.
>
> Interestingly, women do not seem to feel that to succeed in
> public office they have to sacrifice their femininity and become
> hard-nosed and aggressive. Rather than imitating these tradi-
> tionally "masculine" traits they feel that women in public office
> should use their "feminine charm and diplomacy" in positive
> ways. (p. 31)

How do the convention participants compare with American
women in general in their perceptions of female politicians? In contrast to the 46 percent of Harris's respondents who felt that women in
politics would be more idealistic than men, only 32 percent of the
convention participants felt this way, and 48 percent disagreed. Over
one-half of the female population answered negatively to the suggestion that women in politics usually are more hard-nosed and aggressive, while nearly one-third agreed with this statement. Only 13 percent of the convention participants saw politically active women in this
light, while 65 percent disagreed with this idea.

The convention attenders overwhelmingly (90 percent) rejected
the notion that women who succeed in politics usually have to sacrifice
their femininity to get there. To a lesser extent (67 percent), Harris's
respondents agreed with the convention women. Harris's women
were more positive toward the idea that women are more sensitive to
the problems of the poor and underprivileged than men are. Seventy-one percent agreed with this statement while 23 percent disagreed. The Iowa caucus participants were somewhat more skeptical

about women bringing any unique qualities into government service, but 78 percent of the respondents did feel that the presence of women in government would change things. One-half felt that women were more sensitive to the problems of the poor than men, and 30 percent disagreed.

There were no significant differences among the respondents according to partisanship or occupational status on any of these items. The convention participants appeared to be "ahead" of the female population in general in believing that there are no unique differences between men and women when it comes to politics. At the same time, they do feel that greater involvement by women in the decision-making process will change things. This belief could follow from the different life experiences of women from those of men which would be brought into the political arena.

Promotion of Equal Rights

The women who were attracted to a convention to promote women's rights and to develop a plan of action to gain equality for women in the political arena must have had some ideas on how they should go about gaining their rights. Did they feel they would have much trouble gaining their rights? Would they have to form a separate political party or perhaps even overthrow the system of government? The convention attenders were asked their attitudes on these forms of political action. Two more moderate means of gaining their rights—gaining control of government by (1) getting more women elected and (2) protesting and demonstrating to make their needs known—were also suggested. One would expect that if the members of the caucus were of the reformist mold as opposed to the more radical elements of the movement, they would reject the more radical means of gaining their rights. At the same time, since they found it necessary to band together as an interest group, it could be predicted that they would disagree with the statement that women would not have much trouble gaining their rights. Their responses indicated that they did fall into this expected pattern.

The respondents rejected the ideas of forming their own political party and of overthrowing the system of government, but well over half (68 percent) believed that they would have to protest and demonstrate to make their needs known. The way to gain their rights, these activists felt, was by gaining control of the government by electing women to office, although picketing to right an injustice was not beneath them, if necessary.

Partisanship, Occupation, and Efforts to Gain Rights

Partisanship produced few significant differences among the respondents on how they should go about gaining their rights. Only on the idea of protesting and demonstrating was there a significant difference. The Republican women were more skeptical about this method as a proper course of action. Over a third of the Republicans disagreed as opposed to 13 percent of the Democrats and 20 percent of the Independents.

The students appeared to be slightly more "militant" than the other groups in the means they would employ to gain their rights. Although only a minority in each group felt women should form their own party, the students were most supportive of this idea. Nineteen percent of the students agreed with this course of action while 4 percent of the professionals, 10 percent of the nonprofessional, and 4 percent of the homemakers supported this idea. And 13 percent of the students felt that women should overthrow the government as opposed to 3 percent of the professionals, 6 percent of the nonprofessionals, and 1 percent of the homemakers.

ISSUE ORIENTATIONS

Whether the increased participation and demand for political equality on the part of women will reinforce the present status quo on issues of public policy or lead to a change is an important area of analysis, particularly for those who seek to influence public policy. Thus the convention participants were asked to assess the importance of several major issues of the day: racism, consumer protection, pollution, wage scales, population control, inflation and unemployment, defense spending, criminal justice, abortion, crime, hunger, child care, drugs, welfare, foreign aid, busing, and gay liberation. Only a marginal amount of information about the respondents attitudes on these issues was gained from these data.

The respondents were first asked to assess the importance of these issues in terms of their importance to them personally. Second, they were to consider the importance of the items as "women's issues"—issues of particular importance to women. Collectively, all the issues except gay liberation were considered important to the caucus participants personally and as women's issues. There was not a significant difference among the respondents in correlating the salience of the items to themselves personally and their importance as women's issues. Asking the respondents to order the issues in relation to their perception of their importance perhaps would have allowed for a more exacting analysis of the orientation of caucus participants to these issues.

Cultural issues stood out as causing the main splits among the convention participants. Gay liberation and abortion were the main issues producing diverse salience ratings, ratings closely linked to partisan and occupational factors. Republican women attached less significance personally to these two issues than did Democrats and Independents. Based on occupation, homemakers attached the least importance to abortion as a woman's issue and as a personal issue. Professionals joined homemakers in not perceiving any importance to themselves of gay liberation in significantly larger numbers than students and nonprofessionals.

The caucus appears not to have transcended party lines in attracting women of similar attitudes toward the main political issues of the day. Although there were differences on only a minority of issues, clearly the presence of a significant minority of Republican women produced these differences. This is an indication that as the caucus continues to place emphasis on becoming a truly multipartisan organization, conflicts over issue priorities could become more pronounced leading to internal stress and lessening outside influence.

There were fewer distinctions among the participants according to occupational status. Since the convention participants regardless of occupational status were nearly all of high socioeconomic status, one could anticipate that differences along occupational lines would be minimal. Perhaps because of their greater isolation in society, the homemakers (who tended to be Republicans) attached somewhat less significance to some of the cultural issues.

CONCLUSION

"Studies of political elites have regularly found an overrepresentation of persons of relatively high socioeconomic status" [2, p. 219]. The caucus participants appear not to deviate from other political elites in this respect. On the items of income, occupation, and education, which are traditionally used to measure socioeconomic status, the caucus participant falls into a relatively high-status category.

The profile that emerges of the Women's Political Caucus participant from this study is one of a fairly young, highly educated, and
ideologically liberal person who has been active in politics prior to the
caucus's inception. However, in addition to what one might call the
average or typical member, there appears to be a wide spectrum of
persons who have become involved. There is the moderate-to-
conservative Republican homemaker, the liberal professionally employed Democrat, and the somewhat more radical student. In Iowa,
the Women's Political Caucus is the only active statewide feminist organization. More radical groups and other reformist organizations
have not been active in Iowa except on some college campuses and in
the state capitol. Thus, the lack of competing groups could account at
least in part for the caucus's attraction for a wide range of individuals.
Studies of caucus members in states where other feminist groups are
prominent could provide a more definitive profile of those persons
drawn to the political arena in search of equality.

Generalizations to the larger population of caucus members nationally and even to the statewide membership in Iowa should be
made with caution. Although a 60 percent sample was obtained and
the respondents appeared to represent the statewide membership
geographically, there was a self-selection process involved both in
terms of those who chose to attend the convention and in those people
who responded to the questionnaire. Since randomness was not
sought in this sample, those persons who chose not to participate
could be quite different from the respondents in this study.

However, the data gathered at this convention should help to fill
a void that now exists in political science research. Little scientific attention has been given to the study of women as political activists. The
Women's Political Caucus is an excellent group from which to begin to
amass knowledge of women as politicians. The Women's Political
Caucus has the potential (and already appears to have had an impact)
for acting as a major force in increasing participation in politics by
women and gaining more positions of power for women. The numbers of women being elected to public office at least at local and state
levels have increased dramatically in the last few years. For example,
the number of women elected to state legislatures in 1972 increased
by 28 percent over 1970, and an increase of 26 percent over 1972 occurred in 1974. The Women's Political Caucus nationally appears to
have been instrumental in this increased female involvement and in
the promotion of heightened political awareness on the part of wom-

en. The role it is playing thus should have a lasting influence on political participation in America.

REFERENCES

1. Maren Lockwood Carden. *The New Feminist Movement.* New York: Russell Sage Foundation, 1974.

2. Edmond Costantini and Kenneth Craik. "Women as Politicians: The Social Background, Personality, and Political Careers of Female Party Leaders." *Journal of Social Issues* 28 (1972): 217–36.

3. Louis Harris and Associates, The 1972 Virginia Slims American Women's Opinion Poll.

4. "The Iowa Poll." *Des Moines Register,* 7 August 1966.

5. "The Iowa Poll." *Des Moines Register,* 7 July 1971. P. 10.

6. "The Iowa Poll." *Des Moines Register,* September 1973. Unpublished.

7. Allan Kornberg, Joel Smith, Mary Jane Clark, and Harold Clarke. "Participation in Local Party Organizations in the United States and Canada." *American Journal of Political Science* 18 (February 1973): 23–47.

8. Marjorie Lansing. "Women: The New Political Class." Manuscript, ca. 1972.

9. Lester W. Milbrath. *Political Participation.* Chicago: Rand McNally, 1965.

10. National Women's Political Caucus. "Report of the Organizing Conference-National Women's Political Caucus." Washington, D.C., 11 July 1971.

11. "Outsiders on the Inside." *Newsweek,* 24 July 1972. P. 32.

12. Judith S. Trent and Jimmie D. Trent. *The National Women's Political Caucus: A Rhetorical Biography.* Bethesda, Md.: ERIC Document Reproduction Service, ED 077 054, 1973.

13. Douglas Truax. Institute for Social Research Newsletter, Ann Arbor, Michigan: University of Michigan. Vol. 1, no. 20 (Winter 1974).

14. U.S. Bureau of the Census. *Census Population: 1970.* Washington, D.C.: Government Printing Office, 1973.

15. U.S. Bureau of the Census. *Statistical Abstract of the U.S. 1973.* 94th ed. Washington, D.C.: Government Printing Office, 1973.

16. Charles W. Wiggins and William L. Turk. "State Party Chairmen: A Profile." *Western Political Quarterly* 23 (June 1970): 321–32.

V

Performance of
Women in Politics

Throughout the struggle to obtain the vote for women, both proponents and opponents of female suffrage contended that American politics would be significantly affected. Sexual stereotyping which associated emotion and irrationality with female behavior was the keystone for arguments that women were by nature unfit to participate in political activity. Politics, it was asserted, required analytical skill, detachment, and the capacity to reason, as well as adventuresomeness and courage. All these characteristics, attributed to the male, meant that politics was and had to be a man's business. If women were to become involved politically, the nature of politics would necessarily be changed. Whim and fancy would become the order of the day, and the stability and well-being of society would be threatened.

Those who fought for the vote for women, on the other hand, argued that those very qualities which women were supposed to possess would raise the moral tone of politics. Of course, the acknowledgment of women's dignity and worth which the franchise implied was important; but, in addition, women's concern with home and family, their moral sensitivity, their lack of aggressiveness, and their propensity for peaceful activities would transform the society and make it better. This controversy over women's suffrage has left a con-

259

siderable legacy insofar as it has provided criteria for the evaluation of women's performance when they began to enter the political arena.

The previous sections have dealt with the impact of sex-role assignment on women's political involvement. They have shown that even women who have escaped or modified those aspects of the socialization process that limit their role to essentially interior or home-centered functions have experienced some measure of role conflict. The readings document the expenditure of time and energy in reconciling societally assigned female roles with that of politician and the often fairly elaborate procedures that have been worked out to minimize stress. While there is now some awareness of the problems that socialization poses for women political activists, judgments about their effectiveness still tend to be addressed to the issues surrounding women's suffrage. Is the woman in politics frivolous? capricious? ineffectual? Does she possess the same qualities as her male peer? Has she changed the nature of politics? raised the moral tone of society? If she has not performed according to expectations, are there extenuating circumstances? What are the reasons for differences between male and female performance?

In "Women as Voters: Their Maturation as Political Persons in American Society," Stucker approaches the question of performance by examining the effects on their voting behavior of the long and bitter struggle to obtain the franchise for women. The initial failure of women to come to the polls after the passage of the Nineteenth Amendment, he feels, was related principally to three factors: local resistance to implementation, racial policies that militated against black women, and the problems of internalizing voting as a habit.

Sex differences in voting are seen as resulting from external cues and societal norms which asserted that woman's place was in the home. Only when these attitudes began to change and girls began to internalize modified norms did women's voting participation increase. To bolster this argument, a breakdown in voting by age cohort is presented. Older women can thus be seen as inflating the category of female nonvoter. Stucker then seeks to explain sex differences that exist in terms of other factors. He takes the position that the separation of political and economic rights for women at the beginning of this century produced a sense of loss and defeat following the adoption of the Nineteenth Amendment. The failure of women to turn out at the polls in large numbers in turn led male politicians to be less responsive to demands for broader reform. Faced with limited access to existing political parties, women, particularly white women, moved into nonpartisan organizations and volunteer groups which emphasized issues of unique concern to them, such as social welfare and education. As a result, white women did not extend their professional political roles despite the gradual increase in their voting participation. In contrast, black women, with no such experience in nonpartisan and volunteer groups and low voting levels, were politicized by protest movements and moved into professional political roles at the same rate as white women.

For Stucker, the key to an expanded political role is economic and career equality. Without it, he believes that women's place in professional politics will continue to remain marginal. In other words, Stucker takes the position that differences can be explained in terms of the socialization of women; the failure to achieve economic rights which affected a sense of political efficacy; and the isolation of women from mainstream, effective political organizations.

Using the case-study method, King examines the same issue: the paucity of women in professional political roles. The emphasis here is on the impact of socialization and on the sexual stereotyping that defines women as unsuitable for holding public office. After discussing the characteristics of women who have stood for election to the Iowa legislature and comparing successful with defeated candidates, the author cites a number of factors as significant in explaining the low representation of women. Like Stucker, she sees the recruitment policies of political parties as pivotal. Women simply are not encouraged to run for elective office except in those districts where their party traditionally loses.

King concludes that, although there is some truth to the allegation that few women are elected because few run for office, party recruitment patterns combined with the fact that women are not heavily represented in those occupational and political groups from which legislators are drawn are primarily responsible. Moreover, when women do seek elective office, their chances of success are less; and they must be regarded as exceptional before they are taken seriously. Since the work experience which provides credentials for holding office and heightens a sense of political efficacy is not common among women, their opportunities in professional politics are limited. Again, female performance must be viewed as a product of sexist attitudes which limit women's chances.

Gehlen, in her article "Women Members of Congress: A Distinctive Role," raises a somewhat different question: female contribution to politics. Her findings indicate that in spite of expectations to the contrary, there is little difference between male and female members of the House of Representatives. This is especially true for those women who have achieved their office through the traditional patterns of political advancement. Yet, even women who moved into the House to fill vacancies created by their husbands' deaths are not really very different in their attitudes, behavior, and role perceptions from their male peers. One factor that has differentiated male and female members of the House is age at the time of entrance. Women taking their seats in Congress for the first time are older. This has had serious ramifications for exercising power. The seniority system has meant that since women generally did not have the same length of service, they were unable to move into powerful committee slots. This may soon change; some representatives already seem to be deviating from this pattern.

While women are more likely to support others' programs, any such generalization is risky. Gehlen feels it may well be just a fluke, although it is, of course, possible that it reflects the socialization of women which defines opposition as unfeminine. Contrary to prevalent notions, no clear or strong sex differences are exhibited in the area of social-reform legislation. When slight differences do exist, Gehlen feels they may be more reflective of the congresswoman's previous experiences as wife and mother rather than of abstract ideological and moral commitments. Thus women do not appear to be morally superior or to make any unique contribution. At the same time, they have not adversely affected congressional politics. The women elected have merely adapted to their new role and its expectations. They have not transformed or modified it. Thus, for Gehlen, the common assumptions about female performance are not borne out by the facts.

The final selection deals with the tensions that the role of wife and politician pose. Female performance is closely related to sex-role expectations. Stoper's research would seem to indicate that the older norms which restricted women in politics still exist. The "new breed" of woman has not yet appeared at the state legislative level. Women still enter politics later and generally do not view legislative service as a steppingstone to higher office. Although there is apparently no difference between male and female legislators in terms of the aid that they received from their spouses, the husbands of female legislators seem to have more favorable attitudes about their spouses running for and holding public office than the wives of male legislators. Successful female political officeholders, however, continue to retain much of their orientation to traditional sex roles. Thus they are likely to be concerned about domestic responsibilities, such as getting home in time to cook dinner, that are not convergent with political roles. Moreover, they are less likely than males to emphasize their families in their political campaigns because of their own uneasiness and guilt about their failure to conform to accepted norms.

As all the articles in this section clearly point out, neither the hopes nor fears expressed during the battle for women's suffrage have been realized. Politics and society have not been destroyed by increased female participation. At the same time, morality has not been augmented. Where differences have manifested themselves, they have been largely the product of sex-role assignments transmitted to and internalized by women and men long before their entrance into politics. Sex stereotyping has made politics arduous for women insofar as it has meant that they must play an inherently contradictory double role: woman in all its home managing, nurturing, and mothering dimensions; and politician. Unless some aptitude is shown in fulfilling the first role, no opportunity exists to play the second. Indeed, although the role of woman is not seen as providing credentials to perform the second, it is a fundamental prerequisite. The criteria used to evaluate male and female performance are the same; but the demands on each are very different. The societal context places the onus of proving competence and special merit on women in politics. It also maintains that women must conform to home-centered, interior roles that contribute nothing positive (although perhaps something negative) to their exterior role. As a consequence, evaluations of female performance raise as many questions as they answer.

Perhaps nowhere in this volume is the marginality of women in politics more clearly documented. The very statement of criteria for evaluation, the doubts expressed about women's ability, the women's responses to the conflicting value systems in which they operate and the problems of personal acceptance illustrate both their objective and experiental marginality. Obviously in the area of performance some focus needs to he placed on manifestations of symptomatic marginality. Such investigations seen within the theoretical framework of the marginal man might go a long way toward explaining the role that women have played and establishing suitable criteria for the role they can play under such a condition of marginality.

15

JOHN J. STUCKER

☆☆☆☆☆☆☆☆☆☆☆☆☆☆☆☆☆☆☆☆☆☆☆☆☆

Women as Voters: Their Maturation as Political Persons in American Society

The point of departure for this discussion is the well-known observation that very few women occupy professional roles in the American political system. This observation remains true whether one defines professional political roles as those of party leadership, elected office, appointed office or the policy-making levels of federal and state civil services. Examples of this situation abound. Another chapter in this volume is devoted to a discussion of black women legislators, a category which counted no more than 35 members during the period 1971–1973. Even if we were to drop the adjective black, however, we are still left with a miserly number of women elected to representative office. As Krause notes, the federal and state legislative assemblies in this nation consisted of no more than 3 percent women during the quarter century following World War II.[1]

The most recent figures released by the Women's Political Caucus seem to suggest some progress. When the legislatures of the fifty states convened in January 1975, 604 of their members, or 7.98 percent of the whole, were women. But according to Murphy, the pace of change has been and remains glacial.[2] As one example, Murphy points out that at the current rate of recruitment and placement of women into the top 100,000 federal jobs, it will take women 150 years to fill even 25 percent of those positions. Indeed, in summarizing her recent review of the literature on women in politics for the *American Political Science Review,* Krause seems resigned to the conclusion that the more things have changed, the more they have remained the same.[3]

Why is it that women have been so slow to participate in professional political roles? The answer is, of course, that a multitude of factors, social, economic and cultural, have inhibited women from becoming involved in virtually all types of professional roles. In addition, there is the political dimension. The political history of women in the United States, particularly in their role as voters, has had important consequences for their current status within the political system, and it is this subject that will be the focus of this discussion.

The traditional literature on participatory political cultures has characterized political participation as an essentially intransitive hierarchy of behaviors in which voting serves as the baseline.[4] According to this model, participation in higher-order political roles is dependent on the development of stable and mature patterns of voting, since the motivation for political activism must be nurtured by the politicizing effects of consistent voting. In the case of women in the American political system, this conventional schematic has only limited application. Clearly, women were barred from virtually all political roles during the period in which they did not hold the franchise. On the other hand, once they were formally inducted into the electorate, not all women wanted to or were realistically able to vote; nor did this legal opportunity to vote lead in stepwise fashion to entrance into professional political activism.

Accordingly, the purpose of this chapter is twofold. In the first instance, we review the history of women's political status in the United States with particular emphasis on the struggle to gain full suffrage rights for women and the psychological and behavioral responses which characterized their induction into the electorate. Second, we explore how the reaction of various groups of women to their status as political persons has led to variations in the predisposition of women to become professionally involved in politics.

LEGAL HISTORY OF WOMEN'S POLITICAL STATUS

During the colonial period in North America women had, on the face of it, no political status. With few exceptions, the franchise qualifications of the several colonies contained no references to sex as a criterion for eligibility.[5] It might be presumed from all this that women in those days were so conscious of what their proper role in society was that they did not need the benefit of the blunt legal reminders which were to confront the women who followed after them. In point of fact, however, it is doubtful that the matter was left quite so much to chance. More than likely, the combination of suffrage qualifications based on proper ownership and the statutory laws excluding most women from the ownership of property provided all the legal means necessary to bar women from the franchise. As John Stuart Mill pointed out, lawmakers have seldom relied upon the forces of nature to ensure that women remain in their naturally subordinate role.[6]

As the young United States approached the start of the nineteenth century, the ideals which had been embodied in the fight for independence began to appear in the laws of the states. In the case of voting qualifications this took the form of the gradual weakening and subsequent dismantling of requirements based on wealth or property ownership. But in at least one respect, the lawmakers adhered very closely not only to the spirit but also the letter of the American Revolution. The Declaration of Independence had said that "all *men* were created equal," and one by one the states inserted the word "male" into their rules defining an eligible elector. As Seymour and Frary noted, this first major movement toward national democracy and the universal suffrage would obviously be limited to white males, a policy that was to be repeated in the wake of the French Revolution.[7]

Before long, however, the first step was taken to extend a limited political role to women. In 1838 Kentucky granted the franchise in school elections to "widows with children of school age in country districts." For almost a quarter of a century Kentucky stood alone with its grant of voting rights to women, but in 1861 Kansas followed suit. During the next fifty years almost two dozen states granted school suffrage to women. One of the more interesting aspects about this phenomenon was that it was national in scope; states in every region of the country participated in this initial extension of the franchise to women (see table 15.1). This contrasts with the decidedly regional bias

TABLE 15.1. Dates When School Suffrage Grants to Women Were
Made Effective by State Legislative Action or
Change in State Constitution

1838	Kentucky
1861	Kansas
1875	Michigan, Minnesota
1876	Colorado
1878	New Hampshire, Oregon
1879	Massachusetts
1880	Mississippi, New York, Utah
1883	Nebraska
1887	Arizona, Kansas, New Jersey, South Dakota
1889	Montana, North Dakota
1890	Oklahoma, Washington
1893	Connecticut
1894	Iowa, Ohio
1900	Wisconsin
1908	Michigan
1910	New Mexico

Source: Mildred Adams et al., Victory: How Women Won It (New York: H. W. Wilson, 1940), pp. 165–66.

in the granting of full suffrage rights to women around the turn of the century; most of the states which made women full-fledged electors prior to the adoption of the Nineteenth Amendment were located in the western United States.

Aside from the fact that this legal status vis-à-vis the voting process was extremely limited, however, a more important point was that it did not involve assigning women a real political role. Their participation in the political system was viewed rather as an extension of a woman's special role in society as a mother and educator of her children. This perspective was most eloquently embodied in the statutes which granted school suffrage to women only in the event they became widows. Presumably, prior to that circumstance, a woman would not need to vote since her motherly concern for the youth of society could be transmitted into the public education system by her asking her husband to exercise his political rights. Needless to say, the suffragettes were incensed with the state of affairs.[8]

The women who met in Seneca Falls, New York, in the summer of 1848, and who subsequently founded the National Women Suffrage Association, had laid out a program for reform that was not just visionary but in fact radical.[9] Their proposals called for sweeping revisions of the laws, mores, and institutions that kept women in a subordinate role in society. In the political domain, they demanded that women be treated as political persons, not as political mothers. The move by the states to grant school suffrage to women not only did not comply with their demands, it actually served to reemphasize the nature of women as second-class citizens.

Beyond the symbolism of this legal change, however, this type of private political role failed to provide women with an experiential basis which would advance the politicization of American women. A number of students of nineteenth-century American electoral processes argue that local politics in the last century generated much more interest and participation on the part of the citizenry than has been demonstrated in the findings of mid-twentieth-century survey research.[10] While we may concede merit to their arguments, it is still hard to conceive that this partial suffrage grant would have the same politicizing effect on women as would a full grant of suffrage rights.

In my research on the adoption of woman suffrage in the United States, I found that the number of years during which women enjoyed school suffrage had no discernible impact on the direction and amount of change which can be observed in several indices of presidential and congressional voting behavior subsequent to the full enfranchisement of women.[11] In other words, those women who had had the opportunity to vote in school board elections seemed no more likely to vote in national elections once the occasion presented itself than women who were confronting the ballot box for the first time. This was so because in great measure women had not exercised their rights to school suffrage; consequently, they had not developed maturity and experience as political persons.

To make matters worse, the legacy of school suffrage eventually became a *Catch-22* trap for the advocates of full suffrage rights. By the turn of the century the opponents of women suffrage were arguing that American women had already shown that they were incapable of fulfilling private political roles given their poor levels of participation in school board elections. Of course, women would never be able to prove their capabilities as political persons until they had had a sustained and meaningful opportunity to act out private political roles— i.e. with full suffrage rights. But the anti's persisted. Why, they argued, should women be given full suffrage rights when they had not shown their ability to exercise even the limited franchise that had been bestowed upon them in so many states?[12]

Eventually, the suffragettes prevailed, but it was not a quick or easy victory. Their first substantial breakthrough came in 1869 when Wyoming was established as a territory with a proviso in its constitution guaranteeing equal suffrage rights for all adults. In 1890 it was Wyoming which once again led the way as it entered statehood with a constitution that maintained this principle of universal suffrage. For the first time, a state had granted women the right to vote for all elective offices, local, state, and national. Within the next six years three more states—Colorado, Idaho, and Utah—had followed Wyoming's lead, but in the decade following 1900 no further progress was made.

During the decade of the 1910s the ferment over women suffrage began to bubble once again. The reform spirit of Progressivism had established itself within the body politic, and the suffragettes had now become successful in identifying their ideals and principles with those of the Progressives. As table 15.2 shows, almost a dozen states had granted full voting rights to women before the decade was out, and twelve other states made the fundamental concession of granting women the right to vote in presidential elections. Finally, in 1919, the U.S. Congress proposed an amendment that would prohibit the denial of the right to vote on the basis of sex. In marked contrast to the current situation surrounding the ERA ratification effort, affirmative

TABLE 15.2. Full and Presidential Suffrage Grants to Women by the States

---

A. *Dates When Full Suffrage Rights for Women Were Made Effective by Legislative Action or Constitutional Change at the State Level*

1890	Wyoming
1893	Colorado
1896	Utah
1897	Idaho
1911	California, Washington
1913	Arizona, Kansas, Oregon
1915	Montana, Nevada
1917	New York
1918	Michigan, Oklahoma, South Dakota

B. *Dates When Presidential Suffrage Rights for Women Were Made Effective by Legislative Action or Constitutional Change at the State Level*

1913	Illinois
1917	Nebraska, North Dakota, Rhode Island
1919	Indiana, Iowa, Minnesota, Missouri, Ohio, Tennessee, Wisconsin
1920	Kentucky

---

action by the requisite number of states (36) was swift in coming; on August 25, 1920, Secretary of State Bainbridge Colby signed the proclamation of the Nineteenth Amendment to the Constitution of the United States.

WOMEN'S RESPONSE TO THE LEGAL CHANGE IN THEIR POLITICAL STATUS

The old adage that "you can't legislate morality" seems to summarize a good deal of what we know about the nature of behavioral responses to structural change; often individuals are slow to modify their attitudes or behaviors to conform with changes in the legal or institutional frameworks which impinge upon them. A classic example within recent memory has been the response of the nation, not just the southern states, to the Supreme Court's *Brown* decision and the legion of lower federal court decisions which have followed. The reality of integrated and equal educational opportunities for all has unfolded very slowly across these past two decades.

The enfranchisement of women in Western democracies during the late nineteenth and early twentieth centuries was also a situation in which the target group responded rather slowly to their new legal opportunities. While the pattern varied from country to country, available evidence indicates that women voted as consistently lower rates than men. In an early study of voting behavior in Western nations, Tingsten reported that the differences in the rates of participation for men and women were as low as 5–7 percentage points in New Zealand and as high as 25 percentage points in Iceland, with differences of 10–15 points in countries such as Germany, Sweden, Finland, and Norway.[13] Since voter registers and election results were not reported separately for men and women in the United States, Tingsten could not present the same analysis for this country.

On the basis of the available evidence, however, he suggested that the differential was quite large; and Chafe, citing some limited data from Chicago and New York City, has shown that in the early 1920s men were outvoting women in general and local elections by as much as a two-to-one margin.[14] Furthermore, this pattern does not seem to have been limited either to the decade of the 1920s or to these two cities. In my research I found that, regardless of the year in which full voting rights were granted to women, the average turnout across all

the states in both presidential and off-year congressional voting declined by ten percentage points between the two elections immediately
preceding and the two elections immediately following the enfranchisement of women in each state.[15]

Why were so many women so slow to respond to the political opportunity which some had fought so long and so hard to secure for
them? Several factors seem to have been operative. For one thing
there was a problem of logistics. With the Nineteenth Amendment
ratified less than three months before the general election of 1920,
there were numerous cases in which local election officials were hard
pressed to enroll women in the voting registers and provide adequate
numbers of ballots and polling stations. In fact, Gosnell reports that in
three states, the legislatures did not enact the necessary legislation to
permit women to register in time for the 1920 election.[16] Timing and
logistics, of course, can not explain all the variance, particularly in
those states which enfranchised women prior to 1920.

A second, and clearly more important, factor had to do with race.
During the turn of the century period when women were finally gaining full access to the ballot box, a movement was under way in the
southern states to reverse whatever limited suffrage gains had been
made earlier on the part of black men. As Key and others have noted,
this effort to disenfranchise blacks had consisted of a variety of extralegal stratagems and had been underway for some time before the
1890s.[17] It was, however, during this decade that the southern system
of election codes was adopted in state after state across the South.
These codes, which featured most prominently poll taxes, literacy
tests, and long durational residency requirements, helped to seal the
fate of black voters throughout this region of the country and subsequently nullified the effects of the Nineteenth Amendment for
southern black women.[18]

As for white women, both North and South, how do we explain
their reaction to being inducted into the electorate? McPhee has articulated a life-cycle model based on learning theory which, if con-
verted to a generational model, can be used not only to explain the
behavioral response of white women but also to interpret some empirical data available on early twentieth-century voting patterns of the
American electorate.[19] Like any behavior, the act of voting can become a pattern or habit, the maintenance of which an individual can
support internally. Developing a habit, however, requires both time
and experience; when one is intially confronted with the opportunity

to vote, the nature of the behavioral response will be strongly influenced by external cues.

Thus, when women as a group were inducted into the electorate, we would expect their behavior to be governed not so much by the legalities of the situation but rather by their norms and expectations regarding legitimate behavior. In this respect, many women must have felt severe inhibitions about the legitimacy of their voting. For one thing, since no women had been able to vote before the law was changed (discounting the effects of school suffrage), there was no overt role model after which to pattern one's behavior. Furthermore, there was a substantial array of social norms and arguments which emphasized that the women's role in society was a domestic rather than a political one. These cultural cues would have been particularly influential among middle-aged and older women whose views regarding women in politics were formed without the benefit of the countervailing cues which were generated as the debate over women suffrage reached a climax in the first two decades of this century. Thus, while some women immediately took up the franchise, many others, especially those who had been isolated from the counsciousness-raising effects of the suffrage movement, remained at home on election day.

Dramatic evidence of this pattern was offered by Merriam and Gosnell in their study of the 1920 general election and the 1923 mayoralty race in Chicago.[20] These analysts found that, while native-born women, particularly those living in the Gold Coast section along the north shore, voted at rates only slightly lower than those of men in general, the participation rate among ethnic women was substantially lower than the male rate. The results from their survey interviews made it clear that immigrant women were far more likely to express the belief that a woman's place was in the home, while it was the man's business to attend to public affairs. This same pattern has been corroborated in my research. Looking at the same percentage-point comparison cited earlier for the nation as a whole, I have found that in the Great Lakes and northeastern regions of the country, average turnout in presidential and off-year congressional voting declined from thirteen to seventeen percentage points between the two elections before and the two elections after the enactment of women suffrage (see table 15.3). Since these were the regions of the nation in which the largest number of immigrants were concentrated, it is not surprising that these difference scores were four to seven percentage points above the national values.

Another example of the effects of social norms is contained in the findings regarding the decline in turnout in the southern states. In this region of the country the percentage-point decline in presidential turnout was equal to the nation as a whole, ten points. On the face of it this may not appear to be an unusual finding, but one must remember that by 1920 the South had undergone some three decades of steep and continuing declines in voter turnout. Thus, just prior to the enfranchisement of women, turnout had declined to such a low ebb that only wholesale abstentions by women on election day could have driven the value of the index down by as much as ten points. While the matrix of poll taxes and literacy tests served to exclude black women from voting participation, it seems clear that the "magnolia curtain" proved to be almost as powerful a barrier in preventing southern white women from exercising their franchise.

Additional evidence of the abstention of southern women from the voting process can be obtained by looking at the other index of electoral behavior continued in table 15.3, the mobilization index. In contrast to the turnout index which measures the total votes cast divided by the number of eligible electors, the mobilization index measures the number of votes cast over the total adult population. Thus, while the denominator of the turnout index changes after women are enfranchised (on the average we would expect it to double), the denominator of the mobilization remains constant in its composition. Where we would expect the turnout index to decline after women are enfranchised, we would expect the mobilization index to increase somewhat, reflecting the impact of those women who begin to vote immediately. (All this is assuming that the participation rate of men is constant; an assumption that cannot always have been valid.) While the mobilization index for the nation as a whole increased seventeen percentage points for presidential voting and ten percentage points for off-year congressional voting after women were given the vote, in the South the mobilization index increased by only five and one percentage points respectively for presidential and off-year congressional voting.

In at least one area of the country, however, it appears as though the mechanism of social norms did not operate to repress women from an immediate exercise of their right to vote; this was the western states. As the results in table 15.3 indicate, the decline in presidential and congressional turnout was negligible. It could be argued that this result is an artifact of arithmetic. While the sex ratio in the rest of the country more nearly approximated 50–50, in the western states the female proportion of the adult population was in the low 30 percentage range during the 1890s and did not climb above 40 percent until close to 1920. Consequently, when women were enfranchised in the western states, the denominator in the turnout index would not have doubled in value, and therefore there would be less pressure on the turnout index to decline sharply. If this reasoning were true, then we would expect an additional artifact of the arithmetic to be a very slight or nonexistent increase in the value of the mobilization index; but an inspection of table 15.3 shows that the mobilization indices in the western states increased as much as any other region of the country. This combination of no-change in turnout and a substantial increase in mobilization (the opposite of the pattern for the southern states) clearly suggests that women were more likely to vote in the West than they were anywhere else in the country.

These findings are not particularly surprising when one considers that this was the "women suffrage" region of the country. With the exception of Kansas and New York, all the states in which women were exercising full voting rights by 1918 were in this part of the country. In fact, only New Mexico of all the Rocky Mountain and West Coast states did not extend full suffrage rights to women before 1920. Consequently, the emphasis placed on woman suffrage in this region of the country must have had a greater politicizing effect on women as they approached their first opportunity to vote. Alternatively, the fact that women were enfranchised so early in the West suggests that the

TABLE 15.3. Percentage Point Difference Scores on Four Electoral Indices, Differences Between Two Elections Before and Two Elections After Women Suffrage, National and Five Regions

	Turnout		Mobilization	
	Pres.	Off-year Cong.	Pres.	Off-year Cong.
National	−.101	−.108	.168	.104
Northeast	−.134	−.151	.188	.127
Midwest	−.135	−.174	.226	.105
Plains	−.105	−.105	.221	.156
South	−.091	−.064	.050	.014
West	−.011	−.036	.211	.153

dominant social motif of this region was not based on the belief that a woman's place was in the home. The exigencies of frontier life made it imperative that women participate both socially and economically in the life of the community. Therefore, when the same principle was extended to the political dimension, the role model for community involvement had already been established for women.

PATTERN OF GROWTH IN PERSONAL PARTICIPATION

What we have discussed thus far relates to the initial response by women to being inducted into the electorate. We must now turn our attention to the years that followed and trace the pattern of growth by which women become increasingly more participatory, at least with respect to the ballot box. Unfortunately, given the problems of data collection mentioned earlier, we cannot systematically trace the early stages of this growth process as Tingsten was able to do for the various Western European nations he studied,[21] but undoubtedly the first substantial increment in female voting rates came about during the New Deal era. For one thing, women were exposed to the same set of stimuli, generated by the Al Smith–Roosevelt coalition, that mobilized large numbers of men into the political process. In addition, Chafe has noted that in many respects the Roosevelt administration had (consciously so) an added appeal for women.[22] The volume of domestic policy issues which confronted the President led him to consult with and to employ numerous women in his administration, including the first woman cabinet member; and throughout the administration, Eleanor Roosevelt continued her long-standing efforts designed to involve women in both governmental and Democratic party affairs.

While progress was made in mobilizing women voters during the Roosevelt years, the first tracings of post-World War II survey studies show that a significant difference between male and female participation rates still prevailed. As table 15.4 indicates, the Survey Research Center's 1948 presidential election study showed that women's turnout was thirteen percentage points behind the rate for men. Year by year, however, turnout for women increased bringing it closed to the rate for men, and as table 15.5 demonstrates, the gap has now, for all practical purposes, disappeared. Although there is still a perceptible difference in the South, for the rest of the country and the nation as a whole the differences of one and a half to two percentages points are negligible.

TABLE 15.4. Sex Differences in Voting in Presidential Elections, 1948–72

	1948	1952	1956	1960	1964	1968	1972
Male Turnout	69	72	80	80	73	76	76
Female Turnout	56	62	69	69	70	73	70
Percentage Difference (M–W)	13	10	11	11	3	3	6

Source: Center for Political Studies data reported in Majorie Lansing, "The American Woman: Voter and Activist," *Women in Politics*, ed. Jane Jaquette (New York: Wiley, 1974).

All the more interesting to look at are the differences in male-female voting rates by age group and by race. Table 15.6 is a reproduction of a table from Marjorie Lansing's excellent summary of contemporary voting patterns of American women. The upper half of the table makes it clear that within the younger age cohorts women are just as likely to vote in presidential elections as men and that this pattern has held true across the last three presidential elections. Two other aspects of these age differences are also interesting to note. A comparison of the older and younger age cohorts demonstrates the effects of the generational model, outlined earlier, which predicted that the gap in turnout.rates for men and women would gradually close as women, exposed to the pre-1920 attitudes toward women in politics, grew older and left the population.

Second, by comparing the differences in voting by sex for the age cohorts below 65 years of age with those of the cohorts 65 and over, we can see eloquent support for the proposition that the New Deal had a substantial effect in mobilizing women to vote. While women 65 and over have generally voted at a rate 10 percentage points or more

TABLE 15.5. Sex Differences in Voting in 1972 Presidential Election, National and Regional

	Nation	South	North & West
Male Turnout	64.1	57.3	67.1
Female Turnout	62.0	53.7	65.8
Percentage difference	2.1	4.3	1.3

Source: U.S. Bureau of the Census, *Current Population Report, Population Characteristics* (October 1973), table 1.

TABLE 15.6. Sex Differences in Presidential Voting by Age Group, 1964, 1968, and 1972

Age Group	1964 Male	1964 Female	1968 Male	1968 Female	1972 Male	1972 Female
18–24					48	49
21–24	53	52	53	53	50	52
25–29	66	65	63	63	58	58
30–34					66	67
35–44	75	72	74	72	66	67
45–54	79	75	78	76	72	70
55–64	80	74	79	74	72	69
65–74	78	67	79	69	73	64
75 and older	67	50	68	51	67	49

Source: Adapted from table 15.4, Lansing, *American Woman*.

below males of the same age group during the last three elections, women below 65 have for the most part been very close or equal to men of their same age cohorts in their voting rates. Since women in the age cohorts 45 to 54 and 55 to 64 were coming of age during the decades of the 1930s and 1940s, it seems clear that the stimulus of the Smith-Roosevelt campaign coalition had a substantial impact in leading these women to higher levels of voting participation than was characteristic of women who came of age during the 1920s or earlier.

With respect to race, table 15.7 shows the turnout rates, by age group, for the total population and then for blacks and whites sepa-

TABLE 15.7. Sex Differences in Voting in 1972 Presidential Election by Age Grouping and Race

Age Group	Total Population Male	Total Population Female	White Male	White Female	Black Male	Black Female
18–20	47.7	48.8	51.0	51.0	25.6	35.2
21–24	49.7	51.7	51.2	53.8	38.4	38.0
25–29	57.6	58.9	58.8	59.5	50.1	49.8
30–34	62.1	61.7	63.1	63.2	56.1	54.3
35–44	65.9	66.7	67.2	68.0	57.8	60.8
45–54	72.0	69.9	73.1	71.1	62.6	61.8
55–64	72.4	69.2	73.4	70.2	62.1	61.1
65–74	73.2	64.3	74.8	65.3	59.8	53.9
75 and older	65.9	49.1	67.7	50.6	49.4	32.5

Source: U.S. Bureau of the Census, *Current Population Reports*, table 1.

rately. We can see that black women are less likely to vote than white women even in the younger age cohorts, a clear indication that the extension of suffrage rights to women in the late nineteenth and early twentieth centuries was, for all intents and purposes, an extension of suffrage rights to white women. What is worth noting, however, is that younger and middle-aged black women equal or exceed the participation of black men in the same age groupings. In a recent discussion of the voting patterns of American black women, Lansing has shown that this tendency for black women to vote at higher rates than black men is true only in certain age groups, but that it also shows up in certain educational and occupational strata as well, as she goes on to argue that the rate of participation among black women is likely to increase in the coming years.[23]

To summarize, we have seen that large numbers of white women refrained from voting when they first received their full suffrage rights during the period from 1890 to 1920; while for black women, the adoption of the Nineteenth Amendment was by and large irrelevant. In the intervening years the participation rate of white women increased steadily, helped along substantially by the politicizing effects of the New Deal era. Black women did not begin to participate in substantial numbers until the passage of the 1965 Voting Rights Act, and consequently their voting race still lags behind that of white women. Overall, by the 1972 presidential election, the differences between male and female voting rates in national elections had virtually disappeared. The question that remains is, what has been the politicizing effects of this voting history on women in the American political system?

THE POLITICAL EFFECTS OF VOTING RIGHTS

In order to understand the politicizing effects that voting had on American women, it will be necessary for us to consider the systemic context within which women struggled for, achieved, and then began to exercise their right to vote. What we have come to call the woman suffrage movement first began in earnest in the 1840s, and its objectives regarding the status of women in society were quite revolutionary for the times.[24] The feminists of the mid-nineteenth century wrote and spoke about the need for economic, social, sexual (particularly as relates to childrearing) as well as political reforms. In short, they were calling for complete equality for all women in society. But it should be noted that already a wedge was being driven between black and white on the question of political reforms. In an action that was to foreshadow a similar movement by the southern states a half century later, most northern states during the period prior to the Civil War adopted restrictions against voting by free-colored.[25]

The controversy over abolition, the Civil War, and the sectional conflict which marked the decade and a half after the war all served to delay serious consideration and response to the feminists' proposals; and as the debate over women's rights dragged on, a new generation of feminists came forward around the turn of the century. This group of women seemed more disposed to compromise and to accept a change in the laws relating solely to voting rights rather than the broader sweep of reform proposals put forward in preceding years.

In consequence, victory for women was finally sealed in the passage of the Nineteenth Amendment to the Constitution, but in the aftermath of this achievement there was a sense of loss and defeat. For a brief while there had some discussion about the desirability of organizing a woman's political party to carry on the fight for women's rights, but the disappointing performance by women as voters in the wake of their enfranchisement quickly vitiated this possibility. Furthermore, the poor voting record of women led many male leaders of the two established parties to question the need for them to offer serious legislative responses to the various reform proposals being pushed by women's groups. As a result, the League of Women Voters, a nonpartisan and non-office-seeking group, soon became the dominant voice for women in politics in the United States, calling upon women to focus on those issues of unique concern to them—social welfare and education.[26]

Two other developments subsequently strengthened this regressive trend moving women away from the central arena of professional politics. As noted, the Roosevelts, both Franklin and Eleanor, gave the political status of women a boost during the 1930s, but as it happened, this boost only served to reify further the principle of women concentrating on "women's issues." Most of the women who came to positions of prominence in the administration or in the Democratic party brought with them the perspectives of social workers or educators, which is exactly what so many of them were. As Chafe has pointed out, no women were placed in charge of the major boards, commissions, and agencies which directed our nation's war effort in the

1940s, nor were women to be found in the decision-making councils which planned the conversion back to a peacetime economy in this country or the political and economic revitalization of Western Europe and Japan.[27]

A second factor enhancing the isolation of women from professional political roles was the development of volunteerism in our society, a process which was symbolized by the growth of the League of Woman Voters. "Volunteerism" is actually somewhat misleading. At issue is not the fact that women volunteer their free time to participate in some organized activity; some men engage in volunteer activities as well. The question is, what is the form and the content of the activities which are undertaken? There are clearly significant differences between participation in the Council on Foreign Relations and joining the local hospital auxiliary.

The National Organization for Women has provided a cogent description of what these differences are in their distinction between "service-oriented" and "political or change-oriented" volunteering.[28] Service-oriented volunteer activities are those which are person or situation directed, as opposed to change-oriented volunteering which is directed toward inducing change in the broader social, political or economic system. "Service-oriented" volunteering became the unique province of women, especially white women, because, as many persons argued, it was the type of work that would otherwise not get done.

As for black women, many of them could not afford to engage in volunteer activities because their circumstances forced them to seek employment. Others, however, did engage in service-oriented volunteer activities, but they did so with a twist. They undertook these activities because they felt that the white society would not, through its governmental agencies, respond to the legitimate needs of black people for social services. Once they perceived that the government was prepared to respond, their efforts swiftly turned to change-oriented goals and active protest against the broader system. As a result, the government assumed responsibility for supporting many activities which blacks had previously had to support out of their own volunteer resources.

So once again we see differences in the political experiences of black and white women, differences which, it can be argued, have had important consequences in their politicizing effects on American women. Obviously, the steady growth in voting participation on the part of white women has not led to significant levels of participation by these persons in professional political roles. On the other hand, black women, who only recently have begun to vote in larger numbers, are participating in professional political roles in roughly the same proportion as white women. Clearly it would seem that the politicizing effects of their involvement in the protest movement and in efforts to extract a larger share of benefits from the political system have more than made up for their lack of experience in the traditional act of voting.

What will be the pattern of women's involvement in professional political roles in the coming decades? It is worth noting that many white women (e.g., the mothers of Southie in Boston) have come to embrace nontraditional means of political involvement in order to induce change in the system, but this phenomenon has remained relatively limited, focused on the issue of busing in northern, urban school districts. It would seem that more and different types of politicizing experiences will not be sufficient to move women across the threshold to rapid advancement in professional politics. What is now required is a focus on the question of private economic roles.

As noted, the feminists of a century and a quarter ago viewed the progress of women's rights as whole cloth. They did not see that political equality could be sustained in the absence of economic and social equality. In this light, the achievement of equal voting rights without equal standing in economics could be viewed as an artificial concession by men in our society. What is needed is the fundamental achievement of equality in career and income opportunities. While black women have long since established themselves in economic roles, their occupational (and income) horizons have been severely limited. As for most white women, particularly middle-class white women, they have hardly begun to establish an economic identity separate from but equal to that of their husbands.[29] Until women compete with men for economic roles within the system and thereby come to view politics, as men do, as one of several career alternatives, it is difficult to envision them competing equally with men for professional roles in the political arena.

NOTES
    1. Wilma R. Krause, "Political Implications of Gender Roles: A Review of the Literature," *American Political Science Review* 68 (December 1974): 1706–23.
    2. Irene L. Murphy, *Public Policy and the Status of Women* (Lexington, Mass.: Heath Lexington Books, 1974).

3. Krause, "Political Implications of Gender Roles."

4. Some examples of the literature that have dealt with this subject are Lester Milbrath, *Political Participation* (Chicago: Rand McNally, 1965); Gabriel Almond and Sidney Verba, *The Civic Culture* (Princeton, N.J.: Princeton University Press, 1963); and Sidney Verba and Norman H. Nie, *Participation in America* (New York: Harper & Row, 1972).

5. Jerrold G. Rusk and John J. Stucker, "An Historical Review of Suffrage Legislation in the United States," in *Behavioral Guide to the Study of American Electoral History*, ed. W. D. Burnham et al. (Cambridge, Mass.: MIT Press, forthcoming).

6. John Stuart Mill, "The Subjection of Women," in *Essays on Sex Equality*, ed. Alice Rossi (Chicago: University of Chicago Press, 1970).

7. Charles Seymour and Donald P. Frary, *How the World Votes*, 2 vols. (Springfield, Ill.: C. A. Nichols, 1918).

8. Mildred Adams et al., *Victory: How Women Won It* (New York: H. W. Wilson, 1940).

9. William H. Chafe, *The American Woman: Her Changing Social, Economic and Political Roles, 1920–1970* (New York: Oxford University Press, 1972).

10. Among the writers who have addressed this topic are W. D. Burnham, *Critical Elections and the Mainsprings of American Politics* (New York: Norton, 1970); Richard J. Jensen, *The Winning of the Midwest: Social and Political Conflict, 1888–1896* (Chicago: University of Chicago Press, 1971); Paul J. Kleppner, *The Cross of Culture: A Social Analysis of Mid-western Politics, 1850–1900* (New York: Free Press, 1970).

11. John J. Stucker, "The Impact of Woman Suffrage on Patterns of Voter Participation in the United States; Quasi-Experimental and Real-Time Analyses, 1890–1920" (Ph.D. dissertation, University of Michigan, 1973).

12. U.S. Senate Committee on Woman Suffrage, *Hearing before 63rd Congress, 1st Session* (1913).

13. Herbert Tingsten, *Political Behavior* (London: P. S. King, 1937).

14. Chafe, *American Woman*.

15. Stucker, "Impact of Woman Suffrage."

16. Harold F. Gosnell, *Why Europe Votes* (Chicago: University of Chicago Press, 1930).

17. V. O. Key, Jr., *Southern Politics* (New York: Knopf, 1949).

18. Jerrold G. Rusk and John J. Stucker, "The Effect of the Southern System of Elections Laws on Voter Participation: A Reply to V. O. Key," in *The History of Popular Voting Behavior in the U.S.*, ed. Joel Sibley et al. (Princeton, N.J.: Princeton University Press, forthcoming).

19. William A. McPhee and Robert A. Smith, "A Model for Analyzing Voting Systems," in *Public Opinion and Congressional Elections*, ed. William McPhee and William Glaser (New York: Free Press, 1962).

20. Charles E. Merriam and Harold G. Gosnell, *Non-Voting: Causes and Methods of Control* (Chicago: University of Chicago Press, 1924).

21. Tingsten, *Political Behavior*.

22. Chafe, *American Woman*.

23. Marjorie Lansing, "The Voting Patterns of American Black Women" (Paper presented at the Annual Meeting of the American Political Science Association, New Orleans, Louisiana, 4–8 September 1973).

24. Adams, *Victory;* and Chafe, *American Woman*.

25. Rusk and Stucker, "An Historical Review of Suffrage Legislation."

26. Chafe, *American Woman.*

27. Ibid.

28. National Organization for Women, Report of the NOW Task Force on Volunteerism (Washington, D.C., November 1973).

29. Judith Stiehm and Ruth Scott, "Female and Male: Voluntary and Chosen Participation Sex, SES, and Participation" (Paper presented at the Annual Meeting of the American Political Science Association, Chicago, Illinois, 29 August–2 September 1974).

ELIZABETH G. KING

16

☆☆☆☆☆☆☆☆☆☆☆☆☆☆☆☆☆☆☆☆☆☆☆☆☆

Women in Iowa Legislative Politics

Legislators—male or female—are elites. They disapportionately come from the higher income brackets, the highly educated, and the white Anglo-Saxon Protestant components of society.[1] Most legislators, especially at the state level, can also be considered "localists," since they have deep roots in the community they represent.[2] A great number come from the "broker" occupations.[3] The majority do not seek office until after they are thirty, which may reflect a desire to become somewhat established in their occupation before risking leaving it. Most women, however, do not seek office until after they have passed the child-rearing years.[4]

Beyond there demographic and attitudinal similarities, there are further parallels in the socialization process; yet no clear pattern emerges. Some evidence suggests that state politicians' concern with the political arena does not necessarily stem from their childhood and thus is not dependent upon the political climate in the home,[5] and Kornberg and Smith have reported that U.S. congressmen feel that the school was a more important agent in the development of their political interest than was the family.[6] Also, not all legislators are recruited in the same manner.[7] Though they may not have held an elective office, many legislators have had some sort of political experience before their election. At the congressional level it appears that the

284

"background of the regularly elected U.S. Congresswoman includes pre-legislative experiences typical of congressmen."[8]

Since both male and female legislators come from the same general type of background, one is led to wonder if sex or some other condition might explain why women have not been elected to legislatures more than they have. Except for the numerous works that point out that women are not as politically aware or concerned as men,[9] there has been little research in which scholars have compared the female legislator with her male counterpart.[10] In addition, most of the articles dealing with women in politics examine only the backgrounds of women who are serving or have served in government and ignore those women who were defeated in primary and general elections.[11]

This article examines women in legislative politics in Iowa. It makes some comparisons between the attributes of the female members and those of the average Iowa legislator and between the women who won and the defeated female candidates in the 1972 election. It also attempts to assess the status of women in Iowa legislative politics.

THE AVERAGE IOWA LEGISLATOR

The Iowa legislator is likely to be well educated relative to the general population, middle-aged, white, Protestant, male, Iowa-born, and either a farmer, a businessman, or a lawyer. Before reapportionment in 1964, he usually was a Republican from a rural district; the chances that he will be a Republican are still more than 50 percent.

In the 1960s approximately two-thirds of the legislators had some training beyond high school,[12] and in 1970, 72 percent had such education.[13] More than half of those serving between 1945 and 1963 were fifty or older.[14] Recently the average age of the legislature has been a little lower; the average age of the current body is forty-seven.[15] Only five blacks have ever served in the Iowa legislature.[16]

Usually more than 90 percent of those serving in each session are Protestant, and around 80 percent are native Iowans.[17] A very large proportion of Iowa legislators have been self-employed, and according to Harlan Hahn, lawyers and farmers have always been principal groups in the Iowa legislature, with the farmers being from rural areas and the lawyers from urban areas or small towns.[18] For example, in 1961, 45 percent of the members were farmers; 21 percent, businessmen; and 11 percent, lawyers.[19]

Today farmers still constitute the largest single group in both Houses of the state legislature. Twenty-two percent of the senators are farmers compared with 28 percent for the House. Lawyers make up 14 percent of the Senate membership, 9 percent of the House. Most of the remaining members may be classified in various white-collar occupations—businessmen, service occupations, salesmen, etc. In this residual category only a small percentage own their own businesses. In relation to previous sessions, it appears that the number who are self-employed has decreased. Very few representatives are from blue-collar occupations—only around 2 percent in the Senate and 3 percent in the House.

Throughout this century, the Iowa legislature has been predominately Republican. Except for the New Deal years, Republicans controlled a majority in the Iowa General Assembly until 1964, when both houses were captured by the Democrats.[20] The Senate remained in Democratic hands in 1966 though control of the House returned to the Republicans. In 1968 the GOP regained control of the Senate and legislative politics are again, at least numerically, under Republican dominance.

Until reapportionment most legislators were from rural districts since "the rural areas, on the basis of population, [were] definitely overrepresented in both the House of Representatives and in the Senate, as is illustrated by the fact that in the 1950s more than 40 percent of the total population [was] concentrated in sixteen counties, which elect[ed] only 25 of the 108 members of the House of Representatives."[21] As late as 1967, Patterson and Boynton found that "the very smallest towns and villages (those under 2,500) were quite overrepresented by legislators."[22]

In regard to the socialization of the Iowa legislator, Patterson and Boynton found that only one-third of the legislators had a model to emulate in an immediate family member who had held public office.[23] More than a third of the legislators also claimed that their earliest recollection of politics came in adulthood.[24] Half had never held public office before, either elective or appointed.[25] Most legislators claimed that the primary reason they sought public office was the urging of party leaders, and most felt that they were motivated by a political or a civic obligation. Few mentioned concern with a particular issue or policy as a motivating force.[26]

Patterson and Boynton gained the general impression from interviewing legislators in 1967 that there were few self-starters. Since party organization is weak in Iowa, recruitment contacts often come from other elite groups in addition to those from the parties. Sources of contact include businessmen, county party chairmen, former legislators, local public officials,[27] and lobbyists, who appear to do less recruiting than other agents.[28] Once in office, the chances are 50/50 that the legislator will retire voluntarily.[29]

THE WOMAN LEGISLATOR IN IOWA

One purpose of this paper is to determine how the Iowa female legislator compares with the "picture" of the average Iowa legislator.

To date, thirty-three different women have been elected to the Iowa General Assembly.[30] Twenty-five served only in the House; three in the Senate only, and five in both chambers. There are currently ten women in the Iowa legislature: two Republicans and two Democrats in the Senate, and four Republicans and two Democrats in the House (6.7 percent of the total legislative membership).

Of those women elected, approximately 87 percent had some education beyond high school, more than half had graduated from college, and approxiamtely 20 percent had some form of advanced college work. Eighty percent of those currently serving have a college degree. The average age of all the women at the time of their first

TABLE 16.1. The Iowa Legislator

	Average	Woman
Education	College	College or grad. work
Age	Middle-aged	Middle-aged
Race	White	White
Religion	90% Protestant	70% Protestant
Birth	80% Iowa	70% Iowa
Occupation	Farmer Lawyer	Housewife previous: Education
Socialization	No set pattern	No set pattern
Recruitment	Party and/or friends	Party and/or friends
Retirement	50% voluntary	60% voluntary

election was approximately 47.[31] The average current age of those presently serving is 48.8. The youngest women ever elected was 26 and the oldest was 65. Two of the thirty-three women elected were black. Seventy percent were born in Iowa, and of those who listed religion approximately 70 percent were Protestant. Only two of the elected women have been single—a Republican of 55, and a Democrat of 29. Of the other women, twenty-four were married, and seven were widows when elected. Four of the widows' husbands had served in the legislature.

Though most of the women were housewives and not working at the time of their election, many of them had been employed previously. Approximately 45 percent had been engaged in some sort of educational work. Nine percent were lawyers and 6 percent had worked for the news media. Most of the women were also active in organizations, partisan and nonpartisan, which could help them develop "vocal skills" and allow them to gain organizational experience. For example, approximately 45 percent were active in their local party organizations and some 18 percent were members of the League of Women Voters. Thirty-three percent had been on local or state governmental advisory boards.

Werner's article on "Women in State Legislatures" reports that most female representatives came from the minority party.[32] Seventeen of the thirty-three women elected in Iowa have been members of the Democratic (minority) party; sixteen have been Republicans. Yet, Democrats have been chosen by the electorate thirty times, while Republican women have been selected thirty-four times.

From the election of 1928, the first time that a woman was elected, through that of 1962, the thirteen times that women were elected they were members of the majority party of their district. All were Republicans. Seven were members of the minority (Democratic) of the district that chose them. Competitive districts have sent Democratic women to the General Assembly six times and on three occasions have chosen Republican women.[33] Viewed in this manner, more women of the majority party have been elected. Until reapportionment, the county was the basic unit of representation. Beginning with the 1964 election when reapportionment first took effect, Iowa has adopted different apportionment plans for each subsequent legislative contest. Consequently, it is difficult to determine the party alignment of the (until now) constantly changing districts. However, it appears that most women chosen in the post-reapportionment period are also members of the majority party of their district.

The election pattern of women also generally reflects the political urban-rural apportionment of the period. Sine women have been eligible to serve in the General Assembly, urban districts have chosen women as state legislators in equal proportion to rural ones.[34] Yet, when the time dimension is also considered, the results are somewhat different. In the pre-reapportionment period, twenty-nine women were sent to the legislative body, twenty-four of whom came from rural districts. From the 1964 election to the present, thirty-five women have been chosen, twenty-seven of them from urban districts. It is interesting to note that five of the women currently serving come from rural districts and five from urban ones. Except for the election of 1972, it appears that women in urban areas have been more successful in the political arena in recent years.

Thirty-three percent of the thirty-three women legislators had a political model to emulate either in their husbands or a male relative, and 50 percent of those currently serving had a male exemplar who had held either political or party office. Though all the mothers of those women currently serving voted and a few were active in political activity at the ward or precinct level, none of them were full-time careerwoman—political or otherwise. Each of the legislators came from homes in which politics was discussed; however, few of the women were active in precollegiate or college politics. In fact, several stated that they did not become really interested in politics until their college years or their late twenties. However, even during their school careers the future representatives were "joiners" of nonpolitical organizations.

None of the women felt that they had decided to run for office on their own. Most stated that both friends and party members were the sources of their recruitment; none claimed that they were asked to run by an interest group. In addition to being asked to seek office, other reasons given in answer to the question of why they decided to run for office were: a sense of civic duty; confidence that they could do the job; concern with specific policy areas, e.g., problems of the aging, conservation.

The committees that have seen the most service by women since they have entered the legislative halls are those dealing with education, those concerned with social welfare issues, and appropriations. The women currently serving hold a variety of committee assignments many of which could not be viewed as typical areas of interest for women. It appears that most women currently serving view themselves as politicos since most of them claimed that when an issue directly affected their constituency they felt they were obliged to play the delegate, but when the issue was broad and they felt that they had more knowledge of the subject, they acted as a trustee.

Those women who have voluntarily retired from the General Assembly have a slight edge over those forced to do so by the electorate. It appears that women have been retired by the electorate less often than the average legislator.

It appears that women legislators in Iowa fit the general model of the Iowa lawmaker fairly well. They are, however, slightly better educated than the average legislator, and their occupational backgrounds are quite different. It appears, therefore, that if a woman is going to be elected, she will possess many characteristics of the model legislator to a large degree. Consequently, it will be interesting to see if there is a great deal of difference between the women candidates elected in 1972 and those who were defeated.

THE DEFEATED CANDIDATES

In 1972 there were eighteen women (D.-13, R.-5) defeated in the general election. The following discussion is based on questionnaires from fifteen (83.3 percent) of them (D.-11, R.-4).

Slightly more than 70 percent of the defeated candidates had some college education; however, only 40 percent had college degrees compared to 80 percent for those elected. The average age of the defeated candidates, 43.5 years, is some what lower than that of the women currently serving in the Iowa legislature. The defeated candidates approximate the average legislator model in regard to religion;

TABLE 16.2. Women Retired from the General Assembly

		By the Electorate	Voluntary
House	D.	7	7a
	R.	3	8
Senate	D.	0	1
	R.	1	2
Total		11 (37.9%)	18 (62.1%)

aTwo of these retired voluntarily from the House but lost in their bids for the Senate.

75 percent are Protestant. However, only 50 percent of the losing candidates were born in Iowa. Two-thirds of the losing office seekers were married or widows compared with 90 percent of the women legislators.

Since one-third of the defeated candidates were not married, they could not rely upon their husband's name to aid them in their election bid; and since most of the husbands of the married women were not active in politics and/or not in occupations that would make them widely known, it is doubtful that the married women benefited from their husbands' names as much as the winning women may have done.

Most of the married women were not working at the time they sought office. The other women were either secretaries, in educational work, or retired at the time they sought office. At one time or another, approximately 34 percent had been engaged in some type of general office work, and approximately 27 percent were in some form of educational occupation. These occupations are not ones that would give women much preparation for political office or a great deal of public exposure.

As was the case with the women legislators, no set pattern of political socialization can be discerned. In general the defeated candidates did not come from as highly politicized backgrounds as the winning candidates. In fact, approximately 60 percent did not even belong to the same political party as their parents. Only 20 percent had a political model to emulate in their families. Nevertheless, all were active in their local party organizations, and approximately 47 percent had held a party post. Though some were also active in other voluntary organizations, only one had ever been elected to a public office, and none had ever served on any governmental advisory board.

In response to the question of whether any individual or group played an important role in their decision to run for the legislature, only one candidate did not mention either friends, a party official (usually the county chairman), or a current legislator. From the perceptions of the winning and losing candidates, it appears that the political party played a more significant role in the recruitment of the losing women to candidacy than in that of those who were elected. Though one candidate listed the League of Women Voters as a source in her political recruitment, none mentioned an economic interest group as playing a role in their recruitment. Also, none of the defeated women listed a concern with a particular issue as the motivating force in her decision to seek office.

Though there are similarities and differences between the elected and the defeated women candidates, in general it appears that the defeated candidates do not fit the model of the average Iowa legislator as closely as the women who were elected do.

WHY SO FEW WOMEN HAVE BEEN ELECTED: POSSIBLE EXPLANATIONS

In answer to the question of why they thought there were so few women in politics, both the winning and losing candidates gave a wide range of answers, e.g., socialization patterns, lack of money, fear of competition, the low salary that often makes it difficult for the single woman.[35] But one of the most important reasons why so few women are in public life, according to the women legislators, is that not enough women give it a try.

An attempt will be made to determine what factors have contributed to the low percentage of women that have been elected to the Iowa legislature and to ascertain whether the explanation given by the winning women candidates may indeed be one of the prize reasons for the status of women in Iowa politics.

Recruitment Patterns?

Since there are few self-starters in Iowa legislative politics, it is possible that the recruitment patterns of the parties may act to the detriment of women. The defeated candidates and winners were in general agreement that neither party has done enough to recruit women at the state and local level. However, there was a slight difference in the responses of Democratic and Republican women. More Democrats felt that some improvement was being made in the recruitment of women in their party. It appears, moreover, that the Democratic party does (or at least in the past did) more recruiting than the Republican party in general. According to Patterson and Boynton, the Democratic party leadership plays a large role in legislative recruitment in competitive and especially Democratic districts. The Republicans also recruit in Democratic and competitive districts but do little recruiting in the safe Republican districts.[36] Yet, as has been pointed out, a large proportion of the districts were and many still are safe GOP territory; consequently, it appears that the Republican party does not do as much recruiting as the Democratic one in the districts from which most of its members are elected.

When he studied primary recruitment in Oregon, Seligman found that the minority party often had to conscript candidates into the primary.[37] One cannot help but wonder whether the Democrats may have done this in the past for the general elections in Iowa and that when they could not find a man willing to play the sacrificial lamb, they chose a woman. Twenty-nine women who had not run in the primary have run under the Democratic label in the general election. A large percentage of these women (82.7 percent) were members of the minority party of their district—a condition that makes entrance of the race in many instances nothing more than a suicide mission. It is difficult to imagine that one would recruit oneself for such a task unless one is lacking presence of mind.

As the strength of the Democratic party has increased in Iowa, there is evidence to suggest that the conscription of women to run in the general election is not as prevalent as in the past. This may be due to the fact that now the Democrats have a better chance of being elected in Iowa the party leadership does not have as much difficulty in finding acceptable male candidates. In 1972 four women—two Republicans and two Democrats—were recruited to run by either the party convention or the central committees after the party primary; all lost in the general election.

Subjective Factors?

Much of the literature on political participation stresses the importance of psychological factors and attitudinal predispositions in determining whether one will be politically active. Some authors contend that an individual's self-perception influences to a large extent whether he will choose a political path and his chances of success on it.[38] Consequently, one cannot help but wonder whether certain subjective factors may at times work against a candidate in his quest for political office.

It is interesting to note that a majority of the defeated candidates felt that most people desire to be represented by a male, while a majority of those who hold legislative seats do not. There is also some disagreement between what the legislators and the defeated candidates see as assets and as liabilities for women candidates.

A large majority of the defeated candidates did not feel that being a woman was the primary cause of their defeat. Rather than sex, the losing women indicated that membership in the minority party in their district, and/or their opponent's incumbency, played the major role in their defeat. Nevertheless, some of the comments made by the

losing candidates reveal that they perceive their sex as a handicap
when it comes to running for office.

> One liability I found was being unable to get into men's service
> clubs *to speak* or before groups of predominantly men to say what
> I thought about issues.

> Rural people don't like women in politics.

> Women distrust women.

> Most voters have more faith, for some reason, in men.

> I think opposition to a candidate who is a woman is like an
> iceberg—mostly under surface and rarely spoken aloud.

> . . . I do not think the public will give a woman a chance to show
> what she can do or how effective she can be. Many of the older
> generation still believe, I think, that a woman's place is basically in
> the home.

Women in office felt that their biggest asset as a candidate was that
they as women had "a better understanding of community needs,
especially welfare, education and recreation"; the defeated candidates
also felt that this was an asset but mentioned with about as much frequency that "women are not easily swayed from causes they believe in"
and that "women have a unique advantage in that their business future is for the most part not tied up in what they do politically." One
defeated candidate felt that unless a woman was running against
another woman, the female candidate, as a novelty, often has the advantage of receiving a lot of press coverage.

Regarding liabilities, elected candidates stressed that (1) "men
want women on the precinct level to campaign for them, but they do
not want to compete with them for public office"; (2) "women have to
be exceptionally worthwhile and work harder than men in comparable political office." Defeated candiates listed the latter as a liability,
and added three others in about equal frequencies: (1) "there is a dis-
trust of the female politician by (both male and) female constituents";
(2) "women cannot mix in crowds of men—at poker games and stag
parties where a great deal of informal political discussion goes on";
and (3) "a woman in politics fears any neglect of family duties especially if children are involved."[39]

One wonders if Kingdon's concept of the congratulations-rationalization effect may be present in this case and that the candidates made these assessments after the votes were tabulated[40] or whether the candidates held these views of assets and liabilities at the outset of the campaign and that they may have affected the manner in which the candidates campaigned and the image they projected. To this writer it appears that the assets and liabilities set forth by women in office are not only more realistic but also to a degree reflect a more optimistic outlook, while some of those listed by the losing candidates are similar to long-standing clichés.

The Republican Control of the State?

Some might argue that one reason why so few women have won in Iowa is Republican control of the state, since it could be contended that Democrats, usually perceived as being more liberal, would be more likely to elect woman. On the other hand, it could also be argued that many individuals are liberal on economic issues while conservative on social ones and that a large proportion of the strength of the Democratic party comes from the working class—a group that often is characterized by an attitudinal pattern hostile to women in politics. It is interesting to note that Carroll, a rural county, and Dubuque, an urban one, which are the two most Democratic counties in Iowa, have never elected a woman to the state assembly. In fact, very few women have even entered the legislative foray in these areas. This situation may be due in part to the recruitment pattern discussed earlier.

From 1937 through 1973, Democratic women have held a higher proportion of the Democratic seats in the Iowa House than Republicans women have of the Republican seats, even though the ratio of Republican women who ran and won was greater than that for the Democratic women. Both are lower than the success rate of their party.

At first glance it appears that the chances of women of being elected in Iowa legislative contests is not as great as their male counterparts. Somewhat similarily, Jennings and Thomas found that women did not fare as well as men in general elections in Michigan.[41] Though both may be the case, one should not automatically conclude that the differences in success rates are due to sex.

Lack of Favorable Attributes?

Three conditions probably would enhance the chances of winning of any candidate—male or female: (1) incumbency or previous

TABLE 16.3. The Iowa House 1937–73

	% of Entire Membership	% of Party's Seats Held by Women	% of Women Who Were Successful
R.	71.4%	1.9%	58.0%
D.	28.6%	3.7%	18.9%

Source: Data compiled from the Book of the States and the Iowa Official Register.

TABLE 16.4. Favorable Attributes of Candidates

	Man More Attributes	Equal Attributes	Woman More Attributes
Woman wins	5.9% (5)	53.8% (7)	89.5% (17)
Man wins	94.1% (80)	46.2% (6)	10.5% (2)

service which bring voter recognition and publicity, (2) candidacy of the majority party of the district, and (3) the coattails effect—being a member of the party that carries the district's vote for the Presidency.

A matching of the favorable attributes of all women candidates with those of her opponent, who in several cases was also a woman, in the pre-reapportionment period resulted in the pattern shown in table 16.4. Though men were elected slightly more often when they did not possess the greater number of the favorable characteristics than women were when they did not possess them, women were elected more often when the factors were equal.

During the pre-reapportionment, candidacy of the majority party of the district was the most important factor in determining who was elected; incumbency was the second most important. Usually being a member of the winning presidential party made a difference only in those elections in which a party virtually swept the state, e.g., 1932, 1952. Though a precise matching is difficult in the post-reapportionment period due to the multimember districts used in 1964 and 1966 and to the difficulty in determining with certainty the nature of each district because of changing district lines, it appears that the favorable attributes are playing a similar role in the post-reapportionment elections. For example, in 1964 several defeated women candidates shared the experience with the male counterparts in their party. In that contest two Republican women went down to defeat in the Democratic landslide. In 1966, two of the Democratic House candidates first elected in 1964 were defeated as the House returned to Republican control. In the 1972 election, seventeen of the eighteen losing candidates were defeated by opponents with at least one of these attributes on their side; thirteen of the defeated candidates lost to incumbents or men with previous legislative service.

When the favorable traits of the women and men candidates are matched, the results are such that one would hesitate to conclude that women are automatically handicapped because of their sex in Iowa once they have captured their party's primary. Consequently, an important thing to determine is a woman's chances of winning primary contests.

Failure to Win Majority Party Primary?

In the pre-reapportionment period, Democratic women won 86 percent of the primaries they entered; it is interesting to note that in 88 percent of these they were the only candidate. Though this record may appear outstanding, it must be recalled that during this period, any Democratic candidate did not stand much of a chance of winning the general election. Consequently, it is significant that only 40 percent of the Republican women won the primaries they entered; 55 percent of these victorious women were the only candidate in the primary race. It appears that sex may have been a detriment to winning the majority party primary in the pre-reapportionment period.

The Rural Nature of Most Previous Districts?

Though more women won primary races in rural districts than in urban ones (approximately 6 to 1) in the pre-reapportionment period, more than 90 percent of the women were selected in noncontested races and most of these were members of the minority party. It also appears that women did not fare as well in contested primaries in rural areas as they did in urban ones during this period.

In contested primary races the chances of women to lose were greater than those to win in all districts, but they were even greater in rural districts. The reader should take note of the fact that there were only twenty-two urban counties compared to seventy-seven rural ones at the time of reapportionment and that these rural counties were over-represented in the Iowa General Assembly. Surprisingly, there is little difference in the proportion of women losing the general elec-

TABLE 16.5. Contested Primaries

	Rural Counties	Urban Counties
Women winning	19.4% (7)	40% (8)
Women losing	80.6% (29)	60% (12)

tion in rural areas compared to those losing in urban areas. This may be due to the fact that nearly all the defeated candidates were members of the minority party of their district, whether it was rural or urban.

TABLE 16.6. Pre-apportionment General Elections

	Rural Counties	Urban Counties
Women winning	24.2% (24)	25% (5)
Women losing	75.8% (75)	75% (15)

Malapportionment?

It has been seen that women did not succeed very often when they entered the legislative foray during the pre-reapportionment period; consequently, it will be interesting to see how women have done in the post-reapportionment period. There has not been much change in the performance of Democratic women in their party primaries since reapportionment. They have won around 80 percent of the primaries they have entered compared to approximately 72 percent for the Republican women, which is more than a 30 percent improvement. Both Democratic and Republican women have fared better in the general elections since reapportionment in the sense that the proportion of the seats that they have won has increased; nevertheless, the rate of GOP women's success has declined in the post-reapportionment period if based on the percentage of women who ran and won. It is evident, however, that a lower rate of success will result in a larger proportion of seats if the number of candidates seeking office is greater than in the past.

Level of Participation?

It appears that reapportionment has facilitated party competitiveness in Iowa which in turn has helped to increase the number and proportion of Democratic women elected. Yet, democratic women are not the only group of women that is being elected with greater frequency; the opportunities for legislative service for Republican women have also improved. It appears that the increase in the proportion of Republican women elected is in large part due to the heightened participation of Republican women in recent years.

TABLE 16.7. The Iowa House 1937–73

		% Membership	% Women Membership	% of Party's Seats Held by Women	% Successful Women
Pre-reapportionment	R.	77.4%	.9%	1.2%	70.0%
	D.	22.6%	.6%	2.6%	13.4%
Post-reapportionment	R.	55.4%	2.6%	4.7%	46.9%
	D.	44.6%	2.3%	5.1%	26.7%

Source: Data compiled from the *Book of the States* and the *Iowa Official Register* (some vacancies were presented and they are reflected in the tabulations).

As is indicated by table 16.8, Democratic women still participate more than Republican women, and there has also been an increase in their participation since reapportionment; however, their increased participation has not resulted proportionately in as many victories as has that of the Republican women.

TABLE 16.8. Participation of Women in Legislative Elections 1920–72

		Primaries		General Elections		Elected	
		%	N	%	N	%	N
Pre-reapportionment; 22 races, 2,926 seats	R.	1.5%	(45)	.7%	(21)	.6%	(16)
	D.	3.2%	(94)	3.3%	(98)	.4%	(13)
Post-reapportionment; 5 races, 754 seats	R.	7.0%	(53)	5.2%	(39)	2.4%	(18)
	D.	8.8%	(66)	8.1%	(61)	2.3%	(17)

CONCLUSION

There does seem to be some validity in the argument that one of the reasons few women have been elected to the legislature in Iowa is that relatively few have entered legislative contests. It is more difficult to say with certainty why this is the case, though several explanations may be offered.

Few women are found in groups—occupational and political—from which legislators are drawn. The small number of women in the professions is politically significant because it appears that work experience heightens a woman's sense of political efficacy and civic obligation.[42] Jennings and Thomas also found that in Michigan "employed women were much more likely to enter electoral contests and somewhat more likely to succeed in them than the unemployed."[43]

Though most U.S. congresswomen have been career women, many women state legislators view themselves as housewives. Consequently, one must also look for explanations of why so few housewives have become involved in politics. One reason might be the widespread belief held by both men and women that politics is an unsavory profession and/or pastime. Other reasons might be that many women do not possess the educational, socioeconomic, and psychological characteristics associated with participation in groups; that many who do possess these attributes and become active outside the home prefer nonpartisan activities;[44] and that those that do become involved in partisan affairs often prefer a career *within* the political party rather than public office.[45] But, perhaps, the most important reason is that a large proportion of women enjoy playing the role of wife and mother for which they have been socialized since birth and thus lack the ambition often deemed necessary for embarking on a political career.

Even when women enter political races, their chances of being elected may not be as great as men in their own party; however, more research is needed before it can be concluded that sex is the primary reason why women are not elected more than they are. In any event, it does appear that public resistance to female candidates is still strong and that an aspiring woman politician has to be exceptional before she is taken seriously by the electorate.[46] Sex-role stereotyping, which is prevalent in American society, works against female representation in the legislative halls in two ways. Relatively few women venture out of their "traditional role" to enter political contests, and those who do often face an electorate that has also been taught that politics is unfeminine. Nevertheless, it appears that, at least in Iowa, both the number of women participating in politics and their chances of being elected are increasing.

NOTES

1. Donald R. Matthews, *The Social Background of Political Decision-Makers* (Garden City, N.Y.: Doubleday, 1954), pp. 20–32; *U.S. Senators and Their World* (New York: Vintage, 1960), pp. 11–67.

2. James D. Barber, *The Lawmakers: Recruitment and Adaptation to Legislative Life* (New Haven: Yale University Press, 1965), p. 6.

3. Herbert Jacob, "Initial Recruitment of Elected Officials in the U.S.—A Model," *Journal of Politics* (November 1962): 709; the occupation that he feels most adequately fits the broker model is that of the lawyer. Works dealing with lawyers in politics include Heinz Eulau and John Sprague, *Lawyers in Politics* (Indianapolis: Bobbs-Merrill, 1964); and Joseph A. Schlesinger, "Lawyers and American Politics: A Clarified View," *Midwest Journal of Political Science* 1 (May 1957): 26–39.

4. Emmy E. Werner, "Women in Congress: 1917–1964," *Western Political Quarterly* 19 (1966): 21.

5. See Heinz Eulau, "Recollections," in John C. Wahlke et al., *The Legislative System: Explorations in Legislative Life* (New York: Wiley, 1962), pp. 77–95.

6. Allan Kornberg and Norman C. Thomas, "The Political Socialization of National Legislative Elites in the U.S. and Canada," *Journal of Politics* 27 (November 1965): 763.

7. Samuel C. Patterson and G. Robert Boynton, "Legislative Recruitment in a Civic Culture," *Social Science Quarterly* (September 1969): 243–63; Lester G. Seligman, "Political Recruitment and Party Structure: A Case Study'" *American Political Science Review* 60 (1961): 77–86; Harmon Zeigler and Michael A. Baer, "The Recruitment of Lobbyists and Legislators," *Midwest Journal of Political Science* 12 (November 1968): 493–513.

8. Charles S. Bullock III and Patricia Lee Findley Heys, "Recruitment of Women for Congress: A Research Note," *Western Political Quarterly* 25 (September 1972): 423.

9. Gabriel Almond and Sidney Verba, *The Civic Culture* (Boston: Little, Brown, 1965); Wendall Bell, Richard J. Hill, and Charles R. Wright, *Public Leadership* (San Francisco: Chandler, 1961); Bernard Berelson, Paul F. Lazarsfeld and William N. McPhee, *Voting* (Chicago: University of Chicago Press, 1954); Angus Campbell, Phillip E. Converse, Warren E. Miller, and Donald E. Stokes, *The American Voter* (New York: Wiley, 1960); Maurice Duverger, *Political Role of Women* (Paris: UNESCO, 1955); Robert E. Lane, *Political Life* (Glencoe, Ill.: Free Press, 1959); and Lester W. Milbrath, *Political Participation* (Chicago: Rand McNally, 1965).

10. S. Breckenridge, *Women in the 20th Century: A Study of Political, Social and Economic Activities* (New York: McGraw-Hill, 1933); Martin Gruberg, *Women in American Politics* (Oshkosh, Wisc.: Academica, 1968). This work is not, however, limited to data on women in political office; Ingunn Norderval Means, "Political Recruitment of Women in Norway," *Western Political Quarterly* 25 (September 1972): 491–521, and "Women in Local Politics: The Norwegian Experience," *Canadian Journal of Political Science* 5 (September 1972): 365–88; Annabel Paxton *Women in Congress* (Richmond: Dietz, 1945); E. Roosevelt and L. Hickok, *Ladies of Courage* (New York: Van Rees, 1954); Emmy E. Werner, "Women in Congress: 1917–1964," *Western Political Quarterly* 19

(1966): 16–30, and "Women in the State Lesiglatures," *Western Political Quarterly* 21 (1968): 40–50. A few articles do, however, deal with differences between male and female political activists: Edmond Costantini and Kenneth H. Craik, "Women as Politicians: The Social Background, Personality, and Political Careers of Female Party Leaders," *Journal of Social Issues* 28 (1972): 217–46, in part deals with differences between male and female party leaders in California, and M. Kent Jennings and Norman Thomas, "Men and Women in Party Elites: Social Roles and Political Resources," *Western Political Quarterly* 12 (November 1968): 469–92, compares Michigan male and female delegates to the 1964 national party conventions.

11. However, Bullock and Heys, "Recruitment of Women for Congress," does compare the regularly elected Congresswomen with those reaching office by widow's succession.

12. Patterson and Boynton, "Legislative Recruitment in Civic Culture," p. 245.

13. Charles W. Wiggins, *The Legislative Process in Iowa* (Ames: Iowa State University Press, 1972), p. 8.

14. Charles W. Wiggins, *The Iowa Lawmaker* (Ames: Iowa State University Press, 1970), p. 8.

15. Based on data from *Legislative Directory: Sixty-Fifth General Assembly* (Des Moines: State of Iowa, 1973).

16. William J. Peterson, "Twenty Years After," in *The Negro in Iowa*, ed. Leola Nelson Bergmann (Iowa City: State Historical Society of Iowa, 1970), p. 92.

17. Wiggins, *Iowa Lawmaker*, p. 8.

18. Harlan Hahn, *Urban-Rural Conflict: The Politics of Change* (Beverly Hills, Calif.: Sage, 1972), pp. 135–36.

19. Wiggins, *Iowa Lawmaker,* p. 8.

20. Hahn, *Urban-Rural Conflict,* p. 134.

21. Russell M. Ross, *The Government and Administration of Iowa* (New York: Crowell, 1957).

22. Patterson and Boynton, "Legislative Recruitment in a Civic Culture," p. 247.

23. Ibid., pp. 247–48.

24. Ibid., p. 248.

25. Ibid., p. 250.

26. Ibid., p. 251.

27. Ibid., p. 255.

28. Ibid., p. 257.

29. Wiggins, *Iowa Lawmaker,* p. 9.

30. The discussion of the social characteristics of the women legislators and the electoral data that follows is based on information taken from the *Iowa Official Register* for the years 1920–27, *The Legislative Directory for the Sixty-Fifth General Assembly,* the Secretary of the State's Office, Des Moines, Iowa, and interviews with or questionnaires answered by the women elected legislators in 1972.

31. Not all the women who have served listed their date of birth.

32. Werner, "Women in State Legislatures," p. 46.

33. From the election of 1920, when women first entered the legislative foray, through that of 1962, the county was the unit for legislative districts. Based on how the counties voted in House races during this period, using a 60–40 percent breakoff for competitiveness, and taking party alternation into account, the following breakdown was discovered: 79 Republican counties, 15 competitive ones, 4 Democratic ones; Polk,

the most populous, was Republican during the first three decades under consideration and Democratic during the last one. It is interesting to note that despite a constitutional provision in the Iowa Constitution until 1926, which prevented women from serving in the General Assembly, that women began to enter legislative contests in 1920.

34. The urban-rural classifications for 1920–70 are taken from the appropriate years of the U.S. Census.

35. In 1970 the annual salary of an Iowa legislator was $5,500.

36. Patterson and Boynton, "Legislative Recruitment in a Civic Culture," pp. 259–61.

37. Seligman, "Political Recruitment and Party Structure," p. 84.

38. The reader may want to check Earl R. Kruschke, "Level of Optimism as Related to Female Political Behavior," *Social Science* 44 (April 1966): 67–76.

39. The list of assets and liabilities that the candidates were asked to rank was taken from Werner, "Women in State Legislatures," pp. 48–49.

40. John W. Kingdon, *Candidates for Office: Belief and Strategies* (New York: Random House, 1966), pp. 14, 147.

41. Jennings and Thomas, "Men and Women in Party Elites," p. 481.

42. Morris Levitt, "The Political Role of American Women," *Journal of Human Relations* 15 (First Quarter 1967): 33.

43. Jennings and Thomas, "Men and Women in Party Elites," pp. 481–82.

44. Ibid., p. 277.

45. Costantini and Craik, "Women As Politicians," p. 217.

46. Donald E. Stokes and Warren E. Miller, "Party Government and the Saliency of Congress," *Public Opinion Quarterly* 26 (Winter 1962): 543.

FRIEDA L. GEHLEN

☆☆☆☆☆☆☆☆☆☆☆☆☆☆☆☆☆☆☆☆☆☆☆☆☆☆

17 Women Members of Congress: A Distinctive Role

Much has been made lately of the manner in which women are systematically excluded from or discriminated against in those areas of life that have the greatest prestige and power. We now have the concept of "institutionalized sexism" as a part of the sociological jargon at least, and much of the research energy of the feminist movement is going into documenting its existence and studying its impact.

There is, however, another kind of question related to increased participation. What is (or will be) the impact on the various institutions of society if they do become equally open to women? Are women likely to change the dominant character and thrust of the professions, politics, education, or business? Or will they simply act as men have always acted in these same situations—and with the same wide range of behavior patterns?

The speculative answers to that question depend greatly on the particular set of stereotypes that one holds about woman. Even within the current feminist movement there is no consensus. One common position is that women are no different from men aside from those characteristics related to reproduction. Women, it is asserted, are *not* necessarily more emotional or irrational; they do not rely more on in-tuition than on logic: and there is no reason why they should be more comfortable in, or adaptable to, subservient roles than are men. Cultural stereotypes die hard, however—whether based on reality or not. Many women as well as men assume that the above characteristics are an inherent part of female human nature.

But while the feminists do not agree to that stereotype, some accept another set of characteristics often associated with women in our culture that has a more positive image. In this view, woman are supposed to be more moral, more humane, more oriented to the needs of individuals. In the political sphere, for instance, they are assumed to care more about the moral issues involved than about political prag-matism, to be less willing to support war and other oppressive activi-ties, and to give their support on the basis of conscience, not power. They can thus be expected to be more independent in action—less regular in party support. Above all, they see politics as a means of aid-ing individual people.

Whether any of these views is an adequate basis for projecting the kind of impact that women will have if they gain a sizable representa-tion can only be answered completely in the future. However, a study of the way in which women now perform in traditionally male posi-tions may provide at least some interesting suggestions.

The institutional area selected for study is politics. The particular position under investigation is that of member of the U.S. House of Representatives, the highest political office in this country that has been attained by more than a handful of women.

Most of the data on which this paper is based come from case studies of two different Congresses—the 88th (1963–64), and the 91st (1968–69). The earlier study was exploratory and fairly comprehen-sive both in scope and research technique. Data were gathered by interviews, observation, and analysis of a wide variety of documents. A matched sample of two men for each of the eleven women was used as a control group in analyzing the behavioral data gathered from the documentary sources: election statistics, legislation introduced, and other legislative activities. In the case of the 91st Congress the new data are all documentary. A random sample of thirty men serves as a control group for statistical analysis.

In addition to the case-study material, some aggregate descriptive data are presented about the personal and background characteristics of all women who have ever served in the House. Including them provides some help in understanding the manner in which the women have performed.

GROUP BACKGROUND DATA

Altogether there have been sixty-nine women elected to the U.S. House of Representatives from 1916 to the present.[1] The first, Jeannette Rankin, was elected in 1916 to the 65th Congress and served one term before being defeated in a bid for the Senate in 1918. Since then, the number of women members has risen slowly and erratically to an average of approximately ten woman per session. The largest number of women to serve at any one time is seventeen, the number reached in the 84th,[2] 86th, and 87th Congresses. The 88th and 91st Congresses, with which this paper is basically concerned, had twelve and ten women members respectively.[3] Twelve women are serving in the 92nd Congress.

In an institution where length of tenure is all important to the role that one can play, three facts stand out about the amount of time served by women. First is the wide variation. Terms have ranged from two months to thirty-five years. Second is the fact that while a few women have served long terms, the majority of women have served three terms or less. Six years is not sufficient time to gain much influence in the House. Neither of these facts differs greatly from the pattern for the men, however. In the 91st Congress alone, the variation in tenure among men ranged from less than one complete term to forty-eight years. Furthermore, the attrition rate among new male members is fairly high.

The third fact is that the average length of continuous tenure for women has risen more or less consistently. This pattern would be of no great significance if it continued only until that point where the original women members were no longer simply adding to their tenure. But the pattern has continued. Average tenure of the women members in the 84th Congress was 6.7 years; in the 86th, 8.8 years; the 88th, 10.4 years; and in the 91st, approximately 11 years. Average tenure for all men in the 88th Congress was 11.3 years. For the random sample of men in the 91st Congress average tenure was 9.4 years. This would seem to indicate that the pattern of tenure for women is not greatly different now than it is for men.[4] If there turns out to be some significant difference in role performance, it cannot be accounted for by differences in the number of years served.

One factor that is logically related to length of tenure, as well as the type of expectations held for behavior, is the age of the woman at the time of her initial entrance into the Congress. Using grouped data, forty-five to fifty years of age is both the median and model age for women to begin their terms of service in the House. This is beyond the age when most women are intimately involved in child rearing, but it is also a bit late in life to begin to accumulate the kind of seniority needed to gain much power under present House traditions (see table 17.1).

TABLE 17.1. Age of the Women Members of the House of Representatives at the Time of Their Initial Election: 1916–69

Age in Years	Number of Women
30–35	2
36–40	10
41–45	12
46–50	15
51–55	11
56–60	7
Over 60 years	6
Information not available	2

With regard to marital status, the single career woman has never been an important part, numerically or otherwise, of the female contingent in the Congress. Of the sixty-six women who had served through the 91st Congress, only seven had never been married when first elected.[5] On the other hand, over two-thirds of the women were not currently married at the time of their initial election. As none were divorcees when first elected, widows were a major source of recruits (see table 17.2).

In looking at the figures in table 17.2 it is easy to see why even students of Congress have been caught in the trap of stating that "most" of the women members have been widows of congressmen who died while still in office. While *most* have not been, many have; and the largest single category in terms of marital status is that of congressional widow. It is hard to assess what impact there may have been on role expectations for women due to this group.

The second largest category is that of the currently married. Moreover, this would seem to be an increasingly common situation. Of the eleven regular members of the 88th Congress, six were mar-

TABLE 17.2. Marital Status of the Women Members of the House of Representatives at the Time of Their Initial Election, by Party, 1916–69

Marital Status	Democrats	Republicans	Total
Single[a]	2	5	7
Married	13	6	19
Widow of a congressman[b]	15	14	29
Other widows	6	2	8
Information not available	2	1	3
Total			66

[a] Includes Mrs. McCarthy, who was single when elected.

[b] Includes Ruth Hanna McCormick, whose husband had most recently been in the Senate, though he served some years previous to that in the House; and Leonore Sullivan, who lost her bid to succeed her husband at the special election, but at the next regular election defeated the interim incumbent.

ried at the time they were first elected. Eight of the ten women in the 91st Congress were currently married when elected initially.

It is evident from table 17.3 that no one area of the country has a monopoly on sending women members to the House. Looking strictly at the totals, however, is a bit deceptive. The pattern differs from area to area on one significant point. The women from the South are predominantly the widows of Democratic congressmen. Although this particular table does not indicate this, none of these southern congressional widows ran for a complete term in her own right.

Relative to the rest of the female population of the country, the women who have served in Congress have been well educated, and the level of education is rising. The women do not fare quite so well as a group if compared to their male colleagues, but the comparison is not drastically unfavorable. The general educational backgrounds of the women are given in table 17.4. Werner[6] notes that the most frequent college major was education, and the most frequent preincumbency occupation was teaching.

On the grounds that the women's role in Congress might be distinctive if they came from distinctive types of districts, the districts of the 88th Congress which were represented by women were checked on a variety of demographic characteristics: degree of urbanization, type of economic base, educational level, income level, population growth, percentage of blacks and foreign-born. No pattern emerged at all. Neither was the wide range of difference in these characteristics

TABLE 17.3. Marital Status of the Women Members, by Area of the Country and Political Party, 1916–69

Marital Status	North Central–Northeast and Mideast[a]		Midwest[b]		South and Border[c]		West[d]	
	D.	R.	D.	R.	D.	R.	D.	R.
Single	—	1	1	3	1	—	—	1
Married	3	4	3	1	1	—	6	1
Widow of congressman	4	3	1	5	10	3	—	3
Widow	2	2	1	—	1	—	2	—
Information not available	—	—	—	1	1	—	1	—
Totals	9	10	6	10	14	3	9	5
	17		16		17		14	

[a]*North Central–Northeast and Mideast:* Maine, Vermont, New Hampshire, Connecticut, Massachusetts, Rhode Island, New York, Pennsylvania, New Jersey, Maryland, and Delaware.

[b]*Midwest:* Michigan, Ohio, Indiana, Illinois, Wisconsin, Minnesota, North Dakota, South Dakota, Nebraska, Kansas, Missouri, Iowa, and Oklahoma.

[c]*South and Border:* West Virginia, Virginia, North Carolina, South Carolina, Georgia, Florida, Kentucky, Tennessee, Mississippi, Alabama, Arkansas, Louisiana, Texas.

[d]*West:* Washington, Oregon, California, Alaska, Hawaii, Montana, Idaho, Utah, Nevada, Arizona, Wyoming, Colorado, New Mexico.

attributable to a clustering of the congressional widows at one pole and the nonwidows at the other.[7]

EMPIRICAL DATA ON WOMEN AND ROLE BEHAVIOR

The following section attempts to test the hypothesis that women do play a different kind of role in the Congress once elected. The data are from the 88th and 91st Congresses entirely.

Having been alerted to the fact that the pattern for congressional widows might be atypical for women elected on their own, it is worth noting here that five of the twelve women of the 88th Congress were congressional widows. However, the only two who were still in the 91st Congress were rather different from the other widows and could, presumably, be expected to act more like the nonwidows in many ways.[8] From the type of data available for the 88th Congress, it is quite

TABLE 17.4. Educational Background of Women Members of the House: 1916–69[a]

Background	Members
Graduated from business college	4
Graduated from teachers' college	2
Attended a woman's college but did not graduate	6
Graduated from a woman's college	3
Attended a university but did not graduate	10
Graduated from a university with an A.B. or B.S.	10
Took postgraduate work at a university but no degree	5
Obtained a graduate degree from a university	11
Obtained no post-high school education	13

[a]Adapted and modified from Werner, "Woman in the U.S. Congress: 1917–64," p. 22.

easy to separate the widows from the others, and it is felt that the inclusion of Mrs. Sullivan and Mrs. Reid in the group data on the 91st Congress should not radically alter the findings.

The first area of investigation is a very simple one, perhaps even inconsequential. But it is interesting. It could be hypothesized that the women politicians would be more interested than their male colleagues in supporting equal opportunities for women to achieve high-status positions. One way in which they can do so is through legislation, and all but one of the women in the 88th Congress did support the amendment to the 1964 Civil Rights Act forbidding discrimination on grounds of sex.[9] This was a much higher percentage than was true for men. Also, by February 1964, midway in the 88th Congress, five of the eleven women had introduced the Equal Rights Amendment. Only about one-fourth of the men had done the same. At least in the area of legislation, the women do seem to be more concerned about women's rights than do the men.

Is this greater interest and involvement still the case when it comes to something the women can personally control—the hiring of their office staffs? *The Congressional Directory* for each session includes the names of the administrative aide and main office secretary for each of the members. (The term "administrative aide" is usually used to denote the top-ranking staff member.) Two of the women, 20 percent, had a woman's name listed for the position of administrative aide in the *Directory* for the second session of the 91st Congress. Of the 425 male members, 92 listed female administrative aides—20 percent. In this particular area it would seem that the women do not act any differently than their male counterparts.[10]

More important than their behavior with regard to their office staffs, however, is their participation in the decision-making process. The interview protocols offer some clues as to "style" of action and degree of actual participation. The formal record of how they voted is another type of measure. While voting records are not the most informative type of data, they are at least available. They are also used very regularly by behavioral scientists studying the Congress. Consequently this paper also attempts to use voting studies as one possible measure of difference between the men and woman members of the House.

Six voting studies were taken from the *Congressional Quarterly Almanac, 91st Congress:* voting participation, party unity, bipartisan support, and three measures of support for the President's program—foreign policy support, domestic policy support, and overall support.[11] The voting scores were given as percentages, and the *t*-test was used to compare the means for the women and the random sample of thirty men. Given the variety of cultural stereotypes about how women might be expected to perform, a two-tailed test was selected with .10 being the level of significance.

The first issue is basically one of attendance. In 1970, the first session of the 91st Congress, the women answered an average of 75.1 percent of the 266 roll-call votes. The range was between 48 percent and 96 percent. For the sample of men the average response was 79.8 percent, with a range of 30 percent–100 percent. Taking all roll calls of the 91st Congress, 443 votes, the women voted on the average of 78.2 percent of the time, the men 83.9 percent. The range of participation for women was 55 percent to 97 percent, and for the men 49 percent to 100 percent. The hypothesis that the women are more conscientious certainly receives no support. Neither can they be charged with being unconcerned—at least statistically. The difference in means is not significant at the .10 level. Thus the hypothesis of any difference is rejected.

One further check was made on voting participation. On the grounds that with such a small number of women, one person with a very low voting record could conceivably lower the arithmetic mean disproportionately, a comparison of medians was made also. The difference turned out to be greater than was true of the means. In 1970 the median voting score for the women was 74.5 percent, for the men

TABLE 17.5. Percentage of Votes Supporting Various Programs, Men Compared to Women, 91st Congress

	Men Mean	Range	Women Mean	Range	Difference in Means	t-score	Statistically Significant at .10[f]	
							Yes	No
Party unity[a]	57.33	18–91	60.20	32–89	2.87	.39		X
Bipartisan[b] agreement	69.73	37–95	69.90	35–85	.17	.03		X
Foreign[c] policy	53.00	9–100	64.74	18–82	11.70	1.43		X
Domestic[d] policy	54.66	24–71	55.50	25–77	.84	.17		X
Overall[e] presidential support	54.23	26–69	56.30	25–74	2.07	.43		X

[a]Party unity, 91st Congress. Percentage of 127 House party-unity roll calls in 1969 and 1970 on which representative voted "yea" or "nay" in agreement with the majority of his party. Failures to vote lower both support and opposition scores.

[b]Bipartisan support, 91st Congress. Percentage of 314 "bipartisan" roll calls in 1969 and 1970 on which representative voted "yea" or "nay" in agreement with majorities of voting Democrats and voting Republicans. Failures to vote lower both support and opposition scores.

[c]Foreign policy support score, 91st Congress. Percentage of 11 Nixon-issue roll calls in the field of foreign policy in 1969 and 1970 on which representative voted "yea" or "nay" in agreement with the President's position. Failures to vote lower both support and opposition scores.

[d]Domestic policy support score, 91st Congress. Percentage of 101 Nixon-issue roll calls on domestic matters in 1969 and 1970 on which representative voted "yea" or "nay" in agreement with the President's position. Failure to vote lower both support and opposition scores.

[e]Overall support score, 91st Congress. Percentage of 112 Nixon-issue roll calls in 1969 and 1970—both foreign and domestic—on which representative voted "yea" or "nay" in agreement with the President's position. Failures to vote lower both support and opposition scores.

[f]The t-score must be ≥ 1.69 for a two-tailed test at .10 level of significance with $38df$.

82 percent. The median figure for the men in the total congressional session rose to 84.5 percent. The median score for the women rose two percentage points likewise, to 76.5 percent.

If there is no real difference in the regularity with which women and men vote, what about the way in which they cast their votes? Is there any evidence for the idea that they are more independent either of party or the administration? Or conversely that they are more

TABLE 17.6. Percentage of Votes Opposing Various Programs, Men Compared to Women, 91st Congress

| | Men | | Women | | Difference | t- | Statistically Significant at .10[f] | |
	Mean	Range	Mean	Range	in Means	score		
							Yes	No
Party unity[a]	28.30	6–69	18.90	6–55	9.40	1.48		x
Bipartisan[b] support	11.50	0–23	7.80	3–18	3.70	1.91	x	
Foreign[c] policy	30.93	9–91	15.30	0–36	15.63	2.46	x	
Domestic[d] policy	32.33	16–44	28.40	13–43	3.93	1.17		x
Overall[e] presidential support	33.13	16–58	27.40	13–41	5.73	1.78	x	

[a]Party unity, 91st Congress. Percentage of 127 House party-unity roll calls in 1969 and 1970 on which representative voted "yea" or "nay" in agreement with the majority of his party. Failures to vote lower both support and opposition scores.

[b]Bipartisan support, 91st Congress. Percentage of 314 "bipartisan" roll calls in 1969 and 1970 on which representative voted "yea" or "nay" in agreement with majorities of voting Democrats and voting Republicans. Failures to vote lower both support and opposition scores.

[c]Foreign policy support score, 91st Congress. Percentage of 11 Nixon-issue roll calls in the field of foreign policy in 1969 and 1970 on which representative voted "yea" or "nay" in agreement with the President's position. Failures to vote lower both support and opposition scores.

[d]Domestic policy support score, 91st Congress. Percentage of 101 Nixon-issue roll calls on domestic matters in 1969 and 1970 on which representative voted "yea" or "nay" in agreement with the President's position. Failure to vote lower both support and opposition scores.

[e]Overall support score, 91st Congress. Percentage of 112 Nixon-issue roll calls in 1969 and 1970—both foreign and domestic—on which representative voted "yea" or "nay" in agreement with the President's position. Failures to vote lower both support and opposition scores.

[f]The t-score must be ≥ 1.69 for a two-tailed test at .10 level of significance with 38df.

"under the thumb" of the leadership or subservient to the leadership's wishes? Tables 17.5 and 17.6 give the data from the other voting studies in summary form.

The analysis of party unity shows that in the 91st Congress the men voted in agreement with the majorities of their parties 57.3 percent of the time. The women supported the majorities of the parties 60.2 percent of the time, a difference that is nowhere near statistical significance at the .10 level. With regard to party opposition, the average disagreement score for the men was 28.3 percent. The difference between the men and women proportionately was much larger here than in the support category with an average opposition score for the women of only 18.9 percent. The difference is still not significant, but it more nearly approaches it. If the women are "unbought and unbossed" to any greater extent than the men, it does not show up in greater independence from their party positions.

Bipartisan support shows the same pattern in even more exaggerated form. The average bipartisan support score for the women was 69.9 percent, for the men 69.7 percent. On the other hand, bipartisan opposition scores show that the women were less apt to oppose the majorities of both parties than were the men. The difference in means is again greater in opposition than it is in support. The men had an average opposition score of 11.5 percent, the women 7.8 percent. This time the amount of difference is statistically significant at the .10 level.

Looking at the issue of support for administration programs, the same pattern appears. The woman support the President at a slightly higher level than do the men, but the difference is not statistically significant. Opposition to the President's programs is always less, and by a much larger margin. In two of three cases it is significantly less (see tables 17.5 and 17.6).

The most consistent finding from all the studies is the evident reluctance of the women members to oppose programs which they cannot support. More so than the men they seem to have a tendency to "opt out" rather than to go on record as opposed.

Looking at the data from one other angle, if sex is a decisive factor in the decision on voting, then one would expect this to be reflected in voting patterns that cluster together. The range of difference should be fairly small. Yet in looking at the figures in tables 17.5 and 17.6 it seems quite obvious that the women are as diversified in their opinions as are the men. In only one category, opposition to presidential foreign policy, do the women show a strikingly more compact distribution than the men. Whether this is due to a solid difference in perspective related to the content or is primarily a function of the small number of bills involved needs further investigation.

If women don't vote in a significantly different fashion on the bills as they are finally considered, perhaps they differ in their input into the legislative arena. Maybe they introduce different kinds of legislation than men do. An analysis of the bills introduced in the 88th Congress does lend some support to this idea. The bills were first categorized to the committees to which they were assigned and then a rank order correlation computed. In this test the men and women showed no difference—women no more apt to send bills to the Education and Labor committees, for instance, or Veterans Affairs than the men. The Spearman Rank Correlation was a strong .95.

Classifying the bills by content orientation produced some difference between men and women, however. The bills were separated into twenty-four different content categories and again the rank correlation determined. The correlation this time was .44—decidedly lower than when committee assignment was the criterion.

One further test was run. The bills were again divided into content categories, but this time only three groupings were used: traditionally feminine areas of interest, traditionally male areas of interest, and a "neutral" or "leftover" category. Admittedly the groupings were arbitrary, but they were consistent. Using a chi-square test there was a significant difference between the men and women, with the women's legislation more apt to fall into the category of traditional feminine interest. This is not to say, however, that most of the women's legislation fell into this category. It did not. It was just that a greater percentage did than was true for men.

As a further check on the idea that there is an area of legislative specialization unique to women, or at least in which women are predominantly interested, the question was put directly to the women members as well as to several of the men who serve in Congress. Only three of twenty-three men gave a decisive "yes" to the question as to whether the women members specialized in "women's interest areas." (All three, it might be noted, are considered strong conservatives politically.) Three others gave a sort of "qualified" yes answer, but indicated that they did not mean that women were limited to such areas.

The women disagreed with the notion entirely. Perhaps one woman member put it best when she stated:

> Maybe connected with that [her initial entry into politics] a woman brings to her service in politics some specialized interest in what we call social welfare legislation. . . . Not that a man isn't interested, but the whole field is so huge, and he comes from a background where his interests have evolved with his profession. So it is probably a true statement that a woman does take a deeper interest in these fields, at least originally. But much of the time

may not be taken in that initial interest. I can't imagine a woman being successful in Congress if she narrows her interests to these fields.

Or as another woman put it:

People back home get the idea we are here as social workers— that we are for all the welfare programs and interested in juvenile delinquency, etc. We are, but so are the men. We are interested in the broad-based programs as well that keep this country strong. I wouldn't think that as a group we are narrow in our interests.

There appeared to be greater willingess to admit that women might bring a "feminine viewpoint" to bear on some problems. Both men and women agreed to this in larger numbers, although still more than half of the men said "no." Those women who did agree put in terms of a limited number of areas. Again quoting one of the women,

The thing which you bring to it is the experience which you have had. My experience has been that of a man. My background is much the same as theirs—with perhaps a little more variety than many of them have had. . . . Most areas here don't take a "woman's view." Your opinion is valued as an expert, not as a woman or a man.

If the women do not at least admit to any great legislative specialization, and the objective data are unclear, what about the area of private relief bills? One might hypothesize that a woman would be more apt to introduce legislation relating to the individual needs of her constituents. In fact, the interview data did suggest, impressionistically, that the women are somewhat more interested in individual constituent problems than are men. But a check of the number of private relief bills introduced indicates that on this measure there is again no significant difference between the men and the women. In the 88th Congress the 11 regularly elected women members introduced a total of 111 such bills, or an average of 10 each. The matched sample of 22 men introduced 263, or not quite an average of 12 each. In the 91st Congress almost the same figures apply. The 10 women averaged 11.5 relief bills each, the male sample 12.8. For both men and women the range in the numbers was very wide.

The final area of investigation in the search for some kind of distinctive role for the women members is a more subjective one—and harder to document. It has to do with the concept of style. Granting that the women represent a wide range of political philosophy, that they do not limit themselves to social welfare concerns, that they do not vote in a greatly different fashion from men, they may still play a distinctive role if their style is unique. They may make a special contribution in terms of the informal functioning of the House.

Rather than trying to operationalize the concept of style and then quantitatively measure it, the approach here is simply to look at the interview data for comments about the manner in which the women operate, to note the degree to which there is consensus about the individuals; and to question whether there is any great similarity overall.

On the first question, the interview data are remarkably consistent for most of the women. The male members, press corps, and other interviewees tended to give very consistent pictures of the individual women. But that same degree of consistency does not hold in comparing one to another. The characterizations range from "a very attractive woman, but you wouldn't try to hold an intelligent political conversation with her" and other similar comments about one of the widows to "very sharp, very knowledgeable" about one of her colleagues. On another dimension, one woman was noted as being able to bring her male colleagues into harmony when they were tending to get too acrimonious; she was referred to as the "oil on the troubled waters." In contrast, another woman was regularly referred to as totally impossible to get along with. There is nothing to indicate that they all operate in the same fashion or have the same effect on their fellow members.

DISCUSSION AND CONCLUSIONS

To the initial question of "what difference does it make" if women are elected to political office, the answer would seem to be "very little." Particularly is this true of those women who are elected on their own and have come up through the same political processes as have the men. The congressional widows may play a somewhat more distinctive role than the others, but to the extent they do, it tends to be a relatively inconsequential one as far as the functioning of the legislature is concerned.

Women have traditionally started their careers in the House at an age that limits the degree of power they can obtain through seniority, but even this may be changing if Mrs. Mink and Mrs. Heckler are examples of a new trend. If so, the personal power of some women will be greater, but given the other indications, the impact on the system will not be greatly different. Certainly the women now seem as apt as men to make a long-range commitment to, and career of, Congress.

On most objective measures the women seem to be very similar in behavior to the men. Only in the pattern of not opposing others' programs do they consistently show a difference in performance. This may be a kind of "fluke," but the cultural traditions in which women are socialized in this society are such that it would not be surprising if women were more uncomfortable than men in opposing someone. This might, indeed, have some impact at times on the outcome of legislation, although it is unlikely to be of major consequence.

While there is some support for the notion that women may be more interested than men in social reform legislation, even this is not a strong pattern. If, indeed, to the extent this interest exists it is of their previous experiences as housewives and mothers rather than as professionals, even this may be expected to decline as educational and occupational backgrounds more nearly equal those of men.

For those who would argue that increasing numbers of women ought to be elected to political office because of their unique contributions and their moral superiority, this paper offers little in the way of support. On the other hand, for those who fear that too many women would mean too much tampering with the system, too many do-gooders who don't understand the realities of life, there is little support either. At least in the past, those women who have attained high political office seem to have adapted to the role and its expectations as they exist rather than modifying the role greatly to fit more traditional feminine values and habits.

NOTES

1. This total includes the delegate from Hawaii, Mrs. Farrington, who served while Hawaii was still a territory. It also includes 10 women who were elected in special elections to fill very short unexpired terms of deceased members—usually their husbands—but who actually served six months or less in the House. In one case the woman was not even sworn in because Congress was never in session during her two-month term. In all, 15 of the 69 women have served less than one complete two-year term.

2. Includes the delegate from Hawaii.

3. There were eleven women elected to the 88th Congress at the regular elec-

tion in November 1962. The twelfth, Mrs. Irene Baker, was elected early in 1964 to fill the remainder of her husband's unexpired term. She let it be known early that she did not intend to run again in the fall and consequently played very little role in Congress. She is not included in most of the analyses.

4. If the Women's Liberation Movement is successful in getting large numbers of new women into office at once, this will, of course, lower the average tenure until such time as equilibrium in numbers is reestablished. On the other hand, it seems quite likely that some women now serving will continue to do so for some time to come.

5. This figure includes Kathryn O'Loughlin McCarthy, who was single when elected but has since married the man she defeated in the primary.

6. Emmy E. Werner, "Women in the U.S. Congress: 1917–1964," *Western Political Science Quarterly* 29 (March 1966): 16–30.

7. For a more complete discussion of district characteristics, see Frieda L. Foote, "Role Stress and Cultural Resources: A Study of the Role of the Woman Member of Congress" (Ph.D. dissertation, Michigan State University, 1967), pp. 244, 281–90.

8. Lenore Sullivan was denied the nomination by the party organization in St. Louis at the special election of 1951 to fill the seat of her deceased husband. She gained the seat at the next regular election by winning in the primary and then defeating the Republican interim incumbent. She can thus be considered more of a politician in her own right than most of the widows.

In Charlotte Reid's case, her husband died in August 1962 after having won the Republican nomination for Congress in a heavily Republican district. Persuaded by the party organization to run in his place, Mrs. Reid won in the regular election in November. Consequently, the seat has been strictly her own—although it is unlikely that she would have chosen to run in other circumstances.

9. Edith Green voted against the amendment, not because she did not favor it, but because she feared that its inclusion would cause some men to vote against the final bill who might otherwise have supported it.

10. Some women stated that a male administrative aide could make some informal contacts of value among other men that the woman could not.

11. See the notes to table 17.5 for a more complete description of the studies.

18

☆☆☆☆☆☆☆☆☆☆☆☆☆☆☆☆☆☆☆☆☆☆☆☆☆☆

Wife and Politician: Role Strain Among Women in Public Office

To be a wife is a dream, a goal, a central focus of life for most American women. Over 90 percent of women marry at some point in their lives. Very few young girls do not eventually hope to marry.

A desire to be a politician is extremely rare among women—perhaps because the requirements of the role of politician are directly· in conflict with those of wife.[1] The traditional wife devotes herself in private to meeting the physical and emotional needs of her husband and children. Her currency is not power but service and love. The role of politician is public, power oriented, and egoistic (in that the politician must seek recognition and preeminence for him/herself, no matter how altruistic his/her purposes). Thus, the two roles are neither "congruent"[2] (easily harmonized with each other) nor "convergent"[3] (requiring similar skills and personal qualities).

Therefore it is not surprising that until fairly recently most women politicians at the national level attained political office in a way incidental to and usually subsequent to their wifehood—that is, as

320

widows of politician-husbands who died in office or while campaigning or as stand-ins for husbands somehow unable to run.[4] A second pattern, most common at the state level, was for women to establish political careers of their own but only at a much later age than men, as a kind of afterthought to twenty or more years of being a wife, mother, and volunteer. Jeane Kirkpatrick describes this pattern in great detail in her landmark study, *Political Woman.*[5]

Today, some writers speak of a third pattern followed by a "new breed" of women politicians whose careers more closely resemble those of men: they start when the women are young, they are consciously planned and prepared for, they play a central role in the woman's life script—and, in most cases, they are combined with an ongoing marriage and child rearing. Examples of the new breed are Representatives Margaret Heckler of Massachusetts and Patsy Mink of Hawaii.[6]

Today, family roles no longer seem to prevent women from engaging in political activity short of officeholding. Women now vote virtually as often as men.[7] Employed women have a rate of political participation that is virtually equal to that of men[8] and college-educated women are actually more active than college-educated men.[9] Yet the number of women officeholders, even at the local level, is still a tiny fraction of the number of male officeholders. That fraction is rising at the state level, but at an extremely slow rate; in Congress it reached a peak in 1961 and has been holding steady in the last few years in spite of massive efforts by the National Women's Political Caucus and other feminist groups to increase it.[10] It seems clear that women will not hold political office in large numbers until they have found a way to deal with the problems raised by the noncongruence of officeholding and family roles—or until social changes occur which make those roles more congruent.

The study on which this paper is based was designed to explore these problems. The hypotheses, results, and findings are organized under three broad headings, focused around the following general questions:

1. To what extent is there a new breed of younger, more career-oriented women state legislators, whose careers are more like those of men?
2. The remaining two sections explore ways in which many women's sex roles in the family limit their political careers to the

afterthought pattern described by Kirkpatrick. What kinds of help do women legislators receive from their spouses? How (if at all) does this help differ from the aid received by male legislators from their spouses? Also, how do the attitudes of husbands of legislators differ from those of wives?

3. Do family roles present different kinds of problems with the voters for women than for men legislators? Are the problems handled differently?

THE METHOD

A questionnaire was sent out in the fall of 1973 to a nationwide random sample of 424 of the approximately 7,700 state legislators. This office was chosen because there were large enough numbers of women serving in it (424) to get meaningful results. It is true that thousands of women serve in county and city posts, but these offices vary a great deal in their level of responsibility and power; the office of state legislator offered many fewer problems of comparability. The sample consisted of half of all the women state legislators (212), plus an equal number of men state legislators, who were included so that the problems faced by politician-husbands could be compared with those faced by politician-wives. The return rate, after a follow-up in the spring of 1974, was a little over 50 percent (215 questionnaires). There were 58 items on the questionnaire, all but 3 of which required a forced choice or called for only a word or two in answer.

Fifty-five percent of those who responded to the questionnaire were females; 43 percent were males (the remaining 2 percent did not answer this question). There was good representation from all regions of the country, but none of the answers to the questions about problems and attitudes correlated significantly with region. There were only 16 blacks (and one "other"), not enough to produce any meaningful correlations. Only 13 of the legislators who responded were divorced, again too few to produce meaningful correlations.

Eighty-one percent of the respondents were married; 62 percent had been married more than twenty years. Moreover, the respondents had a large number of children: 48 percent had three or more, 26 percent had two or more, and only 7 percent had no children. However, 48 percent of the respondents had all their children over age 18; only 9 percent had all of them under 12. Not surprisingly, males were more likely to have younger children. Nevertheless, such a large percentage of married legislators with children gave an adequate sample for finding meaningful correlations.

The main weakness of the study is the self-selection of the sample. However, I have no reason to believe that the respondents are not representative of the population. No hint was given to the legislators of what results were hoped for, or even of the fact that men and women were being compared. The author's sex was hidden behind initials. Accordingly, the following analysis treats the data as if they have come from a random sample.

Due to the repeated application of chi-square tests, there is also a problem of interpreting results as being statistically significant at the specified level of significance. To deal with this difficulty, I have generally reported significant results only where the data are relatively extreme.

THE NEW BREED

The first set of hypotheses was that, as in previous studies,[11] the women legislators would be significantly older than the men, would have started running for the legislature at a later age, would have older children, would be less likely to be married and would be less likely to have careers in business or law. In short, I hypothesized that the so-called new breed is not yet very large. Kirkpatrick had found very few young women with young children and high ambitions even among the fifty very effective women legislators whom she studied.[12]

Results
All these hypotheses were confirmed, as the first five tables show. Ninety-four percent of the men and only 73 percent of the women were married. The modal woman state legislator is in her fifties; the modal man is in his forties. By far the most significant of the correlations in this section was the one between sex and present ages of children (see table 18.5).

Discussion
These results make clear that the new breed is still a small percentage of women politicians. However, the differences in age, occu-

TABLE 18.1. Marital Status of Legislators

Number Answering	No Sex Given	M	F
Married	0	87	87
Widowed	1	1	16
Divorced	1	2	10
Never married	1	3	5
Other	0	0	1

TABLE 18.2. Ages of Legislators

Number Answering	M	F
No Answer	1	0
18–29	0	5
30–39	16	12
40–49	34	28
50–59	28	42
60–69	8	28
70 or over	6	4

N = 212 (95 men and 119 women)
Chi square = 25.49 with 12 degrees of freedom
          (significant at better than the .05 level)
Contingency coefficient = 0.33

TABLE 18.3. Ages of Legislators When First Ran for Legislature

Number	M	F
18–25	5	5
26–35	28	22
36–45	38	33
46–55	11	32
55 or over	8	17

N = 199 (90 men and 109 women)
Chi square = 12.82 with 4 degrees of freedom
          (significant at better than the .05 level)
Contingency coefficient = .25

TABLE 18.4. Occupation of Legislators (other than politics)

Percent Answering	M	F
No answer	4	4
Business	55	24
Law	16	6
Education	7	9
Homemaker	1	38
Other	17	19
N = 212 (93 men and 119 women)		

TABLE 18.5. Present Ages of Children[a]

	M	F
1	6	0
2	8	9
3	31	60
4	6	6
5	31	15
6	18	37
7	0	32

N = 171 (77 men and 99 women)
Chi square = 50.14 with 6 degrees of freedom
(significant at better than the .001 level)
Contingency coefficient = .48

[a]People who had no children gave no answer.

pation, and age when first ran were not as significant as others in this study, nor as large as age differences reported earlier.[13]

By far the most significant correlation in this section was the one between sex of legislator and present ages of children. That is, men legislators were much more likely to have young children than women. This tends to confirm Marcia Lee's finding that responsibility for child care was the most serious obstacle to running for office for young women political activists.[14]

The figures on marriage in table 18.1 make it apparent that one way that many women legislators deal with the noncongruence of marital and political roles is by not attempting them simultaneously. Women legislators are much more likely to be widowed or divorced than men legislators. This does not necessarily mean that they are following the old American tradition of entering politics by being appointed or elected to fill their husbands unexpired term:[15] that pattern was followed by only four people in the entire sample. It is more likely that most of the formerly married women were following an even older tradition in which many women first come into their own as widows, possessing the dignity and property that often go with having been married but also freedom from the dependency and service obligations that go with marriage as well.

It seems clear from these results that the delay in the woman state legislator's career in office is largely caused by familial roles. This delay makes it likely that almost no women will rise to executive office or national legislative office.

AID AND ENCOURAGEMENT

The first hypothesis here was that male legislators received far more help from their wives than female legislators received from their husbands. I expected this to be true because serving one's spouse (in both practical and emotional ways) is central to the traditional role of wife but not to that of husband—in some families to the point where there is even a "two-person career" (that is, the husband has a career, to which the wife also devotes her life, receiving no public recognition and less private recognition than she deserves).[16] In any case, husbands of women politicians would probably be too busy with their own jobs to offer much assistance to their wives. Kirkpatrick had found that the women legislators in her sample expected and received little help from their husbands other than financial, far less than the amount of help provided by the wives of male legislators.[17] A second and related hypothesis was that help given by spouses would be along the lines of traditional sex roles. This is consistent with Kirkpatrick's report that most of the women legislators in her study were quite conventional and traditional.[18] The third hypothesis was that the wives of male legislators would have more favorable attitudes toward their husbands' careers than would the husbands of female legislators. The reasons for this hypothesis will be explained later.

Results
The first hypothesis was not confirmed. As shown in table 18.6, male legislators did find their wives more helpful than female legislators found their husbands—but not to a significant degree.

TABLE 18.6. Answers to Question, "Overall, What Role Has Your Spouse Played in Your Political Career?"

Number Answering	M	F
Helped a great deal	35	27
Helped somewhat	24	26
Did not affect it	4	7
Hindered somewhat	0	4
Hindered a great deal	0	1

N = 128 (63 men and 65 women)
Chi square = 7.04 with 4 degrees of freedom
(not significant)
Contingency coefficient = .23

For the second hypothesis (that help given was along the lines of traditional sex roles) I looked at several measures: the amount of money contributed by the spouse, the allocation of housework, and the amount of aid given in meeting parental and household responsibilities and in keeping the business or law firm going. These last two kinds of help were compared for two situations, prior to running for the legislature and during service in the legislature other than at campaign time. I wanted to find out if spouses increased the amount of aid in areas outside their sex roles in response to a political career. The hypothesis would be confirmed if husbands gave more money and more help in business and law firms and if wives helped more with parental and household responsibilities and were more likely to do the housework.

In accord with the hypothesis, women legislators received a lot more money from their spouses than male legislators (see table 18.7).

Table 18.8 shows that male legislators received far more help from their wives in meeting parental and household responsibilities than female legislators received from their husbands, again as the hypothesis predicted. However, it is interesting to note that the number of husbands who helped a great deal rose from 15 prior to their wives' running for the legislature to 35 during her service. In other words, 20 husbands stepped out of their traditional sex roles to help their wives step out of theirs. (The comparable figure for wives was only 7.) Still, it seemed unlikely that husbands were really taking over substantial responsibility for housework. Who did perform this necessary job?

TABLE 18.7. Answers to Question, "Has Your Spouse Contributed Money to Your Campaign or Otherwise Financially Aided Your Political Career from His/Her Own Income?"

Number Answering	M	F
A great deal	0	22
Somewhat	9	34
A little	10	16
Not at all	64	19

N = 174 (83 men and 91 women)
Chi square = 62.05 with 3 degrees of freedom
    (significant at better than the .001 level)
Contingency coefficient = .51

TABLE 18.8. Answers to Questions, "Has Your Spouse Helped with Parental and Household Responsibilities . . ."

Number Answering	M	F
1. ". . . prior to your running for the legislature?"		
A great deal	74	15
Moderately	11	30
A little	1	28
Not at all	1	17

N = 181 (88 men and 93 women)
Chi square = 87.47 with 3 degrees of freedom
    (significant at better than the .001 level)
Contingency coefficient = .57

2. ". . . during your service in the legislature (other than at campaign time)?"		
A great deal	81	35
Moderately	6	26
A little	0	23
Not at all	1	9

N = 181 (88 men and 93 women)
Chi square = 49.7 with 3 degrees of freedom
    (significant at better than the .001 level)
Contingency coefficient = .46

Looking at table 18.9, we see that more than a quarter of the women legislators do their own housework with no help from servants or family members. In addition, more than a third get help but do some of their own housework. Only 15 of the 88 men (16 percent) say they do any housework at all.

Finally, table 18.10 examines the amount of aid given by spouses in the legislator's business or law firm. There is not a significant difference between the sexes in the amount of aid given to the legislator's business or law firm. Of course, many fewer women answered this question, reflecting the fact that many fewer women had business or law firms (see table 18.5). There was also almost no change in the pattern before and during service in the legislature.

In sum, then, the hypothesis that aid was given along the lines of traditional sex roles is mostly confirmed: men give money; women do housework and child care; neither sex steps out of sex roles very much to accommodate a spouse's political career. However, husbands and wives are about equally likely to help out if their spouse has a business or law firm.

The third hypothesis in this section was that the wives of legislators would have more favorable attitudes toward their husbands' careers than the husbands of legislators would have toward their wives' careers. I assumed this for several reasons. First, it is part of the

TABLE 18.9. Answers to Question, "Who Does a Substantial Part of the Housework in Your Family?" (Check as many as apply.)

Number Answering	M	F
a. Yourself	2	33
b. Spouse	44	2
c. Children	0	0
d. Servants or other	2	15
combination of a + b + c	4	7
combination of a + b or c	8	19
combination of a + d	1	17
e. b + d	15	3
f. Spouse and children	12	0

N = 184 (88 men and 96 women)
Chi square = 108.88 with 8 degrees of freedom
(significant at better than the .001 level)
Contingency coefficient = .61

TABLE 18.10. Answers to Question, "Does (or Did) Your Spouse Help Out in Your Business or Law Firm . . ."

Number Answering	M	F
1. ". . . prior to your running for the legislature?"		
A great deal	14	8
Moderately	15	7
A little	10	4
Not at all	43	28

N = 129 (82 men and 40 women)
Chi square = .66 with 3 degrees of freedom
　　　　　　(not significant)
Contingency coeffiicient = .07

	M	F
2. ". . . during your service in the legislature (other than at campaign time)?"		
A great deal	17	7
Moderately	12	4
A little	8	5
Not at all	42	29

N = 129 (82 men and 40 women)
Chi square = 2.05 with 3 degrees of freedom
　　　　　　(not significant)

traditional role of a wife to give encouragement to her husband's work, whatever it might be; husbands are not traditionally expected to give parallel support, except for home roles. Politics is an area where husbands might find it particularly difficult to give encouragement to their wives (and not vice versa) because politicians are necessarily prominent and well known, a privilege usually reserved for males. Even husbands who initially felt goodwill toward their wives' political careers might be so cruelly teased that their attitude would change. Congresswoman Bella Abzug's husband, for example, had been portrayed in a New York nightclub show as a tiny man wearing an apron, dwarfed by an ungainly woman. Representative Sissy Farenthold's husband is called "Mr. Sissy."[19]

So I fully expected this hypothesis to be confirmed. But it was not. Table 18.11 shows that wives of male legislators had significantly less favorable attitudes toward their service in the legislature than did husbands of female legislators. Both private and public attitudes were examined. They were very significantly correlated so I've presented only the data on private attitudes.

TABLE 18.11. Answers to Question, "How Would You Describe Your Spouse's Present or Most Recent Attitude (in Private) Toward Your Service in the State Legislature?"

Number Answering	M	F
Highly favorable	40	65
Mildly favorable	23	17
Neutral	7	5
Mildly unfavorable	17	5
Opposed	1	0

N = 180 (88 men and 92 women)
Chi square = 13.91 with 4 degrees of freedom
(significant at better than the .01 level)
Contingency coefficient = .27

Discussion

The second set of hypotheses had been designed to explore exactly how women's familial roles functioned as so much more of an obstacle for them than men's. I had hypothesized that men legislators received considerably more of both aid and encouragement from their spouses than women legislators received from theirs. Why was neither one of these hypotheses confirmed? It is not clear how it is possible that men legislators did not receive significantly more help overall from their spouses than women, since in all specific areas except financial support they received more help, including two which were not reported for lack of space, child care and performance of duties in the legislature. Even in the area of help in business or law firm, they received more help because they more likely to have a business or law firm. My suspicion here is that when the men legislators answered the question on "overall help," they did not give their wives enough credit. Perhaps they took for granted the help given in meeting parental and household responsibilities. This suspicion is borne out by the fact that for men legislators, overall helpfulness failed to correlate significantly with five of the seven specific kinds of helpfulness; whereas for women, overall helpfulness correlated significantly with all the specific kinds of helpfulness.

The hypothesis that men's spouses would have more favorable attitudes than women was even more strongly disconfirmed: the opposite was true. This is less difficult to explain. It is probable that women are just less likely to run for the legislature at all unless their spouses feel highly favorable about such a venture. People rarely do things that are very much at variance with traditional marital roles unless their spouses are unusually supportive.

Answers to two open-ended questions on the reasons for spouse's unfavorable attitudes shed some light on this point. The questions were: "What aspect of your marriage makes the greatest problem for your role as state legislator?" and "What was the cause for a change for the worse in your spouse's private attitude toward your service in the legislature?" Thirty-three men and 43 women mentioned a problem in reply to the first question; 15 men and 9 women, to the second. Both men (29) and women (26) mentioned time away from home or separation from spouse as a problem far more often than any other single factor. The important point here is that the men mentioned no other problem more often than three times, whereas a number of women wrote of other problems, almost all of them arising from their sex roles. For example, 9 women and no men mentioned meeting home responsibilities (such as keeping the house clean or getting meals cooked). In addition, 5 women described problems which clearly fit into the category of spouse's difficulties with handling the role reversal, and 8 other women mentioned spouse's jealousy, mostly jealousy of attention they were receiving (only 2 men had mentioned jealousy).

A few particularly poignant examples should make the point clearer. One woman saw her "growing sense of individualism, ambition and independence" as a problem! Another woman, whose husband resented the time she devoted to the job of legislator and the attention the title gave her, wrote, "Clare Boothe Luce said she always saw to it that Henry was involved first, before she assumed her responsibilities for the day—I haven't managed that yet."

Still a third woman spoke of her husband's "role reversal from head of household to husband of Senator." She said he received "wry sympathy from friends whose wives are private and subservient" and was continually subjected to questions and comments like, " 'How can you allow your wife to be a politician?' 'Do you tell your wife how to vote?' 'You must be henpecked,' etc."

A fourth woman, who said her marriage was unhappy and not entirely because of her political role, still regretted her "lack of time—for constant and ever present attendance on my husband. . . . He is a fine, strong individual and I know he would be happier if I didn't do anything."

A divorced man wrote bitterly, "It's not worth losing your family to serve in public office—a total waste of life." But in general male responses to the open-ended questions were stereotyped expressions of regret at the lack of time to spend with family. Although time was also the most common problem for women, they gave a great variety of other responses, most of which were clearly connected to the fact that they were stepping out of a traditional role.

ATTITUDES OF VOTERS

The final area I looked at was relationships with the voters. Regardless of the actual situation in the family, voters might perceive an incompatibility between politics and women's family roles. In their presentation of family roles to the voters, how do women deal with this potential loss of votes? It seemed reasonable that women would place more emphasis on their family roles than men because it would be particularly important for them to let the voters know that they were normal women with normal families which did not feel neglected.

An earlier study found that during campaigns women state legislators are frequently asked if their husbands and children approve of their running, whereas no one knew of any men candidates who were asked similar questions.[20] Pat Schroeder, who ran for Congress from Colorado with children aged 6 and 2½, forestalled hostile questions from voters by starting her campaign speeches with, "Hi there, I'm that radical you've all heard about, who doesn't shave under her armpits and leaps over barricades screaming obscenities. I keep both children in the freezer, and my husband is short, has feathers, and goes 'cluck, cluck.' "[21] So my hypothesis was that other women candidates would emphasize their family roles in their campaign materials in order to reassure the voters a bit more conventionally.

Results
The hypothesis was not confirmed. Men emphasized these roles in their campaign literature significantly *more* than women did (see table 18.12).

334 ☆ EMILY STOPER

TABLE 18.12. Answers to Question, "In Your Campaign Materials, How Do You Present Your Role as a Spouse and/or Parent?"

Number Answering	M	F
Emphasize greatly	20	6
Emphasize somewhat	42	29
Very little emphasis	24	43
Never mention	1	19

N = 184 (87 men and 97 women)
Chi square = 33.5 with 3 degrees of freedom
      (significant at better than the .001 level)
Contingency coefficient = .39

Discussion

There are clues in my own data as to why this was disconfirmed. For both men and women, but considerably more for women, guilt about neglecting family responsibilities correlates significantly (at better than the .01 level) with how often the voters asked about the candidate's role as a spouse or parent (chi square = 40.35 for women, 22.6 for men, both with 9 degrees of freedom). Candidates can—and do—influence the frequency with which they are asked about this role. My data show that for both men and women, the more the candidate emphasizes marital and parental roles in his/her campaign literature, the more often the voters ask about these roles (chi square = 21.29 for women, 39.6 for men, both with 9 degrees of freedom, which is significant for men but not for women at better than the .01 level). Thus, many women candidates deemphasize familial roles in order to discourage guilt-producing questions—but at a cost. For legislators of both sexes, greater emphasis on these roles in campaign literature correlated significantly with the degree to which these roles were felt to enhance his/her standing with the voters (chi square = 32.42 for women, with 9 degrees of freedom, 28.43 for men with 6 degrees of freedom—both significant at better than the .01 level). In other words, candidates who deemphasize family roles cannot use them to put across an image to the voters as normal, warm-hearted, responsible, and all the other qualities that supposedly go with being a family man or woman.

SUMMARY

There were the three main findings:

1. Most women politicians could not be described as members of a new breed whose political careers more closely parallel those of men. My guess is that such a trend will emerge only over a very long period of years, as a more sharing pattern of marriage increases in popularity, a pattern in which husbands and wives share responsibility for both financial support and parental and household responsibilities. There is some evidence from public-opinion polls that such a pattern is emerging,[22] but in the meantime most women state legislators seem to fit the pattern described by Kirkpatrick of rising to the legislature relatively late in life than using legislative service as a basis for a more ambitious career.
2. Men legislators did not receive significantly more aid from their spouses than women legislators. However, women legislators have spouses with more favorable attitudes, perhaps because attitude of spouse is a more crucial factor for them in deciding whether to run for the legislature at all.
3. Women legislators place less emphasis than men on their family roles in their campaign literature, partly in order to avoid guilt-producing questions.

The general conclusion of this study is that even women who have broken free of sex roles sufficiently to run for and win political office are limited by these same sex roles, particularly the family-related ones, from shaping a full political career. A woman will rarely run for the legislature unless her husband's attitude is highly favorable—and even then she may receive less overall aid from him than a man would receive from his wife, although her attitude is probably less favorable. Moreover, women tend to wait until their children are older before they run, much more than men do—thus getting a late start on their political career. And even after they run and win, many of them still do their own housework and worry about getting home in time to cook dinner—both activities which are in no way convergent with the role of legislator. In spite of the fact that they shape their careers around family roles, women still feel guilty when voters ask them questions about their families—and so they try to avoid discussing these roles in public, which probably puts them at a further disadvantage. More research along these lines would doubtless reveal many other ways in which traditional sex roles handicap women who attempt political careers.

NOTES

1. A number of recent works on women in politics have chapters or sections on "the husband problem." They include Martin Gruberg, *Women in American Politics* (Oshkosh, Wisc.: Academia, 1968); Peggy Lamson, *Few Are Chosen* (Boston: Houghton Mifflin, 1968); Jeane Kirkpatrick, *Political Woman* (New York: Basic, 1974); Martin Tolchin and Susan Tolchin, *Clout—Womanpower and Politics* (New York: Coward, McCann & Geoghegan, 1973).

2. Kirkpatrick, *Political Woman*, p. 230.

3. Heinz Eulau and John D. Sprague, *Lawyers in Politics: A Study of Professional Convergence* (Indianapolis: Bobbs-Merrill, 1961).

4. Kirsten Amundsen, *The Silenced Majority* (Englewood Cliffs, N.J.: Prentice-Hall, 1971), p. 68. All ten women who have served in the U.S. Senate have been widows of politicians, as have almost half the women who have served in Congress. It was not until 1974 that a woman was elected a governor in her own right (Ella Grasso of Connecticut). The three other women who have served as governors were a widow of a politician (Nellie Taylor Ross of Wyoming) and two stand-ins for husbands (Miriam A. Ferguson of Texas and Lurleen Wallace of Alabama).

5. Kirkpatrick, *Political Woman*, p. 29.

6. Lamson, *Few Are Chosen*, p. 88.

7. Marjorie Lansing, "The American Woman: Voter and Activist," in *Women in Politics*, ed. Jane S. Jacquette (New York: Wiley, 1974), p. 8.

8. Kristi Andersen, "Working Women and Political Participation," *American Journal of Political Science* 19 (August 1975): 442.

9. Lansing, "American Woman," p. 22.

10. Emmy E. Werner and Louise M. Bachtold, "Personality Characteristics of Women in American Politics," in Jacquette, *Women in Politics*, p. 76.

11. See Kirkpatrick, *Political Woman*, p. 29; also see *Women State Legislators: Report from a Conference for Women in Public Life, May 18–21, 1972* (Center for the American Woman and Politics, Eagleton Institute of Politics, Rutgers—the State University, New Brunswick, N.J.), p. 7.

12. Kirkpatrick, *Political Woman*, p. 67.

13. *Women State Legislators*, p. 7.

14. Marcia M. Lee, "Why Few Women Hold Public Office: The Incompatibility of Democracy and Traditional Sex Role Assignments" (ms., 1975), p. 16.

15. Amundsen, *Silenced Majority*, p. 68.

16. Hanna Papanek, "Men, Women and Work: Reflections on the Two-Person Career," in *Changing Women in a Changing Society*, ed. Joan Huber (Chicago: University of Chicago Press, 1973), pp. 90–110.

17. Kirkpatrick, *Political Woman*, p. 227.

18. Ibid., p. 42.

19. Tolchin, *Clout*, p. 98.

20. *Women State Legislators,* p. 14.

21. Tolchin, *Clout,* p. 87.

22. Forty-six percent of women and 44 percent of men now believe that a marriage in which husband and wife share responsibilities for both earning a living and rearing children is "the most satisfying and interesting way of life." Virginia Slims American Woman's Opinion Poll (1974), p. 31.

VI Black Women: A Minority Within a Minority

Over the long period of the American political experiment, politics has been "man's business" with very limited officeholding by women. In addition, for the major portion of the history of this country, politics has also been "white folks' business." As a consequence, black women have been doubly excluded from the political arena. This section deals with those special problems that accrue to black women as a result of this dual discrimination. More specifically, black women who are political activists experience a dual pattern of marginality, one resulting from a kind of suspension between two sets of norms related to sex and another related to race.

What are the special problems of sexism compounded by racism confronted by black women in the political arena? To what extent are black women and white women socialized to conflicting norms of femininity? To what extent does racism militate against a coalition of interests among black women and white women? Are the experiences of black women and white women in the political arena so radically different as to defy the utilization of common central concepts and frames of reference? Are there aspects of the thrust for greater politi-

339

cal political participation by white women that are antithetical to black women's liberation? Are there special tensions that come into play for black women as they interact with the larger female community? These questions are of critical relevance to any assessment of the present and future political status of black women in particular and American women generally.

Because political socialization theory has been especially useful in the examination of women's participation in the political system, it might be well to consider research done on the political socialization of blacks in quest of findings relevant to black women as a special category of political being.[1] Studies suggest, for the most part, that black adults tend to relate to the political system rather differently from whites. Blacks experience a far greater sense of personal alienation and political futility; tend to be less trusting of their political systems (local and national); and are inclined, in surprisingly large numbers, to feel that the country is not worth fighting for in time of war. Moreover, blacks have a lower rate of political efficacy and exhibit a pattern for development of the political self different from that of whites.

When findings on children are examined, these racial differences prevail.[2] Studies of white children reveal that political orientations begin to develop at a very early age and are indiscriminately positive. Further, basic political values are fixed by the end of elementary school with little alteration in later stages. Benevolence is attributed to political authority figures by white children, and the overwhelming majority of them express great pride in America. Findings on black children reveal political attitudes substantially different from those of whites. For example, while both black children and white children express positive attitudes toward political authority figures in early grades and with age experience a decline in such feelings, the decline among black children is much more pronounced, especially in the case of policemen. At least one study indicates that this decrease in affection is more accelerated in the more perceptive black youngsters. Black children express lower rates of political efficacy and higher levels of cynicism than white children. Sex differences found in early studies of whites did not appear on those measures used to study black children. The cumulative impact of these findings would seem to support the contention, implicit in the organization of this volume, that black women may be a unique type in American politics.

The concept of marginality has been applied to the black experience in America by a number of writers. Over the years these efforts have been greeted with varying degrees of acceptance and rejection. The black sociologist W. E. B. DuBois, in *The Souls of Black Folks,* sets forth this phenomenon with extraordinary clarity:

> One ever feels his two-ness,—an American, a Negro;
> Two souls, two thoughts, two unreconciled strivings;
> Two warring ideals in one dark body. . . .
> The history of the American Negro is the history of this strife,—this longing to attain self-conscious manhood, to merge his double self into a better and truer self. In this merging he wishes neither of the older selves to be lost.[3]

Everett V. Stonequist, in his *The Marginal Man,* recognizes the applicability of this concept to the black experience. He describes the American Negro as one "who carries on his face the tell-tale evidence of an alien background, but whose inner personality may be indistinguishable" from that of the average white. The marginal man's dual social connections, Stonequist advances, will be reflected in his life style, the nature of his achievements and failures, his conception of himself, and his social attitudes and aspirations—in fact, he is a kind of dual personality.[4]

Similarly, J. Saunders Redding writes,

> . . . there is something very personal about being Negro in America. It is like having a second ego which is as much the conscious subject of all experiences as the natural self. It is not what the psychologists call dual personality. It is more complex, and, I think more morbid than that. In the state of which I speak, one receives two distinct impacts from certain experiences and one undergoes two distinct reactions—the one normal and intrinsic to the natural self; the other, entirely different but of equal force, a prodigy created by the accumulated consciousness of Negroness.[5]

This psychological disequilibrium associated with the black experience is a frequent theme in the works of Frantz Fanon, Eldridge Cleaver, James Baldwin, and others. In addition, another manifestation of the concept of marginality related to race, the tragic mulatto, has permeated American fiction and nonfiction for nearly two hundred years.[6]

In the aftermath of the 1965 Voting Rights Act, blacks elected to public offices in the South quickly became aware of some of the incongruities associated with their separate statuses as blacks and as officeholders.[7] Maintaining credibility in the black community through appropriate expressions of outrage at differential standards of services, for example, while engaging in the kind of compromise and conciliation necessary to obtain some tangible benefits for their constituencies represented one of their major problems. To fail at either of these tasks would be equally dysfunctional for achievement of longevity in office or, perhaps more significantly, achievement of upward mobility.

The selections that follow broach some of the more critical elements in the black woman's political status and behavior in the context of American politics. In "The Politics of Sexual Stereotypes" Mae C. King examines the political implications of the stereotyped images of the American black woman in an effort to delineate substantive differences between the racial oppression and sex discrimination she faces as compared to the selective sex discrimination experienced by white women.

Using stereotype to refer to any "exaggerated belief associated with a category in order to justify or rationalize behavior in relationship to that category," King identifies three major images that have emerged: the "nonfeminist," the "depreciated sex object," and the "loser." Each is painstakingly placed in historical context and subjected to analysis for its wider social and political implications in a system which, she contends, is founded on racial oppression and organized on the caste principle. The "nonfeminist" image depicts black women as tough, hard-working domestics who assume a role of dominance in their homes but revise that role to one of appropriate submissiveness in their relationships with the white world. This image facilitates the economic exploitation of black females, the psychological castration of black males, and the idealization of those opposing characteristics embodied in the stereotypical images of white women. The major political function of the "depreciated sex object" image is that of excluding black women as acceptable marriage partners for white men by providing these men with a psychological protective device against any "momentary passion" or "compassion" which might result from their physical contact with black women. Stifling or destroying the self-esteem, self-respect, and aspirations of black women is the political effect of the "loser" image, according to King.

Inez Reid's article "Traditional Political Animals? A Loud No" conveys the deeply ingrained disaffection of a sample of black "so-called militant" women with the recent administration of Richard M.

Nixon. In addition to probing their generalized feelings, Reid examines their attitudes regarding specific proposals and personalities associated with that administration. Her reporting provides some insight on such concerns as the levels of political information and sophistication these women possess, the extent to which they resemble other women political activists, and how they perceive of themselves in the context of American politics. Not surprisingly, an overwhelming majority of these women, employing "very vivid and colorful" language, expressed exceedingly hostile feelings toward Nixon and Agnew as individuals, toward policies and personnel associated with the Nixon administration, and toward the political system as a whole. Most were confident that the administration was not destined to become more responsive to black needs. With unexpected acuity perhaps, some even suggested terms and notions that were to surface later in relationship to the former Chief Executive—"mania," "power mad," "ego trip," "Nixon frightens me." Except for some favorable remarks about Robert Finch, disapproval was virtually universal. Reid projects that these women are not likely to become "traditional political animals," largely because of lack of confidence in traditional politics.

Using data on recent presidential elections, Marjorie Lansing seeks to illuminate voting behavior patterns of black women in relationship to age, education, region, occupation, and status as head of household. Voting behavior of black women is also compared with that of black men, white men, and white women, using essentially the same variables. How do black women compare with their white counterparts? Are there striking differences between the voting behavior of black men and black women? If so, what are the possible sources of these behavior differentials? Given the widespread attribution of a "matriarchal pattern" to black family life, what impact does the head-of-household role have on the propensity of black women to cast ballots in presidential elections?

While Lansing's work offers some valuable insights on these questions, its major contribution might well be the significant concerns that are generated in quest of greater understanding of the political behavior of a rather nontraditional voting bloc through utilization of basic canons of traditional voting behavior research theory and methodology. For example, Lansing finds that black women's voter participation has increased at a rate greater than that of any other sex/race group, that there is a narrower gap between voting levels of black men and women than between white men and women, with

344 ☆ GITHENS AND PRESTAGE

women approaching parity by 1972, and that among younger blacks, women have outvoted men in recent elections. Especially noteworthy is the striking inconsistency between these findings and what would seem to be dictated by extant voting research theory.

Officeholding by black women is a rather recent phenomenon in American politics. Edward T. Clayton observed in 1964 that few black women had made a dramatic success at politics; less than a dozen across the nation had gained elective office in the sense that they had political constituents. By 1973, this figure had increased to 337. Herrington J. Bryce and Alan E. Warrick report on the number and regional distribution of these officeholders, the offices held, and their tenure in office and also make some limited comparisons of black women and white women officeholders.

Among black officeholders, women account for 12 percent of the total. By contrast, when the total population is considered, only about 3 percent of the offices are held by women. The South ranked first in number of offices held; those states with the greatest numbers of black females elected were generally the ones with the greatest total numbers of blacks in office. The heaviest concentration of women was in offices related to education. Black women were least visible in county- and federal-level positions.

The first black woman to serve in a state legislative body was Crystal Bird Fauset of Pennsylvania, elected to that state's lower house in 1938. Cora Brown became the first black female state senator, in Michigan in 1952. These women and those who have followed them in the various state houses constitute an elite cadre in the American political arena. "Black Women State Legislators: A Profile" focuses on 32 of the 35 legislators in office between 1971 and 1973. Social backgrounds, career patterns, tenure in office, future plans, and selected political orientations are explored in what might be viewed as a pioneering effort in this field of inquiry. This study of the social milieu out of which these women have emerged, their paths to legislative position, family life styles, ambitions for the future, and attitudes on selected political concerns provides some answers to existing questions and simultaneously raises others, possibly more complex and agonizing.

NOTES
1. For studies on black adult attitudes, see Dwaine Marwick, "The Political Socialization of the American Negro," *Annals* 361 (September 1965): 112–27; National

Advisory Committee on Civil Disorders, *Report of the National Advisory Commission on Civil Disorders* (New York: Bantam, 1968); Charles S. Bullock III and Harrell R. Rodgers, Jr., eds., *Black Political Attitudes* (Chicago: Markham, 1972).

2. See, for exanple, James E. Conyers and William Farmer, *Black Youth in a Southern Metropolis* (Atlanta: Southern Regional Council, 1968), p. 13; Joan E. Laurence, "White Socialization: Black Reality," *Psychiatry* 33 (May 1970): 174–94; Edward S. Greenberg, "Orientation of Black and White Children to Political Authority Figures," *Social Science Quarterly* 51 (December 1970): 562–71; Schley Lyons, "The Political Socialization of Ghetto Children," *Journal of Politics* 32 (May 1970): 288–304; Milton Morris, "The Political Socialization of Black Youth: A Survey of Research Findings," *Public Affairs Bulletin* (Carbondale, Ill.: Southern Illinois University, May–June 1972).

3. W. E. B. DuBois, *The Souls of Black Folks: Essays and Sketches* (Greenwich, Conn.: Premier, 1961), p. 17.

4. Everett V. Stonequist, *The Marginal Man: A Study in Personality and Culture Conflict* (New York: Scribner's, 1937), pp. 3–4.

5. J. Saunders Redding, *On Being Negro in America* (New York: Bantam, 1964), p. 3.

6. See Frantz Fanon, *The Wretched of the Earth* (New York: Evergreen, 1966); Frantz Fanon, *Black Skin White Masks* (New York: Evergreen, 1967); Eldridge Cleaver, *Post Prison Writings and Speeches* (New York: Vintage, 1967), pp. 58–59; James Baldwin, *Nobody Knows My Name* (New York: Dial, 1961), esp. pp. 1–12; Leonard Broom and Norval Glenn, *The Transformation of the American Negro* (New York: Harper & Row, 1965), p. 188. Examples of the mulatto theme are the works of the novelist Charles W. Chestnut, including *The Conjure Woman;* Sinclair Lewis, *Kingsblood Royal* (New York: Random House, 1947); E. B. Reuter, *The Mulatto in the United States.* Among the films taking this theme are *Pinkie, Imitation of Life, View from Pompey's Head.* The preoccupation with mulatto influence has been more prevalent among whites studying the black experience than among black writers.

7. See *Conference Proceedings, Southwide Conference of Black Elected Officials* (Atlanta: Southern Regional Council, 11–14 December 1968).

MAE C. KING

19

☆☆☆☆☆☆☆☆☆☆☆☆☆☆☆☆☆☆☆☆☆☆☆☆☆☆

The Politics of
Sexual Stereotypes

The position of the woman of an oppressed people has historically been a delicate and a potentially strategic one for both the oppressors and the oppressed. In America the physical access that some slave women had to the personal environment of the oppressors, demeaning though this status was, placed them in a position to carry on subversive activities geared to the liberation interest of their people[1]

Conversely, this same situation made them vulnerable to being corrupted, i.e., identifying with or internalizing the values of the oppressors. If this occurred, the slave woman could become a valuable supportive instrument of the latter and thereby contribute to the perpetuation of the oppression of her own people. Hence, intrinsic in this position were the contradictory human possibilities of betrayal and devotion. The suspicion, guilt, and degradation generated by such a predicament gave birth to a legacy that uniquely burdens the black female in her relationship with males in American society. This legacy is manifested today in several stereotyped images and myths associated with black women. These female racial stereotypes appear to be indispensable to the maintenance of the racially stratified order in America.

The purpose of this paper is to explicate the stereotyped images

346

of the black woman in the context of the American system, and to look at the political implications of these images for the maintenance of power in a system based on racial determinism. This approach will also enable us to delineate the substantive differences between racial oppression, compounded by sex discrimination, which has victimized the black woman, and the selective sex discrimination experienced by white women in American society. These two different phenomena must not be confused under the appellation of "women's liberation." To do so would be to equate historically structured legalized cruelty with selective socioeconomic constraints. Furthermore, the assumption of such a position would tend to relieve the white female of any responsibility for the role that she plays, in partnership with the white male, in defending and perpetuating the system of racism in America.

The stereotyped images of the black woman discussed in the paper are: the "nonfeminist," the "depreciated sex object," and the "loser image." These stereotypes are in turn complemented by what appears to be an otherwise general policy of invisibility by the mass media with respect to black women. In our discussion, a stereotype refers to "an exaggerated belief associated with a category. Its function is to justify (rationalize) our conduct in relation to that category."[2] This definition points to the interrelatedness of stereotypes, images and myths. Furthermore, these function against the background of a racial caste system, and the latter will be examined, also.

It should be noted at the outset that a critical examination of the aforementioned images in the context of the American system should not be construed as an acceptance of the desirability of the values that the system assumes. Rather, an understanding and an appreciation of the systemic support provided by images that denigrate the black female necessitates analysis that assumes the role definition of the female in American society. Such role expectations constitute the basis for the creation of the images of the American woman (meaning white). These, as we will see, are in sharp contrast to those of the black female stereotypes. At this point, a look at the function of myths and images as control and influence agents of a political system, will help illuminate the significance of the black female stereotypes in the American order.

Every political system has its myths. Some are more dominant than others. These myths serve as a means of explaining and justifying the way of life of the society. Myths associated with racial identity are predominant in the United States and they have given birth to a caste system. Caste, based on race, has been the dominant principle for organizing American society. A belief in the ideology of race provided the theoretical rationale for the caste organization. The caste system "is defended by a set of myths that are used to justify the restrictions, different levels of privilege, and practices of etiquette that separate the various groups from one another."[3] The groups that concern us here, of course, are the blacks and the whites, and the image of the female both within and without each of these respective components of the caste system. It is our contention that the black female stereotypes and their concomitant myths are indispensable to the maintenance of the caste system.

Meanwhile, the essentiality of the myth to caste is reflected in Edelman's definition of myth. He states that "the word myth signifies a belief held in common by a large group of people that gives events and actions a particular meaning. It is typically socially cued rather than empirically based."[4] This definition suggests that the influence of a myth in establishing the boundaries of power, or in determining the "authoritative allocation of values"[5] and resources is not necessarily contingent upon the intrinsic veracity of the myth itself. In fact, myths are more often ill-founded beliefs uncritically held by those who benefit from them in status, wealth, and their concomitants. Where such myths coexist with a racial caste system, the latter tends to provide stability and security for the myth believers. The inflexibility of caste serves to protect myth beneficiaries from threats to their existing status and privileges. This point is supported in the statement that caste is designed to "freeze various levels of status, opportunity and privilege in a society. Inherited and inescapable biological characteristics, whether physical, mental, or both, are ascribed to the various castes, and there is generally some notion of untouchability."[6] Consequently, if one is "frozen" at the top he remains there and vice versa. Injustices, and the power iniquities that sustain them, are also frozen. At least, as long as the caste system and the myths that undergrid it, remain intact. There is no social mobility outside of one's caste.

The political implications of the stereotyped images of the black woman cannot be fully understood without noting the role that racial caste has played in maintaining societal equilibrium in America. The term "equilibrium," according to Emmet:

> should only be used where it is possible to show that customs, institutions, and social activities related to them dovetail in

together in certain specified ways so that one provides a corrective to disruptive tendencies in another. It should also be possible to show how if these functional relationships are lacking, a form of social life will break down, and also how a reacting tendency may go too far.[7]

In this connection, the racial caste system defines the role (i.e., social activities) of black women as inferior to that of white women. This definition reflects the racist norms (i.e., customs) of America, and the black female stereotypes are employed to help ensure mass conformity to these norms by all components of the caste system. Families, schools, churches, corporations (i.e., institutions) have all institutionalized these norms. Exceptions notwithstanding, they have historically been, and still are, organized along racial lines with black institutions subordinate to white, with black roles subordinate to white ones, or in another sense, with white on top of black.

Utilizing Emmet as a frame of reference, then, if any one of these elements, i.e. customs, institutions, or social activities, becomes substantially disoriented from the racist norm, the entire American system, which is based on racial determinism, is threatened. The equilibrium will be upset.

It should be stressed that classes exist within both the upper and the lower castes, and in America white males generally constitute the ruling class. They are the powerholders in the system. And the caste order that they control and serve has generated a variety of images and symbols depicting members of the lower caste both male and female as inferiors and undesirables, who of course, are harmless as long as they "stay in their place." The use of such metaphorical language, like the stereotyped images and myths, performs the crucial function of simplifying and giving meaning to otherwise complex and conflicting observations and experiences. As a result, the metaphors, images, and myths, false though they may be, become central in determining political values, perceptions, and attitudes.[8]

Against the background of racial castism in America the projection of negative black female stereotypes becomes inevitable. They are indispensable to maintaining caste restrictions especially those against intermarriage between members of the upper and lower castes. At the same time, these negative images permit the imposition of intercaste sexual terror by male members of the upper caste. To reiterate, the stereotyped images most frequently portrayed of the black woman are those of the "nonfeminist," which incorporates the matriarchy idea;

the "depreciated sex object"; and "the loser." In the absence of these negative visual presentations, American society has generally decreed the black woman invisible. Collectively, these images and the "invisible orientation" are calculated to deprive black women of their womanhood, self-respect, and social status and hereby to dissuade any contemplation by members of the white male *ruling class,* of marriage with females of the lower caste.

While creating an environment that bars by custom, and previously by law, intercaste marriage, the derogatory images simultaneously permit white males to use their power position to satisfy their lusts, without jeopardizing their status or violating the "white ethics" that sustain their power. Therefore, as Frazier points out:

> An apparent contradiction in the attitudes of whites toward race mixture disappears when the element of status is known. A white man may have children by a colored woman whom he supports as well as his white children. This behavior and its results are not considered mixing of the races or race mixture unless the white man would marry the Negro woman. Such marriages are forbidden by law. Thus, race mixture is forbidden within the legal and moral order. When it occurs outside of the legal and moral order, it is a purely biological phenomenon and racial status is not involved.[9]

Similarly, Angela Davis, placing such behavior in a political and historical perspective asserts that the slave master "knew that as female this slave woman could be particularly vulnerable in her sexual existence. Although he would not pet her and deck her out in frills, the white master could endeavor to reestablish her femaleness by reducing her to the level of her biological being. Aspiring with his sexual assaults to reestablish her as a female *animal,* he would be striving to destroy her proclivities toward resistance."[10] Further emphasizing the political function of this system protected sexual exploitation, Davis asserts that:

> In its political contours, the rape of the black woman was not exclusively an attack upon her. Indirectly, its target was also the slave community as a whole. In launching the sexual war on the woman, the master would not only assert his sovereignty over a critically important figure in the slave community, he would also be aiming a blow against the black man. The latter's instinct to protect his female relations would be frustrated and violated to

the extreme . . . clearly the master hoped that once the black man was struck by his manifest inability to rescue his women from sexual assaults of the master, he would begin to experience deep-seated doubts about his ability to resist at all.[11]

Likewise, James Baldwin on national television in the 1960s exposed the sordidness of the myth that undergirds America's white ethics. When John Kilpatrick, "Southern genteel, aristocrat from old Virginia," suggested a concern that the black thrust for equality might be misinterpreted, and that some (meaning whites) might be fearful less blacks marry their daughters, Baldwin "stared long and hard" and astutely observed, "you're not worried about me marrying *your* daughter. You're worried about me marrying your *wife's* daughter. I've been marrying your daughter since the days of slavery."[12] Baldwin's statement is another reminder of the amoralism inherent in a system of racial determinism. It also points to the persistent fear by white male "representative powerholders" that interracial sex might have a social meaning restored to it through the union of black males and white females. Indeed, without a status to jeopardize or a power position to protect, black men cannot be trusted to keep intercaste sex at the biological level.

Historically, the most brutal physical force was employed and sanctioned by white male "caste keepers" as punishment for black males who engaged in or whom they imagined as engaging in sex relations with white females. At the same time, the private nature of sex, and the possibilities of human love, excluded any certainty that white women could be counted on to remain loyal to the caste system in the face of humane sexual contact with black men. After all, although relative material well-being, respect, dignity, security and protection are bestowed upon white women under the American system, these women generally are not the holders, controllers, or directors of power. They are the recipients of the "fruits" rather than the makers. The difference between these positions can be an important one.

Meanwhile, to destroy the risk of sex becoming a weapon used by female members of the lower caste as a means of weakening the power of the caste keepers, white males stripped sex between themselves and black females of any social significance and placed it exclusively in the realm of the biological. The political implications of this action must not be overlooked. For in a larger sense, the invention of the current stereotyped images of black women is but a continuation of the same cruel slave control method clothed in the garments of modern technology. Changing conditions demand new methods of control. Hence, the racial stereotypes are the reformed, more sophisticated techniques used by moon-age America for maintaining the essence of both the slave and caste systems, i.e., white domination of blacks or the exercise of power on a racist basis. At this point, a more specific examination of the nature of the black female stereotypes is in order.

First, the nonfeminist, depreciated sex object, and loser images are in sharp contrast to those of the American woman (i.e., white). The latter is variously described as feminine, i.e., "small," "delicate," "soft," and "light." She may also be "dull, peaceful, relaxed, cold, rounded, passive and slow."[13] She is also portrayed as the ideal housewife, and the symbol of love and motherhood. So much so that Alice B. Rossi has declared that "for the first time in the history of any known society, motherhood has become a full-time occupation for adult women."[14] Such a reference, of course, obviously ignores the economic situation of black women.

Conversely, the "nonfeminist" image connotes negative opposites. Black women are featured as tough, hard-working domestics who assume the role of matriarch in the home but somehow always manage to know their place and remain appropriately submissive in the white world. Such an image permits the most outrageous exploitation of black females as a cheap labor source. By "defeminizing" them, America could subject them to the most harsh and unsafe working conditions without violating the white ethics that sustain the system.

The matriarch concept is a concomitant of the nonfeminist image. Essentially, this concept holds that the black woman is the dominant figure in the black family. This deviation from the "American patriarch" standards, of course, led, it is suggested, to the psychological castration of the black man. This resulted, it is implied, in negative consequences for the black man, such as low educational achievements and the inability to earn a living for his family, personality disorders, and delinquency. This myth as well as its subsidiaries, e.g., the myth of black female education and employment,[15] have been thoroughly refuted by research. Recently, Robert Hill found, for example, that (1) most black families, whether low income or not, are characterized by an egalitarian pattern in which neither spouse dominates but each shares in decision making and the performance of expected tasks; (2) in 85 percent of poor black families, husbands out-earn wives.[16] Consequently, the husband is the provider in the overwhelming majority of the cases. Notwithstanding the refutation of the stereotypes, the black woman still bears the brunt of the negativisms associated with such images.

The fact that the matriarchy myth was popularized and widely accepted in this country by all segments of society is a reflection of the depth of the cruelty that America from its inception has inflicted upon the black woman. For this myth, if carried to its logical conclusions, tends to make the black woman responsible for the creation of the social, educational, economic, and political institutions in this country which, historically, explicitly and implicitly, have been structured to deny equality in all of these areas to *all* black people. Another inference of the matriarchy notion is the exemption of white America from responsibility for the oppression of blacks and the conditions that inevitably resulted from this action. Instead, the black woman who is at the very bottom of the economic scale, earning an average wage in 1966 of $3,487 a year as compared to $4,580 for white women[17] is blamed for the consequences of white America's systematic efforts to dehumanize blacks. The absurdity of this myth is astounding, superseded only by its cruelty. After all, matriarchy in its historical usage denotes a position of power which, of course, neither black women nor black men have secured in America.

Politically, then, in addition to permitting exploitation of black female labor and shifting responsibility for oppression from the oppressors to the oppressed, the nonfeminist image also allows continuous brutality and insults against the black woman without generating mass hostility which could lead to systemic disequilibrium. In the absence of such a threat, there is no compelling reason to rectify the inhumane conditions that support her abuse. It is most noteworthy, for example, that the United States Congress was never moved to pass legislation abolishing lynching when confronted with evidence showing how often black women fell victim to this American barbarity. For, while in America rape of black women was "as common as whistling 'Dixie' in the South," almost equally as common was the lynching of black women. For example, from:

1891–1921, the South lynched forty-five (the acknowledged number) Negro women, several of whom were young girls from fourteen to sixteen years old. One victim was in her eighth month of pregnancy. Members of the mob suspended her from the tree

by her ankles. Gasoline was poured on her clothes and ignited. A
chivalrous white man took his knife and split open her abdomen.
The unborn child fell to the ground. A member of the mob
crushed its head with his heel.[18]

Likewise, Walter White testified: "In 1918 a Negro woman about
to give birth a child was lynched with almost unmentionable brutality
along with ten men in Georgia. I reached the scene shortly after the
butchery and while excitement still ran high."[19] Such atrocities, of
course, did not engender corrective action by the white male powerholders because the social, political, and economic system that they
guard excludes black women from its definition of womanhood,
motherhood, and femininity. Furthermore, the depravity of these
power arrangements still prevail. And, acting out of this same tradition, white America made the Boston Strangler (to whom some white
women fell victim) a household word, while in 1972 the brutal, pat-
terned murder of six little black girls in the Washington, D.C., area,
and systematic, mutilated slayings of five black women in Connecticut,
hardly received a footnote on national television.

Second, the image of depreciated sex object also serves a political
function. Perhaps more than the nonfeminist image, it excludes black
females as potential marital partners of white males. In other words, it
is a powerful psychological weapon which is designed to accomplish
the same results as the historical use of physical brutality against black
males accomplished in placing white females beyond their practical
consideration as marital partners. Indeed, in lieu of statistics on interracial marriage, one might speculate that the psychological weapon is
more effective than the physical approach. In a deeper political sense,
the depreciated sex image is intended to protect white males against
momentary passion, compassion, or compunction that might result
from his physical contact with black females. For such humane feelings sometimes lead to marriage which in turn entails partnership,
legal obligations, respect, dignity, and responsibilities. Marriage, then,
between members of the ruling class and those whom they oppress,
inevitably undermines the rationale for the basis of oppression,
whether the oppressive determinant be race, religion, culture or some
other such factor. In this connection, it is necessary to point out without apology, notwithstanding the pernicious violation of the dignity
and security of the black woman that such a position recognizes, that
the controversy over interracial marriage does not emanate from op-

position to the "mongrelization of the races." The latter is a custom that predates by far the U.S. Constitution. Rather, when stripped of its emotionalism, interracial marriage is a raw power question.

This point is reflected in a statement made by the U.S. President, Abraham Lincoln, who has been erroneously labeled as the "Great Emancipator" of black people. In the famous Lincoln-Douglas debates, Lincoln asserted that:

> I will say then that I am not, nor ever have been in favor of making voters or jurors of negroes, nor of qualifying them to hold public office, nor to intermarry with white people; and I will say in addition to this that there is a physical difference between the white and black races which I believe will forever forbid the two races living together on terms of social and political equality. And inasmuch as they cannot so live, while they do remain together there must be the position of superior and inferior, and I as much as any am in favor of having the superior position assigned to the white race.[20]

Especially noteworthy is the linkage Lincoln makes between power that flows from officially sanctioned social rights, such as marriage, and those that emanate from the possession of political rights. Consequently, he infers that the power of the vote, the power to hold public office, the power of judicial judgement (i.e., the right to serve on juries) as well as interracial marriage are all equally as threatening to the superior power position which he has chosen to assign to the white race.

In accordance with Lincoln's position, many senators, especially southern ones, objected to blacks being seated in the U.S. Congress. They also insisted that social and political rights were intertwined, and that full racial and political equality would also mean full social equality between the races. Therefore, both must be denied. They also argued that those whites who pretended to favor political equality were both hypocritical and inconsistent in their position. This point is stressed by Senator Garrett David of Kentucky. When Senator James W. Nye of Nevada criticized Davis for his vehement opposition to the seating of Hiram R. Revels, the first black to serve in the U.S. Senate, Davis declared: "I have never known a solitary Senator who is so clamorous in favor of the rights of the negro and the equality of the races, that he has made sedulous court to any one fair black swan and offered to take her to the alter of Hymen."[21]

Historically, the political implications of marriage, i.e., its effect, whether positive or negative, on power symbols (e.g., England's monarchy), or on the actual power arrangements, have been fully recognized. Subsequently marriage has frequently been employed as a political weapon for securing property and power which otherwise would not be forthcoming. In feudal society, for example, marriages among the nobility were generally arranged to maintain or extend fiefs.[22] Frederick I of Germany, Holy Roman Emperor, attempted to use marriage as a means of extending the power of his kingdom. Therefore, after he was defeated in his attempt to conquer Italy by force, "he arranged a marriage between his son, the future Henry VI, and Constance, heiress to the Kingdom of Sicily. He hoped that by surrounding Rome and Northern Italy with Hohenstaufen possessions, his son might succeed where he failed."[23] This marriage in 1194 linked the Italian Kingdom with the German dynasty.

European history is replete with such political marriages. Some, of course, did not always accomplish their power purpose. For example, the political marriage of Louis VII of France to Eleanor, heiress of the duchy of Aquitaine, proved to be a mismatch. Louis was forced to procure an annulment. About two months later, Eleanor married Henry II of England and by this marriage he obtained control of Aquitaine for the English crown. This marriage culminated in England extending control over about two-thirds of France.[24]

Ancient history offers memorable examples of how marriage was used to break, obtain, or consolidate power. The story of the biblical Jewish queen Esther is probably a familiar one. Esther, through the efforts of her uncle Mordecai, was brought to the palace of the King of Persia, Ahasuerus. The king loved her and made her queen. Meanwhile, Haman, chief of the princes of Persia and confidant of the king, considered the Jews a threat to the kingdom because of their different customs and laws. With the initial consent of the king himself, Haman decreed that all Jews be destroyed. Upon hearing this decree, Esther petitioned the king to reverse it; pleading "for how can I endure to see the evil that shall come to my people? or how can I endure to see the destruction of my own kindred."[25] Responding to her appeal, the king not only reversed the decree, he conceded to her wish to have Haman hanged along with his ten sons. Esther's uncle Mordecai was chosen to take over the position that was previously held by Haman. The king further granted the Jews the right to organize to defend themselves and "to destroy, to slay, and to cause to perish all the power of the people and the province that would assault them, little ones and women."[26] The Jews proceeded to exercise the power that flowed from this grant. Politically, then, Esther used the influence derived from her queenly status to break the oppressive power that held the Jews in bondage.

One of the most celebrated ancient political romances is that of the black African queen, Cleopatra. Probably it is because of the political implications of her love affair with the Roman, Mark Antony, that countries adhering to racism have insisted on painting her white. However, as Clarke notes, "she was not a white woman. She was not a Greek. . . . Until the emergence of the doctrine of white superiority, Cleopatra was generally pictured as a distinctly African woman, dark in color."[27] Also Shakespeare refers to her as dark in color (tawny) in the opening paragraph of *Antony and Cleopatra.*

This love affair between the representative of the Roman Empire and the queen of Egypt, which was at the time a Roman protectorate, threatened the power of the empire. Denouncing the bond between Antony and Cleopatra, Octavius Caesar informed his sister (Antony's wife by Roman law) that Cleopatra had won the heart of Antony and that ". . . he hath given his empire up to a whore, who now are levying the Kings o'th earth for war."[28] Nevertheless, Octavius' anger notwithstanding, the fact is that Cleopatra, like Esther, used the influence derived from her personal relationship with a ruler, and previously with Julius Caesar himself, to protect her people, and the interests of Egypt. Describing this situation, Clarke states that Cleopatra, who was born in 69 B.C.,

> came to the throne that she shared with her brother Ptolemy III, when she was 18 years old. Egypt, now a Roman protectorate was beset with internal strife and intrigue. Cleopatra aligned herself with Julius Caesar, who reinforced her power. Their political and sexual relationship was a maneuver to save Egypt from the worst aspects of Roman domination. After Julius Caesar was murdered, Cleopatra, still in her early twenties, met Mark Antony and a love affair strongly motivated by politics began.
>
> Her effect on Mark Antony was profound. This noble Roman turned traitor to his own people when he attempted to save the country of this fascinating black queen from Roman domination. After Antony's death, the victor, Octavius, assumed full control of Egypt, and Cleopatra, now without a protector or companion, committed suicide.[29]

Hence, history is a constant reminder of how sexual bonds between man and woman based on mutual respect and dignity, tend to transcend otherwise divisive forces. Moreover, they have led to the undermining of the status quo that sustain power arrangements, including those that are oppressive.

In a political system organized on the racial caste principle, dignified and respectful intercaste sexual relationships between the holders of power and their victims may undermine the power base. For example, one might reasonably pose the question as to whether interracial families occupying the offices of the executive, judicial, and congressional branches of government would exercise America's power in the racist manner in which it is now exercised? In raising this question, one should by no means ignore the fact that blacks, as well as whites, strongly oppose interracial marriages. However, the commonality of this opposition is itself based, it seems, on diverse power perspectives. Notwithstanding historical abuses and insults, blacks object to such unions because they are likely to weaken their ability to resist oppression. Especially since there is no assurance that such marriages will be positively politically targeted. Conversely, whites object because such occurrences may weaken or jeopardize the power that is, while blacks seek to break it.

Third, the loser image is not without its political function. It aims to stifle or destroy the very self-esteem, respect, and aspirations of the black woman. This image is activated whenever the black woman attempts to "move out of her place." In other words, whenever she competes for a position or status, whether social or economic, that is generally identified with whites, especially white women, she is featured as a failure. A reference to the images of the black woman projected by one or two motion pictures will suffice to demonstrate this repeated occurrence. Indeed, the daily experiences of those who care to observe will probably testify to this point.

For example, as long as the black woman remains a domestic, America's media portray her as a happy figure, scattered-brain perhaps, but happy. This was true of Butterfly McQueen who played servant to "Miz Scawlett" in *Gone With the Wind,* and also of Hattie McDaniels who performed the same function for "Miz Alice" in the radio television *Beulah* series. On the other hand, Diana Sands in the movie *Georgia, Georgia* becomes a tragic figure, and her romance with a white man predictably leads to a tragic end. This same scene is repeated in the *Omega Man.* While *For Love of Ivy* portrays a black woman succeeding in her love affair with Sidney Poitier, Abbey

Lincoln, to be sure, is featured as a maid to a white suburban family. Deviations from depictions of this type relating to the black woman are rare exceptions indeed.

The loser image is directed at imposing and reinforcing a frame of reference for black females which psychologically constrains. Simultaneously, it intimidates her with the penalty of pain by depicting tragic experiences for those of her kind who dare venture beyond the boundaries of the constricted roles of members of a lower caste. At the same time, this image is calculated to deprive her of the will to fight back. For the environment in which it is projected is populated by beings who have been socialized to treat her as a thing *not* of value. Consequently, rejection of her presence, and violations and abuses of her person become rather routine responses of these inhabitants. Assuming the validity of this assertion, the loser image is one that white America finds congenial to its own way of life. Furthermore, the constraining effect of this image will most likely militate against black women enjoying any substantial benefits that might result from a societal redefinition of the role of "women."

Lastly the "invisible orientation," i.e., a kind of nonrecognition by America of the black woman's existence, tends to prevail in the absence of the negative stereotypes. Such a posture discourages any serious consideration by the country of the unique problems black women that are engendered by the caste environment. In fact, there appears to be a kind of unspoken understanding among white "castees" that the black female is America's "other woman." By relegating her to this culturally derogatory status, the country can, without compunction, ignore her pleas and problems. Thus, one is reminded again of the fact that, despite repeated pleas from the victims, the U.S. Congress never passed a law abolishing lynching which savagely sucked the life drops from black women as well as black men. Yet, responding to a far lesser complaint from "American women," of economic discrimination and social boredom, the Congress passed a proposed constitutional amendment designed to correct this unpleasant situation. However, consistent with racist tradition, the Congress most recently passed legislation which would force poor women, most of whom are probably thought to be black, "off the welfare roles" into a nonexistent job market to work for slave wages. Since the suggested jobs do not exist, the implications of this legislation encourages exploitation, insult, and intimidation.

The mass media regularly exemplify their apparent commitment to the aforementioned nonrecognition policy. One example is sufficient to demonstrate this rather prevalent situation. On March 26, 1972, the Columbia Broadcasting System (CBS) carried a special feature on discrimination against "women" on its "60 Minutes" series. Not one black woman was featured. A white female reporter ended this special by concluding that it was true that America has placed its women on a pedestal. But there are now indications, she admonished, that a large number of these women are no longer satisfied with this position. The protection and security that it once offered, she asserted, no longer obtain for a significant number of them. However, since America has never placed the African-American woman on a pedestal, nor provided her with protection or security, such a statement characteristically ignores the black woman's situation. Worse still, it is yet another indication that America is not prepared to rectify the conditions that she has erected, which continue to exploit, affront and wantonly to insult black women.

The nonrecognition attitude also penetrates academia and the "women's liberation" movement. In fact, there is a tendency to appeal to the white male powerholders' belief in the ideology of race in order to gain support for "women's rights." White male castees are admonished by the females of their group, that evidence of the depth of the "oppression" that they inflict upon "women" is illustrated by the former's act of sometimes preferring blacks over women. This position is reflected in a statement by Alice Rossi who writes:

> The tenuous hold academic women without doctorates have enjoyed by way of part-time college teaching or as high school teachers without the master's degree, may therefore be reduced in the future as school systems can hire doctorates holders and what they believe to be more stable employees, men. There is growing awareness of this possibility among counselors of girls and women, and it is joining yet another source of concern to produce a good deal of anxiety among women concerning their future employment opportunities in academia. This is heightened among women in graduate and professional schools as the latter search their souls and markets for qualified blacks. This has lent an air of pressing and conflicting concerns in many circles of women. I have had several letters from women teaching in graduate schools on this point. They say it is hard enough to keep up the morale of male students to push through to the degree, but they despair of giving genuine encouragement to their women students, many of whom feel a double disadvantage; they are not black and not male.[30]

This statement not only indicates a tacit nonrecognition and disregard of black women; it is a subtle, academic appeal to racism. As such, it upholds the racist tradition that has historically inflicted the "women's movement."

At this point, it is appropriate to stress the intracaste nature of the "women's liberation movement." For it is this distinguishing aspect that dictates the incidental character of benefits that might seep through to black women as a result of an intracaste sex battle at the upper power level. However, this should by no means be interpreted to suggest that sex discrimination does not exist within the lower caste (it does), or that the white male castees do not extend their multiclawed tentacles beyond caste boundaries to duplicate in a brutal fashion their sexist tradition (they do). Rather, the point is that until racial castism is abolished in America, no coalition between disadvantaged groups of whites and racially defined exploited and oppressed blacks will be sufficient to liberate the black element of the coalition. This is true because the white male powerholders, in accordance with their power maintenance interests, will offer to reward the white element of the coalition. In so doing, they simultaneously neutralize the latter's opposition and activate their racism. As a result the movement turns conservative, i.e., racist.

This was true of the Woman Suffrage Movement. This fact is substantiated in a 1903 statement by the national board of directors of the National American Woman Suffrage Movement. The statement was a response to an accusation by the news media that the women were going soft on racism. In an attempt to disassociate themselves from what they apparently viewed as un-American behavior, the women declared:

> Like every other national association (we are) made up of persons
> of all shades of opinion on the race question and on all other
> questions except those relating to its particular object. The
> northern and western members hold views that are customary in
> their sections. The southern members hold views that are
> customary in the South. The doctrine of states rights is
> recognized. . . . The National American Woman Suffrage Associ-
> ation is seeking to do away with the requirement of a sex
> qualification for suffrage. What other qualifications will be asked
> for, it leaves to other states.[31]

In a similar vein, a woman suffrage advocate had earlier asserted: "Men and women, in their reciprocities of love and duty, are one flesh and one blood—mother, wife, sister, daughter—come so near the heart and mind of every man that they must be either his blessing or bane. Where there is such a mutuality of interests, such as interlinking of life, there can be no real antagonism of position and action."[32]

Confirming the intracaste nature of the woman suffrage movement and leaving nothing to the imagination regarding its affirmation of racism, Belle Kearney, a noted advocate of woman suffrage, proclaimed before the Suffrage Association's national convention, amidst great applause: "Just as surely as the North will be forced to turn to the South for the nation's salvation, just so surely will the South be compelled to look to its Anglo-Saxon women as the medium through which to retain the supremacy of the white race over the African."[33]

The noted black woman poet, abolitionist, and feminist Francis Harper was cognizant of the fact that white women were no less racist than white men. Having experienced the insults that the woman suffrage movement meted out to black women, Harper declared: "Being black is more precarious than being a woman, being black means that every white, including every working-class white woman, can discriminate against you . . . the white women all go for sex, letting race occupy a minor position."[34]

Such evidence suggests that black women of the 1970s, still burdened by the system sanctioned stereotypes, would be politically naive to discount the decisive role that racism will most likely play in the decision making in the women's movement. There is reason to believe that white women in tle 1970s, like those of an earlier period, will disassociate themselves from the issue of racial justice whenever it appears advantageous for them to do so. Furthermore, there is a fundamental difference between their concerns and problems and those of black women. This difference is derived from the racial caste nature of the American system itself. This fact dictates different problem-solving approaches and programs of action which may be incompatible. In any case, since the system favors white over black, including white women over black women, it is not likely that the former will voluntarily seek to dismantle that which serves their interests and pamper them with privileges. Yet, the problems of black women will defy solution as long as America retains racial castism. Therefore, black women must aim at more than a redefinition of the role of women, they must aim for the abolition of the racial caste foundation of the American state itself.

In conclusion, it should be emphasized that although the

stereotyped images of black women are generally devoid of reality, this actuality hardly diminishes their effectiveness in achieving the political power purposes that they serve. The power of image making is concentrated in the hands of white male castees and, therefore, their victims have little recourse to counteracting the negativisms that derive from this situation. As long as the power relations that sustain this monopoly persist, the reality of the black woman's plight in America will continue to be distorted and suppressed.

In explicating the stereotyped images of black women, we have shown that these images are basic and functional to a political system founded on racial oppression and organized on the caste principle. In America, they serve ultimately as a means of institutionalizing the "power distance" between the white male powerholders and the lower caste victims of their action. Since the stereotypes symbolize system sanctioned degradation, the powerholders are, not only free to, but encouraged to exploit the black woman on an economic, personal and social basis, without incurring cost to their power position, status, conscience, or material well-being. Moreover, although modernized racism theoretically accords legal status to intercaste marital relationships, the negative stereotypes not only limit these to an almost infinitesimal number, but also strip them of political significance. In so doing, they eliminate any potential threat that such relationships may pose to the status quo power arrangements of the American system.

Finally, to focus on the unique position of the black woman in the context of the American system, is surely not to disregard the more frequently examined unique plight of her counterpart in this arena, the black man. Rather, it is to call attention to an aspect of racism in the United States which has virtually escaped political analysis. Yet, the possible power implications of this question are too important to be relegated to the cloakroom of "better forgotten history." Instead, the questions posed by this history, wreathed with strength and courage as well as pain and dishonor, need to be confronted and examined from a power-maintenance perspective. If this paper generates dialogue along these lines, or encourages a more in-depth political analysis of this issue, which in turn could serve as a basis for corrective policy measures in this area, it will have served its purpose.

NOTES
1. For a detailed discussion of this point, see Angela Davis, "Reflections on the Black Woman's Role in the Community of Slaves," *Black Scholar,* December 1971.

2. Gordon W. Allport, *The Nature of Prejudice* (New York: Doubleday, 1958), p. 187.

3. Liston Pope, *The Kingdom Beyond Caste* (New York: Friendship, 1957), p. 53. See his chapter 4 for a discussion of the variability of caste and the inconsistency of caste rules. The latter point is especially pertinent to the American situation.

4. Murray Edelman, *Politics as Symbolic Action* (New York: Markham, 1971), p. 14.

5. David Easton, *The Political System* (New York: Knopf, 1953).

6. Pope, *The Kingdom*, p. 52.

7. Dorothy Emmet, *Function Purpose and Powers* (London: Macmillan, 1958), p. 74.

8. See Edelman, *Politics*, chap. 5.

9. E. Franklin Frazier, *Race and Culture Contacts in the Modern World* (Boston: Beacon, 1957), p. 65.

10. Davis, "Reflections," pp. 12, 13.

11. Ibid., p. 13.

12. Quoted by John O. Killens, "The Black Mystique," in *Black on Black*, ed. Arnold Adoff (New York: Macmillan, 1968), p. 36.

13. Robert J. Lifton, ed. *The Woman in America* (Cambridge, Mass.: Houghton Mifflin, 1965), p. 173. For further discussion of these stereotypes, see Nancy Reeves, *Womankind: Beyond the Stereotypes* (Chicago: Aldine, 1971).

14. Cited in Lifton, *Woman*, p. 106.

15. See Jacquelyne Jackson, "But Where Are the Men," *Black Scholar*, December 1971, for an extensive discussion of this point. See also Robert Staples, "The Myth of the Black Matriarchy," *Black Scholar*, January–February 1970); and Joyce A. Ladner, *Tomorrow's Tomorrow: The Black Woman* (New York: Doubleday, 1971), for relevant discussions.

16. Robert Hill, "The Black Family" (Paper delivered at the 61st annual convention of the Urban League, Detroit, Michigan, July 1971). Research Department, National Urban League, Washington, D.C.

17. U.S. Department of Commerce, Bureau of the Census, CPR 60, no. 66.

18. Maude White Katz, "The Negro Woman and the Law," *Freedomways* II, no. 3 (1962): p. 289.

19. Walter White, "I Investigate Lynchings," in Adoff, *Black on Black*, p. 36.

20. Quoted by Thomas S. Gossett, *Race: The History of an Idea in America* (New York: Schocken, 1965), p. 254.

21. *Congressional Globe*, 41st Cong., 2nd. Sess., 23 February 1870, p. 154. Hymen was the ancient Greek god of marriage.

22. Carlton J. H. Hayes et al., *History of Europe* (New York: Macmillan, 1949), p. 167.

23. Ibid., p. 281.

24. Ibid., pp. 266–67.

25. Esther 8:6.

26. Esther 8:11.

27. John Henrik Clarke, "The Black Woman: A Figure in World History," *Essence* (May 1971): 29.

28. *The Tragedies of William Shakespeare*, ed. Peter Alexander (New York: Heritage, 1958), p. 1021.

29. Clarke, "Black Woman," p. 29.

30. Alice Rossi, "The Road to Sex Equality" (Paper delivered at University of Chicago 10 February, 1969).

31. Quoted by Catherine Stimpson, "Women's Liberation and Black Civil Rights," *Woman in Sexist Society,* ed. Vivian Gornick and Barbara K. Moran (New York: New American Library, 1972), p. 643.

32. "Women's Rights," in *Essays and Addresses on Women Suffrage,* tract 1851, no. 1 (New York: Appleton, 1870), p. 643.

33. Cited by Stimpson, "Women's Liberation," p. 643.

34. Ibid., p. 639.

20

INEZ SMITH REID

☆☆☆☆☆☆☆☆☆☆☆☆☆☆☆☆☆☆☆☆☆☆☆☆☆☆☆☆

Traditional Political Animals? A Loud No

Against a background of urban riots and rebellions, and a deep-seated fear of blacks by whites, Richard Nixon entered the White House as the thirty-seventh President of the United States. His success at the polls occurred without the cooperation of most blacks since about 90 percent of the black vote went to Hubert Humphrey. Unlike Lyndon B. Johnson, Nixon made no apparent effort to include a black person in a cabinet position. Nor did he extend an "open" invitation to any "black leaders" to come periodically to the White House to talk over pressing problems confronting the black population. Indeed, with respect to the black political leadership President Nixon initially adopted a closed-door policy and refused repeatedly to meet with them, a fact which led all twelve black members of the Unites States House of Representatives to boycott the 1971 State of the Union address. Only after the boycott did President Nixon agree to meet with the black congressional caucus.

While some "black leaders" may have chastised Nixon for his cool attitude and nonproductive endeavors with respect to black people, the women of our study employed very vivid and colorful terminol-

366

ogy in describing their feelings toward the Nixon-Agnew administration. Nixon was called everything from "a bunch of shit," to an "ass
hole," to "a dirty old man." And Agnew's labels ranged from
"monkey," to "honky," to "son of a bitch." Some typical comments follow:

1. Nixon—that's my hound dog. I can't stand the guy. I'm
   going to be frank and honest with you. He's not helping no
   one but Nixon himself.
2. Nixon: I think here too is a bunch of shit. I think the most
   swinging thing that's happened—there've been two or three
   things. One when some of his cabinet started to resign and
   got other jobs. Two is when that little gal last week—Princess
   Anne—came to town. I think that's the most dynamic thing
   that has happened since the Nixon administration. When
   that kid went up there on the hill and these old men started
   shuffling her around as to where she ought to go and she
   pulled her arm away from them, I thought that was very significant. The fact that they had her lined up to go to some
   library showing thing at the White House and she said I
   don't want to go there, I want to go where the riots were; the
   word is bad but she knew what she meant and she knew the
   street. When those two limousines from the White House
   took her—and they had to take her because how do you tell
   the Princess she can't go where she wants to go in America?
   They had to take her and when the car was driving fast she
   said slow up I want to take a picture; slow up more. And they
   had to slow to a snail's pace. I thought that was beautiful.
   That was magnificent. While Charles is all charming and
   Mrs. Nixon is trying to make sure there's a romance created
   there, an international romance, this kid was always left
   alone and I'm glad they didn't find her an escort because
   America will always remember that.
3. Nixon, I think he's an ass hole. There's no better word to express it.
4. Well, since I'm on tape I won't say it but you do want my
   honest opinion? Really I do think they (Nixon and Agnew)
   are two crazy motherfuckers.
5. President Nixon is a pig. He's what capitalism is. He's what it
   represents.

6. I think Nixon borders on fascism. I think he's deliberately attempted to organize a really dangerous right around him. Socially all his friends are profascist pigs. The attempt to get Haynsworth and then Carswell into the administration proves he's a really dangerous person.
7. I think he's an ass hole. I think he's a motherfucker. Nixon's not thinking about us but one must always be thinking about him.
8. I think Nixon's just an example of White America, what they represent: white supremacy, middle-class values, narrow isolation philosophy about other countries, just all the negative things that anybody has written about white middle-class America seems to me to be Richard Nixon and everybody that supports him.
9. Agnew? What is my attitude toward the monkey? A monkey would have more sense than this guy. I mean a monkey even has sense enough to clean his tail when he go to the washroom or else whatever he does. Agnew ain't got that kind of sense. He don't have the sense he was born with and I don't see how he got in the White House in the first place, as Vice President.
10. Agnew? He's a nut. I know he's supposed to have this 135 IQ but after all that's not very high. I have two sons with a higher IQ than that. Mine too was higher than that. But I don't see why he keeps going around talking about a 135 IQ—so what? That doesn't prove anything. It doesn't prove that a person has the attitude and outlook that's going to help people. You can be a genius and still not have the attitude and outlook that's going to help people. This matter of going around and flinging high phrases—anybody can hire him a good writer and do this. I feel that if his speeches are an indication of his attitude then we're in a sorry state.
11. Agnew is nothing but a down right, no good, low lifed racist and is only doing his job as far as the power structure is concerned, reflecting what they want him to reflect: the right wing views and to frighten whites more to make them think we, black people, are their enemies and that the power structure is their friend.
12. In one sentence Agnew's a front for nothing. I don't think he's actually nothing.

13. Agnew is a fool, a racist fool.
14. Agnew is a honky.
15. All I know about him (Agnew) is that he's a good friend of Nixon's. Well, he's just another dirty old man to me.
16. (Agnew's) so funny. He deserves all those little watches and all those little tee shirts. It puts him right where he belongs: in a play pen. He's a child. He's a child in an adult body. You laugh at him and forget him. I don't think he really has any political influence. I however think he does have political influence on the crackers and WASPS in Ohio.
17. He's a fool. That's all. (Agnew)
18. Agnew's a pig.
19. Agnew's a joke. He's unbelieveable really. Do I need say more?
20. I'm sorry. I think Agnew is an ass. That's all I can say about him.
21. (Nixon and Agnew)—they're two big idiots.
22. I don't have any feelings about Agnew at all. He's just another Mickey Mouse, Jr.

A few women suggested that President Nixon was mad or insane, or power mad:

1. He's the President of the United States and he represents the silent majority that deals with patriotism and all that. Sometimes I get the feeling that the man's insane. I watch him on TV. He just looks like some people who are just out, just gone that I know. Then a lot of times he acts like a little kid. That whole thing in terms of Carswell. Like he got mad when they didn't approve his people and stomped his foot and then he says your job is not to choose but to approve what I do. They just laughed at that. He doesn't act like a mature adult. I think the man has a lot of problems that have been evident in his whole political career since the Eisenhower days since this tremendous scandal about him taking payola from the people in San Francisco—being bought lock, stock and barrel by the business people out there.
2. First I thought Nixon was an idiot but really now reading some more things about the mass media and rereading *1984* I think he really might be less of an idiot and more of someone that's shrewd and who has the key for bringing this country into a total suppression of all the people or bringing people

into World War III. I think he's mad in a strange way. His madness is toward what someone called saving face. He has a mania toward saving face and he would kill himself to save face. I think the danger is he would do the same thing to the whole country.

3. It's really sad. I don't think the man has all of his senses. I think we are in a very dangerous situation.
4. He's power mad. I feel that the man is very entrenched in the glory of power. I haven't seen him operating as a human. He's operating like a kid you give a bunch of toys for Christmas. It's difficult for him to see the toys as toys. He's so far out on the ego trip, now the toys are his.

Still others advanced the theory that someone else is pulling the strings for Nixon; that is, others are exercising effective political power even though Nixon ostensibly holds the reins of legitimate power. Big business interests were most often identified as the controlling force acting upon Nixon. Yet someone even suggested that Governor Reagan of California represented the real force in the American political system.

1. Like all administrations they are controlled by big business and he's only doing what the power structure tells him to do. He's only a lackey.
2. Nixon actually is only a figurehead. He's part of a system that's out to destroy us. We've been a sore spot to these people here for a long time. I think Nixon is following the policy.
3. Shit. I think he's going to screw everybody up in terms of foreign policy. I think those that are beckoning to him because they feel he is in sympathy with them domestically and so they are giving him the red light on certain foreign policies. It's like he goes to the highest bidder. Nixon is bought off so he's a puppet on a string so far.
4. Nixon isn't even the man in power. Neither is Agnew or Finch. They are mouthpieces that do the work of those that are out to repress black people in this country.
5. Well, President Nixon, he's just a puppet to Reagan. Reagan rules the United States.

An overwhelming majority of women felt that Nixon had done nothing to help blacks. On the contrary, some women were convinced that Nixon's ultimate plan is to send blacks to concentration camps.

1. My feelings about him ain't nothing. I just don't say nothing about President Nixon. He's just done told us so many different things wrong until it's just awful. He's done a good job on poor black people. President Nixon didn't keep a word he said he was going to do for the black people. He just ain't right.

2. Nixon and his administration have lived up to and probably surpassed everything that a lot of black people felt he was going to do which is essentially to support what he calls the silent majority of people and his emphasis on law and order and the protection of property which has always been a very consistent position with him. I don't think there is any question that he cares nothing about the interest and welfare of black people in this country and has demonstrated time and time again that his position is going to be one of containment and if necessary extermination. I think this is very clear.

3. I don't trust him at all. I don't trust him if I was a radical white student. I don't trust him if I was a peaceful, submissive militant black person. I think he's one of those subtle racists. He cut back all the funds across the board for jobs and poverty, housing, everything he cut back—the Headstart and everything. I think he's really cracking down on the black community, especially ghettoes because it's getting real bad and he isn't doing anything to alleviate it. I think it's going to come a time sooner or later that the next riot that they have, if they have a large scale riot like the summer of '64, I think he's really going to start shooting people down 'cause they started already and he's going to give the order. Remember when they had the segregation of the schools and they turned over the bus with those children and he hasn't come out and said anything about that. He's taking his time with the desegregation bit in the south. And his partner Agnew with his comment: 'you seen one ghetto you seen them all!' If there ever was a President that's ready to put black people in concentration camps he's the one, 'cause he has the backing of the so-called silent majority.

4. (Nixon's) really more anti-black than I expected him to be and I didn't expect nothing out of him. I expected him to be anti-black but I guess I didn't expect him to be so open about it.

5. The Nixon Administration stinks. They are all a bunch of fools. They have nothing for the black man. They're not giving the black man anything. They don't want to have nothing to do with the black man. As a matter of fact, they're all racists. That's all.

6. As far as black people are concerned, they are full of shit, like every other administration. As far as white people are concerned, they exemplify their system.

Some women saw the Nixon-Agnew administration in a favorable light in terms of its ability to radicalize people. As one woman said:

The Nixon administration will serve to radicalize a great deal of people. And I think I'm glad Nixon got in rather than Humphrey because I think it will serve to heighten the differences between Johnson and the present administration. I hope more people will wake up as a result and see the seriousness of the situation.

Other women confessed that they had nothing to do with Nixon since he was not the president of blacks. Most of these women simply "tuned out" the Nixon administration completely. One woman admitted that she would not give one second to mourning the death of Nixon.

1. To show how much I've turned him off, I don't listen to him on the radio, on the TV, when he comes on. I don't read any statements that he has made in the newspaper. I don't care. I have no interest in what he is doing and saying because it's so way out.
2. I hate him. I can't even look at the man on television.
3. If he (Nixon) was to die today it would not be one minute of mourning for me and I hope a whole lot of more feel the same way.

Quite a few women believed that Vice President Agnew represented or was the embodiment of Nixon, saying or doing nothing without the approval of the President.

1. (Agnew) is the mouth of Nixon and more than that. He is the next movement of the right. He never knew he could have it so good up there. And now that he's gotten used to it, if he didn't believe it before, he believes it now.
2. I feel whatever (Agnew's) expressing he's been specifically designated to express. I think that's his purpose. He is like the mouthpiece of the things that Nixon would not be able to say and get away with. I think Agnew is a very intelligent person. They realize what they're doing.

3. I actually don't think Agnew think at all. His thoughts I don't think has ever really been projected. I really would hesitate to say what he really thinks because I believe before he goes on a speech Nixon write it for him, or he sit down and have an all night briefing session with him. I feel if he has any feelings of his own he's afraid to buck the administration any way.

Some women were quick to point out their belief that Nixon and Agnew were dangerous individuals who had to be taken quite seriously. This was true, most believed, because the Nixon administration is quite bold and willing to take actions which might have been looked upon with horror some seven or eight years ago.

1. Nixon and Agnew—yuck! Chet Huntley denies this but *Life* quoted him a couple of weeks ago as saying that Nixon frightened him. Well Chet Huntley might not have said it but I say it—Nixon frightens me because this man is very much concerned with Richard Nixon period. It is surprising with his Quaker background. You would think that a bit of the Quaker humanism—and there is some humanism in the friends' theosophy I guess you would call it—you would think that some of that would come out but you never see any of it. Nixon frightens me because he makes these little jokes—"I am the President," type thing that David Frye did him up brown.
2. Agnew is an ass. He's not a very intelligent man at all. They always say an empty wagon makes a hell of a lot of noise. I think he's allowing himself to be used by the President. I think he's falling very much into the qualifications for the Vice Presidency in that you are supposed to parrot or say those kinds of things that the President wants to say but it is not politically advantageous for him to say it. Nixon gets his speech writers to write things Nixon wants to say or Mitchell wants to say and the ass repeats like a parrot what he is told to say. As a matter of fact I think he is so (un)intelligent he really wouldn't have any opinion on almost anything because he doesn't have the intelligence to form an opinion. When a man has to go through and publish his IQ and that whole bit then that means there's some question there as to his intelligence, and I don't think he has any. I think he's dangerous though. Dumb people in positions of power are always dangerous. This country would be in very dire danger if something happened to Nixon and Agnew became President. That's one of the worst kinds of catastrophes I could think of.

3. And Agnew I think is even more dangerous because Agnew is Nixon's alter ego. Agnew is really the old Nixon. He is mouthing what Nixon really wants to say and thinks but Nixon as President can't. So Nixon is really putting on a facade. He is the new Nixon but Agnew is the old Nixon. This Agnew is dangerous because he is appealing to the baser instincts in man's nature. I don't like Republicans generally. Those that you see in the media, the newspapers, the TV, you notice them. They all have narrow eyes, thin lips, and they very seldom smile. I think so often about a quote from Shakespeare: "let me have men about me that are fat, sleek-headed men. On such a sleepy night yon Cassius has a lean and hungry look. He thinks too much. Such men are dangerous." But these fools don't even think. Agnew: the only qualifications he could list for President of the USA was that he was President of the PTA of some school in the suburbs.

4. Agnew? Is it allowed? I think he is a blooming idiot. I think people should take him seriously. He is dangerous, very dangerous.

5. It's been thrown out that (Nixon) will cancel the '72 elections. Just as an attorney he really knows better. This Manson thing (about Manson being guilty) which I think he put out there to see what the climate was. That was nothing but a test case and if that can be acceptable, which it seems to be, because of the extreme nature of that, he can do whatever he wants.

In an effort to see how deeply ingrained the disaffection of black women for the national administration might be, we asked them to indicate their attitude toward Nixon's Family Assistance proposal and toward former Secretary of Health, Education, and Welfare Robert Finch. In terms of the Family Assistance proposal (designed ostensibly to assist lower socioeconomic levels of the population which include a heavy proportion of blacks) we felt that a positive reaction to that guaranteed income package would negate many of the negative comments on the Nixon administration—especially with respect to the treatment of the black community. Of those who had heard of the proposal (and many had not) the overwhelming majority merely confirmed the disaffection of blacks for the Nixon administration. The Family Assistance proposal was scored time after time as a grossly inadequate crumb thrown out to appease the black populace. As some women contended:

1. That's jive time. It's very superficially dealing with the needs of poor people. When he talks about guaranteed income or a base of 1,600 bucks in this inflationary time he's—it's being stupid. I mean 1,600 bucks ain't even poverty. It's like desperation. It's like people starving to death. I don't think he is sincere because when he talks about people working and then he cuts back on employment, he cuts back on federal programs that would provide employment, then it's jive time. If you want people to work you're going to have to give people a job. I think what it was was people from various elements of this country putting pressure on him to come out with dealing with social welfare and he got some of his "brain childs" to come up with something that might look good on paper, might sound fairly decent but means nothing.

2. I think this income thing is a joke. It's a joke. It's a hoax and every other thing you want to call it. There's a gimmick to that thing. Whatever they say it takes to maintain a family your size, whatever you're making or whatever occupation they find. Now fuck the fact that you may not be able to swing it. If you don't do it you don't get the money—not to mention that the amount of money that they've designated per size of family is not enough anyway. He's not doing anything for black people. He doesn't have the slightest intent of doing anything for blacks. He's a poor redneck. Now what has a poor redneck ever done for a black man?

3. It's just a whole lot of talk. Now this guaranteed income, the reason it looks so pleasing to some people like in Mississippi in the South, it's more than what they have now but for the people out here in California, and in New York it's less than what they have now. But what he intends to do is supplement that. He intends for every able bodied person to be out there working. Now with the state of the economy as it is now, where are these people going to get a job? These people are old. Some of them are crippled. Some of them are mothers who don't have anybody to keep their children and mothers without any skills. It looks good: we're going to guarantee every mother or every able-bodied person a job. It sounds good but where are you going to get a job?

4. I think it's something he's throwing out here just like the poverty program to pacify the people and make them feel that they are getting somewhere under this present system. Just like the poverty program it will not be a success.

5. I feel like (Nixon) should go home and live on it a couple of

days. It doesn't even take a week, just a couple of days. Then the whole thing would be chánged.
6. Now you know Nixon spends more on his dogs feeding them and we're supposed to be a little above them. We should be entitled to more than that. It's just not worth a damn.

We chose to question the women about Robert Finch because he was pictured in some quarters as the "good guy" of the Nixon administration, that is a "good guy" in the sense that he was viewed as more in tune with the social needs of black people. Yet most women had never heard of Robert Finch or had not heard enough to comment one way or the other. Those who did make a statement on Finch were divided in their evaluation of him. Some accepted the "good guy" image and felt that Finch had tried to help black people.

1. I heard quite a bit about him helping the black people with this program they had. I think he's a nice man.
2. I think Finch was an idealistic man. I think that he wanted to do a lot of things and he would have done a lot of things if his hands had not been tied but his hands were tied and Finch could not and I say it's the best thing that he's no longer there.
3. Finch was the type of person that was helping the black people. That's why he was fired. Any white man that helps the black man is either killed or taken from his job.
4. His job has probably made him more liberal. He's now been made a minority and he's beginning to see how it feels. And one thing about white people, they're not used to being mistreated and they come out fighting. We haven't heard the last of him. If he leaves that administration he'll be the one to tell all.
5. I think he was a little white boy who was just trying, who really was coming from his principles, dealing on that whole level that they taught him when he was a kid and the stuff he read in the Constitution, on the level you can't do it if you're white. You're not supposed to do that. They call you nigger lover like they used to call folks Indian lovers. He was coming from a straight HEW line. This is what HEW is supposed to do and this is what we were told. "No, that ain't what you're supposed to do. You're supposed to keep them niggers in check, not give them niggers more money, not fund this program and that program."

Others concluded that Finch was just another white man who could not be trusted. Moreover, they viewed him as incapable or unwilling to go against the wishes of Richard Nixon.

1. All I know is that he got burned by his buddy. I understand he wasn't as big an s.o.b. as Mitchell is but I'm sure he's done his little tricks in his day too. I'm not really too concerned about white folks.

2. I think he kept the same type of double image of trying to be a poor struggling liberal but under the attack of all these moderates and conservatives. I think he was just the President's boy and he was there. There was no way possible he could have brought off any significant health, education, and labor reforms because Nixon himself didn't want them to go through and the people he had given him to work with weren't going to approve them and put them into practice. So he was put in a hamstring type of position and he was demoted and now put into a position of presidential advisor. It just adds to that thing of giving false illusions to the American people and he let himself be used in that way. I just see him as being someone who is aiding and abetting the eventual increased suppression of people.

3. I never met the guy. I never seen the guy. All I know I hate the guy. He does so many things that just don't agree with my way of being and my way of thinking. I understand he's white. A lot of things that really need attention to and a lot of proposals that's sent in to him to get rents and this type of thing, they always come back without any help for it. He's out to help just me and my white folks and that's it.

4. I think Finch is just like the rest of the little puppets Nixon has around. When things got too tough for him he cut out like most of them do. He's secretary of HEW and we want to talk with him. We were advocating this guaranteed income and a lot of policies that can be set by him but he just didn't want to deal with it. He was afraid of the people for one thing. He was afraid of Nixon. He didn't want to lose his white-collar job so we in turn went down and took over the office. I think Finch began to realize welfare rights was organized. We have a membership of 45,000 people across the country. He knows that we are beginning to speak up for our rights and he just got scared. He even had a heart attack or whatever that was that put him in the hospital. I think we did it.

5. Finch is not a liberal. Finch is a Californian and a Reagan man. He ain't no different from all them other exploiters. He's a tool of the military-industrial complex. He was never a liberal.

He was a liberal to Reagan but shit, what is that? He's to the left of Reagan and not to the left of Nixon. He has no guts. When it was finally demanded that he meet with his people he had a nervous breakdown.

It is apparent, then, that most women surveyed have written off the national political administration and dismissed any possibility of Nixon, Agnew, or any member of the cabinet being helpful to black people. Some women were so disenchanted with the national political scene that they refused to comment on it. Then, too, several women abstained from offering remarks about national politicians—apparently because they feared their words would end up in the wrong hands and result in possible reprisals against them.

MARJORIE LANSING

21

☆☆☆☆☆☆☆☆☆☆☆☆☆☆☆☆☆☆☆☆☆☆☆☆

The Voting Patterns of American Black Women

PERSPECTIVE

The voting patterns of American black women over the last decade run directly counter to the expectations of voting behavior research. The 11 million black females are the most disadvantaged in the country in terms of their socioeconomic status. A high proportion of black women are disproportionately poor and unemployed; at the same time, more than one-quarter are heads of households who support themselves and their children at earlier ages than white women. On the basis of data from the 1972 presidential election from the Center for Political Studies, it is clear that black women, in comparison to black men and both white sexes, held the lowest levels of political efficacy and the lowest levels of trust in the federal government, and viewed sex discrimination as sharply affecting them. Yet the voting records of black women over the past decade show that the rate of increase in voting by black women has been greater than that of any other sex/race group in the population. In the 1950s black women voted in all regions at rates from 10 to 20 percent lower than those of black men.

379

Since 1960 the voting rate of white men has been declining. Moving ahead of black men by 1960, in 1964, 1968, and 1972 black women voted at the same rates as black men. (It should be noted that the rate for black citizens is still considerably lower than the rate for white men and women.) Thus, the voting rate of black women is incompatible with several canons of voting behavior research, in which the dependent variable (voting/nonvoting) is considered to be influenced by income, education, occupation, and social class. The explanation for this paradoxical behavior could easily be described as linked entirely to the removal of illegal barriers to voting by blacks and to the transfer of black power objectives to politics. But this fails to account for the fact that black women are increasing their rate of voting faster than black men. The thesis of this study is that black women are increasing their vote not only because of race, but because of perceived sex discrimination; in effect, a double jeopardy. Second, we suggest that some black women hold a role-reversal relationship to black men, which makes voting appropriate behavior for the independent, aggressive black female.

Before the 1960s, no more than one-third of black women voted (not only in the South but also in other regions of the country). We agree that the increasing politicization of black women can be linked to the removal of legal and other intimidating restraints on voting. And the participation of black women of all classes and ages in the protests of the 1950s led to a resocialization in political behavior which has, apparently, led to a pattern of increasing voting. But we would add that increased voting by black females is indirectly related to their rising expectations for change in their status and role as women.

This study seeks to explain the increase in voting by the most disadvantaged group in America. Who are the black females who are increasing their rate of voting? Who are the nonvoters?

DATA

As the black population is no more than 13 percent of the total, the number of blacks falling into survey samples is not usually large enough to permit analysis. For this reason we have taken some of our basic data from the Bureau of the Census for 1964, 1968, and 1972, the presidential election years for which their large voter surveys are available. The principal survey data are from the 1956, 1968, and

1972 national election studies conducted by the Center for Political Studies of The University of Michigan. The data were made available by the Inter-University Consortium for Political Research, which bears no responsibility for the interpretation in this study.

It should be noted that the measurement of turnout is from survey data which are dependent on postelection self-report and vary somewhat from official statistics. For comparative purposes the over-report and underreport are internally consistent. The proportion of women in these samples tends to be slightly higher than the proportion of men since the excluded population elements are disproportionately male.[1]

The proportion of blacks in the sample for 1968 includes a weight for the Center data, but the result is still not a true random sample of blacks. The data for 1956 have a limited number of blacks which do not permit extensive cross-tabulation. In this study the Ns will be noted when they are small. Despite the limitations of the data from the Center for Political Studies, their archives appear to have the most extensive survey data which include blacks.

Differences in political behavior between men and women in the total electorate have been documented from survey data.[2] But there has been very little systematic study of black women, although there has been extensive investigation of the black citizen in relation to protest movements and politics. No extensive studies at this time give the voting statistics by black women except on regional or local bases.

METHOD

We examine the vote by black women exploring the relationships of age, education, region, and occupation. We also discuss the effects of a possible sex-role reversal by black Americans in relation to a comparison of female heads of household, and also for professional women.

This section examines voting by race and sex for the 1956, 1964, 1968, and 1972 presidential elections. The data for 1964 and 1968, taken from the Bureau of the Census surveys, demonstrate that black women in the younger age groups outvoted black men. Black women in the middle-age groups voted in numbers comparable to black men. We compare the 1964 and 1968 figures with the Matthews-Prothro study of the South, with data collected in 1961, which found voting rates for black females far below that for black males. Data from the Center for Political Studies, comparing 1956–72, also illustrate that voting by black women in numbers comparable to black men is a recent phenomenon. We include comparative figures for white voters for the presidential elections to demonstrate that the gap between the sexes was larger for the white community for 1956, 1964, and 1968. We describe the 1968 election, providing census figures for region, age, education, and occupation.

BACKGROUND: THE BLACK WOMAN
VOTER BEFORE 1964

A black woman reared in the South who was sixty years old in 1973 probably was not allowed to vote until she was in her thirties, and quite possibly not until she was over fifty. The white primary was not outlawed until the *Smith* v. *Allwright* decision in 1944. Voting figures are difficult to find. An estimated 12 percent of the black population voted before 1940.[3] Ralph Bunche, researching the problem for Gunnar Myrdal's *An American Dilemma,* estimated that only 250,000 voted in the South in 1940.[4] The Commission on Civil Rights estimated that the total number of black voters in the South had doubled by 1955 and by 1964 the figure had climbed to slightly more than 2 million.[5] Insofar as this researcher can determine, the earliest reliable figure comes from Matthews and Prothro, the first to analyze the southern black voting patterns by sex (1966). They reported from data collected in 1961:

> In terms of voting alone, 47 percent of Negro males and 38
> percent of Negro females would qualify as participants (including
> voting). . . . At every level of education, and for all forms of
> political participation, more Negro men than women are active.[6]

The major change did not come until 1965 with the Voting Rights Act, which among other provisions, provided direct federal assistance in registration and voting. The act is generally seen as the most significant step since the Fifteenth Amendment in opening opportunities for black people to register and vote.

If a black woman did vote before 1964, she probably had moved to the North or West, to a state where blacks had voted prior to 1964.

These were the years of the massive migration: the Census Bureau reported that 3.5 million blacks left the South between 1940 and 1966.[7] (Fifty-three percent now remain in the South.[8]) Thus, older blacks, especially from the southern states of the Old Confederacy, male and female, have generally begun to vote only late in life—if they vote at all. It is our contention that in this process of political re-socialization the younger black women have adapted more easily than older women.

THE VOTING RECORD OF BLACK WOMEN IN 1964 AND 1968 BY AGE

Matthews and Prothro found that black women in 1961 reported that they lagged behind black men in all forms of political participation, including voting. As table 21.1 makes clear, in the 1964 presi-

TABLE 21.1. A Comparison by Sex, Age, and Race of Eligible Persons Voting for President in 1964 and 1968 (in percent)

Age in Years	1964 Negro[a]			1968 Negro		
	Men	Women	M−W	Men	Women	M−W
21–24	39	49	−10[b]	36	42	− 6
25–34	58	62	− 4	56	57	− 1
35–44	64	62	+ 2	65	65	0
45–54	65	66	− 1	66	66	0
55–64	65	60	+ 5	65	60	+ 5
65–74	57	48	+ 9	51	32	+19

Age in Years	1964 White			1968 White		
	Men	Women	M−W	Men	Women	M−W
21–24	53	52	+ 1	53	53	0
25–34	66	65	+ 1	64	63	+ 1
35–44	76	73	+ 3	73	71	+ 2
45–54	80	75	+ 5	77	75	+ 2
55–64	80	74	+ 6	79	69	+10
65–74	79	51	+28	68	51	+17

Source: Bureau of Census, *Current Population Reports, Population Characteristics,* Series P-20, no. 143, 25 October 1965; and no. 192, 2 December 1969.

[a]The census defined Negro differently from nonwhite.

[b]Percentage of difference in score (percent men minus percent women).

dential election black women up to age 54 voted at rates comparable
to or higher than black men. In 1968 the pattern was repeated. In the
youngest cohort, aged 21–24, 10 percent more women than men
voted in 1964, and 6 percent more women in 1968. Voting was about
the same for the middle cohorts (ages 24–54) for both sexes. For
people born before 1919—the oldest cohorts—black men voted pro-
gressively at higher rates than black women: 5 percent more in the
55–64 group, and 9 and 19 percent in the 65–74 group in 1964 and
1968.

This pattern does not appear to be the same for white voters in
the same elections. The voting rates for white women and men appear
to have been about the same—slightly less for women up to 55 years
of age. In the two oldest age groups, men voted considerably more
than women—6 and 10 percent in the 55–64 group, and 28 and 17
percent in the 65–74 group. None of the white female cohorts voted
in higher percentages than white men. The overall voting pattern for
black men and women in 1968 was the same. This same pattern continued into 1972.

Table 21.2 presents a comparison of voting by black women in
1956 and 1972 from the data from the Center for Political Studies.
Although the Ns are small, we note that 29 percent of black women
voted in 1956 and 46 percent of black men voted in 1956. This figure
doubled by 1968 and increased slightly in 1972.

REGION

If we examine a breakdown of the black vote by region for 1968,
we find that the pattern of the black vote for the whole country is reversed when age is considered (see table 21.3). For the youngest

TABLE 21.2. Differences by Race and Sex in Voting for President
(in percent)

Race	Sex	1956	1968	1972
Black	Women	29	60	63
White	Women	72	76	71
Black	Men	46	77	68
White	Men	82	78	76

Source: Center for Political Studies, The University of Michigan.

TABLE 21.3 A Comparison by Sex, Negro Race, Age, and Region of Eligible Persons Voting for President in 1968 (in percent)

Age in Years	North and West		South	
	Men	Women	Men	Women
21–24	39	47	37	32
25–44	61	61	56	56
45–64	71	69	57	59
65 and over	59	52	37	49

Source: Bureau of the Census, *Population Reports, Population Characteristics*, Series P-20, no. 192, 2 December 1969.

cohort, 5 percent more men than women voted in the South, contrasting with 8 percent more women voting than men in the North and West. For the next two cohorts, here combined, both sexes voted at similar rates in both regions. In the older cohorts, the pattern is reversed in the South, with 2 percent more women than men voting in the North and West. For the next two cohorts, here combined, both sexes voted at similar rates in both regions. In the older cohorts, the pattern is reversed in the South, with 2 percent more women than men voting in the 45–64 group, and 12 percent more women than men ages 65 and over voting, contrasting with 3 percent and 7 percent more men voting in the North and West.

Verba and Nie found (1967 survey data) that "blacks vote almost as regularly as whites in the North, much less regularly in the South. And when one takes out the effects of social class one finds that in the North blacks are more active in voting than their class would predict, whereas in the South they are less active than their class would predict. Clearly this reflects the fact that historical legal discriminations against black voting in the South still make a difference."[10]

To explain this pattern further, we can examine the record of the youngest cohorts. Two general directions could be taken in explaining why young black women are increasing their vote at higher rates than black men. It could be understood as a decrease among men, explained by evidence of higher levels of alienation of the political system, or self-concern over the war in Vietnam, or unemployment. Or it could be seen as a relative increase among young women. We have chosen the latter alternative, as we shall demonstrate. Black women in 1972, for example, had lower levels of trust in the federal government and political parties than did black men. Black females responded positively to sex discrimination in 1972, especially in the area of job discrimination.

One source of evidence of increasing politicization of young black women is Matthews and Prothro's study of the civil rights movement (1966). They found that no large gap existed in participation rates between black males and females in the student protests. In their data, demonstrations against segregation in 1960 and 1961 included almost as many young women as men: 48 percent of the student participants in the sit-ins and freedom rides were females. The Matthews and Prothro study of levels of participation found 30 percent of male students and 21 percent of females at the "most active" level, and 12 percent of males and 17 percent of females at the second level of involvement. Well over half—57 percent—of blacks enrolled in predominantly black institutions at the height of the sit-ins were women—a fact, Matthews and Prothro suggest, which reflects the special position of women in the black subculture.[11]

EDUCATION

Strong evidence for the increasing politicization of black women, and further explanation of their voting patterns, can be found through an examination of changes in the level of education among blacks in the last twenty years: the average number of years in school jumped from 7 in 1950 to 11 in 1970. The number of blacks aged 16 and 17 in high school increased from 77 percent in 1960 to 86 percent in 1970; 16 percent of young blacks were attending college in 1970. Black women have had more years in school at all levels for the past two decades.[12] One of the best-documented findings in voting research describes the close relationship between level of education and voting. Black women of elementary education in 1968 voted at rates slightly higher than white women of comparable education (see table 21.4), 7 percent higher with 0–4 years of schooling and 8 percent higher with 5–7 years of school. Further, the gap between the sexes is smaller for blacks than whites. Black women with the lowest level of education voted 4 percent less than comparable black men; white women with the lowest level voted 13 percent less than comparable white men. Blacks (of both sexes) with more than four years of school vote at similar rates, white women remain about five percentage

TABLE 21.4. A Comparison by Sex, Race, Education of Eligible Persons Voting for President in 1968 (in percent)

Education in Years	Black			White		
	Women	Men	M−W	Women	Men	M−W
Elementary						
0–4	39	43	−4	32	45	−13
5–7	53	54	−1	45	60	−15
8	54	56	−2	59	68	− 9
High School						
1–3	56	57	−1	60	65	− 5
4	65 .	67	−2	73	73	0
College						
1–3	74	73	+1	80	78	+ 2
4	80	79	+1	83	84	− 1
5 or more	91	87	+4	88	86	+ 2

Source: Bureau of Census, *Current Population Reports, Population Characteristics,* Series P-20, no. 192, 2 December 1969, p. 18.

points behind white men up to four years of high school. Thus black women tend to vote in percentages slightly higher than their levels of education would predict—if the prediction is based on the performance of white women.

YOUTH

The pattern of an increasing female vote does appear in the youth vote (table 21.5). For the states of Georgia, Kentucky, Alaska,

TABLE 21.5. Voter Participation of Persons 18 to 24 Years Old by Race, Sex, and Region, November 1968 (in percent)[a]

White		
	male	52
	female	52
Negro		
	male	35
	female	41

Source: Current Population Reports, *Population Characteristics, Characteristics of New Voter, 1972* (Bureau of the Census), Series P-20, no. 230, December 1971, p. 23.

[a]Civilian noninstitutional population of persons 18 to 24 years old in Georgia and Kentucky, 19 to 24 years old in Alaska, 20 to 24 years old in Hawaii, and 21 to 24 years old in all other states.

and Hawaii—which permitted voting by citizens below the age of twenty-one—white men and women voted in equal rates in 1968, while 6 percent more black women than men voted.

NONVOTERS

An alternative way to examine the question is to compare nonvoters. Flanigan, using data from the Center for Political Studies, has reported that the most dramatic reductions in permanent nonvoters have occurred among blacks, both in the South and non-South. He found 87 percent of black women in the South reporting themselves to be nonvoters in the 1952 presidential election. With a steady decline, this figure dropped to 31 percent in the 1968 election. For black men, the figure dropped from 65 percent in 1952 to 25 percent in the South in 1968. For the non-South, the figures were 28 percent black women reporting themselves as nonvoters in 1952 (1956, 32 percent; 1960, 28 percent; 1964, 18 percent) and 17 percent in 1968. For black men, the figure was 17 percent reporting as nonvoters in 1952, with no reliable figures in 1968, which Flanigan attributed to sampling difficulties in the central cities of the North.[13] (Self-reporting on voting/non-voting involves recall which varies with actual statistics.)

SUMMARY

We have suggested that a pattern exists in terms of the percentages of black Americans voting in the 1964 and 1968 presidential elections. For the youngest cohort, aged 18–24, black women voted at higher rates than black men—our figure ranges from 6 to 10 percent. Among the middle-age groups, 25–54, the two sexes voted at similar rates. This pattern differs from that for whites. Among cohorts over 55 years of age, black men outvoted black women at rates ranging from 5 to 19 percent higher. We have so far isolated only variables that relate to the pattern: race, as the pattern is confined to blacks, and region, as the pattern does not appear in the South.

SEX-ROLE REVERSAL

One explanation of black women's increasing voting can be investigated by exploring the sex roles of black men and women. One theory suggests that black women have always occupied more aggressive roles than white women or white men, and have been more achievement-oriented than black men. Thus given a chance to vote, they tend to exercise it.

Joyce Ladner provides a statement of the difference in roles:

> . . . women in American society are held to be the passive sex, but the majority of black women have perhaps never fit this model, and have been liberated from many of the constraints that society has traditionally imposed on women. Although this emerged from forced circumstances, it nevertheless allowed black women the kind of emotional well-being that Women's Liberation groups are calling for.[14]

A great many black families simply could never afford the luxury of an unemployed wife. Chafe, in his excellent history of the roles of American women since 1920, described the economic position of black women before the Second World War, documenting what Ladner referred to as "forced circumstances":

> In the years preceding the war (II) black women were twice as likely to be employed as whites, but their economic horizons were severely limited. Over 70 percent worked as domestic servants in private homes, and another 20 percent toiled in the fields, picking crops and hoeing gardens on small farms. For them the war represented in some ways a second emancipation. The manpower shortage broke down rigid employment barriers and gave them an unparalleled opportunity to advance.[15]

There has recently been considerable controversy over the exact nature of black sex roles and family structure—Moynihan's "matriarchy" thesis is well known. We are simply interested in discovering whether a connection can be traced between black women's active roles and their political participation. There are two areas which we can quantify from our data which relates to this question. We look first at a comparison of voting/nonvoting by women who described themselves as heads of households and women who reported that they were wives of the heads of households. Our second table examines a comparison of black men and women by occupation.

Matthews and Prothro looked at the first question in their survey in the South in 1961. From their general finding that for all forms of political participation more black men than women were active, they went on:

> The idea that responsibility for acting as head of the household might carry over into political activity receives uneven support. Negro women who are heads of their households exceed Negro housewives in political activity by only a very small margin. . . . Being head of the house does not necessarily increase the probability that Negro women will become politically active, but the combination of such responsibility with outside employment does seem to lead to a modest increase in political participation.[16]

If head of household were controlled for black females, the expectation would be that on the basis of income, education, social class, and occupation, these women probably would not vote. On the other hand, according to our notion of role reversal, it seems likely that holding the position of head of household would increase voting. But the results from table 21.6 neither confirm nor deny. Black female heads of household voted in 1968 at the same rates as wives of household heads. In 1972 there was a slight difference—5 percent—that is, 68 percent of black female heads of household voted as compared to 63 percent voters among wives of head of household.

TABLE 21.6. A Comparison of Female Heads of Household and Wives of Heads of Household by Race Voting for President, 1968 and 1972

| | | Black | | White | |
		Female Head of Household	Wife of Head of Household	Female Head of Household	Wife of Head of Household
1968	voted	(50) 63%	(43) 61%	(159) 74%	(343) 78%
	not voting	(30) 38%	(28) 39%	(56) 26%	(97) 22%
		N = 82	N = 74	N = 238	N = 493
1972	voted	(48) 68%	(33) 63%	(215) 65%	(552) 75%
	not voting	(23) 32%	(19) 37%	(115) 35%	(185) 25%
		N = 85	N = 59	N = 387	N = 861

Source: Center for Political Studies, The University of Michigan.

The voting rate by black female heads of households is 5 percent higher also than for the total number of black women voting in 1972. In the white community, female heads voted at about the same rate as wives of heads (4 percent less). In 1972, white female heads of households voted at a rate which was 10 percent lower than voting rates for wives of heads of households.

We can press the sex-role reversal notion a little further by investigating the voting behavior of black women who are at the high end of the economic continuum. Among blacks classified by the census as "Professional, technical, and kindred workers," women exceeded the male rate of voting by 8 percentage points (women, 87 percent voting; men, 79 percent voting). Epstein (1972) concluded from a survey of thirty-one black female professionals that the double prejudices of racism and sexism can work to the advantage of a select few women at the top. Although there are few black women in the ranks of lawyers, doctors, and business executives, their numbers are proportionately greater than for white women. She wrote that black women are less likely to arouse traditional sexist hostilities in the primarily white, male professional world—the suspicion that the women are looking only for a husband. Even among black male professionals, sexism is less prevalent because black men are more accustomed to the image of working women.[17]

If we examine voting by occupation from census data for the 1964 and 1968 presidential elections, we find that black women in white-collar and manual occupations slightly exceeded the voting rates of black men found in those occupations (white-collar: women, 82 percent; men, 77 percent; manual workers: women, 68 percent; men, 61 percent). In 1968, black women voted at a rate of 5 percent more than men who were in the same white-collar occupations, and also in manual occupations. Table 21.7 notes also that in 1964 black men who were service workers voted at 8 percent higher rates than black women, although they voted at the same rates in 1968. In 1964, black men voted at 10 percent higher rates than black women. It is interesting that farm workers, of both sexes, voted at drastically lower rates than other occupations.

SUMMARY AND CONCLUSIONS

Black women in America were voting for President in 1964, 1968, and 1972 at the same rates as black men. Using 1956 as a

TABLE 21.7. Comparison of Negroes by Sex and Occupation of Eligible Persons Voting for President in 1964 and 1968 (in percent)

Occupation	1964			1968		
	Men	Women	M−W	Men	Women	M−W
White-collar workers	77	82	− 5	77	82	−5
Manual workers	61	68	− 7	58	63	−5
Service workers	68	60	+ 8	62	61	+1
Farm workers	34	24	+10	44	B	

B. Base less than 75,000

Source: Bureau of the Census, Current Population Reports, Population Characteristics, Series P-20, no. 192, 2 December 1969.

baseline for comparison, we have noted that less than a third of black women voted and that this rate was doubled by 1968 and 1972. While some 29 percent of black women voted in 1956, 46 percent of black men voted. Thus in the 1960s black women have increased their rate of voting at higher rates than black men, and more than either white sex—for whom turnout has been declining since 1960.

Using census data for 1964 and 1968, we noted that the youngest black female cohort voted at slightly higher rates than their male counterparts (black women, 10 percent more than men in 1964 and 6 percent more in 1968). The middle-aged female cohorts voted at about the same rates as black men. Only at ages 55 and over was there a sharp increase in voting rates by black men as compared to black women (black men, 5 percent more in 55–64 age group, and 9–19 percent in the 65–74 group in 1964 and 1968).

We extended the investigation to report that black women in white-collar and manual occupations voted at slightly higher rates than black men in those occupations. This was reversed for service and farm workers. Black women in the professions and technical fields voted at 8 percent higher rates than men in those occupations. Black female heads of household did not vote at higher rates than black wives of heads of household.

Black women of elementary education voted at rates slightly higher (7 percent in 1968) than white women of comparable education. The gap between the sexes by education is smaller for blacks than for whites at lower levels.

Overall, a key finding is that black Americans, and especially

black female Americans, do not fit the model of voting from the pre-
dictions developed over several decades. The themes of alienation,
interest theory, mass participation theory, feminist theory—all relate
to the mosaic of voting as described in this presentation. A deeper
understanding of the specific relations among these factors will become feasible only when more extensive data become available—data
designed specifically to explore black culture and not the white super-
culture.

NOTES

1. For a more rigorous explanation, see Aage R. Clausen, "Response Validity,
Vote Report," *Public Opinion Quarterly* 32, no. 4 (Winter 1968–69): 588–606.

2. The literature on sex-related differences in political behavior would include
Harold F. Gosnell, *Democracy: The Threshold of Freedom* (New York: Ronald, 1948), chap.
4; Maurice Duverger, *The Political Role of Women* (Paris, UNESCO, 1955); Robert E.
Lane, *Political Life* (Glencoe, Ill.: Free Press, 1959), pp. 209–16; Angus Campbell, Philip
E. Converse, Warren E. Miller, and Donald E. Stokes, *The American Voter* (New York:
Wiley, 1960), pp. 483–93; Gabriel A. Almond and Sidney Verba, *The Civic Culture* (Bos-
ton: Little, Brown, 1965); Kirsten Amundsen, *The Silenced Majority: Women and American
Democracy* (Englewood Cliffs, N.J.: Prentice-Hall, 1971); *A Sampler of Women's Studies*
(Center for the Continuing Education of Women, University of Michigan, 1973); Jane
Jaquette, ed., *Women in Politics* (Wiley, 1974); William H. Flanigan, *Political Behavior of
the American Electorate* (Boston: Allyn & Bacon, 1972).

3. These estimates are rough approximations because of the decentralized organization of records: *Report of the United States Commission on Civil Rights, 1959* (Washington, D.C., 1959, 1961); Commission on Civil Rights Report, *Voting*, bk. 1 (1961); *New
York Times*, 22 November 1964. Hanes Walton, Jr., *Black Politics* (Philadelphia: J. B. Lip-
pincott, 1972), pp. 225–39, gives an extensive bibliography on black politics but unfortunately these references do not generally provide statistics on the voting patterns of
black women.

4. Gunnar Myrdal, *An American Dilemma* (2nd ed.; New York: Harper & Row,
1962), p. 488.

5. *Report of the Commission on Civil Rights*, p. 243.

6. Donald R. Matthews and James W. Prothro, *Negroes and the New Southern Poli-
tics* (New York: Harcourt, Brace & World, 1966). See section on the rise in negro voting
since 1944, pp. 17–20; see section on sex and political participation, pp. 65–70. The
South, for purposes of their study, was defined as the former Confederate states:
Alabama, Arkansas, Florida, Georgia, Louisiana, Mississippi,North Carolina, South
Carolina, Tennessee, Texas, and Virginia.

7. See summary, *Newsweek*, February 1973; census data.

8. Ibid.

9. Bureau of Census, *Voting and Registration in the Election of November, 1972*, Series P-20, no. 253 (Washington, D.C.: Government Printing Office, October 1973).

10. Sidney Verba and Norman H. Nie, *Participation in America; Political Democracy
and Social Equality* (New York: Harper & Row, 1972), chap. 10.

11. Matthews and Prothro, *New Southern Politics*, pp. 416–19.

12. A good source on published data is Tobia and Nampeo McKenney, "Negro Women in the United States" (Population Studies paper, 18–20 April 1968).

13. Flanigan, *Political Behavior*, p. 23.

14. Joyce A. Ladner, *Tomorrow's World: The Black Woman* (New York: Anchor, 1972). This sociological work has an excellent bibliography.

15. William Henry Chafe, *The American Woman: Her Changing Social Economic, and Political Roles* (New York: Oxford University Press, 1972).

16. Matthews and Prothro, *New Southern Politics*, p. 66.

17. Cynthia Fuchs Epstein, "Black and Female: The Double Whammy," *Psychology Today* 7, no. 3 (August 1973): 57–61, 89.

HERRINGTON J. BRYCE and ALAN E.
WARRICK

☆☆☆☆☆☆☆☆☆☆☆☆☆☆☆☆☆☆☆☆☆☆☆☆☆☆

22 Black Women in Electoral Politics

We are awakening to the extent of female exclusion from full participation in many areas of
professional life. Black women have been constrained from entering
many fields, partly because of sexual discrimination which handicaps
all women, and partly because of racial discrimination which handicaps all blacks.

Although there are approximately 7 million black women of voting age in the United States today, a study of the latest *National Roster
of Black Elected Officials,* published by the Joint Center, shows that
black women hold only 337 of the more than 520,000 elective offices
in the country. However, there has been about a 160 percent increase
in the number of black women officeholders since 1969, when only
131 such women were listed in that year's *Roster.*

The increase for black men, from 1,099 in 1969 to 2,293 in 1973,
was 108 percent. Thus, today, black women account for 12 percent of
the 2,629 black elected officials in the country. In 1969 they were 10
percent of the national total of black elected officials.

NUMBER AND REGIONAL DISTRIBUTION

In 1973, as in 1969, about 45 percent of all black women in elec-

395

tive offices are in the South. In 1973 the states of the Old Confederacy alone account for roughly 34 percent of all black women in elective offices. In 1969 this figure was 39 percent.

The decline in the Old Confederacy's share, from 39 percent in 1969 to 34 percent in 1973, occurred because the number of black women elected officials in other parts of the country increased more rapidly. For example, the number of female black elected officials in the Northeast increased more than fourfold, from 21 to 94.

The continued concentration of black female as well as black male elected officials in the South undoubtedly reflects the concentration of blacks in small southern communities, vigorous registration and voter education projects, and the protections of the Voting Rights Act of 1965.

New York is the state with the greatest number of black women elected officials, with 37. In 1969 there were 3. Michigan, with 30, and Mississippi, with 22, rank second and third in the number of black women holding elective offices.

These three states with the greatest number of black female elected officials are also the ones with the greatest number of black male elected officials. Moreover, these states rank among the top ten in the percentage of blacks of voting age.

All but two of the 37 black females who hold elective offices in the state of New York serve on school boards, mostly in New York City where blacks account for roughly 20 percent of the voting-age population. In Mississippi the black women are not concentrated in any specific town in that state. In Michigan most black women elected officials are members of school boards, and most reside in the greater Detroit area, where blacks account for 39 percent of the voting-age population.

OFFICES HELD

The most common elective offices held by black females are those related to education, primarily on local school boards. In the nation as a whole, about 44 percent of all black female elected officials are in that category. The concentration of women in education is greatest in the Northeast. There, 69 percent of all elected black women are in offices related to education, compared with 28 percent in the South, 35 percent in the Midwest, and 52 percent in the West.

The fact that black women are concentrated in education is related to the high proportion of educated black women who are teachers and the traditional concern of women with the welfare of children. It is also related to the perception by the electorate that education outside the university is primarily a female function. Only 27 percent of black male elected officials are in offices related to education.

The second most common offices held by black women are those on the municipal level. About 31 percent of all black women elected officials are in municipal offices. This compares with about 41 percent of black men. Thus, while black women are concentrated in offices related to education, black men are concentrated in offices on the municipal level.

Like black men, black women are least visible at the county and federal levels. This is particularly distressing since many governmental responsibilities of critical importance to blacks are discharged on the county level, such as water and sewer, zoning, education, health, and welfare. In a sense, blacks are acutely underrepresented at the level where global and national decisions are made (the federal level) and on the county level where men and women make the "nitty-gritty" decisions—many of which loom large with the new thrusts of revenue sharing, the "new federalism" and local government reorganization.

UPWARD MOBILITY AND TENURE

Often one elective office is a steppingstone to a higher office. However, this study finds that there was little upward mobility among black women elected officials between 1969 and 1973. Most notable among those who did move upward were State Senator Barbara Jordan of Texas and State Assemblywoman Yvonne Brathwaite Burke of California, both of whom moved from state legislatures to the U.S. House of Representatives, and Doris A. Davis, who became mayor of Compton, California, after serving two terms as city clerk.

This lack of observed mobility may be due, in part, to the fact that some of the incumbents who took office in 1969 may not have completed their terms of office by April, 1973, the printing deadline for the latest *Roster*. But this does not appear to be too important, because only about 61, or roughly 46 percent, of the 131 women who were in office in 1969 are also in office in 1973. This suggests that the rate of

BRYCE AND WARRICK

attrition among black women in elected office was nearly 54 percent over a four-year period. That is, about half of the black women listed in the first volume of the *Roster* are no longer in the offices they held in 1969.

The lack of tenure in office is a significant drawback since long-term service is often an important element in the acquisition of power. This instability in office is an ominous sign, even if some of these black women have been replaced by other blacks. The real objective should be the retention of current black political gains and the expansion of the total number of capable black officeholders.

Black females in county-level offices are the least likely to be building up seniority. The retention rate of black women in these offices between 1969 and 1973 was 14.2 percent—meaning that nearly 86 percent of all black women who held county-level offices in 1969 do not hold similar offices today. The retention rate is highest among those black women elected officials who hold offices related to education. Nearly 60 percent of those who held these offices in 1969 hold similar offices today.

COMPARISON OF BLACK AND WHITE WOMEN

It would be interesting to compare black women and white women elected officials along several dimensions. However, the available data on white women are incomplete. While we do not have complete data for white women, black women account for an impressive 25 percent of all women in federal offices—the House of Representatives. But they account for only 6 percent of the 466 women in state-level positions.

CONCLUSIONS AND DISCUSSIONS

In just four years the black female has more than doubled her presence among elected public officials. While this is impressive, we are sobered by the reality of her continued underrepresentation. She accounts for an infinitesimally small percentage of all elected officials and only about 12 percent of black elected officials.

Why is the black female so underrepresented? There are several possible explanations.

Certainly one of the most important explanations lies in the society's discriminatory attitudes toward women which only recently have begun to give way and to tolerate female entry into various male-dominated occupations, including electoral politics. Women won the right to vote just over fifty years ago—in 1920 through the Nineteenth Amendment to the U.S. Constitution. Seven years later, Mrs. E. Howard Harper was appointed (to succeed her deceased husband) to the state legislature in West Virginia. Mrs. Harper's position was, at that time, the highest elective office held by a black woman, and she was the first black woman to reach that plateau.

It was not until 1938, however, that a black woman, Crystal Bird Fauset, was elected to a major public office. She was elected to the Pennsylvania Assembly.

In 1968 black women achieved an important breakthrough on the national political scene with the election to the U.S. Congress of Shirley A. Chisholm, who became the first black woman to serve in that body. Today there are four black women in the U.S. House of Representatives: Mrs. Chisholm, Cardiss Collins, Yvonne Brathwaite Burke, and Barbara C. Jordan.

Today there are at least four black women mayors: Lelia Foley of Taft, Oklahoma; Doris A. Davis of Compton, California; Ellen Walker Craig of Urbancrest, Ohio, and Sophia Mitchell of Rendsville, Ohio. Mrs. Mitchell, former president of the city council, was appointed by the city council following the resignation of the previous mayor. (Because she was not elected to office, she is not included in our tally of elected officials.)

In addition to sexual discrimination, a major explanation for the underrepresentation of black females in elective offices is racial discrimination. It was not until the passage of the Voting Rights Act of 1965 that some of the racial barriers to black political participation began to crumble. This act was buttressed by vigorous private voter registration and voter education efforts. Partly as a result of these, blacks, including black women, made important gains in electoral politics. Yet blacks account for less than one-half of one percent of all elected officials.

Gains by black women appear likely to continue in the future as sexual and racial discrimination ease; as black women gain easier access to funds and to the political fund-raising mechanisms; as their level of awareness of the political process moves upward through political socialization, and as there is an increase in the number of educated black women willing to hold political office and willing to assume the responsibilities inherent in winning and holding public service positions.

It is interesting that the educational factor seems to have less impact on the success or failure in politics of black men and many white men—especially on the local level. For example, black men, whose educational attainment is comparable to black women and whose voting age population is roughly 1.9 million less than black women, hold just over seven times as many elective positions. But, both black women and black men are seriously underrepresented in electoral politics.

JEWEL L. PRESTAGE

23

☆☆☆☆☆☆☆☆☆☆☆☆☆☆☆☆☆☆☆☆☆☆☆☆☆

Black Women State Legislators: A Profile

Discrimination on the basis of race and sex in American politics has resulted in very limited participation by black women. Prior to the late 1960s the only period of widespread black involvement in politics was the period of Reconstruction in the South when women were still denied the franchise. Black women, therefore, did not experience with black men this brief stint of voting and officeholding, which was mostly restricted to the South.[1] By 1920 when the Nineteenth Amendment marked the beginning of constitutional protection of the franchise for women, racial barriers to voting nullified most benefits that might have come to black women. It was not until after the passage of the Voting Rights Act in 1965 and its subsequent enforcement in the South that black females first experienced any substantial participation as voters or officeholders. This study focuses on a segment of the black women who have served in one category of offices.

The purposes of this paper are: (1) to review available literature on political behavior of black women; (2) to examine social and political backgrounds and some political orientations of black women state legislators who were in office between 1970 and 1974; and (3) to offer some projections regarding research possibilities in this area.

REVIEW OF LITERATURE

Despite the centrality of the black female in extant social science literature on black America, only minor attention has been devoted to her role in the political arena. This neglect has continued to be reflected in the recent rash of scholarly publications under the separate rubrics of Black Politics and Women in Politics.

Tensions created by efforts to study the politics of the black female in the equality movements (both black and women) have perhaps been partially responsible for this limited research effort. In fact, the suggestion that black women deserve attention as a special case in the study of the politics of blacks or politics of women is almost certain to evoke, at minimum, serious questions of motives or, at worst, cries of "Treason."

In probing sexual differences in political behavior of adults, one widely offered explanation has been the sexual differences in childhood political socialization patterns.[2] Alleged matriarchal family style and its impact have been the theme of most literature on the black family and the black female.[3] While much has been written about sexual differences among white children and the impact of family structure and style on black children and youth, there is not a substantial amount of evidence to support sex differentiated political orientations among young blacks.[4] Nor have differences in political orientations been found among American blacks on the basis of whether or not the father is present in the home.[5] Also, more recent studies have failed to yield support for such sex differences among black or white children.[6]

To date, I have been unable to locate any thorough analysis of black women in politics, even though those elected to Congress are in *A Minority of Members* by Hope Chamberlin,[7] and Judge Constance Baker Motley is included in Peggy Lamson's *Few Are Chosen*.[8] Both are collections of biographies of women politicians. In an August 1973 issue of its monthly newsletter, *Focus,* the Joint Center for Political Studies published a brief tabulation of black women holding political offices with a breakdown by region and offices held.[9] At the time, black women held only 337 of the more than 520,000 elective offices in America; the majority were offices related to education and were concentrated in the South. In the main, black women held offices primarily in those states with the largest numbers of black males in office and were least visible in county and federal positions.

Widespread female participation is revealed in the investigations

of protest activity of black college students in the 1960s.[10] Strong
female participatory orientations have apparently persisted over time
as evidenced by occurrences on at least two campuses experiencing
killings of students by police. In one case a male student, testifying
about the incident in which two black male students were shot by
police, estimated that well over half the students in the area at the
time were female.[11]

Sexual differences in adult political attitudes and participation
were reported by Matthews and Prothro in the 1960s as well as in a
later study of blacks in New Orleans. While earlier studies
documented measurable sex differences, in the latter study only minimal overall variations in protest and traditional participation were
found for black men and women.[12]

Inez Reid's *"Together" Black Women,*[13] a study of black women with
a reputation in the community for "militancy," yielded at least five
fundamental findings:

1. The adoption of the concept "together" as a substitute for
   militant
2. The feeling of "together" black women that their interests are
   almost diametrically opposed to those of the Women's Liberation Movement
3. The gross disenchantment of "together" black women with national and local political and social conditions in the United
   States
4. The willingness of "together" black women to embrace violence as the only viable solution to black oppression
5. The "state of limbo" in which many "together" black women
   find themselves while awaiting the next stage of the black
   struggle

In Reid's perceptive study, "militant" was discarded as an "alien
phenomenon imposed on the black community." "Together" was
adopted as a term which connotes "having one's mind free of confu-
sion, to be positive, functional to emerge as a whole person." "To-
getherness" is further characterized by a spiritual closeness in a common endeavor to erase oppression and a refusal to take uncritically
the total value structure of the white community. A profile of the "together" black woman is one who is relatively comfortable in economic
terms, relatively young, apolitical traditionally speaking, semireligi-
ous, working at a variety of jobs, exposed to some college education,

and possessive of a high degree of black or social consciousness. Further, she is committed to the black struggle, involved, selfless, fearless, and confident.[14]

In a study of voting patterns of black women, Marjorie Lansing concludes that in the 1960s black women increased their rate of voting at higher rates than black men, and more than either white sex.[15] Especially noteworthy was the finding that black women with elementary school educations voted at rates slightly higher than white women of comparable education and that the gap between females and males by education is smaller for blacks than for whites at lower levels. In this same reporting, black women were found to have lower levels of political efficacy than black men or whites of both sexes.

Edward T. Clayton in his 1964 study of *The Negro Politician* devoted a chapter to "The Woman in Politics."[16] He observed that the majority of Negro political workers were females who outnumbered men in performing grass-roots tasks. The rewards to women, however, were found not to be commensurate with their contributions to party efforts. A dismal "score or so" of Negro women were found to have made a dramatic success at politics, as there were in 1964 less than a dozen across the nation who had gained elective office in the sense that they had political constituents. Mostly, black women had elevated themselves to positions of power within their parties.

Clayton examines the political careers of about a dozen women officeholders. The diversity of personalities, geographic locations, social backgrounds, and political styles among these women thwarted his efforts to discover any pattern for success to offer black women aspiring for high places politically. He did note that the late Congressman Dawson once commented: "The Negro woman has been the salvation of Negroes politically . . . they are unbending, cannot be easily swayed and cannot be bought. This is in contrast to the Negro male who is susceptible to money."[17]

Shirley Chisholm's *Unbought and Unbossed* gives an account of the political career of the first black woman to be elected to the U.S. Congress after overcoming a double disadvantage, race and sex, to win. She discusses the comparative impact of these inpediments and her propensity to speak out and to break the rules.[18]

METHODOLOGY

Data utilized in this study were obtained principally through interviews with the legislators, ranging from 45 minutes to 2.5 hours. In addition, printed materials were supplied by legislative research agencies in the states and biographical and other printed information were made available by the legislators' offices. Newspapers, periodicals, statistical data, and professional literature were also consulted.

Between 1971 and 1973, 35 black women served in American state legislatures. The sample on which this study is based included 32 of these lawmakers. Twenty-nine are currently serving terms in state houses, of whom 27 are interviewees. Most of the 32 women (28) were in the lower house with only 4 in the upper house.

The 60-item interview schedule solicited information on geographic origin, age, marital status, family size, education, occupation, family background, interest in politics, political experience, basis for contesting for legislative seat, and character of campaign for office. Further, respondents were probed as to perceptions of role, policy priorities, quantity of bills introduced, committee assignments, relations with other legislators, and an assessment of their work as legislators. Other areas of concern were attitudes toward the Women's Liberation Movement, future plans and political ambition, perceptions of the future of blacks and women in the political arena, and views on the liabilities and assets of women in elective office.

In this reporting, concern is limited to consideration of the following dimensions of the data assembled:

Geographic origins and distribution
Family background
Early political socialization
Education
Occupation
Age
Marital status and family size
Prior political experience
Tenure and future plans
Political orientations
Political party affiliation

FINDINGS

Geographic Origin and Distribution
The 35 legislators came from 23 states, while the 32 interviewees

were located in 21 states. The black population in these states, the number of black women serving in the legislature, and the total black membership of the legislature for the 1970–72 period and for the current terms are given in table 23.1.

As the table reveals, the Midwest is most fertile for females seeking careers in legislative service. A greater degree of success seems to be associated with those areas where the black percentage of the population is less pronounced. This observation would seem to have interesting research implications reminiscent of V. O. Key's thesis rel-

TABLE 23.1. Black Women Legislators, Total Black Legislators, and Black Percentage of Population by State

	Black Percentage of Population	Black Women Legislators		Total Number of Black Legislators	
	1970	1972	1974	1972	1974
Arizona[4]	3.0	1	0	4	2
California[4]	7.0	1	0	6	7
Colorado[4]	3.0	0	1	3	4
Connecticut[3]	6.0	0	1	6	6
Delaware[3]	14.3	1	1	3	3
Florida[1]	15.3	1	2	2	3
Georgia[1]	25.8	1	2	15	16
Illinois[2]	12.8	0	1	19	19
Indiana[2]	6.9	0	1	2	7
Iowa[2]	1.2	1	0	1	1
Kentucky[2]	7.2	3	3	3	3
Louisiana[1]	29.8	1	1	8	8
Maryland[3]	17.8	3	3	18	19
Massachusets[3]	3.1	0	1	3	5
Michigan[2]	11.2	4	3	16	13
Missouri[2]	10.3	2	2	15	15
New Jersey[3]	10.7	1	1	5	7
New York[3]	11.9	0	1	12	14
Oklahoma[4]	6.7	1	1	6	4
Pennsylvania[3]	8.6	1	0	11	13
Tennessee[1]	15.8	0	1	8	9
Texas	12.5	1	2	3	8
Washington[4]	2.1	1	1	3	2
Totals		24	29	206	236

Sources: U.S. Bureau of Census, Congressional District Data, Districts of 93 Cong. CDD-93X; National Roster of Black Elected Officials, vol. 4 (Washington, D.C.: Joint Center for Political Studies: 1974).

NOTE: Area code is as follows: 1 = South, 2 = Midwest, 3 = Northeast, 4 = Far West

ative to proportion of blacks in the population and black political participation patterns.[19] Among other possibilities are racial residential patterns and the politics of apportionment in these areas.

The urban South is the region of origin for the greater portion of the women in this study (43.7 percent). Equal portions come from small to moderate-size cities and large cities in the North (21.8 percent from each) and the remaining indicate they grew up in small to moderate-size cities in the South. None grew up in the rural South.

Family Background
The educational levels of fathers and mothers of the legislators and those of the legislators are compared in table 23.2.

Educational data reveal that while 40.5 percent of the fathers and 40.5 percent of the mothers had less than a high school education, all the legislators had some post-high school education. Further, according to 1972 census data, the median school years completed by persons of all races, 25 years or older, was 12.2 and for all women 12.2. A lower figure of 10.3 years was the median for all blacks, while black women had completed 10.4 years and black men 10.1 years. A bachelor's degree was the minimum education of 52.9 percent of the women in the study. Educationally these women resemble their white counterparts from a study of women legislators serving in 1963–64. That author found that most had some form of post-high school education, but less than half graduated from college.[20]

TABLE 23.2. Education of Legislators and Fathers and Mothers of Legislators (in percent)

Education Level	Fathers	Mothers	Legislators
Some elementary	18.7	6.2	—
Elementary completed	21.8	34.3	—
High school completed	18.7	28.1	—
Special/vocational postsecondary	—	—	12.5 (*N* = 4)
Attended college	6.2	12.5	34.3 (*N* = 11)
Bachelor's degree	21.8	15.6	31.2 (*N* = 10)
Master's degree	—	—	9.3 (*N* = 3)
Law degree	—	—	9.3 (*N* = 3)
Ph.D., M.D., D.D.S., or equivalent	6.2	—	3.1 (*N* = 1)
Failed to respond	6.2	3.1	—

Early Political Socialization

Dawson and Prewitt identify the family as the key agent through which the political culture is transmitted from one generation to the next.[21] In an effort to ascertain the impact of family on the political socialization of these legislators, three probes were made.

First, the subjects were asked to respond to this item: "Is there anything you would like to say about your family as it affected your political involvement?" Family impact was reported by 59.4 percent. Of these the father or grandfather influenced 18.7 percent while mother or grandmother influence was dominant in the case of 6.2 percent. Some 21.8 percent indicated that both parents were politically active and this parental activity had an impact on them. One respondent attributed interest in politics to her early detection of differential treatment of blacks and whites. The largest single category of responses was from women indicating no family impact on their political involvement, 40.6 percent of the group.

The second area of investigation was initial interest in politics. The item was stated as: "Now, about your interest in politics, what was your first recollection of interest in politics (including childhood)? Was there some special person or event?" Responses were coded to show whether interest occurred during early childhood, during teen years, during college, or during adulthood. Over half the legislators (53 percent) stated preadult political interest, 34.3 percent recalling such interest in childhood, 12 percent in teen years, and 6.2 percent while in college. Political interest did not surface in the other 46.8 percent until adulthood.

A third inquiry was: "Have any other members of your immediate family been involved in politics? For example, holding elected or appointed office?" Results revealed only limited political officeholding by other members of legislators' families. Only 12.5 percent ($N = 4$) indicated that other members held political office, while 84.3 percent had no relatives in office. Of the four with officeholding relatives, two cases involved mothers and two were brothers. For the most part, then, for whatever reasons, politics was not a family avocation; in their families, these women are atypical.

Legislators were asked to disclose the number of sisters and brothers and to give their location in the family progeny. Counting the legislators themselves, their 32 families had a total of 162 children, or an average of 5.62 per family. Only 2 legislators were the lone offspring in their families; the largest family was one of 15.

In terms of location in the progeny, 8 were the eldest child and 6 the youngest child. The other 16 were distributed throughout their respective families. There were 5 families in which there were no brothers and 3 families in which siblings included no other girls. Generally, then, these legislators grew up in family environments that were sexually heterogeneous and above average in terms of numbers of children. Exactly half of them were either the only child, the oldest child, or the youngest child. The other half, of course, were spread throughout the sibling groupings.[22]

Association between religion and black political involvement has been investigated by several studies.[23] All the legislators indicated a religious preference. Twenty-six (81.25 percent), indicated a Protestant orientation, and 6 (18.75 percent) were Catholic. Especially noticeable was the presence of several religious persuasions during a lifetime on the part of a number. Generally such moves are consistent with upward mobility, not only among blacks but for the American population generally.

Occupation

As shown in table 23.3, these legislators come from a variety of jobs and professions.

A substantial number had engaged in more than one occupation. A single interviewee, for example, had been a secretary, a teacher, a social worker with the Red Cross overseas, and a newspaper publisher. Another, a master's degree holder, had been teacher, princi-

TABLE 23.3. Occupation/Profession of Legislators

Profession/Occupation	Number of Legislators
College professor	1
Lawyer	3
Teacher	3
Librarian	1
Social worker	5
Journalist	1
Nurse	3
Businesswoman (owner of)	6
Managers	2
Clerical	2
Consultant/public relations specialist	2
Housewife	1
Incomplete response	2

pal, and lawyer. One legislator from a midwestern state had been a French teacher, a research biochemist, and a law librarian. Only one legislator listed housewife as sole occupation.

Age

Ages ranged from the 20s to the 70s, consistent with earlier studies of women in Congress and state legislatures. On the interview instrument legislators were asked to supply ages in ranges rather than to give exact ages. Therefore, no average can be computed. A majority of the respondents were above the age of 40, the oldest past 70 and the youngest 29 (see table 23.4).

TABLE 23.4. Age Ranges of Legislators

Age Group	Percentage
20–30	6.2
31–40	25.0
41–50	34.4
51–60	15.6
60 years or older	18.7

Marital Status and Family Size

Among the women, just less than half (49.9 percent) are either presently married or widowed.

TABLE 23.5. Marital Status of Black Women Legislators

Marital Status	Percentage
Single	6.2
Married	34.3
Divorced	37.5
Widowed	15.6
Legally separated	6.2

Of the divorced women, ($N = 12$), 5 were divorced prior to campaigning for office, 3 others disclaimed any relationship between political endeavors and divorce. One of 2 legal separations reported is directly attributable to conflict over political officeholding. The current divorce rate in America is 44 out of every 100 marriages. Thus this pattern seems consistent with current trends in the general population which causes America to rank second in divorce in the world.

Family Size
Table 23.6 gives information on family size. About two-thirds of the legislators are mothers, but only 15 percent have children under 18 years. Most of the legislators are without young children.

TABLE 23.6. Number of Children in Families of Black Women Legislators

Number of Children	Percentage
None	31.2
1	18.7
2	21.8
3	15.6
4	6.2
5	—
6	3.1
7 or more	3.1

Prior Political Experience
Until recently, most congresswomen have come as replacements to serve out terms for which their husbands had been chosen.[24] This pattern has also prevailed in state legislatures. Only one of these legislators had come to office as a widow replacing her husband. Even she later ran and won election to this position in her own right. Another ran when her husband withdrew as party nominee following a primary victory. The others came to office with no special advantage related to previous officeholding by their husbands.

Forty percent of these women entered the legislature as political novices. Table 23.7 presents data on this aspect of the study.

The women's views of their expertise and special competence upon entering the legislature for the first time are given in table 23.8.

TABLE 23.7. Political Experience of Black Women Legislators

Type of Experience	Percentage
Elective office	9.3
Appointive office	18.7
Salaried employee	6.2
Political party position	21.8
Civil rights organizations	3.1
None	40.6

TABLE 23.8. Views of Personal Expertise and Special Competence by Black Women Legislators

Response	Percentage
Yes, special expertise	84.3
No	12.5
Uncertain	3.1

Despite absence of experience in political office, most (84.3 percent) felt they brought with them special expertise and competence.

Tenure in Office and Future Plans
The fate of the 24 legislators who ended terms in 1972 was as follows:

> 2 were elected congresswomen
> 2 retired
> 1 defeated (when her old district was eliminated)
> 1 defeated when she decided not to seek reelection to the House but to run for a Senate seat
> 18 reelected

Eleven of the 29 legislators in office in 1974 were serving their initial terms. The 18 incumbents in the legislatures now have served an average of 6.8 years (123 years of total service). One who retired in 1972 had completed over 18 consecutive years in her state house.

Reliable estimates are that close to one-half of the approximately 7,600 American state legislators must be replaced every two years because incumbent legislators refuse to seek reelection.[25] These legislators' reelection plans are shown in table 23.9.

TABLE 23.9. Reelection Plans for Black Women State Legislators

Response	Percentage
No response	3.1 (1)
Yes	71.8 (23)
No	3.1 (1)
Uncertain	15.6 (5)
Retired	6.2 (2)

The interviewees were asked if they planned to seek higher office, thereby seeking their upward mobility aspirations. Due to the recency of black women in legislative posts, any suggestion about upward mobility prospects and possibilities might appear premature. However, Joseph Schlesinger contends that "ambition lies at the heart of politics. Politics thrives on the hope of preferment and drive for office".[26] Table 23.10 reveals the extent to which these lawmakers aspire for higher office.

TABLE 23.10. Ambitions for Higher Office of Black Women Legislators

Responses	Percentage
Yes	31.2
No	31.2
Uncertain	31.2
Retired	6.2

Especially striking is the level of ambivalence reflected in these data. However, the knowledge that three of the four black congresswomen are former state legislators does reveal the potential of these posts.

Political Orientations
Opinions on the future of blacks in American politics, on women in American politics, and an assessment of the Women's Liberation Movement were solicited. Table 23.11 conveys the optimistic views on the political future of blacks and women.

Regarding the Women's Liberation Movement, the most widespread attitude is that the movement has some merits but must be ac-

TABLE 23.11. Views on Future of Women in Politics and Blacks in Politics

Opinion	Future of Blacks	Future of Women
Very bright	53.1	71.8
Moderately bright	28.1	15.6
Not very bright	12.5	6.2
Uncertain	6.2	6.2

corded very low status among policy priorities. Only 15.6 percent assigned the movement high priority while 12.5 percent were opposed to the movement. Another 18.7 percent were neutral, and 53.1 percent, a majority, accorded low priority.

A typical stance on the movement was that of a legislator who expressed her feelings as, "It is good and bad. Good in areas of employment and profession. . . . Black women haven't been turned on to it because we have always worked and have no need to identify. Biggest fight for blacks is racism. NOW and other women's groups will not work for black issues like busing."

Among those opposed to the movement, a typical response was, "Women's liberators scream for equality. . . . who is to be liberated from what? To what? White women from homes while black women take care of their kids?"

A more supportive view expressed was, "They have their hangups. We can get a certain amount of success working with them in child care and equal pay. Coalition was necessary for victory in my case and in others. Black women will prosper from it."

Political Party Affiliation

All respondents were Democrats. Seventy-one percent of the legislators served with the majority party in their respective houses, 25 percent were in the minority party, and for the rest party control fluctuated.

SUMMARY

Black women's political fortunes have been most marked in those states where black men have also enjoyed some measure of success in their bids for public office. In only one state black women served without either white females or black colleagues in the legislature. Three of the four black women senators were without white female or black colleagues. All other respondents were accompanied by other women or other blacks.

Moderate-size to large cities in the South served as the region of origin for most of the women. In their elective posts the women were concentrated outside the South, and all represented urban districts. These legislators are comparatively well educated, have followed a number of occupations or professions, with over 90 percent following careers outside the home. Approximately 60 percent indicated that their families had some impact on their interest in politics while about 53 percent stated preadult political interest. Only minimal political involvement by other family members was reported. These women grew up in families that exceed the American average in size.

Black female lawmakers are universally religious, mostly above 40 years of age, were or are now married, have one or more children mostly over the age of 18, and did not enter politics in their husbands' footsteps. Inconsequential prior officeholding and absence of conventional political experience seem inconsistent with the prevailing self-assessment by these women that they brought to their legislative posts expertise or experiences that gave them special advantage in some policy area.

While only four of the interviewees exceed ten years of service in office, most expressed a desire to run again. All are Democrats, most serve in legislative chambers in which theirs is the majority party. They are ambivalent about seeking higher office but optimistic about the future of women and blacks in American politics. Women's Liberation is viewed with reservations, not opposed but not given high priority.

RESEARCH IMPLICATIONS

The preceding findings on black women legislators provide a preliminary profile and suggest a need for more research in a number of directions. At least four concerns seem to be especially promising topics for further study.

First, there is a critical need to come to grips with the problems involved in attempting to assess the effectiveness of black women legislators. Given their double minority status, what are the traits and skills that will permit them to achieve some success in "acting in the interests of the represented, in a manner responsive to them."[27] Male legislators from the dominant group are usually assessed in terms of success in translating policy priorities into legislative enactments. As a general rule black legislators and women legislators are not too successful with this task. What are other possible means for evaluating the efforts of these legislators? Are the policy priorities of black women legislators (policies which are responsive to needs of blacks and women) primarily responsible for lack of success in getting legislation passed? Does absence of legislative enactments sponsored by these legislators mean that they have been without impact on their respective legislative chambers?

Second, the upward mobility aspirations and patterns of achievement of black women legislators seem to be a promising field of inquiry. If ambition is the source of politics, then how do the upward mobility goals affect the policy priorities, operational styles, and peer preferences of these politicians?

Third, compatibility of political officeholding and family responsibility for women has been a persistent topic in the study of women in politics. These black women legislators have grown up in large families, the majority have families of their own, and black families have a tradition of role flexibility among males and females. These facts would seem to render the exploration of black family life interesting for women officeholders generally.[28]

Fourth, a pressing need exists for increased data on black legislators and women legislators to permit comparisons between these legislators along racial and sex lines. Approximately 412 white women and 207 black males served in state legislatures in 1974.

When Crystal Bird Fauset was elected to the lower house of the Pennsylvania legislature in 1938, she became the first black woman to enter an American state house as a lawmaker. Not until 1952 did a black woman become a state senator, Cora M. Brown of Michigan. Thirty-six years after the historic entry of black women into state legislative chambers, 29 are serving in these bodies. While this increase might be less than spectacular, it is a beginning. In 1974 there are unprecedented numbers of black women contesting elections, many for legislative seats. In light of increased interest on the part of women and the continued interest in reelection bids by incumbents, a projection of at least incremental advances for black women in these offices seems reasonable. While the overall reaction of black females might be impatience, others are more prone to accept the advice offered by the black female politician and diplomat of the Truman era, Edith Sampson, with regard to token advancement for black women: "As a Negro, I found out a long time ago that part of something is better than all of nothing."[29]

NOTES
1. John Hope Franklin, *From Slavery to Freedom* (3rd ed.; New York: Knopf, 1967), pp. 315–23.

2. For an extensive discussion, see Fred Greenstein, *Children and Politics* (New Haven: Yale University Press, 1965), "Sex Differences in Political Learning," pp. 107–27.

3. For summary and assessment of these studies, see Robert Staples, "The Myth of the Black Matriarchy," *Black Scholar* 1 (January–February 1970): 8–16; also Herbert H. Hyman and John Shelton Reed, "Black Matriarchy Reconsidered: Evidence from Secondary Analyses of Sample Surveys," *Public Opinion Quarterly* 33 (Fall 1969): 346–54.

4. Fred Greenstein, "Sex-Related Political Differences in Childhood," *Journal of Politics* 23 (May 1961): 353–71; Robert D. Hess and Judith Torney, *The Development of Political Attitudes in Children* (Chicago: Aldine, 1967), pp. 173–94; David Easton and Jack Dennis, *Children in the Political System* (New York: McGraw-Hill, 1969), pp. 288–304; see also Joan Laurence, "White Socialization: Black Reality," *Psychiatry* 33 (May 1970): 174–94; Schley Lyons, "The Political Socialization of Ghetto Children: Efficacy and Cynicism," *Journal of Politics* (May 1970): 288–304.

5. However, some differences have been found among black Jamaican children. See Kenneth Langton, *Political Socialization* (New York: Oxford University Press, 1969).

6. Anthony Orum, Roberta S. Cohen, Sherri Grasmuck, and Amy Orum, "Sex, Socialization, and Politics," *American Sociological Review* 39 (April 1974): 197–209; see also Lynne Iglitzin, "Sex-Typing and Politicization in Children's Attitudes: Reflections on Studies Done and Undone" (Paper presented at the Annual Meeting of the American Political Science Association, Washington, D.C., 5–9 September 1972).

7. Hope Chamberlin, *A Minority of Members* (New York: Praeger, 1973).

8. Peggy Lamson, *Few Are Chosen* (Boston: Houghton Mifflin, 1968).

9. Herrington Bryce and Alan Warrick, "Black Women in Electoral Politics," *Focus* 1 (August 1973).

10. Among the studies of black student protest activity are Donald R. Matthews and James Prothro, "Negro Students and the Protest Movement," in their *Negroes and the New Southern Politics* (New York: Harcourt, Brace & World, 1966), pp. 407–40; Freddye Hill, "Black Nationalism: A Case Study at a Predominantly White Northern University" (Ph.D. dissertation, Northwestern University, 1974); E. C. Harrison, "Student Unrest on the Black College Campus," *Journal of Negro Education* 41 (Spring 1972): 113–20; and John Orbell, "Protest Participation Among Southern Negro College Students," *American Political Science Review* 41 (June 1967): 446–56.

11. The estimation of female participation was reported in testimony to Black Committee of Inquiry, Baton Rouge, Louisiana, 1972. Transcribed but not published.

12. Matthews and Prothro, *Negroes and Southern Politics*, pp. 65–70; and John Pierce, William Avery, and Addison Carey, Jr., "Sex Differences in Black Political Beliefs and Behavior," *American Journal of Political Science* 17 (May 1973): 422–30.

13. Inez Reid, *Together Black Women* (New York: Emerson Hall, 1972).

14. Ibid., p. 29.

15. Marjorie Lansing, "The Voting Patterns of American Black Women" (Paper presented at the Annual Meeting of the American Political Science Association, New Orleans, Louisiana, 4–8 September 1973).

16. Edward T. Clayton, *The Negro Politician: His Success and Failure* (Chicago: Johnson, 1964), pp. 122–48.

17. Ibid., p. 122.

18. Shirley Chisholm, *Unbought and Unbossed* (New York: Avon, 1970).

19. V. O. Key, Jr., *Southern Politics* (New York: Knopf, 1949).

20. Emmy E. Werner, "Women in the State Legislatures," *Western Political Quarterly* 21 (1968): 40–50.

21. Richard Dawson and Kenneth Prewitt, *Political Socialization* (Boston: Little, Brown, 1969), p. 107.

22. Birth order and success has been the focus of numerous studies. For example, E. E. Sampson, "The Study of Ordinal Position: Antecedents and Outcomes," in *Progress in Experimental Personality Research,* ed. B. A. Maher (New York: Academic, 1965), pp. 175–228; W. D. Alters, "Birth Order and Its Sequelae," *Science* 15 (1966): 44–49; J. R. Warren, "Birth Order and Social Behavior," *Psychology Bulletin* 65 (1966): 38–49; Gordon B. Forbes, "Birth Order and Academic Behavior Among Seriously Disadvantaged Adults," *Journal of Social Psychology* 93 (1974): 301–2; and G. B. Forbes, "Birth Order and Political Success: A Study of the 1970 Illinois General Elections," *Psychology Report* 29 (1971): 1239–42.

23. See Joseph H. Fichter, "American Religion and the Negro," in *The Negro American,* ed. Talcott Parsons and Kenneth B. Clark (Boston: Houghton Mifflin, 1965), pp. 401–22; Gary T. Marx, "Religion: Opiate and Inspiration of Civil Rights Militancy Among Negroes," *American Sociological Review* 32 (February 1967): 64–72.

24. Martin Gruberg, *Women in American Politics* (Oshkosh, Wisc.: Academia, 1968).

25. Daniel R. Grant and H. C. Nixon, *State and Local Government in America* (Boston: Allyn & Bacon, 1968), p. 242.

26. Joseph A. Schlesinger, *Ambition and Politics: Political Careers in the United States* (Chicago: Rand McNally, 1966), p. 1.

27. Hannah Pitkin, *The Concept of Representation* (Berkeley: University of California Press, 1967), pp. 154–55.

28. See Robert Hill, *The Strengths of Black Families* (New York: Emerson Hall, 1972); and Andrew Billingsley, *Black Families in White America* (Englewood Cliffs, N.J.: Prentice-Hall, 1968).

29. Quoted in Clayton, *Negro Politician,* p. 127.

VII Women in Politics

24

MARIANNE GITHENS AND JEWEL L. PRESTAGE

☆☆☆☆☆☆☆☆☆☆☆☆☆☆☆☆☆☆☆☆☆☆☆☆☆☆☆☆

Conclusion

Research included in this volume has emphasized, explicitly or implicitly, the marginality of the American woman as a participant in the political process. Fundamental to this marginality is a socialization process that transmits to women attitudes, values, and behavior patterns inconsistent with political involvement. Women who seek involvement confront special hurdles at every step in the process. At the recruitment stage are problems of access to organizations that have traditionally facilitated the launching of successful political careers. Problems related to knowledge acquisition, analytical skills, and informal linkages arise once women assume political office. Assessment of their input and impact on public policy is made on the basis of criteria devised for male officeholders. And, in a variety of ways, policy outcomes reflect the limited political involvement of women. Of course, if the question of allocation of resources is at the core of politics, then the relationship between the quantity and quality of female participation in that process and the character of female existence in the society becomes even more obvious. Throughout, this volume has examined the theme of marginality, its ramifications for women political activists and its implications for the study of women in politics.

Particularly striking is the extent to which the image of the woman political activist emerging from the reported research resembles the sensitive portrayal of the marginality of the American black found in Stonequist's *The Marginal Man*. At least three similarities are

421

suggested: absence of a traditional or folk culture, an acute sense of frustration, and the "conceptual lag" characteristics of the dominant group. Stonequist writes:

> Unlike most other racial and national minorities they have not a traditional culture of their own making. The immigrants, the Jews, nationality minorities in Europe or elsewhere, have a distinctive language. When such groups have become racially conscious and have reacted to the attitude of the dominant group by some collective movement, they have turned inward and revived their peculiar customs and speech. By this action they have sought to differentiate themselves from the other group. It has been a means of giving expression to their collective self-respect and pride.[1]

Because of their estrangement from Africa, Stonequist argues, American blacks cannot return to a folk culture, revive a venacular, or idealize an ancestral land.[2]

> Consequently coloured people are forced to express themselves in the only culture they know, that of white America. This means that the Negro's effort to improve himself and his race necessitates his becoming more like the white man, not in differentiating himself. By equalling the white man he demonstrates his ability and refutes the stigma of inferiority.[3]

Yet the effort blacks make to prove their equality and competence arouses hostility, for white America has a definite notion about what blacks are and ought to be. This stereotype limits what blacks can do and restricts their options. When blacks, particularly educated and ambitious blacks, do not conform to the stereotype, there arises "a sense of frustration, of injustice and a consciousness of prejudice".[4]

> They live on the same level of culture as the corresponding white classes, but they are subject to the attitudes and treatment which the white man bestows upon less advanced Negroes. In their own race they occupy a high status; from the white point of view they are inferior.[5]

Stonequist further contends that "the white man's conception of the Negro lagged behind the latter's cultural advance" and that the Negro affected by this attitude was marginal because "his conception of himself is in conflict with the white man's conception of him."[6]

Today women find themselves in an analogous situation. Lacking a culture of their own, women do not have the opportunity to differentiate themselves. Women's history, positive role models, an inspiring common cultural heritage, and the like are largely absent from the contemporary woman's consciousness. Elizabeth Gould Davis's *The First Sex* represents an effort to idealize feminist culture; but in many respects it resembles Garvey's "Back to Africa" movement for blacks insofar as it asks women to take pride in a culture that has little meaning for them. Women, like blacks, thus "are forced to express themselves in the only culture they know."[7]

Because differentiation from men only accentuates stereotypes of inferiority, women find themselves in a position where they must behave like men in order to demonstrate their ability. However, there is a place for women and a feeling that women ought to stay in their place, just as there is a place for blacks. Hostility and resentment follow when either subgroup seeks to move beyond that assigned role. At best, women and blacks may serve as spokespersons for their group; but nothing more. In politics this means that women may speak on those issues that have been traditionally associated with female concerns—social welfare, child care, etc.—but not on matters that range further. The increased educational opportunity for women, the consequent increase in skill and competency in areas unrelated to the traditional female role in the home, and a sense of relative deprivation that advanced education has created in women have not yet permeated man's concept of women. Woman's view of herself is in conflict with man's concept of her. Thus the educated and ambitious woman, like her black counterpart, finds herself in a marginal situation.

These misconceptions are perpetuated by the nature of interaction between groups. White men speak their minds freely; blacks and women listen and observe. Reserve is a protection for them. Unknown and misunderstood "advanced" and "educated" women and blacks live on the same level of culture as the corresponding class of white males, yet both are treated as though they had all the qualities of the less-advanced stereotype. In other words, both are defined a priori as inferior.

If the concept of marginality does offer a viable frame of reference for studying the condition of women, particularly political women, then some new research emphases would seem to be in order. Three possible areas of emphases are suggested by the major research findings in this volume.

First, the data that have been accumulated focus largely on aspects of objective marginality stemming from the positions that women in politics hold and on perceptions of these women that reflect their feelings of experiential marginality; but virtually no work has been done on symptomatic marginality. True, some effort has been made to categorize the personality characteristics of women in politics, but it has not dealt with the relationship of these characteristics to marginality and has often lacked specific focus. For Park and Stonequist, as well as for more recent social scientists who have used the concept of marginality, personality is substantially affected. The condition of marginality can stimulate specific behavioral responses. One set of characteristics concerns the development of a novel perspective that permits the marginal person to view events differently and thereby escape the limitations of an existing culture. The second revolves around behavioral responses stemming from the rootlessness, isolation, and anomie of marginality.

Fundamental to both responses is the notion that the marginal person standing between two groups has no clear guidelines for behavior and experiences problems in intimate relationships. On the one hand, this means that the marginal person is freer from cultural constraints than the ordinary individual. As a consequence, the marginal person is more capable of thoughtful introspection, more willing to move away from traditional patterns of behavior, and more experimental than the ordinary individual. Marginal persons must find new ways of behaving, ways that are compatible with the different situation in which they find themselves. On the other hand, lacking clear directives for behavior, marginal persons are often unable to make decisions, hypersensitive, irritable, lacking ease in interpersonal relationships, and inconsistent in behavior.[8] Research on symptomatic marginality in women in politics might permit a clearer picture to emerge of both the marginality of political women and its impact on their behavior. It would allow an examination of the extent to which the condition of marginality has stimulated women to develop new perspectives on the role of woman and the role of politician. At present, evaluations of political women stress the degree to which they conform or deviate from the political behavior of males. Perhaps a more appropriate concern is the definition of the role of woman and of politician that women in politics have or are developing. Female patterns may well be emerging that are the vanguard for political behavior rather than deviant in the pejorative sense or the products of deficiences in skill and expertise (which longer experience in politics will obliterate). In fact, if women in politics are marginal, such a contribution can be expected. As Stonequist described the marginal person's role:

> The practical efforts of the marginal person to solve his own problem lead him consciously or unconsciously to change the situation itself. His interest may shift from himself to the objective social conditions and launch him upon a career of nationalist, conciliator, interpreter, reformer or teacher. In these roles he inevitably promotes acculturation, either upon a basis of larger political and cultural unity, or in terms of a modified political and cultural differentiation.[9]

At the same time, characteristics such as inconsistency, irritability, and the like ought to be examined to determine the extent to which the anomie of marginality affects women in politics. For example, Robert Park argued that the creative qualities of the marginal might exist side by side with the other set of responses, while Melvin Seeman contends that creative qualities appear when individuals solve their marginality problem.[10] The role and contribution of women in politics might not only be elucidated by the theory of marginality, but also might provide some further insight into the role of marginals and the prerequisites for creativity.

A second fruitful area of investigation seems to be Stonequist's three-part typology of responses to the condition of marginality: the Nationalist Role, the Intermediary Role, and Assimilation and Passing. The Nationalist Role consists of a total identification with the subordinate or oppressed group, with perhaps the assumption of a role of leadership in that group. Often a leader of the subordinate group not only seeks to revive the traditional culture of the group, but also to modernize it. Those who adopt this nationalist style act as agitators who remind the group of old issues and point out new ones. As Stonequist describes this marginal, "he prevents accommodation on any particular level from becoming too fixed and crystalized, thereby helping to raise the ultimate status of his group. His extreme and destructive views promote concessions to the moderates who appear mild in comparison."[11] This response to marginality is seen as springing from a strong identification with the dominant group, perhaps a lack of knowledge of the group's previous interactions with the dominant group, and a sharp rebuff from the dominant group.

Under these circumstances, an intense, militant role may be assumed.

A second form of adjustment to marginality is the Intermediary Role. The marginal who assumes this role seeks to promote accommodation and rapprochement and thus becomes associated with the functions of interpreter, conciliator, reformer, and teacher. According to Stonequist, "he may appear timid, compromising, or opportunistic to impatient temperaments; yet his persistent and steady pressure is an essential part in the progress of the subordinate group. His method has the further virtue of softening or undermining resistance."[12]

Partial or complete incorporation into the dominant culture is a third form of adjustment. An important distinction within this third response is made between assimilation and passing. In the first case, the process is largely unconscious; in the second, it is conscious and deliberate. When assimilation is possible, the marginal stage is relatively short but sometimes acute. With passing, the problems of marginality are particularly acute; passing may be advantageous for some points of view, but it may create as many problems as it solves.[13]

This Stonequist typology may well provide a new framework for examining the political behavior of women, and may be especially useful in viewing the behavior of women political activists. Obviously considerable work needs to be done in refining these types and modifying them to fit the category of marginal woman; but the results may well be worth the effort.

Third among research directions suggested is exploration of benefits that may accrue from examination of the peculiar "marginality" of the black woman and its resultant impact on the dominant American culture. In "Marginality and Social Change" Charles V. Willie suggests that Moynihan's and Jensen's solutions to the problems of blacks is assimilation, that is, the rejection of specific black characteristics that perpetuate the distinctiveness of blacks as a group. Dissenting, Willie argues that the marginality of blacks (and of black women in particular) and their adjustment to it may have contributed to the growth and development of the dominant culture. The dominant group has, he believes, benefited from the creativity and transcendence of blacks adjusting to marginality. Speaking of black women in this context, he says:

The employment of black women outside the home as workers in the national labor force was a pioneering marginal activity over the years, which eventually resulted in an increasing number of white women being employed outside the home. Had blacks been made over in the image of whites as prescribed by some social scientists, white women would not have been able to observe the creative effects of work for pay as the work experience of black women enabled them to do. However, white women probably are unaware of the fact that they may be modeling their behavior after blacks.[14]

The role of black women as pioneers combined work outside the home with the traditional roles of wife and mother and thus unconsciously affected white women, demands that special attention be given to black women in their capacity as political activists. Research focusing on black women in politics needs to be done not only by black women but also by white women. Just as the black woman adopted dual roles, so too the pattern of political behavior of black women may offer important clues for adjustment to white women in their political activity. Concern for and knowledge of the political behavior of the black woman reflects more than a mere sensitivity to the racial issue. It is important to know and understand the black woman's response to marginality, which she has acutely perceived for a long time, so that white women who are becoming increasingly aware of their own marginality may facilitate their adjustment.

As the research on women in politics contained in this volume indicates, much has been done in this critical subject matter area in a very short time. Nevertheless, what has been done is much less impressive than what remains unexplored. Like the initial efforts, exploration will probably be conditioned by the increased sensitivity of academia to the need for such efforts and by a determined cadre of scholars, mostly female, willing to forgo the rewards of more traditional research and teaching in the pursuit of truths that flow from the study of unconventional subject matter or "scholarly trail-blazing."

NOTES
1. Everett V. Stonequist, *The Marginal Man: A Study in Personality and Culture Conflict* (New York: Russell & Russell, 1961), p. 106.
2. Ibid., p. 107.
3. Ibid.
4. Ibid., p. 108.
5. Ibid., p. 110.
6. Ibid., p. 108.
7. Ibid., p. 107.

8. Ralph Turner, *The Social Context of Ambition: A Study of High School Seniors in Los Angeles* (San Francisco: Chandler, 1964), p. 6.

9. Stonequist, *Marginal Man*, p. 221.

10. Melvin Seeman, "Intellectual Perspective and Adjustment to Minority Status," *Social Problems* 3 (January 1956): 442–53.

11. Stonequist, *Marginal Man*, p. 174.

12. Ibid., p. 182.

13. Ibid., p. 184.

14. Charles V. Willie, "Marginality and Social Change," *Society* 12, no. 5 (July/August 1975): 12.